More Than Just Grit

More Than Just Grit

*Civil War Leadership,
Logistics and Teamwork
in the West, 1862*

Richard J. Zimmermann

McFarland & Company, Inc., Publishers
Jefferson, North Carolina

LIBRARY OF CONGRESS CATALOGUING-IN-PUBLICATION DATA

Names: Zimmermann, Richard J., author.
Title: More than just grit : Civil War leadership, logistics and teamwork in the West, 1862 / Richard J. Zimmermann.
Description: Jefferson, North Carolina : McFarland & Company, Inc., Publishers, 2023. | Includes bibliographical references and index.
Identifiers: LCCN 2023001733 | ISBN 9781476688718 (paperback : acid free paper) ∞
ISBN 9781476646640 (ebook)
Subjects: LCSH: United States—History—Civil War, 1861-1865—Campaigns. | Command of troops—History—19th century. | United States—History—Civil War, 1861-1865—Logistics. | United States—Strategic aspects. | Southern States—Strategic aspects. | BISAC: HISTORY / Military / United States | HISTORY / United States / Civil War Period (1850-1877)
Classification: LCC E470.4 .Z56 2023 | DDC 973.7/301—dc23/eng/20230117
LC record available at https://lccn.loc.gov/2023001733

BRITISH LIBRARY cataloguing data are available

ISBN (print) 978-1-4766-8871-8
ISBN (ebook) 978-1-4766-4664-0

© 2023 Richard J. Zimmermann. All rights reserved

No part of this book may be reproduced or transmitted in any form or by any means, electronic or mechanical, including photocopying or recording, or by any information storage and retrieval system, without permission in writing from the publisher.

On the cover: *insets* General Grant and his staff between 1861 and 1865 (Library of Congress); John Alexander McClernand, 1862 (Library of Congress); Equipage and baggage train on the Louisville and Nashville Railroad "Frank Leslie's illustrated newspaper," 1862 (Library of Congress); *background* map from *The Century War Book People's Pictorial Edition*, New York: The Century Co., 1894 (Civil War Museum of Kenosha, Wisconsin)

Printed in the United States of America

McFarland & Company, Inc., Publishers
Box 611, Jefferson, North Carolina 28640
www.mcfarlandpub.com

For Karen
Without her encouragement and steadfast support,
this project would be impossible.

Acknowledgments

The author gratefully acknowledges the assistance provided by the following individuals and organizations: Greg Biggs, Larry Daniel, Bruce Klemm, Christopher L. Kolakowski, and Dr. Timothy B. Smith of the University of Tennessee at Martin read portions of or all the manuscript and offered valuable suggestions. Tom Cole, Mark Wheeler and National Park Service guides (especially Paul Holloway and Ben Blevens) answered numerous queries on the battlefields themselves.

Good friends also offered encouragement at key moments and inspired the author with new ideas and insights. Dr. Thomas R. Stone, Colonel, U.S. Army (Retired), offered helpful suggestions throughout this process. Dr. Richard Heaps provided economic insights, much-needed goodwill and candid observations. Doug Dammann, curator, was a welcoming presence at the Kenosha, Wisconsin, Civil War Museum and shared valuable insights as well. Gina Radandt, curator at the museum, graciously provided important resources from their extensive collection.

Librarians at the Wisconsin State Historical Society; the University of Wisconsin–Madison, the University of Wisconsin–Milwaukee, and the Racine, Wisconsin, Public Library; and the Western Reserve Historical Society in Cleveland all contributed useful materials. Margaret McDonough, at the Prairie School in Racine, Wisconsin, undertook the original editing process that strengthened the final manuscript.

Margaret A. Zimmermann patiently illustrated the manuscript with maps, charts and diagrams.

The folks at McFarland expressed interest and support for a hopeful author throughout the publishing process. Despite all this assistance, the author takes full responsibility for errors of omission and commission found within the book.

Table of Contents

Acknowledgments — vi
Contents — vii
Preface — 1
Introduction — 3
Prologue: The Mexican War — 9

1. Mill Springs: Triumph of Professional Leadership — 21
2. Forts Henry and Donelson: Combined Arms with Gunboats — 34
3. Pea Ridge: Arkansas Travelers — 49
4. Opening the Mississippi River — 65
5. Shiloh: The War Comes of Age — 74
6. Richmond, Kentucky: Kirby Smith Wins for the Confederacy — 92
7. Perryville, Kentucky: Strategic Failures for Both Sides — 103
8. Corinth: The Confederacy Strikes Back — 123
9. Prairie Grove: Arkansas Once More — 138
10. Stones River: Fatal Flaws in Confederate Strategy and Leadership — 153
11. Reflections on Civil War Leadership — 170

Appendix I: Distribution of Food and Ammunition — 177
Appendix II: Artillery Improvements — 181
Chapter Notes — 183
Bibliography — 197
Index — 205

Preface

During the Battle of Mill Springs, Kentucky, January 19, 1862, a horseman approached the lines of the Union 10th Indiana Regiment. In the fog, rain and confusion, it took a moment for the Union soldiers to realize he was a Confederate officer. Then he was shot dead with three bullet holes in him. After Felix Zollicoffer, the second-in-command of the Confederate forces, was killed, the battle eventually degenerated into a Confederate rout. Except for one action at Richmond, Kentucky, and a closely fought engagement at Perryville, the Confederates lost engagements that year at locations throughout Kentucky, Tennessee, Mississippi and Arkansas. Some writers have claimed that the Confederates were outnumbered, overmatched in many other areas and had almost no chance of winning their independence. They have suggested that, though Southern generals and soldiers exhibited great bravery and grit, the North produced more steel, possessed more miles of railroad track, raised more food, and supported more people, more ships, more of everything, perhaps, except cotton and slaves. The true story, however, tells a different tale.

In 1862, a strange dichotomy emerged from the two theaters of war. In the East, the South began winning an entire string of victories throughout the spring and summer; while in the West, except for a few minor skirmishes, the South lost one engagement after another in a disastrous series of defeats that brought the entire war effort and independence movement to the brink of extinction. The South usually brought as many men into western combat as their Northern counterparts, they trained with the same drill manuals, they armed themselves with many of the same weapons, and many of their generals were also West Point–trained. What was different in the West?

A careful study of Civil War leadership suggests that a successful general required more than passion, resilience, or demonstrations of inspirational courage. Several other conditions were necessary ingredients for providing effective leadership in a campaign or battle. With many studies, most of these items are often missing or referred to only in brief passages. What emerges from this study is the story of both sides seeking sound leadership for the West, or even competent midlevel officers, and a search for other conditions that helped a commanding general achieve success in battle. For example, a lack of teamwork or the inability to fully mobilize resources for battle challenged both sides. Many Civil War studies on leadership emphasize the "great man" theory of successful generalship. The winning commander was more determined, "clear-headed, quick and daring," as one writer declared. These characteristics make for interesting anecdotes, but the serious student of history is left with some basic questions. Other than exceptional generalship, what observable elements of Civil War leadership in combat led to victory or defeat? Are they replicated from one battle to the next? Do these actions follow a pattern that might help the reader understand *why* a particular battle was won or lost? In the case of this book, six measurable phenomena emerge from the study and influenced the decision reached in battle. While the North won most of the engagements described in the book, the same queries apply to both sides.

The book suggests that victorious generals were (1) able to achieve a clear and attainable objective, (2) successful in seizing the initiative at the close of the action, (3) sustained by their lieutenants, (4) reinforced by a competent staff that effectively supervised logistical support, (5) skilled at committing all their resources in a timely fashion, and (6) achieved true strategic success by the end of the campaign. Whenever most of these factors were accomplished, an army was triumphant. While the extent of a general's victory was frequently determined by producing a favorable result in several of these areas, a defeated leader had only limited success in a few of them. The evidence suggests that there is a remarkable congruence from one battle to another; these six occurrences or phenomena can be found in every battle for 1862, and this approach provides an original and thoughtful refinement for analyzing the titanic struggle that was the American Civil War. To the author's knowledge, no previous book on the subject has deliberately emphasized these elements and connected them to a range of disparate engagements.

In writing this book, the author has relied on thoughtful visits to all nine Civil War battlefields, explored archives, libraries and other collections of documents while searching online for information that would have a bearing on these battles and the six elements that greatly influenced the outcome of each.

Introduction

As Richard McMurry explored the reasons for success or failure of Civil War armies in *Two Great Rebel Armies,* he compared the military structure and tactics used by Confederate forces in the East and West. Other historians have attempted to examine political and social issues that may have impacted the result. Unfortunately for "The Cause," Southern army leadership in combat was often not as effective as the Northern leadership "on the other side of the hill." Even untried, and at times mediocre, Northern leadership combined with effective teamwork frequently proved superior in combat. Northern strategic failures in 1862, however, served to lengthen the war, and those errors proved every bit as egregious as the mistakes of their opponents.[1]

When the war opened in Virginia, President Jefferson Davis focused much of his energy on the Eastern Theater. Richmond was a mere 90 miles from Washington, and in Davis's eyes and those of most Confederates, it could not be allowed to fall. Much of the Confederacy's limited manufacturing capacity was concentrated in Richmond plants (such as the Tredegar Iron Works). Strong and unified Southern leadership emerged in the East as well. After Joseph E. Johnston was wounded in combat, Robert E. Lee served as the commanding general for an army that evolved to become the Army of Northern Virginia. Lee, Stonewall Jackson, James Longstreet and J.E.B. Stuart formed an unbeatable team for over a year, and Lee worked jointly with President Davis throughout the war. The same could not be said about commanders in the West. All the Confederate forces in the West (usually three to four separate armies) never truly served under one leader, and individual commanders failed (on most occasions) to coordinate their actions with other armies (not to mention with naval forces).

This book examines strategic and operational decisions made by both sides in the West and the resulting outcomes when combat followed. Northern leadership and teamwork made an important difference in determining the outcome of battle. The pivotal year 1862 saw twelve consequential actions throughout the states west of the Appalachian Mountains, and the North was strategically, and often tactically, victorious in nine of those actions. This was not an accident, nor was it the simple result of bringing superior resources to bear, but rather the outcome resulting from more effective Northern leadership on and off the battlefield. After 1862, the South could make the argument that the North brought superior forces to bear, but in 1862 the South had significant opportunities for achieving independence. Their failure to win often resulted from strategic, operational and, at times, tactical mistakes on the part of Confederate military leadership in the West—"unforced errors," to use a tennis term.

But how should a person undertake the study of leadership in a military setting? Army leadership should not be treated as an isolated series of behaviors on the part of one person. The idea of singular or solo leadership does not adequately describe the complexities of the art of command during the Civil War. Studies of staff effectiveness, subordinate performance, and logistical expertise must all be considered when determining the ability of the army commander to succeed in combat. In today's world, we use terms such as cooperative and collaborative behavior to describe these efforts, but in the nineteenth century, this terminology was not used. But how can effective leadership be observed and then evaluated?

Broadly speaking, the art of military leadership divides itself into two major categories: individual behaviors of the commanding general and then the establishment of trusting and professional relationships with immediate subordinates and staff. Individual traits include the following: collaborating with a superior officer or political leader in establishing clear objectives, achieving a victorious initiative at the close of a battle, committing all possible resources, and securing a strategic victory at the close of the battle. The commander must delegate authority where practicable, collaborate where appropriate, and take charge as needed. Even a sampling of the literature leads to lists (often redundant) of leadership characteristics.[2]

The study of military history furnishes us with numerous examples of successful leadership, and military historians have created many "lists" of these traits and characteristics; we should also note that at one point the U.S. Army assembled a catalog of items termed "Principles of War." Beginning with Field Manual 100–1 in 1949, the army outlined nine principles that it considered of critical importance for training its officers. Other armed forces, notably the British, adopted their own principles, often quite similar, but on occasion adding their own variations. For example, in 1946 the British under the direction of the Chief of the Imperial General Staff added, among other items, the concept of army "Administration," which they suggested was synonymous with "Logistics." Until 2008, the U.S. Army principles survived with only slight variations. As the army faced increasingly sophisticated challenges in the twenty-first century, some of its more experienced officers expressed concerns that trainees might simply memorize these traits in rote fashion and then fail to exercise the flexible judgment needed for decision making under the stress of actual combat. For the purposes of this study, several of these principles are indeed quite useful. Many appear to be measurable while others remain subjects for continued debate and discussion.[3]

If we use U.S. Grant as an example of a successful military leader, the challenge of measuring these traits becomes much clearer. For example, on April 12, 1864, Lieutenant Colonel Theodore Lyman wrote to his wife, Elizabeth, "Grant is a man of a good deal of rough dignity; rather taciturn; quick and decided in speech. He habitually wears an expression as if he had determined to drive his head through a brick wall, and was about to do it." Now the problem with this quotation is the section concerning Grant's determination or willingness to "drive his head through a brick wall." One might also suggest that Grant was lucky. How can we possibly measure these traits?[4]

Was Grant more determined than, say, Albert Sidney Johnston? If so, how can this trait be measured or compared between the two leaders? Was one leader more effective at brick wall bashing than the other? We can also read this observation from Grenville M. Dodge: "The great distinguishing qualities of General Grant were truth, courage, modesty, generosity and loyalty." How can one measure modesty or loyalty, and what do those qualities have to do with winning battles?[5]

Finally, Adam Badeau describes Grant at the close of the first day at Shiloh. He

Introduction 5

writes, "When it was apparent that the battle was waning, Grant was at Sherman's front, and gave orders to renew the attack on the morrow.... He could not urge his jaded troops that night into any further assault, but his resolution was unshaken, ... he gave positive orders to take the initiative in the morning."[6]

Again, we can draw the conclusion that Grant was resolute and able to function well under pressure, but how does that compare to his opponent A.S. Johnston at Shiloh? Was Johnston somehow less resolute? Or was he simply unlucky and killed before he could demonstrate the same staying power or other determined, purposeful, steadfast, stalwart and tenacious qualities? So the question repeats: How can we measure and compare successful leaders? What shared and possibly measurable characteristics emerge from a welter of detail and from a series of individual battles, fought at different times, under varying conditions sometimes called the "fog of war," where military plans went awry, often at the first shot? Does an analogous pattern emerge? The year 1862 is particularly important, for the North had not yet amassed its later advantages in numbers, technology and industry. At least six phenomena (many of them observable) emerge from this study as we seek to answer these questions. These inquiries as formulated require a straightforward conclusion. Either the North or the South achieved, or failed to achieve, the desired outcome. In some cases, while precise measurement is impossible due to the complexity of the circumstances, a reasonable, or at least arguable, conclusion can still be reached.

1. Does the nation's political leadership (or the theater commander chosen by the political leadership) create a clear and attainable objective for the commanding general? In a strategic sense, the commander of a Civil War army drew support from his superiors, political or military. They could assist the commander by providing reinforcements, supplies and especially encouragement in helping him carry out his duties. The commander and his superiors needed to trust and support one another and establish "clearly defined" and attainable goals. When political leaders chose commanding officers, they also faced the challenge of selecting talented and experienced officers who could be expected to reach those objectives. Selecting competent commanders was a critical component of that necessary strategic support. The commander also required enough authority to accomplish the mission he was given. While this question may not always have a completely measurable response, it remains a critical issue.[7]

2. At the close of combat, does the commanding general hold the initiative? A commander may be on the defensive at the beginning of an action, but if he seizes the initiative by the *end* of the battle, sometimes on the second or even third day of combat, he can achieve success as a result. Oftentimes we hear of one side or the other taking the initiative at the beginning of a campaign or a battle, but again, the side that is advancing at the close of the campaign or battle is clearly closer to achieving its mission and has probably prevailed.[8]

3. Unity of Command. Does the commanding general have the competent and effective support of his immediate subordinates? It was essential for an army commander's lieutenants to act intelligently, cooperatively and professionally. The term Unity of Command and the effort needed to achieve it suggest that a commanding general and his subordinates were required to work together harmoniously. Even if a general committed serious errors, intelligent lieutenants who overcame the general's mistakes could rescue him. With competent or gifted subordinates, a successful commander might even be able to achieve a kind of synergy where his assistants carry much of the burden associated with victory. In any event, they were required to trust one another to achieve positive results. Are most of the subordinates helpful even though a few are not? On balance, were a commander's deputies useful in helping to win the battle?[9]

In an additional tactical sense, success in battle required that the commanding general be a dynamic presence on the battlefield working with his subordinates to achieve victory. At times the general was forced to make immediate tactical decisions affecting the outcome of battle. Adjusting a single cannon in the front line of combat was unhelpful. But if the general gave the signal for attack or withdrawal or provided advice and counsel during the battle to his immediate subordinates, he could help sway the course of combat. If he rode too far forward for too long, the commander placed himself in great danger of being injured or killed, while if he remained too far to the rear, he would stay isolated from the battlefield and ignorant of important battlefield events. For Civil War battles, it could be suggested that the commanding officer was either "on his horse or in the house." To be successful, the commanding officer needed to be reasonably close to the critical areas of combat where he could intervene forcefully and direct or correct the course of battle. In the West, however, with the largest armies seldom exceeding more than 40,000 men, a commander needed to be visible among his soldiers.

4. Working with the commanding general, does the staff effectively supervise logistical support for the army to ensure proper distribution of food and ammunition? In this study, discussion is limited to covering primarily two facets of logistical support: the availability of food and ammunition and their distribution before and during combat. This book does not attempt to delineate all aspects of logistical support that could include forage for animals, military transportation (such as wagons, railroads and steamboats), and quartermaster stores (such as shoes, uniforms and leather goods). Other writers have covered these topics in detail. But while an army may have a bountiful supply of food and ammunition generally available, if proper distribution is lacking, an army will suffer. This aspect of logistics also has a direct bearing on the extent that the commanding general and his staff form a partnership or team. On several occasions during 1862, the failure to distribute food and ammunition turned the tide of battle decidedly in one side's favor and intensified the loss to the other force. Given the economic and technological changes occurring at the time along with the infinitely greater distances covered in the American West, an effective staff was required to manage the complexities of the Civil War battlefield. While this book does not delve into all the topics inherent in the macro study of logistics as a whole, it seeks to review the immediate question of distribution for these essential items.

The nature of logistics was explored in two recent studies: Larry Daniel's *Conquered* and Earl Hess's *Civil War Logistics*. Frank Vandiver also discussed the topic in a chapter-length treatment for his book *Rebel Brass*. The more granular challenge of distribution, however, remains an important one for Civil War discussion and study. Understandably, this question is among the less measurable parts of the study. But if starving soldiers were brought onto the battlefield or if their ammunition supply for small arms or artillery ran low during the contest, the day would not end well. In several western engagements of 1862, the ability or failure of one side or the other to properly distribute necessary supplies for their men meant the difference between victory or defeat. In attempting to limit this topic, the author feels that the larger question of blockade running, or which army (Northern Virginia versus the armies in Tennessee, Mississippi and Arkansas) received more favorable treatment, has already been examined elsewhere at some length. The challenge of distribution, however, is a fundamental factor for obtaining a successful outcome in battle. This requires an energetic and competent staff working together within the organization. A team of capable individuals needed to complement and amplify the actions of the general. One quote, often repeated, comes to mind here: "Amateurs study tactics, professionals study logistics."[10]

5. Did the general commit all his resources to battle? Throughout military history, the ability of one side to employ its resources more or less simultaneously to win a battle remains critically important. Larger armies, using piecemeal tactics or utilizing only part of their forces, risked defeat by smaller forces committing the whole of their resources to battle. If a general sent some of his forces away from a potential battlefield for a raid or other diversion, engaged only a modest portion of his force at one time, or kept a large and unused reserve, he risked defeat. In a sense, this question combines the principles of bringing "overwhelming combat power" to bear or at least employing "all the combat power available."[11]

6. Following the battle, did the general achieve strategic success? Finally, the question of a strategic outcome complicates the conclusion of many Civil War battles. One often wonders if the bloodletting made a difference. For the most part, armies were seldom destroyed or captured in their entirety on the field of battle. If at the close of combat, however, one side chose to withdraw, then the other side was able to claim victory, both militarily and morally. The retreating army and its general then dealt with plummeting morale, negative newspaper comments and falling civilian morale at home. While this topic does not always provide a measurable outcome, the author once again ventures to suggest that a commander who achieved strategic success through victory in battle enhanced his achievement significantly, even if an optimistic "body count" or other means of claiming victory were not present. It is somewhat ironic to note that after the Confederates achieved a major success at Richmond, Kentucky, and at least a draw at Perryville, neither side could claim a successful strategic outcome. This question also completes the circle surrounding the first question. Was the original objective attainable, and if so, did success in achieving that objective lead to a positive strategic outcome?

To achieve an answer, the six elements described as questions in this book often require straightforward responses. While equivocation is possible for any one of these areas, if all six are asked carefully and answered thoroughly for each contest, a clear picture emerges that indicates the extent to which a compelling victory has been won and suggests why this occurred. Many other variables were tested and found wanting in one way or another. For example, almost all commanding generals in the West were brave and almost all of them had attended West Point. A commander's age, the weapons used by both sides, class rank at West Point or branch of service after graduation were all examined and then discarded as bearing little or no relevance to this study. By comparison, the six elements described in this book were all observable phenomena.

Other qualities or behaviors not included in this study might surface in the years ahead, or perhaps they have simply gone unnoticed or untested by this author. Under enormous pressures, a commander had to organize, support, move and fight his forces so that they would succeed. Victorious commanders had to possess several important personal character traits and, of vital significance, they were required to create successful teams of subordinate officers and staff members to help them accomplish their objectives.

Each chapter is divided into three parts:
- An introduction that sets the stage for the contest
- The battle narrative
- An analysis of the ways in which the six factors influenced the outcome of the action

As a result of this process, however, the somewhat stunning pattern that emerges from this study suggests that with few exceptions, the North was able to win most of the consequential engagements in the West during 1862. Some of the victories were entirely strategic in nature, requiring limited tactical engagements, but many of the victories resulted from a combination of the six circumstances described above. The extent of the victory was often defined by the fact that the commander on one side was able to achieve success in all or many of the six standards listed, while the defeated general had very limited success in any of these areas. In the end, the opening question needs to be addressed: Other than exceptional generalship, what observable elements of Civil War leadership led to victory or defeat?

Prologue

The Mexican War

One might well ask: Why does a book on the Civil War begin with a description of the conflict with Mexico? Why is this useful? From 1846 to 1848, the United States was engaged in a war, now long forgotten by most, with the nation bordering the American Southwest. In fact, the current Southwestern United States, including California, New Mexico, Arizona and parts of Texas, belonged to Mexico until this conflict wrested the territory from our neighbor to the south. Understanding the war with Mexico, however, serves as a foundation for better comprehension of the Civil War as a whole and the battles that follow this prologue. The six factors used to identify the extent of victory in battle were all present during this war, and the two generals who led American armies displayed behaviors that were later emulated by an entire generation of officers that led military forces during the Civil War.

Major General Winfield Scott at Veracruz, 1847 (Library of Congress).

Barring age and health issues, service in Mexico foreshadowed additional service in the Civil War for many men. Nine battles are detailed in this Civil War study. Within these nine battles, 14 commanding generals, seven Union and seven Confederate, served in

Mexico; two of these men, Grant and Bragg, each led armies in two of the battles analyzed here. Of the 14 army commanders in this Civil War study, seven served under Taylor, five under Scott alone, and two saw service under both leaders. Only William Nelson served in the U.S. Navy during the Veracruz landings, and three other officers saw no Mexican War action. In summary, a remarkable number of western generals saw service under either Zachary Taylor or Winfield Scott. It is fair to claim that both Taylor and Scott had a significant impact on the young officers who later led armies in the Western Theater of the Civil War.[1]

During the war with Mexico, these two men exercised very different types of leadership. Appointed by President Polk and charged with winning the war, both generals sought to establish achievable goals for their soldiers, interacted with their immediate lieutenants in an attempt to form victorious teams, and utilized different approaches to staffing as they labored to support their forces. They animated their soldiers as they led their armies into combat, attempted to take the initiative in attacking Mexican armies, and sought a strategic outcome that would bring the war to a quick and victorious close. Demonstrating remarkably different styles of leadership, they went about these efforts while being watched closely, and later emulated in some ways, by the young men who would later lead Civil War armies. Without an understanding of how army leadership superintended the Mexican War, it is much more challenging to determine why many generals in the Civil War behaved as they did. Practices and habits developed during the Mexican War naturally found their way into Civil War operations. However, some of the lessons learned in the Mexican War disappeared as the Civil War opened, and only time and experience would lead to the same or greater levels of sophistication and execution resuming once again. This prologue summarizes that great undertaking and the efforts that Taylor and Scott made to assemble an effective American army.

Coincidentally, just as rivers played a crucial part during the advent of the Civil War in the West, they played a major role when the Mexican

Major General Zachary Taylor, engraved portrait (Library of Congress).

War was launched earlier as well. As the United States and Mexico disputed a common boundary, the land between the Rio Grande River to the south and the Nueces River to the north was inextricably bound up with the dispute. Where did the U.S. boundary end and Mexican jurisdiction begin? A large piece of territory was caught up in this dispute, land that would be crucial in linking the American southwest with coveted space in California. Slavery was an issue during this conflict as well. Would the U.S. expand not only its sovereignty but also the practice of slavery after its "Manifest Destiny" was fulfilled?

With the advent of settlers moving to Texas, the groundwork was laid for conflict. While Mexico secured its independence from Spain in 1821, Moses Austin and the first settlers from the United States received permission to move into Mexican Texas. Following Mexican independence, however, in 1829, the Mexican government abolished slavery throughout its own country and Texas as well. Further disputes between the Texan province and Mexico led to the revolt of 1835–36. When Texan independence was assured after the Battle of San Jacinto in 1836, the American government annexed Texas as the 28th state in 1845. For a time, Mexico recognized neither the annexation of Texas nor any boundary line between the two parties. As a Democrat from the slave-holding state of Tennessee, President Polk understood that an expansion of U.S. territory in the southwest would also improve the opportunities for an expansion of slavery.

* * *

Realizing that this dispute would probably lead to hostilities, Polk ordered Brevet Brigadier General Zachary Taylor and his small army into Texas as a Corps of Observation established on the Rio Grande River, well within the territory that Mexico considered hers. By April of 1846, Mexico recognized the annexation of Texas but continued to dispute the boundary between Mexico and the U.S. Ordering the Americans out of the territory between the Nueces River and the Rio Grande without success, a Mexican force surrounded a United States cavalry detachment and destroyed it, killing 16 and capturing several more. President Polk, sensing the opportunity, asked for and received a declaration of war from Congress. When war was declared on May 13, 1846, Zachary Taylor was already in the area, and owing to the result of his earlier success in Florida during the Seminole War, he became the logical choice to continue as the commanding general. Mexico resisted American demands to surrender its land, forcefully, but the U.S. was now prepared to pursue the war and conquer the available territory. Two men were anxious to provide leadership in the coming contest: Taylor and Winfield Scott, his immediate superior in Washington.[2]

Major General Winfield Scott, the other principal officer in this story, waited in Washington as Commanding General of the army, impatient for his turn at command as well. Having fought heroically in the War of 1812 and now as the country's first soldier, he felt the responsibility should be his. At some point, both men would eye the presidency as a possible prize to reward a successful campaign. But James K. Polk, the sitting president and commander-in-chief, had his own agenda—and the final say over military leadership. For reasons he alone best understood, Polk alternated between the two. As a result, both men would cast very different shadows of "leadership style" over the soldiers who would ultimately succeed them in the next conflict. Both generals were successful in battling a poorly trained and equipped Mexican army. Both men engaged several young lions as officers serving under them, and those men in turn eagerly observed their every move to see how war should be conducted. The observations of these young men would turn into lessons and experiences they would carry into the next war. This writer, however, is not anxious to replicate a Russian novel with its multiple characters and is concerned that crowding the story with all the youngsters might detract from the overall impact of the two masters. Therefore, this prologue will deal principally with the behaviors of the two commanding officers.[3]

After the destruction of the small, American cavalry unit, Mexican forces besieged an American fort on soil they claimed for Mexico. Zachary Taylor began marching his small force of American regulars to relieve the garrison. In two battles, Palo Alto and Resaca de la Palma, Taylor's army defeated the Mexicans. Other actions in California and the New Mexico territory also led to Mexican defeats. As Taylor advanced, he occupied the towns of Matamoros and Camargo, and finally, after stiff resistance, he captured Monterrey (September 21–24, 1846). On February 23, 1847, another Mexican army, under the leadership of Santa Anna, attacked Taylor's force at Buena Vista and was defeated. During and after these actions, Taylor was both celebrated and criticized for his methods of waging war. Celebrations occurred every time he defeated the Mexican army. Criticism erupted when he suffered high casualties or separated his already compact force into still smaller pieces. He was also feared by President Polk and fellow Democrats, as they felt that, based on his victories, he could secure a successful candidacy for the presidential election of 1848. Finally, after Taylor's victory at Buena Vista, Mexican guerrillas destroyed his supply train and with it any opportunity he might have enjoyed for a further advance. Winfield Scott, as general-in-chief in Washington, was also both jealous and critical of Taylor's victories.[4]

In his memoirs, Scott gives the reader a clear view of Taylor's deficiencies as Scott saw them: "This selection of the commander was made with the concurrence of the autobiographer [Scott], who, knowing him to be slow of thought, of hesitancy in speech, and un-used to the pen, took care, about the same time, to provide him, unsolicited, with a staff officer…. With a good store of common sense, General Taylor's mind had not been enlarged and refreshed by reading, or much converse with the world.…. His simplicity was childlike."[5]

On the other hand, U.S. Grant provides this picture of Taylor from his memoirs: "General Taylor was not an officer to trouble the administration much with his demands, but was inclined to do the best he could with the means given him. In dress, he was possibly too plain, rarely wearing anything in the field to indicate his rank, or even that he was an officer; but he was known to every soldier in his army, and was respected by all."[6]

Justin Smith describes Taylor at the Battle of Buena Vista "huddled rather than mounted … on Old Whitey, with arms folded and one leg unconcernedly thrown across the pommel of his saddle."[7]

It is from these descriptions that we see a clear picture of Zachary Taylor as a leader of men. He was brave to a fault. He dressed plainly and never sought to attract attention to himself for purposes of show. K. Jack Bauer suggests that Taylor brought his army to the battlefield, remained visible and alert during each battle, and demonstrated his personal bravery, while at the same time letting his immediate subordinates manage their own assigned parts of the engagement. Most sources seem to agree that he let his appointed chief of staff manage the day-to-day affairs of the army. When Taylor began his advance on March 8, 1846, he brought 307 wagons (one wagon for every ten men), 1,900 horses and mules along with him. Oxen pulled 84 wagons. He apparently used only the most informal staff system to manage his little force at first. When he finally engaged a much larger Mexican army at Buena Vista, he adopted the staff officers serving under General Wool, whose forces made up the bulk of the American army. He won every battle in which he was engaged, and he was able to use these victories as a successful gateway to the presidency. U.S. Grant and some of the other young officers were obviously enamored with some of Taylor's personality traits. There was also another lesson to be learned by some of the officer novices who observed Taylor: On occasion, military victory can be won without the commanding officer rising to the level of a battlefield genius. For every Napoleon or U.S. Grant, one can also find men of more average caliber who succeed when matched against other leaders of lesser ability. Thus, in observing Taylor and some of his foibles, some very ordinary officers could believe and hope that they might do well in command of an army. This was not a lesson taught in a military academy.[8]

In some ways, this description mirrors behaviors that Grant himself practiced during the Civil War. Young officers who would later fight in that conflict learned a great deal from the examples set by these two men, Scott and Taylor. Both men would cast very different shadows of "leadership style" over the officers, who would ultimately succeed them in the next conflict, but it is Scott who left the more indelible impression of the two, and we will concentrate on his efforts to win the war.

Winfield Scott provided the leadership that won the Mexican War. He first worked closely with the U.S. Navy by launching a remarkable, combined arms landing at Veracruz. By employing a professional staff, he planned and executed a series of maneuvers that outflanked heavy Mexican opposition, he supplied his army on a challenging march from the coast to the gates of Mexico City, and he used a force of scouts and spies to secure reliable information about an unknown land. These lessons were taken to heart by only a few Civil War generals. As K. Jack Bauer has written, "Winfield Scott without question was the ablest American soldier to appear in America between Washington and Sherman." Even at the time of his campaign, others, such as the Duke of Wellington, observed his professional qualities from afar and commented on them: "His campaign was unsurpassed in military annals. He is the greatest living soldier."[9]

To capture Mexico City, Scott proposed to transport his army to Veracruz, take the city and then march directly to the Mexican capital. In doing this, he needed to move his force by sea, land it on a hostile shore, capture a fortified city, and then undertake an exhausting march into the heart of a hostile country. In accomplishing his mission, Scott was very successful in assembling a team of men who would support his efforts. A naval force under Commodore David Connor not only provided transportation and armed support, but also included 65 specially constructed surfboats (designed in a joint effort between Scott and a naval lieutenant, George M. Totten). They quickly landed Scott's entire army in the face of armed opposition. As a combined arms exercise, the landing was brilliantly conducted. It was no accident that Scott made it part of his planning to carefully include the U.S. Navy as a key part of the process. While Scott has been accused of being a difficult personality, he was able to work comfortably with a wide variety of professionals in both services. Once ashore, his staff, including Robert E. Lee in a prominent role, provided important reconnaissance support, and while the staff helped plant batteries and supported the infantry, the U.S. Navy once again stepped up and landed heavy artillery for the successful siege of the town. As his campaign unfolded, Scott was carefully monitored by President Polk, who even sent Gideon

Pillow, a trusted ally, to serve as the commander of a volunteer brigade and to spy on Scott at the same time. After seizing Veracruz, Scott proceeded to march successfully across the interior of Mexico and capture Mexico City. Along the way, he was victorious at engagements that included Cerro Gordo on April 18, Battles of Contreras and Churubusco on August 20, capture of Molino del Rey on September 8, and finally the assault of Mexico City and its surrounding fortifications on September 13 and 14, 1847.[10]

After reviewing the Mexican War, it is now possible to apply the six questions introduced in the Preface. While the experiences of General Taylor offer interesting anecdotes in each of these areas, it appears that Taylor delegated many of the staff and tactical decisions to subordinates, and his formal advance beyond the Rio Grande ended after the Battle of Buena Vista. Following his capture of Mexico City in 1848, Scott was able to prosecute the war to a victorious conclusion.

* * *

Unfortunately, President James K. Polk, a Democrat, mistrusted both (Whig) commanders and failed to set a clear objective or even useful parameters for Zachary Taylor, and later quarreled with Scott over the process for ending the conflict. In Taylor's case, the general turned in a high casualty count, particularly after the Battle of Monterrey. Once Taylor occupied the northeastern corner of the country, the President hoped that Mexico would simply give up and sue for peace. When this did not happen, Polk began searching for a different approach that would bring the war to a successful conclusion. His ruminations failed to include Taylor. Eventually Taylor was deprived of almost all his regiments of regulars and left standing in a barren land. Most importantly Taylor did not appear to have a clear objective once the war opened. While he could defeat Mexican armies that attacked him, Taylor was not positioned to capture Mexico City, a journey of over 700 miles, through truly forbidding terrain. Taylor did not have a clear and attainable objective.

In Winfield Scott's case, both President Polk and the general agreed that an achievable objective presented itself: Mexico City. While he faced challenging conditions, he could land his army successfully in Veracruz and march 200 miles to Mexico's capital. As President Polk tried to provide all the physical resources for Scott, he was also aware that Scott was a member of the opposing political party and a potential political rival. Without question, neither Polk nor Scott trusted the other man, and this complicated relations between them. As Winfield Scott was a potential rival, Polk was at first reluctant to appoint him to command an American army in Mexico. In the end, however, Polk was pressured by his own advisors into asking Scott to take charge of the expedition. Even so, President Polk looked for other individuals to command the army. When Polk seriously entertained the thought of appointing Senator Thomas Hart Benton, he proposed that Benton be named as commander and given the rank of lieutenant general. When Scott found out, he declared that he "smelt the rat." This was only the beginning of the Polk/Scott controversy that continued throughout the entire campaign. While Polk was finally willing to let Scott command the expedition, he did everything possible to embarrass his commanding officer both during and even beyond the war. Both Scott and the President, however, agreed on Mexico City as the objective, and Scott successfully captured it.[11]

Under Zachary Taylor, his little American army was poised to take the initiative throughout the early months of the Mexican War. While the Mexican army attempted to attack Taylor on more than one occasion, it was Taylor's aggressive forward movements that encouraged the Mexican attacks. Until Taylor's supplies were finally destroyed during the Buena Vista campaign, he was able to move about forcefully in occupying Mexican territory. After this battle, however, Taylor was simply unable to follow up his victory and very quickly lost any opportunity to retain the initiative.

Following Scott's primary campaign across Mexico, it is clear he seized and held the initiative throughout the duration of the war and continued to take the offensive for each action that he fought. After he landed in Veracruz, Scott never surrendered the offensive initiative for the rest of the campaign. There were occasions when he paused after the Mexicans requested a period of truce or when Scott needed to bring up additional reinforcements or mark time waiting for supplies, but he never completely gave up his offensive campaign.

Achieving unity of command was a challenge for Zachary Taylor. He struggled to gain the active support of his generals. The professionals and amateurs all quarreled with one another and with Taylor on several occasions. Early in the war, a dispute broke out between Generals Worth (holding a brevet rank) and Twiggs (holding a regular army rank), and both reported to Taylor. "Who was the senior officer?" they asked, and each one claimed that title. Taylor supported Twiggs while Worth appealed to President Polk. Polk sided with Twiggs and Worth resigned shortly after receiving the verdict. He later calmed down and returned to duty. Commanders of volunteer regiments often quarreled with the regulars, and Taylor appeared to lose control over his army at times when widespread looting occurred.[12]

Another incident occurred after the Battle of Monterrey; Taylor resolved to discharge his Texans. Their behavior away from the battlefield had been atrocious and uncontrolled. Portions of Texas and northeastern Mexico had become a virtual wasteland. Homes were destroyed, innocent civilians raped, killed or badly injured and whole villages ruined. Taylor was quick to send his Texan volunteers home.[13]

Prior to the Battle of Buena Vista in February of 1847, Taylor and his second-in-command, General Wool, got into a major dispute over where to fight the battle. Wool wished to fall back on the ranch of Buena Vista. General Taylor favored a defensive stance where the army stood. One source tells us that "Rough and Ready raved and told General Wool to 'go to h—l in his own way.'"[14]

Even while the Battle of Buena Vista was exploding in violence, Taylor's own regimental commanders argued with one another. General Joseph Lane ordered his brigade to charge, but Colonel Bowles, commanding the 2nd Indiana, gave the order to retreat. His regiment broke and "fled like deer," throwing away their arms.[15]

Finally, near the end of the day, still another episode transpired. As the enemy neared Taylor's ordnance wagons at a gallop, two volunteer colonels in charge of protecting them, Yell and Marshall, spent the time arguing over seniority. Colonel Marshall ordered the men to fire in defense while Yell wished to wait until the enemy drew closer. Some men fired while others retreated. Colonel Yell was then impaled on a Mexican lance, and that ended the dispute. A regiment of regular cavalry finally drove off the Mexicans.[16]

Taylor's withdrawal from the Buena Vista battlefield was not a pretty sight. One witness called the retreat that of a mob. Officers and men were apparently drunk, and men, women, horses and mules became intermingled during the march. In Taylor's defense, it must be said that he was apparently quite visible during each of his engagements with the Mexican army. While he did not personally lead soldiers into combat, he was close enough to the action to be in some danger from time to time and to respond to any needs that arose during the battle.[17]

As he strove to achieve unity of command, Winfield Scott also faced challenges from his immediate subordinates. Five generals commanded Scott's force. Two of them were regulars who failed to get on well with one another. The other three, whom the professional military men in the army often viewed with contempt, were volunteers turned soldiers. Chief among the civilian soldiers was Gideon Pillow, later serving as a major critic of the commanding general, although it took Scott some time to find this out. This group plus Scott's chosen aides made up his official family. It would be difficult to command a more challenging group, but Scott combined these disparate personalities into a team. During actual battles Scott never seemed to expose himself directly to enemy fire but remained within easy reach of his staff and subordinates. While it is possible to find fault with Scott for a variety of reasons (his vanity, his love of food, and his willingness to talk—unceasingly), he made this group of individualists work tirelessly for one goal—the conquest of Mexico. He succeeded brilliantly.[18]

Justin Smith paints word pictures of these men in somewhat uncomplimentary terms. David E. Twiggs: "Scott had already said that he was not qualified 'to command an army—within the presence, or in the absence of an enemy.' His brains were, in fact, merely what happened to be left over from the making of his spinal cord." Robert Patterson: "Patterson, who led [the Volunteer Division], seemed, however, by no means eager to accept the responsibility of command.... No confidence whatever was felt in Pillow, the second in rank." General William Worth was a friend of Scott's and their friendship dated back to the War of 1812, but after Scott ordered Worth into a bloody attack during the battle of Molino del Rey, their friendship ended. After the war, Worth joined Gideon Pillow in attacking Scott. While in the heat of battle, however, these officers appeared to follow orders to the best of their abilities. Scott suffered a variety of self-centered and self-serving individuals, but he was able to command their loyalty during the battles he fought and achieve the goals of his campaign. It wasn't until after the conquest of Mexico City that his management was truly challenged.[19]

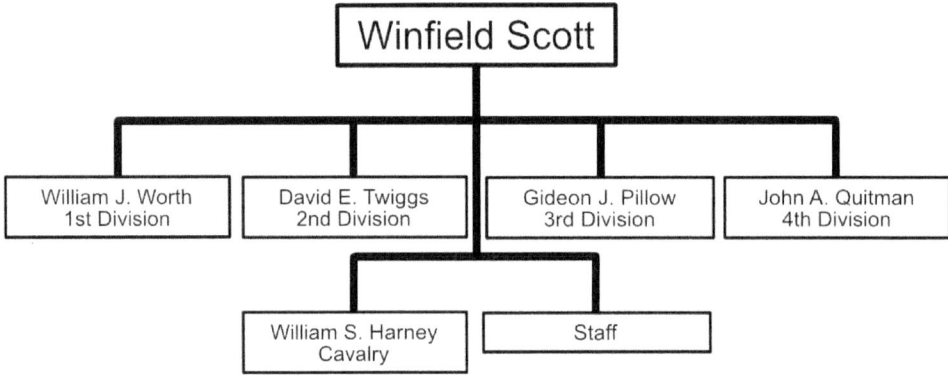

Army organization under Major General Winfield Scott in Mexico. Except for General Pillow, all the other immediate subordinates were members of the U.S. Regular Army (courtesy Margaret A. Zimmermann).

Scott demonstrated his habit of making careful preparations before the Battle of Molino del Rey. "Captain Mason and Lieutenant Foster of the engineers daringly reconnoitered the Mexican position, and, although Casa Mata—standing on low ground and partially masked by its earthworks and the maguey—was not adequately made out, they analyzed the situation correctly otherwise. Then, to prevent errors, Brevet Lieutenant Colonel Duncan and two engineers did the work a second time; and Scott and Worth also made observations." At age 60, even though Scott sent others on scouting missions, he didn't hesitate to conduct his own reconnaissance as well.[20]

Zachary Taylor has often been blamed for running an organization that was, at times, less than professional in performance, particularly in logistical support. A look at his staff appointments suggests, however, that he used the best professional support he could find. Unfortunately for Taylor, the Quartermaster's Department was very weak. Major Charles Thomas struggled to equip Taylor's force originally. Then Taylor's next quartermaster, Trueman Cross, disappeared on April 10, 1846, and was ambushed alone outside of Taylor's camp. After his death, the army's Chief Quartermaster Jesup appointed Brigadier General Henry Whiting to join Taylor in August of 1846. With one exception, these men were all West Point graduates, and a review of their service records through Cullum's *Register* suggests that all of them were experienced practitioners in the staff assignments they held. Despite their professionalism, however, Taylor failed to provide adequate protection for his supply train.[21]

On February 24, 1847, a large government train consisting of 110 wagons and 300 pack mules was attacked; the escort consisted of only 34 soldiers. They apparently surrendered to the guerrillas and the entire train was lost. This disaster, coming at the same time as Buena Vista, ended any hope Taylor might have had for moving forward. Taylor's staff efforts must be ruled a failure.[22]

Even with the staff challenges posed during the Mexican War, these staff assignments suggest that by comparison, Civil War generals used very modest staff organizations to assist much larger armed forces. The size of Taylor's or Scott's little armies seldom reached above 10,000–15,000 men where the standard Civil War army in the West often surpassed 40,000. While Taylor and Scott used experienced West Point graduates almost exclusively, Civil War generals often faced great pressure to use West Point graduates in combat roles. As a result, both sides used men with extensive civilian backgrounds, and it will be seen later that those backgrounds differed significantly between North and South. The evidence also suggests that the North obtained more effective logistical results, and these results were often tied, in part, to choices made by commanders in their staff appointments.[23]

General Winfield Scott used the best, handpicked staff members he could find to carry out his orders and provide logistical support. Men such as Robert E. Lee, Joseph E. Johnston, Pierre G.T. Beauregard, George B. McClellan, Joseph Hooker and George Gordon Meade all played important roles. Scott commented on members of his supporting staff in his autobiography that included "Colonel Totten, Chief Engineer, Lieutenant Hitchcock, acting Inspector-General, Captain Robert E. Lee, Engineer and First Lieutenant, Henry L. Scott, acting Adjutant General." He relied on this group throughout the campaign for their professionalism and support. In his memoirs, Scott also carefully lists his general staff, engineer corps, and the six staff departments that supported his army's efforts as it advanced toward Mexico City. Scott enjoyed a particularly able and active staff. Comparing early Civil War staff assignments with those of Scott, staff effectiveness apparently regressed early in the conflict. In Scott's memoirs, we find references to no less than 36 officers (exclusive of his Pay and Medical Departments) serving as his professional staff. Scott's ability to march overland from Veracruz to Mexico City, bringing sufficient ammunition and securing necessary food and forage along the way, suggests that the staff performed exceptionally well.[24]

Supplies of ammunition remained plentiful even as the army learned to live off the countryside. On April 20, 1847, Scott's chief quartermaster reported that 500 wagons and 250 pack mules took the road in support of the expedition. Scott had originally proposed 800–1000 wagons for his army of 10,000. As Scott's staff officers included trained engineers and the U.S. Army did not have a strong or reliable cavalry arm in Mexico, the staff officers scouted ahead of the army and suggested indirect approaches to the Mexican army that would outflank the strong positions they often held. Members of his staff supervised each engagement and became Scott's eyes and ears across the entire battlefield. While Scott had proved his personal bravery in earlier battles, he now remained an appropriate distance away from the actual combat during the drive on Mexico City.[25]

Scott's successful march on Mexico City relied heavily on a group of scouts and spies to gain information about the foreign land the Americans traveled. According to Justin Smith, Scott's Spy Company grew from a handful of five to at least 100 and perhaps as many as 2,000 men by the close of the campaign.[26] In this way, Scott was able to anticipate the terrain, logistical preparations, and the strength of his opponent before any action was undertaken. During the American Civil War, armed forces faced similar challenges with unmapped territories and unknown quantities of food and forage available from the countryside, and effective commanders needed to plan their campaigns carefully to hope for success. Scott's experience should have prepared anyone who soldiered with his army for this type of energetic and thoughtful preparation. Oftentimes, however, Scott's careful planning was not replicated by Civil War generals.[27]

In discussing his landing at Veracruz and the coming siege operation with his staff, Scott wrote the following: "This plan [for taking Veracruz] I had never submitted to discussion [in a council of war]. Several Generals and Colonels-among them

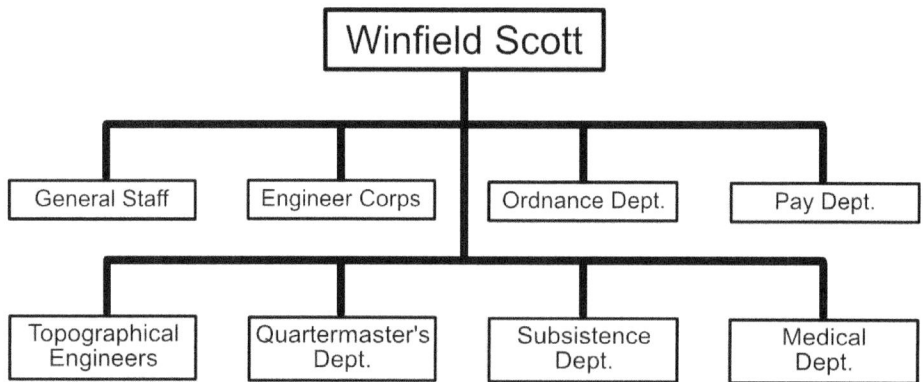

Staff organization under Winfield Scott. For the campaign in Mexico, Winfield Scott utilized the robust staff organization seen in this diagram. Altogether Scott's staff included 66 men. Compare this chart to the lean Civil War staffing usually seen in early 1862. By the time of Stones River, both North and South saw the necessity for adding staff officers at the army level. See note 27 (courtesy Margaret A. Zimmermann).

Major-General Patterson ... solicited the privilege of leading storming parties. The applicants were thanked and applauded; but I forebore saying to them more. In my little cabinet, however, ... I entered fully into the question of storming parties and regular siege approaches."[28]

While Scott did hold councils of war with his leading officers and staff members when he chose to do so, he would also dispense with these formalities when he had already determined his course of action. Councils of war often disappeared during the Civil War or, where commanders used them, they sought only to invite support for actions they wished to take. By including officers in a conversation, a commander could share the responsibility and accountability with his officers. This could be useful when decisions to attack or retreat became controversial. Scott's approach to Mexico City was one such time. "On the morning of the eleventh he inspected these [fortifications] once more, and then had a conference of generals and engineers at La Piedad. It was a solemn gathering. Before them lay the fortified capital of Mexico, a hopeful army of perhaps 15,000, a good equipment of artillery, nearly 700 trained gunners, and a large population, somewhat disillusioned, but excited and vengeful; and in view of the American situation, it was essential, as the commander-in-chief clearly indicated, to strike a vital blow at once. But where? Point by point Scott fully and fairly stated the case."[29]

Zachary Taylor attempted to use all the resources given to him. As he was forced to leave garrisons in his rear to protect line of supply, he was unable to muster all of his men for combat. This was not Taylor's doing, but once again, this problem was a result of Polk's unwillingness to fully support him. By the time Buena Vista was fought, Taylor had been forced to relinquish most of his regulars to Winfield Scott. It would appear that he actively used the resources he still had available to him, and in the end was consistently victorious.

Each time that Scott entered battle, he, too, applied maximum force, used all of the resources available to him and was victorious. While he husbanded his strength for his advance on Mexico City, he also employed most of his army as needed to propel his campaign through to a successful conclusion. He paused to receive supplies and additional soldiers as necessary, but in each of his engagements, he prepared to use his entire military strength at one time to achieve victory. "Here the plans were finally decided upon. Quitman's division and a forlorn hope of about 265 selected officers and men from Twiggs's division, under Captain Casey of the Second Infantry, were to advance by the Tacubaya road; and Pillow's, preceded by a similar party from Worth's division, led by Captain McKenzie of the Second Artillery, was to attack by way of El Molino and the grove. Then every one betook himself to his post." In the end, Scott's entire force was committed to the attack on Mexico City and victory followed.[30]

Unfortunately for Taylor, President Polk and his political supporters believed that a simple show of force would suffice to bring the Mexicans to the negotiating table and achieve strategic success. When this failed, Polk moved on to another plan, Scott's landing at Veracruz. As a result, while Taylor was successful in holding off Santa Anna's host at the Battle of Buena Vista, he was unable to resume offensive operations afterward.[31]

Scott's strategic aim was to secure a favorable peace with Mexico through force of arms, and by capturing the Mexican capital, he positioned the United States to negotiate a favorable treaty and attain the strategic outcome of his expedition. Each battle fought brought him closer to that successful conclusion. In summary, then, we can conclude that Scott was able to achieve his goal in all six areas outlined above. Using the Mexican

War as our starting point, these questions can be applied to Civil War engagements in the West.

Mexico: Six Elements of Victory

Mexico	Clear, Attainable Objective	Operational Initiative	Command Unity
Taylor	Not Achieved	Not Achieved	Not Achieved
Scott	Achieved	Achieved	Achieved
	Logistics/Staff	*Used All Resources*	*Strategic Outcome*
Taylor	Not Achieved	Achieved	Not Achieved
Scott	Achieved	Achieved	Achieved

By setting a realistic goal of capturing Mexico City in winning the war, Winfield Scott successfully employed an army fully supported by a professional staff and ably led by competent subordinates. By comparison and for many reasons he was helpless to control, Taylor struggled to achieve success in several of these areas.

Chapter 1

Mill Springs

Triumph of Professional Leadership

A student of history might think that the Battle of Mill Springs or Logan's Crossroads in Kentucky, fought on January 19, 1862, formed a kind of asterisk or footnote that was heavily overshadowed by far more important events that year. But the battle that occurred there was critically important for both the North and South. It also served to highlight the experience that professional soldiers brought to the battlefield in comparison to the efforts of well-meaning amateurs. To place it into proper perspective and set the stage for the battle, it is necessary to step back in time to 1861.

When the Civil War began with the fall of Fort Sumter in April of 1861, powerful forces were set into motion. Both North and South began gathering their hosts and planning for a hard-fought contest. Both sides thought the war would be brief and that the rebellion would end quickly with a march on Richmond or with a Union defeat that would discourage the North. The South even hoped to bring about foreign intervention for the Confederacy. At this time, three groups of states emerged from the early fog of war: northern, southern and border. While in the East, the states of Delaware and Maryland formed a border between North and South; the West saw the states of Kentucky and Missouri play the same role. West of the Mississippi the state of Missouri experienced its own drama early in 1861. Northern and Southern interests clashed in St. Louis on the Mississippi River, and the North under General Lyon held the city itself; but as soon as Lyon moved his little army well outside the city, he was confronted, defeated, and killed by a Confederate force commanded jointly by Sterling Price, former governor of the state, and Ben McCulloch from Texas. To remain in the Union, Missouri required Northern reinforcements. That left the state of Kentucky entangled in the make-believe state of neutrality.

Kentucky boasted strong commercial ties with the northern states across the Ohio River, but it also sponsored slavery. Both governments in Washington and Richmond coveted Kentucky as a critical state in their wartime planning. For the South, if Kentucky joined the Confederacy, the rebels would hold a natural boundary extending to the Ohio River. For the North, Kentucky represented a gateway for advancing along the river lines of the Tennessee, Cumberland and Mississippi into the deep South. Both sides claimed they would support Kentucky's neutrality, yet each side schemed to control the state's destiny for their own benefit. Who would break Kentucky's neutrality first?

Introducing Bishop Leonidas Polk and Gideon Pillow, two Southern generals of somewhat dubious fame. In a classic demonstration of political maneuvering, Jefferson

Davis and Tennessee Governor Isham Harris appointed two good friends of theirs to critical positions of leadership. Without informing anyone of their plans, however, the two generals sponsored an invasion of Kentucky on September 3–4, 1861. Columbus, Kentucky, on the Mississippi River, was captured and fortified. Now Kentucky was invaded, the Mississippi River was blocked, neutrality was gone, and President Jefferson Davis decided to make the best of it. But Polk (a West Point graduate without military experience) and Pillow (a civilian with Mexican War experience) along with former newspaper editor Felix Zollicoffer, seemed a random lot for such an important theater, and Davis needed a guiding hand. Conveniently for Davis, veteran soldier General Albert Sidney Johnston appeared in Richmond on September 5 after a difficult journey from California, and Davis appointed him to overall command in Kentucky and Tennessee. Born in Kentucky, a graduate of West Point, Johnston had served during the Texas War for Independence, the Mexican War, the Utah War and commanded the Department of the Pacific in California when the Civil War erupted. While Johnston traveled west to take command, events in Kentucky would outpace his ability to control them.[1]

Johnston realized that he was accountable for defending an enormous front, across the entire state of Kentucky, and he set to work immediately. Columbus, Kentucky, with its high bluffs overlooking the Mississippi River, formed the western anchor of the new Confederate line and shielded Memphis to the south. Polk and Pillow were sent there to undertake its defense. Bowling Green in the center of the state guarded Nashville, Tennessee, to the south, and Johnston himself took a small force there for its defense. The Cumberland River shielded eastern Kentucky from Federal incursions, but the Cumberland Gap needed an army to defend the eastern boundary of Johnston's command. Former editor and politician Felix Zollicoffer assembled a small force in that region. While

Brigadier General George H. Thomas. An experienced and professional approach to war made Thomas a formidable opponent (Library of Congress).

Major General George B. Crittenden (courtesy The Civil War Museum, Kenosha, WI).

the South mustered troops to hold these positions, they also attempted to construct no less than six armored warships on or near the Mississippi River and protect a line that ran almost 400 miles across the state of Kentucky.

The North needed to penetrate this line and Union generals began looking for weak points along this front. General Don Carlos Buell was appointed to lead Union forces in Kentucky, and Brigadier General George H. Thomas served under him. Buell was not prepared to undertake a major offensive in Kentucky, but he was not afraid to order Thomas to secure the eastern portion of the state. The first point they tapped was Mill Springs, Kentucky, near the Cumberland River. A small but important engagement would occur here in early 1862 that demonstrated Confederate weakness in several ways. Unfortunately for them, the Confederates made poor choices of commanding officers and then failed to properly equip and train their soldiers. These problems would sorely challenge the Confederates in the months ahead, and their entire independence movement would be endangered.

A favorite of George B. McClellan, commander of all Union armies by the end of 1861, Don Carlos Buell was a native son of Ohio, a state whose troops made up the bulk of his force. As he began assembling a Union force in north central Kentucky, he was willing to take tentative action on the eastern side of the state.

Beginning in October of 1861, the Confederates under Albert Sidney Johnston established their defensive line. Johnston struggled to raise troops, arm and train them, and then hold this great expanse of territory. In this effort, neither Judah P. Benjamin, Confederate Secretary of War, nor Samuel Cooper, Adjutant General, were very helpful. Johnston had the responsibility for the defense of Kentucky but few resources with which to work. Unfortunately for the Confederates, Johnston was forced to concentrate on some very challenging tasks, and he was not able to exercise active oversight in eastern or western Kentucky. In late November, he ordered Felix Zollicoffer to move into eastern Kentucky from the Cumberland Gap, protect that part of the state, and occupy territory just south of the Cumberland River. On December 5, Zollicoffer crossed over to the northern side of the river. Once again, a political appointee took center stage. Zollicoffer lacked even rudimentary military experience, and he moved forward impulsively.[2]

Young John Simpson watched his arrival. "I as a boy of fourteen years, and with a neighbor boy was watching the troops pass.... In a few days a steamboat arrived from Nashville, and General Zollicoffer crossed the river at Mill Springs with most of his army and fortified on both sides of the river." In this way, the Confederates hoped to protect eastern Kentucky from Union forces and shield important Confederate locations in eastern Tennessee, including the Cumberland Gap. Now Zollicoffer would collide with Brigadier General George Thomas, a former Virginian and a professional soldier with a West Point background, but one who stayed with the North.[3]

Thomas brought professional experience with him for this assignment. A veteran of the Seminole wars, the War with Mexico, and conflicts with Native Americans in Texas, Thomas understood what he needed to do in combat and took the time to train his new recruits. Under pressure from both Lincoln and McClellan to move into eastern Kentucky, Major General Don Carlos Buell ordered Thomas to meet Zollicoffer's threat. "On the 17th of January Thomas reached Logan's Crossroads, ten miles north of Zollicoffer's entrenched camp (on the north side of the Cumberland [River], opposite Mill Springs)." At an earlier time under General Robert Anderson and then under the fraying William

Sherman, the North made little headway in Kentucky. Following conflicting orders from each man, George Thomas originally marched about in eastern Kentucky without true direction. At one point ordered forward, then ordered to retrace his steps, he led a small and frustrated band of around 4,000 Union soldiers. Now Buell was in command, Thomas was in place and, with his own force along with additional reinforcements coming shortly to his aid, threatened Zollicoffer.[4]

On December 16, 1861, Zollicoffer, without specific orders to do so, had already crossed the swollen Cumberland River and threatened a further advance. General Buell ordered Thomas forward on December 29. As Zollicoffer's 4,000 men advanced beyond the swollen Cumberland River, Jefferson Davis finally realized that he could use someone with West Point experience and sent Brigadier General George B. Crittenden to direct this force. By sending Crittenden and reinforcing Zollicoffer with additional inexperienced and often unarmed soldiers, Richmond compounded the problems facing the Confederates in Tennessee. Although George Crittenden arrived in Knoxville, Tennessee, in December, he was not informed of Zollicoffer's movement at first. When Crittenden, Zollicoffer and Johnston all failed to communicate their thoughts to one another or back to Richmond, the situation became even more confused.[5]

Confederate leaders felt that Crittenden had gained solid military experience in Mexico and could steady the amateurs. Unfortunately, it was rumored that Crittenden had experience with the bottle as well and therefore was occasionally out of commission at critical moments. He had been court-martialed for this offense in 1848 following allegations made during the Mexican War. Crittenden rode in to join Zollicoffer, but when he arrived in January of 1862, he found the amateur already across the Cumberland River. While technically Crittenden was in charge, Zollicoffer had already made the decisions that committed the Confederates to action. By the 19th of January, Crittenden and Zollicoffer realized that George Thomas was moving toward their position and that strong reinforcements could support him as well. Zollicoffer was in over his head, the weather deteriorated, the river was rising, and now he was trapped on the wrong side. Both Zollicoffer and Crittenden felt they were too weak to defend this poorly selected place. To forestall a unified Federal advance, Crittenden and Zollicoffer marched to

Felix Zollicoffer led Crittenden's force into battle at Mill Springs. By placing the unfordable Cumberland River behind his force and occupying an untenable position, his well-meaning actions helped lead the Confederate army to defeat. Miller, *The Photographic History of the Civil War* (courtesy The Civil War Museum, Kenosha, WI).

attack one portion of Thomas's force near Mill Springs. When the Confederates crossed the Cumberland River, they brought wagons, ammunition and food with them to their entrenched camp. But as they marched out to battle, wagons with additional ammunition did not follow. Food was carried only in knapsacks that were dropped on the ground by soldiers as they moved forward. Major John Lucien Brown, the 60-year-old quartermaster who worked under Zollicoffer, initially saw to it that the soldiers had food and ammunition, but he could not stop them from discarding and misusing the supplies he distributed. Born on March 29, 1800, in Georgia, Brown formerly served as a captain in the Subsistence Department of the U.S. Army during the Mexican War. Now the commanding officers failed to control this wasteful troop behavior and chaos ultimately followed.[6]

* * *

At 6:30 a.m. on January 19, Confederates drove the Federal pickets and cavalry force back to their camp. "It was a smoky, rainy morning; and after the battle had raged for some time, the two armies became confused and ceased firing." Thomas, however, had enough of his little army in place to confront the Confederates, return their fire and, by reaching their flank around ten in the morning, drive them back in disorder. John Scully, one of the participants for the Union, later wrote that Thomas was most active throughout the action. Several sources support this as well. Calming nervous officers, directing the placement of guns, Thomas managed the battlefield with professional skill, even though this was January 19 of 1862 and neither his officers nor men had seen much combat before this day. In his report, Thomas wrote, "I then rode forward myself to see the enemy's position, so that I could determine what disposition to make of my troops as they arrived. As soon as the regiments could reform and refill their cartridge boxes I ordered the whole force to advance." Colonel Mahlon Manson, commanding Thomas's Second Brigade, reported at least three meetings with Thomas during the action. Colonel Fry of the 4th Kentucky Cavalry recorded one meeting on the field with Thomas. Lieutenant Colonel Kise of the 10th Indiana noted one meeting with Thomas in which he received his direct orders. While Thomas did not personally lead charges from the very front lines, he was present on the battlefield.[7]

Most sources agree on the outline of the battle. Wet flintlocks in hand, Zollicoffer led the way with his brigade. Driving in the Union cavalry pickets, they continued until they contacted the first two Federal units in Thomas's force. A Union battery eventually supported the regiments now posted behind a fence line, and Thomas moved his next two regiments onto the rebel flank. The second brigade of Confederates followed about 30 minutes later. As Zollicoffer rode into the Union lines by mistake, he was killed, and the Confederate attack died. While Crittenden marched with Brigadier General Carroll, who commanded the brigade directly behind Zollicoffer, the men of this second brigade saw limited action at first, and there seems to be no clear record of Crittenden's actions on the field of battle. Only suffering about one quarter of the Confederate casualties, it appears that Carroll's brigade was demoralized when Zollicoffer's men withdrew. Crittenden apparently failed to commit all of his men along with the accompanying artillery and cavalry. They remained in the rear, strung out along the road. As Thomas advanced, the 9th Ohio was particularly effective in driving the

Confederates back. As they advanced, we are told that Lieutenant Colonel Kämmerling ordered his regiment to fix bayonets and charge. Then, after an exchange of fire, the Confederates were driven back from their position. The rest of the Federal force followed in pursuit. By noon, Crittenden's little army was crushed and fled all the way back to the river and the Confederate camp. During the night, the Southerners withdrew in disorder across the river, and the remainder of Crittenden's force disintegrated. A St. Paul newspaper crowed for almost a month after the action and wrote stories that included the following: "Active operations in Kentucky have been most gloriously inaugurated, by the complete defeat and death of Zollicoffer, and the dispersion of his forces, and with the loss of all their cannon, camp equipage and stores. They retreated from their entrenched camp towards Tennessee and were vigorously pursued by the Union troops."[8]

With Zollicoffer dead, Crittenden became an important voice in explaining the Confederate actions at Mill Springs. In Crittenden's report after the battle, he suggests that he was outnumbered, his flintlocks were unserviceable, his artillery was outranged by the Union, and his men possessed "a scarcity of provisions" in their camp. For these reasons, he decided to withdraw over the Cumberland River with many of his men returning to their homes. As noted earlier, Brigadier General W.H. Carroll commanded the Second Brigade of the Confederate force. In his extensive four-page official report, he only once mentions General Crittenden, although Crittenden supposedly rode with him and oversaw the action of this brigade. According to Carroll, he himself issued all the orders and oversaw the maneuvers of this brigade as well as the retreating forces of the now-deceased Zollicoffer. Major Rice of the 29th Tennessee confirms that Carroll was giving the orders for combat. Other reports were not included in the Official Records, but enough information exists to support the general sense that Crittenden did not play a demonstrably active role during the battle.[9]

Much has been made of the Confederate small arms challenge of using flintlocks in pouring rain. While this was a problem, it is also true that they were able to keep up an effective fire from dawn until at least 10:00 a.m. and then present a stronger defense line with artillery support from their camp after they had been driven there at the end of the day. Thomas chose not to attack the fortified camp. McKinney suggests that original small arms issues to both sides were almost identical. The North may have preceded the South in re-equipping some muskets with percussion caps, but the rain soaked both sides during the struggle. Captain Alvan C. Gillem was the Union divisional quartermaster and was complimented in George Thomas's report, along with Captain George S. Roper. Captain Gillem "promptly organized an ammunition train and moved it on to the field," while Captain Roper forwarded commissary stores, "promptly organizing his provision train, which supplied the men with rations when they were almost exhausted."[10]

While this was but a small skirmish in a war filled with bloodletting, the strategic results were potentially impressive. Thomas had unhinged the Confederate right wing in Kentucky, leaving both the center of the state and Nashville, Tennessee, in danger from Buell's main force. In east Tennessee, Knoxville was also vulnerable to attack. The strategically important East Tennessee and Georgia, along with the East Tennessee and Virginia, railroads met there as well.

In addition to this, Johnston's left wing was vulnerable at Forts Henry and

Chapter 1. Mill Springs

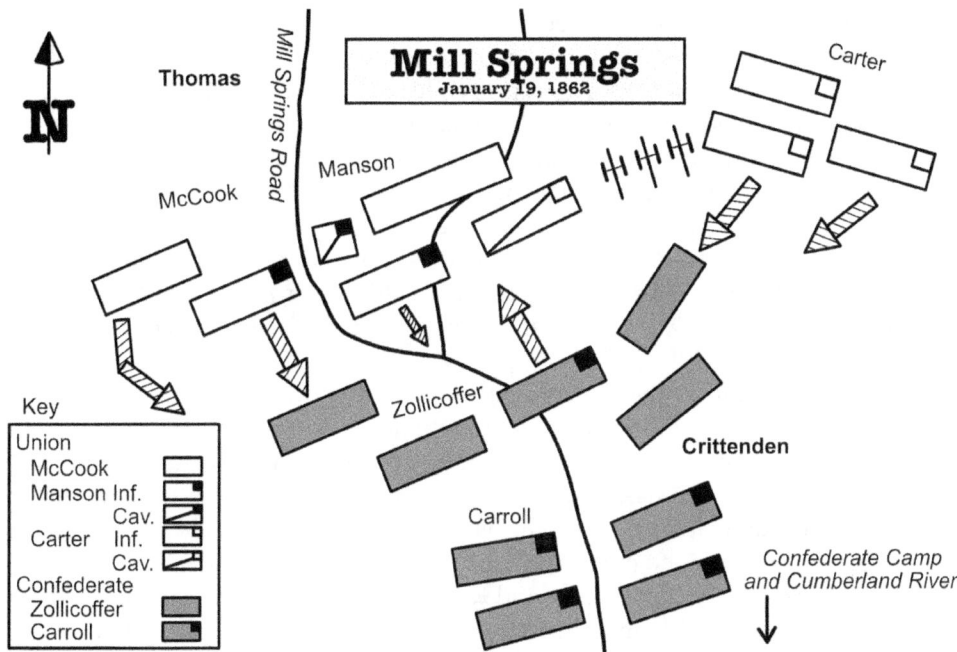

In this conceptual drawing of the battle, only a few regiments were fully engaged. General Thomas had launched a counterattack by regiment following the death of Confederate General Zollicoffer. Note that Thomas used infantry, cavalry and artillery in this action while controlling elements of three separate brigades. As Confederate forces, technically under General Crittenden, initiated a movement toward the Union lines, they found themselves under attack in return (courtesy Margaret A. Zimmermann).

Donelson, and the Confederate dream of defending both Kentucky and Tennessee ended most abruptly.

* * *

At Mill Springs, George Thomas had a very clear objective. Hold eastern Kentucky and defeat Crittenden's force camped north of the Cumberland River. Thomas had done his best to carefully train his men and prepare them for combat. He knew that reinforcements under Brigadier General Shoepf were coming to join him, but he was ready and able to battle Crittenden when the latter advanced on a rainy January 19, 1862. By using all his immediately available force—infantry, cavalry and artillery—he successfully defeated Crittenden and laid the groundwork for further Union success in eastern Kentucky.

On the other hand, George Crittenden experienced a very bad day. Crittenden did not want to advance north of the Cumberland River, but Zollicoffer had preceded him there. The little force they had gathered had no clear objective that was achievable. Even if Thomas had been defeated, reinforcements were on their way to join him, and the Confederates would still be trapped on the wrong side of the river. The Cumberland River was swollen, transportation for a retreat was lacking, and Crittenden was forced to support Zollicoffer's lead into battle. When Zollicoffer literally led the attack and was killed, Crittenden failed to take control of the battle. Without an achievable goal, the day was lost.

At Mill Springs, neither the Federal nor the Confederate central government exerted any real control or support for the actions undertaken by their respective forces. General Thomas had (at various times) three separate superior officers—Anderson, Sherman and Buell—who ordered both marches and countermarches. At the same time, Confederate General Albert Sidney Johnston watched from afar as Felix Zollicoffer acquired a new commanding officer on the eve of battle, but George Crittenden was unable to undo Zollicoffer's folly in crossing the Cumberland to attack the Federal force. Johnston also failed to inform himself about events outside of the Bowling Green area he occupied and provided little help to support Crittenden or Zollicoffer. While the battle occurred on January 19, 1862, Johnston apparently first learned about its outcome in the papers on January 22.[11]

Both Thomas and Zollicoffer sought to seize the initiative. Both Northern and Southern armies undertook offensive action virtually at the same moment and, as a result, both commanders were active in initiating offensive movements designed to aid their respective sides. Thomas, however, was able to maintain his initiative to the very end of the battle, and after the battle, he pursued the Confederates back to their fortified camp. As he maintained pressure on the Confederates, Crittenden's little force dissolved in its retreat over the Cumberland River. For the Confederate force to succeed, they needed to surprise Thomas and commit their entire force early in the struggle. "Mc" the St. Paul newspaper correspondent summarized it well: "Zollicoffer's army had left their entrenchments in the night for the purpose of giving us a night surprise, but … were prevented by the badness of the roads, occasioned by heavy falls of rains which have been nearly incessant for the last three days."[12]

For the Federals, Thomas was obviously in charge, achieved unity of command, and exercised able and active leadership over brigade and regimental commanders. He secured the respect of all his subordinates. He was described in a Minnesota newspaper's laudatory article: "A gruff, tamed bear sort of looking personage is Gen. Thomas, with a face hidden by a profuse growth of 'sandy' beard that gives a wonderfully truculent expression to his countenance, a manner that partakes rather of years of command in camps than of the courtesies in the drawing-room, but that is at least frank and direct."[13]

George Thomas's lieutenants provided intelligent support as combat progressed. Colonel Speed Fry of the 4th Kentucky was in the front line and provided a vigorous defense to open the battle. Colonel Robert L. McCook, commanding a brigade, also followed orders effectively. For a time, it was even thought that Fry shot Felix Zollicoffer when Zollicoffer mistakenly approached the Union lines without reconnoitering. Fry went on to become the Chief of Staff for Don Carlos Buell later in the year. It can be seen, however, that all the regimental commanders that Thomas met or to whom he dispatched orders obeyed his commands intelligently. At this point, Thomas was active directly on the field of battle, but at a proper distance.[14]

For the Confederates, the question arises: Who was in charge? Zollicoffer crossed the Cumberland on his own and pressed for an attack on the Federals. Crittenden, who superseded Zollicoffer without Zollicoffer's knowledge, had ordered Zollicoffer not to do so, and wrote this note to A.S. Johnston: "His [Zollicoffer's] position I consider critical. I ordered him to recross the Cumberland." Afterward Crittenden was officially in command, and while he ordered and supported an attack, he apparently stayed with the rearward brigade when the action began. As Zollicoffer was shot dead early in the

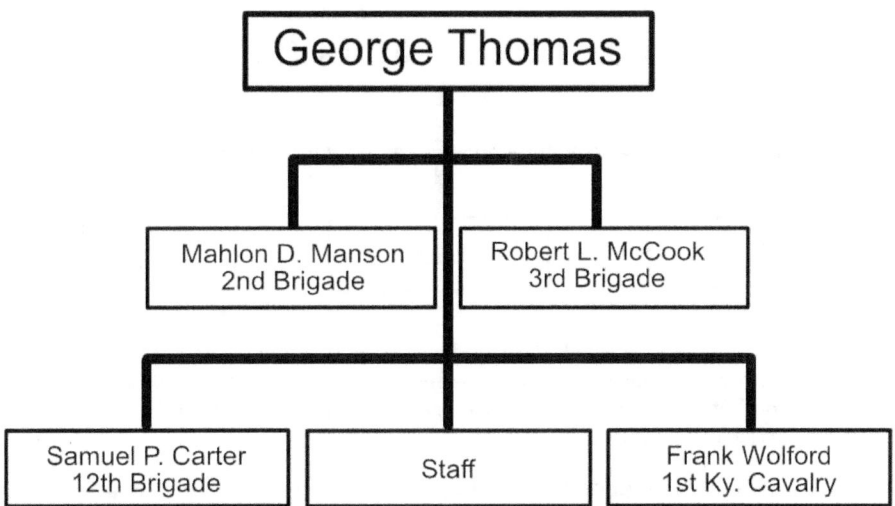

Army organization under the command of Brigadier General George H. Thomas. Both sides committed one regiment after another. As there were only a few regiments committed to action, Thomas was able to move actively about the battlefield, see his subordinates and adjust as needed. See note 14 (courtesy Margaret A. Zimmermann).

action, it is challenging to determine what impact he might have had on Confederate morale during the battle had he lived. While there is a great deal of literature extolling his qualities as an officer, a more sobering analysis is offered by Confederate William Preston Johnston: "What he might have accomplished under other circumstances, it is hard to estimate.... He could not drill a squad himself, nor was his brigade ever drilled or put in line of battle by anybody. Though he had splendid courage, and traits that endeared him to his troops, the cast of his mind was no more military than his training. But he was a good, brave, noble, patriotic man; and his memory deserves well of his country."[15]

Zollicoffer was active in the very forefront of the action, leading his men into battle and then was killed suddenly. After Zollicoffer went down, we have no clear indication that Crittenden exercised leadership during the battle. Afterward Crittenden was accused of drunkenness during the engagement, but some historians believe that his drinking was confined to the previous evening and did not affect his performance during the following day. Drunk or sober, he apparently was not an effective leader during or after the battle. As a result, Crittenden did not hold another combat command during the war. He was, however, arrested and charged with drunkenness on March 31 and later resigned from the Confederate Army. For the Confederates, the second-in-command was killed while failing to scout out the enemy's position, and the other leading brigade commander was later removed from the army for drunkenness along with Crittenden. Not an impressive leadership team![16]

Neither of the Confederate subordinate commanders did well on the day of battle. Zollicoffer was killed and his brigade was routed. Brigadier General Carroll served loyally and dutifully submitted a report after the battle, but it is hard to tell from information readily available how effectively he worked with Zollicoffer or under Crittenden. Carroll's unit suffered few casualties during the battle, and by February of 1863, he had resigned from the army and moved to Canada.[17]

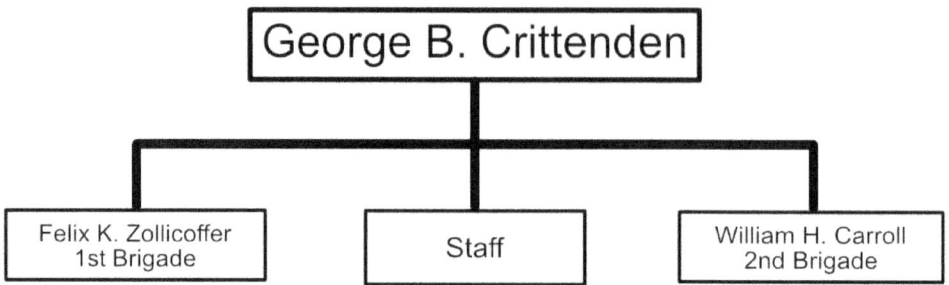

Army organization under George B. Crittenden. While Crittenden had regular army experience, William H. Carroll was the son of a former Tennessee governor and a planter without experience in combat. Felix Zollicoffer was a former newspaper editor and politician. See note 18 (courtesy Margaret A. Zimmermann).

Thomas clearly provided effective logistical support for his little army. Captain Alvan Gillem, Thomas's quartermaster and another West Pointer, provided competent oversight of all the necessary equipment needed to keep Thomas's army in combat.[18] Even though they were short on rations and the weather was miserable, the men were provided with enough ammunition for both muskets and artillery. When Thomas moved forward, he ordered up the 2nd Minnesota and the 9th Ohio Infantry Regiments. "My men replenished their cartridge-boxes," Colonel Kise later reported, "and receiving a new supply of cartridges (the most of our boxes being entirely empty), the men refilled their boxes, and … I put the regiment in motion after the retreating enemy."[19]

The Confederates suffered from too many rain-soaked flintlocks and struggled to re-cross the Cumberland River back to Tennessee on a single steamboat because they failed to allow for that eventuality. Even if Zollicoffer and Crittenden had provided better leadership, the Confederate army fought this action under severe handicap. Yet we have conflicting information. On December 13, 1861, Brigadier General Carroll wrote directly to Samuel Cooper, Adjutant General in Richmond, that his men were armed with about "2,000 ordinary country rifles" and they had not been repaired yet. By January 1, 1862, Carroll reported to Cooper that "Musket situation much improved. 1,620 Tenn. Rifles + 200 muskets [were now available for the brigade]. More coming." This comment would suggest that things were not so critical. Obviously, the whole matter of flintlocks remains a point of contention. But if the men were as poorly armed as Crittenden later claimed, the fact that neither Zollicoffer nor Crittenden paused to re-think their rain-soaked offensive action makes their defeat that much more decisive. This newspaper account also supports that interpretation: "For three hours the firing was incessant on both sides—balls flying like hailstones, cutting off limbs and branches of trees; the roaring of cannon and whistling of shells was awful." A Union brigade surgeon, Sanders, suggests that while the Confederates lacked effective firearms, "a lack of initiative, poor leadership and piecemeal deployments" were critical mistakes.[20]

One final note drops the curtain on Confederate logistics. General Thomas later reported large quantities of supplies discovered in the abandoned Confederate camp, and Captain Wilhelm Stängel of the 9th Ohio wrote in support. He informed his family and newspaper editor back home that besides the food and supplies they found in the rebel camp, they also captured 160 wagons with ammunition and provisions along with 14 pieces of artillery. The Confederates may have lacked the supplies they needed on the battlefield, but without all of this artillery and ammunition, one can understand that perhaps the Confederate challenge was partly one of distribution. For example, as early as November 28, 1861, Zollicoffer wrote to Lieutenant-Colonel Mackall on General Johnston's staff saying, "Mill Springs ... is in a fertile region, with grist and saw mill, wood, water, and capable of easy defense, commanding the ferry. Pork, corn, beef, hay, or fodder, horses, &c, are abundant and cheap here." When George Crittenden wrote his report following the battle, however, he said, "Absolute want of the necessary provisions to feed my command was pressing. The country around was barren or exhausted." This is also a telling evaluation of the extent to which Crittenden and Zollicoffer fully communicated, understood the realities of their challenge, and committed all of their resources to the battle. It was also reported at the time that "the army of the rebels have no uniform. The whole of their killed and wounded had their haversacks crammed with biscuit but no meat."[21]

One of the challenges facing any writer of Civil War history is the problem of defining the role staff officers and subordinates played in providing logistical support for the army's commander. Staff officers needed to do more than simply carry messages across the field of battle. Hundreds of biographies and individual battle histories have emphasized the actions of the commanding general while making scant mention of these other critically important individuals. Occasionally the historian of a particular battle or the biographer will mention the role of these people, but this is often done for the purpose of criticizing their mistakes. In this book, distribution of food and ammunition are reviewed for each battle. The success or failure of campaigns and individual battles often turned in part around the extent to which a staff could efficiently support the desires of the commanding officer or the effectiveness of a commander's immediate subordinates in carrying out his commands. The staff and subordinates either extended the general's ability to win or reduced his effectiveness and helped produce defeat. When both groups of officers acted in concert, the general's faults were minimized, and his strengths multiplied. Numerous accounts simply extol the successful commanding officer's genius or fault his losing counterpart's intelligence or strength of character, but seldom describe staff officers or direct subordinates as part of a team.

Several sources mention Alvan Gillem as a competent staff officer in the Union Army. He graduated from West Point in 1851, 11th in his class. Another officer, Captain George E. Flynt, Assistant Adjutant General, began a combat career with Thomas in 1861, which lasted until Flynt's death in December 1863. While he had a civilian background as a New York merchant, he performed excellent service for Thomas. In summary, Thomas's staff provided for additional ammunition when needed and saw to it that food was brought to the hungry soldiers as the daylight waned. McKinney also provides interesting commentary on the treatment Thomas accorded his staff. At his own dining table, he carefully and respectfully grouped members of his staff—regulars, volunteers and civilians alike.[22]

For the Confederates, it should be noted that staff work was often second-rate. Ammunition ran low without a new supply, and even when the little army retreated to its original camp, there was no food. Yet Union reports noted that over 1,000 horses and mules, over 150 wagons and a large supply of small arms fell into their possession. Additional ammunition was unavailable on the battlefield. Confederate officers noted that they crossed the Cumberland carrying enough food, but when the men dropped their haversacks or blankets when going into combat, the food went missing. Even when

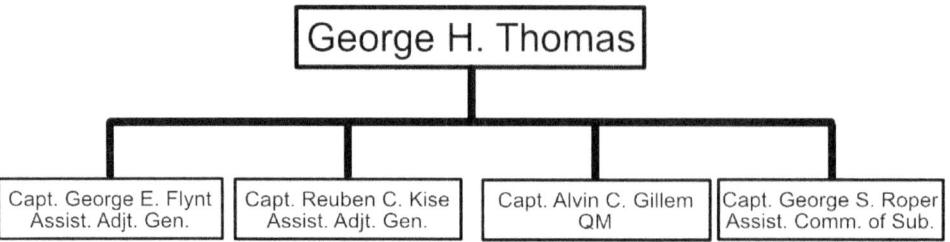

Selected staff of George H. Thomas. Flynt, Kise and Roper all had pre-war experience as merchants in a variety of businesses, while Gillem was an 1851 West Point graduate (courtesy Margaret A. Zimmermann).

the force re-crossed the Cumberland River, food was not to be had on the other side, and Crittenden's force then broke up entirely. It should be noted again that at age 60 the Confederate quartermaster was John Lucien Brown, perhaps one of the oldest men on the battlefield. A West Pointer organized the Union supply effort, and the man who coordinated the entire Confederate effort for Mill Springs served as a regimental quartermaster in the Mexican War. In his defense, it can be said that Brown continued to serve Confederate forces long after the Battle of Mill Springs.[23]

Thomas committed all the resources, both the men and guns he had, for combat. By marching forward in column and then deploying piecemeal into lines of battle, the Confederates never committed more than a fraction of their force at any one time. In some cases, individual regiments were committed one at a time. Also, Crittenden complained that the battleground was not conducive to the use of artillery or cavalry, yet Thomas found a way to use all three arms.

For both North and South, the outcome of this little action was potentially strategic in nature, but the emphasis here is on the term "potentially." With the strategic right flank of the Confederate defenses demolished in this battle, the South now faced the ruin of their entire defensive plan in Kentucky and Tennessee. While the North did not move into East Tennessee following this battle, the road past Bowling Green in central Kentucky lay open straight to Nashville, and the Confederates knew it. Even though the road to East Tennessee was also open, the Union did not move to take it. Strategically it was within their grasp, but neither the central government nor the theater commander, Buell, made this an absolute priority. While the geography prohibited an easy advance, an opportunity was still there, but the North failed to grasp it. In

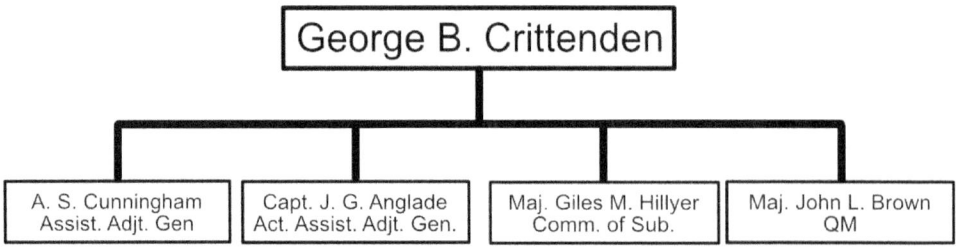

Selected staff of George B. Crittenden. Hillyer was a pre-war attorney and Brown last served in the Mexican War as a commissary officer with the 3rd Tennessee volunteers (courtesy Margaret A. Zimmermann).

Buell's defense, the road conditions were poor and the weather, worse. Thomas himself did not press strongly for an advance into East Tennessee. Also, when A.S. Johnston finally retreated from his own position at Bowling Green, he did not stop to hold Nashville. Even as they sought to hold Fort Donelson and Columbus, Kentucky, the Confederates were already glancing nervously toward the northeast and wondering when Union armies would descend on Nashville from that direction. Had the Confederates made a fight for Nashville, their right flank would have been compromised by the action at Mill Springs. When Buell did eventually enter Nashville, the road had already been opened for him by Thomas's actions.[24]

As a result of this battle, we see that Thomas won a decisive victory with roughly similar numbers to those the Confederates brought to the field of battle. This trend would continue throughout 1862, and this was not an accident. The outcomes of most engagements would end in a roughly similar fashion. The Confederates suffered one defeat after another. While Thomas went on to gain substantial fame for his Civil War victories, other Union commanders, much lesser-known figures, would also experience combat victories that would propel the Union forward during the remainder of the year.

Like the South, the North in 1862 failed to grasp the strategic needs of the war. After Mill Springs, Lincoln continually pressed Buell to drive toward Knoxville and East Tennessee, but Buell disagreed with the President. Lincoln pointed east while Buell moved west—an inauspicious strategic beginning. Some of Lincoln's other commanders in the West (Halleck and later Rosecrans) also behaved in ways that ran counter to Lincoln's strategic thinking, and this goes a long way toward explaining why the war extended for four long years. While we can accuse Southern strategists of trying to hold too much territory with too few resources, we can also see the failure of Northern military strategy to end the war at a much earlier time. It is also possible to see the critical role the six factors played in defining the extent of Thomas's victory.[25]

Six Elements of Victory at Mill Springs

Mill Springs	Clear, Attainable Objective	Operational Initiative	Command Unity
Thomas	Achieved	Achieved	Achieved
Crittenden	Not Achieved	Not Achieved	Not Achieved
	Logistics/Staff	Used All Resources	Strategic Outcome
Thomas	Achieved	Achieved	Not Achieved
Crittenden	Not Achieved	Not Achieved	Not Achieved

By securing the loyal and capable support of both subordinates and staff officers, Thomas was able to win a complete victory.

Chapter 2

Forts Henry and Donelson
Combined Arms with Gunboats

In selecting defensive sites for northern Tennessee, the Confederates sought to protect the furnaces, iron works, railroad lines, and other areas critical to the economic health of the western side of the state. Benjamin Franklin Cooling describes the economic picture of this region in some detail. During 1861, the Confederates were given a full year to prepare the defenses of both the Tennessee and Cumberland Rivers. Both streams flowed south to north in western Tennessee, and both rivers came within a few miles of each other where the rebels decided to construct their first two forts (Henry and Donelson) and then a third (Fort Heiman). Historians agree, however, that after the general sites were selected, little work was done throughout 1861. Albert S. Johnston, coming on board as the area commander, failed to visit the forts and left their construction and the supervision of troops to his subordinates. When Johnston learned as late as January 17, 1862, that the forts were not being constructed quickly enough, he sent his chief engineer, Jeremy Gilmer, to check. Only a few soldiers were present, and even though the authorities pleaded for help, local slave owners were not interested in providing their slaves for government work.[1]

General Polk, commanding in western Kentucky and Tennessee, was consumed with the defense of Columbus, Kentucky, and spent little time thinking about the interior river lines. Polk also wanted to convert a steamboat, the *Eastport*, into a gunboat, and its ongoing construction competed with the work of fortifying the rivers and building other warships at Memphis, Tennessee. Conversations occurred around the idea of planting torpedoes (mines) in the rivers, drawing a chain across one or both, building gunboats, bringing in more troops, implanting heavy guns, bringing in floating batteries, or some combination of all of these ideas.[2]

On the other side of the hill, Henry Wager Halleck took command. Halleck first sought to pacify the St. Louis area and hold a portion of Missouri to protect the western flank of his forces as they moved south along the Mississippi River. To further complicate matters, Don Carlos Buell commanded in central and eastern Kentucky. Both Buell and Halleck reported to McClellan, McClellan to God, and all these men, being good Democrats, felt that a war of position and place, rather than a bloody conflict to defeat Southern armies, was appropriate. As a result, little of consequence took place in 1861 from the northern perspective. It was unhelpful that Irwin McDowell lost his battle at Bull Run in Virginia and that Nathaniel Lyon lost his life at Wilson's Creek in Missouri. All three generals (Buell, Halleck, and McClellan) believed that avoiding defeat involved careful planning along with slow and deliberate movements. When George Thomas

Brigadier General U.S. Grant (Library of Congress).

Brigadier General John B. Floyd (courtesy The Civil War Museum, Kenosha, WI).

(operating under the orders of Buell) won the Battle of Mill Springs in January of 1862, many people were completely surprised. Furthermore, when a little-known brigadier named Sam Grant attacked the Confederates at Belmont in November of 1861, many people thought he had over-reached. Ordering a demonstration against Columbus, Kentucky, from the Missouri side of the Mississippi River, Grant moved a small force of men, with the support of the newly created river squadron of three armed, wooden gunboats and steamboat transportation, against Belmont, Missouri. Grant's men were landed, and at first, they successfully engaged the Confederates at Belmont. While they paused to loot the camps, however, reinforcements from Columbus crossed the river and drove the Federals off. Grant himself barely escaped capture. While Grant lost his first real skirmish with the Confederates, he pronounced the experience a success and would go on to numerous victories after this.

Viewing a modern map or GPS of the United States, we see roads and attractions laid out with a profusion of colorful symbols denoting the number of highway lanes, restaurants and exit points. Putting a twenty-first-century interpretation of this sort on the Civil War geography of the West is pointless. No Civil War army ever travelled a multi-lane, paved roadway, stopped to rest at convenient motels, and refreshed its warriors at drive-ins and fast-food franchises. Our ancestors were much tougher and leaner. In the West, the contested area approximated the size of Europe and required an entirely different kind of warfare. The great river arteries of the West, in conjunction with an ongoing, robust industrial revolution, compelled generals to face a far more complex task of organizing, moving, and fighting their armies than had ever faced American generals in the past. Large masses of volunteers required leaders to depend on others for communication involving larger forces than they were used to seeing, and armies were now engaged on larger battlefields as well. A knowledge of logistics, railroads, the telegraph, armored warships, steamboat transportation and technological changes in weaponry all required a commanding officer to master many new tasks. This new complexity required a true "team" effort. Today on a modern highway or road map, these great waterways, mountains and rail lines are often barely visible.

In the South, secession-minded leaders originally hoped to use the Ohio River as a barrier against invasion, and the Confederates sought to create and fortify other choke points to limit access to the South. These rivers also provided the nutrients for rich crop yields; and if the South converted its land for food production to supplant cotton, these agricultural efforts would succeed in feeding not only the Confederate armies of the West, but those of the East as well. For the North, there was concern that as commerce along the Mississippi River to New Orleans was interrupted, the states of the old Northwest would face economic ruin. Both sides knew that Confederate states west of the Mississippi River needed access across the river to the eastern Confederacy. If the rebels controlled this waterway, the South would remain intact. Lose control of the river, and the South would be divided. As a result, the first Union plan that emerged called for a fleet of armed and armored vessels to accompany the army in its march southward. In like manner the South did its best to prepare for invasion.

The states of Kentucky and Tennessee are "watered and drained" by four major river systems, the Ohio, Mississippi, Tennessee and Cumberland. Unlike Julius Caesar's Gaul, however, or Winston Churchill's Sudan, the American rivers run in various directions, but they all converge in the western portion of Kentucky and greatly affect any military plans that might be prepared for this region. If the North breached the Ohio River barrier or Kentucky failed to secede, the border between Kentucky and Tennessee near the Mississippi River provided the next obvious point of defense. Three of the four major river systems came together within a few miles of one another. By using fortifications, warships, mines and military forces, the South hoped to blockade this junction by the end of 1861.

Following Beauregard's attack on Fort Sumter, President Lincoln called for 75,000 volunteers to put down the rebellion. General Winfield Scott recommended that Federal forces advance purposefully both north and south from each end of the Mississippi River to open New Orleans for western trade and split the Confederacy in two. A blockade was instituted, and his proposal to subdivide and compress Southern territory became known as the Anaconda Plan. Designs were drafted almost immediately to seize the entire Mississippi River Valley, from Cairo, Illinois, to the Gulf of Mexico. Along both the coastlines and rivers, the South was pressed on all sides from the very outset of war and, in the West, the North was working from a very aggressive timetable.

Early in 1861, the North moved to acquire riverboats and construct warships. The Quartermaster General of the Army, Montgomery Meigs, took immediate steps to lease as many steamboats on all four major rivers as he could. With communications disrupted south along the Mississippi to New Orleans, hundreds of steamboats lay idle at riverside wharves throughout the North. Meigs moved quickly. Over the course of the war, he acquired close to 600 vessels for river transport, and by the end of 1861, he moved to secure any vessel floating. Acquiring warships was more complicated, but the North worked on this problem almost from the beginning of the war.[3]

After Lincoln's call for volunteers, a western businessman, James B. Eads, appeared. Growing up in St. Louis, Eads owned a major salvage operation and knew the rivers intimately. In April of 1861, he came to Washington and outlined his proposal to build a squadron of warships. In the West, Northern strategy was very direct; Lincoln's administration envisioned a series of combined arms operations to capture important sites along the major rivers. Other Northerners were equally involved. On May 20, Gideon Welles corresponded with Samuel M. Pook, another shipbuilder, and on June 7, Commodore John Rodgers proposed the building of three gunboats on the Mississippi. On June 21, Charles Ellett proposed the construction of steam-driven rams and offered to both build and command them. By August 16, three sturdy steamboats were converted into wooden gunboats, and the *Tyler, Lexington and Conestoga* floated at Cairo, Illinois, for outfitting.[4]

Eads presented his plans, first to Welles, and then to Lincoln. On August 5, Quartermaster General Meigs let bids, and on August 7, contracts were signed. By November 4, Eads motored four of these newfangled armored boats to Cairo, Illinois, for final fitting. On August 30, Captain and later Flag Officer Andrew Foote was ordered west to command the flotilla. By September 6, Brigadier General Ulysses S. Grant, and Foote, with two of Foote's gunboats and three steamboats, captured Paducah, Kentucky, in the first joint army-navy effort. From inception to completion, the time elapsed was three months. By January of 1862, they were ready for action at a time when the Confederates had failed to finish any warships.[5]

President Jefferson Davis and the Confederate governors determined to defend every state within the Confederacy. Each state looked to its own devices, and each state attempted to shore up weak spots. Nine of the 11 states looked out to sea with fear, but then the consensus ended. Several states could be invaded from any one of several directions. Virginia desired reinforcements from other Southern states, and with the Tredegar Iron Works and the seat of national government both located in Richmond, the Virginians received most of the attention.[6]

The West needed security as well. From Virginia to the Mississippi stretched a long, undefended line of over 400 miles from the Appalachians to Memphis on the Mississippi River. An infant rail network, foundries and broad agricultural lands needed protection. There was even a debate concerning where to draw the defensive lines. Would the Confederacy be able to include Kentucky and secure the Ohio River as a northern border, or would Kentucky remain neutral and force the Confederacy to defend all the other river lines pointed like daggers into the South? The Western Confederacy required forts, ships and heavy guns. When Tennessee finally seceded in June of 1861, Kentucky became the focal point for a great deal of attention. If Kentucky seceded, then the Ohio River would create a natural northern boundary; if it remained neutral, then the more porous Kentucky/Tennessee border must serve. It was a simple line on a map, but natural geographic features failed to provide barriers or defensive advantages for the South below the Ohio River line. President Davis also needed to determine the fate of the land even farther west called the Trans-Mississippi. Finally, each Confederate coastal state bordering the Atlantic Ocean or the Gulf of Mexico also clamored for protection. Now, in 1861, several strategic questions descended simultaneously on President Davis. He was pressed to defend each Southern state: "Missouri and Kentucky demand our attention, and the Southern coast needs additional defense." Later when all were lost, Davis would write, "I acknowledge the error of my attempt to defend all of [the] frontier, seaboard and inland." From the vantage point of the twenty-first century, historians might suggest that the long lines across the heartland of Kentucky as well as the Gulf coastline were too long, the resources to hold it too meager, and the odds of an independence movement succeeding, too great.[7]

On April 20, 1861, onrushing Virginia militia awakened the sleepy town of Norfolk, Virginia. Located there, the only naval dry-dock in North America was the Gosport Navy Yard, where the U.S. Navy repaired and refurbished its miniature but dangerous fleet. Most importantly, if the Virginians captured its accessible vessels and 1,100 heavy guns, they would acquire an instant naval threat. But Virginia wasn't even part of the Confederacy until Fort Sumter fell and President Lincoln called up 75,000 men from the North to subdue the rebellion. Then on April 17, following the bombardment and surrender of Fort Sumter and Lincoln's response, Virginia seceded. On April 20, the Virginia militia descended on Gosport and captured the entire naval base without a struggle. These massive guns could now be redeployed throughout the South and provide firepower for armored warships as well. The story is an interesting one.[8]

Back on July 30, 1861, after General Polk took command in the West, Lieutenant Isaac Brown wrote him from Richmond, "I will go to Norfolk [Gosport Navy Yard] Tuesday evening with an order on the commandant there for fifty heavy 32-pounder guns, and that I shall hurry these West as quickly as I can.... I have 500 shells ordered from Pensacola—the fuzes go from here—and I have the prospect by October of a battery of rifled 30-pounders." But on August 2, he wrote again, "there will be some little delay in getting the fifty guns forward for want of transportation.... I regret to find that these guns will have to be transferred at Bristol, Tenn., to other cars, by which some further delay will be experienced. I shall go to Richmond on Monday to ask from President Davis an order for a share for our river defenses.... Had your requisition been delayed but a few days, the last gun would perhaps have gone from here to defend some creek or inlet which I have never heard of, and which ... could have no influence upon the fate of the war. I fear that all the best guns have gone to places of secondary importance, and that the best projectiles are to follow in the same direction."[9]

Now in July, Brown was determined to move his additional 50 pieces to the west, and General Polk was equally determined to place them on the river at Columbus, Kentucky. Using Robert Black's map from *Railroads of the Confederacy*, one can trace the route of these guns with some accuracy. By reviewing William Peters's little booklet on the disposition of the Gosport artillery, it is possible to see the types of guns that traveled west. Riding over eight different railroads, the artillery would journey successfully, but a later section of this book will highlight problems connected with some of this shared artillery.[10]

Even as the guns made their way west, the Confederate strategic dilemma was highlighted by this move, as a tremendous burden was placed on rail transportation. Polk and Brown were completely entrepreneurial, and one looks in vain for strategic insight and collaboration among Confederate authorities. Each owner of a rail line and each battery commander was a law unto himself. At times the army or navy cooperated and at times they acted independently. While Forts Henry and Donelson were modestly armed, Polk's fortifications at Columbus on the Mississippi River boasted 140 big guns. The Confederates had the artillery, the transportation, the manpower and the *élan* to defend the West. They lacked an overall vision. While Grant and Eads and Foote met to coordinate their efforts, there is no similar record of Confederate collaboration.[11]

By late January of 1862, the strategic picture changed for both North and South. Grant had allied himself with (now) Flag Officer Foote (promoted in November 1861), and Foote's armored gunboats were ready to work together with Grant's forces. P.G.T. Beauregard was coming west to help the Confederates, and Beauregard added a strong voice to strategic and operational thinking in the West. Graduating from West Point in 1838, he commanded the forces that captured Fort Sumter in April 1861, led victorious Confederate forces at First Bull Run on July 21, 1861, and routed the Union army. Arguing with President Davis over Confederate plans in the East, he was now dispatched west to assist Johnston. Halleck was clearly nervous.

At the end of January, the Confederates numbered around 30,781 effectives at Bowling Green, 18,000 at Columbus and 5,000 with Polk—a total of around 53,000 men. Buell could count on 46,150 and Grant could bring 20,679 into battle for a Union total of 66,829. While the North was rapidly recruiting and sending on additional regiments, their advantage in numbers was hardly overwhelming. Also in January of 1862, the Confederates decided to get serious about protecting the high ground across the Tennessee River from Fort Henry, and General Tilghman was ordered to build another fort there (Fort Heiman). Although they labored hopefully on, time had almost run out for the Confederates. By February 1, Fort Heiman had been staked out and Fort Donelson on the Cumberland River could boast a garrison consisting of three Tennessee regiments. Earlier in January, heavy guns and carriages began to arrive from Nashville and the Tredegar Iron Works in Richmond, and a few of the Gosport shipyard guns also emerged. On the negative side of the ledger, the Confederates failed to employ underwater mines (then called torpedoes) with any success—fast-flowing high water and a lack of insulated wire doomed this experiment. The Confederate ironclad, *Eastport,* remained unfinished while labor and raw materials remained in short supply. In the end, the Confederates produced too little, too late in their preparations.[12]

West Point-trained engineer, Brigadier General Lloyd Tilghman, faced Grant. Upon taking command, Tilghman realized immediately that he was short of just about anything needed for successful defense of Forts Henry and Donelson. Both Tilghman and A.S. Johnston sent emissaries to President Davis, pleading for weapons. Finally, Davis exploded at Johnston's messenger with the response, "My God! Why did General Johnston send you for arms and reinforcements when he must know that I have neither?" Tilghman also ran into personality clashes with Gideon Pillow and with his own officers as well. This was not a happy family in December of 1861.[13]

Further complicating matters, Albert Sidney Johnston, the theater commander of Confederate Department Number Two, seldom responded to messages from Tilghman. A busy man, Johnston delegated authority and hoped the commander on the spot could sort out the problems. As Grant initiated a reconnaissance in force beginning in early January of 1862, the Confederates waited and watched for an attack.[14]

Often overlooked, this maneuvering gave the new Union recruits excellent experience in marching and preparation for real combat. While the Union army marched and trained, 17 guns were finally mounted at Fort Henry and the actual layout of the fort was completed. But when would Union gunboats arrive? On three occasions, they had been seen nosing around the area, and concern about their intentions was rising. Their orders were to scout out, as thoroughly as possible, a line of advance for Federal forces. On January 23, General C.S. Smith completed his scouting expedition near Fort Henry and reported to Grant: "I think two iron-clad gunboats would make short work of Ft. Henry."[15]

There was, indeed, reason for Confederate concern at Fort Henry. After the original design had been completed and work begun, Confederate Captain Jesse Taylor visited the fort in September 1861. He noted that high hills on either side of the river commanded the ground on which the fort was built. He also noticed that there were watermarks on the trees near Fort Henry. The rings from high water levels in the past were two feet higher than the walls and embrasures of the fort. In reality, the fort had been constructed underwater! Now it was too late to address the problem satisfactorily. The Confederates could only hope that the water levels for early 1862 would not surge over the walls of the fort. They could hardly abandon the place and start building at another site.[16]

On January 28, Halleck received and pigeonholed Grant's proposal for an attack on Henry and Donelson. On January 29, however, Halleck received word from McClellan that Beauregard was coming west with 15 regiments to reinforce Johnston. (This was not at all true.) Perhaps not coincidentally, on January 30 Grant received Halleck's blessing to prepare an attack on Fort Henry before Beauregard arrived. If the assault worked, Halleck would receive the President's approbation, and if it failed, then Grant and Foote would bear the blame.[17]

* * *

The expedition against Fort Henry was launched on February 2, 1862, and on February 6, Fort Henry, inundated by a rising river and under fire from Foote's gunboats, surrendered. Grant and Foote were pleased, but they faced another question: What next? Grant immediately proposed that they move against Fort Donelson, 12 miles to the east on the Cumberland River. While Grant waited for the rains to cease, Foote's gunboats sailed to the Cumberland to bombard Fort Donelson. Now with both temperatures and snow falling on February 14, Grant's force (about 15,000 strong) finished its overland march from Fort Henry, and Foote's gunboats engaged the fort. During the fight, shore-based Confederate batteries badly damaged the gunboats and wounded the Flag Officer. Unfazed, Grant moved his forces closer to Fort Donelson's outlying earthworks to begin a siege, and then rode off on the morning of February 15 to meet the wounded Foote, assess the situation, and plead for at least one gunboat to remain. Foote's other gunboats all withdrew for major repairs. Given the supine Confederate effort to this point, Grant never suspected a Confederate attack. In Grant's memoirs we read, "I had known General Pillow in Mexico and judged that with any force, no matter how small, I could march up to within gunshot of any entrenchments he was given to hold." By this point in time, Gideon Pillow had other ideas. He urged General John Buchanan Floyd, now in command at Fort Donelson, and, at one point mustering around 5,000 more men than Grant, to attack the Federals. Leaving a strong Confederate force within the works, Pillow marched out to attack Grant's infantry. While Grant and Foote met about seven miles downstream to review the general situation, Pillow's forces advanced and forced open an escape route to Nashville.[18]

When Grant was informed of the clash, he rushed back to Fort Donelson early in the afternoon and prepared a counterattack. Grant set everyone in motion for the attack, even General Charles F. Smith on his far-left flank. The Confederates were hard-pressed to defend their works. At almost the same time, to General Floyd's complete surprise, Gideon Pillow ordered a retreat into the Donelson works. That night after deep discussion, Floyd turned the command over to Pillow, Pillow passed on the opportunity, and now Brigadier General Simon Bolivar Buckner assumed command and prepared to surrender. The two senior commanders, fearing for their lives, fled the scene along with at least four regiments of soldiers. Buckner sent a messenger to ask Grant for terms and felt the sting of Grant's now-famous lines, "No terms but unconditional surrender can be accepted. I propose to move upon your works immediately." As a result, 13,000 remaining Confederates gave up their arms, and Grant's name became a household word in the North.[19]

After witnessing this outcome, however, a basic question remains. With more soldiers than Grant early in the Donelson campaign and well-placed artillery, the Confederates beat off the gunboats, but they still lost the engagement by the evening of February 15. While the Confederates had been largely victorious in the morning and opened an escape route, Pillow's catastrophic decision for retreat slammed the door shut on this early victory. Why did this occur? Several key questions should be raised as a result that will help us make sense of the Union victory at Donelson and gauge whether larger factors con-

Brigadier General Gideon Pillow. At least five generals led Confederate forces at Fort Donelson in the first two weeks of February 1862. One of those men, Gideon Pillow, serving under John B. Floyd on the morning of February 15, led a doomed effort out of the town of Dover to open an escape route for the trapped Confederate army. While Floyd watched, Pillow led. As a Tennessee attorney, Pillow had been instrumental in supporting the candidacy of James K. Polk for the presidency in 1844 and had been rewarded with a major general's commission during the Mexican War. Pillow is shown in his major general's uniform in this photograph. During the Civil War, however, he was heavily criticized when he meekly withdrew his temporarily victorious force back into the lines at Fort Donelson. Just before the garrison surrendered, Pillow fled to safety (courtesy The Civil War Museum, Kenosha, WI).

tributed to the Union victory other than Grant's grit and determination. As the following six key characteristics are applied to the Fort Donelson campaign, they can be used as measurable categories for almost any Civil War campaign or battle.

To examine military leadership and the ability of commanders to achieve clear and attainable objectives in the West, a brief comment on strategy itself is required. While one might look at the question of strategy as a matter of one side or the other undertaking offensive or defensive maneuvers, the question of leadership choice is often overlooked as a matter of strategy. During the American Civil War, the political leaders in Richmond and Washington selected commanding generals in the West. These decisions were strategic and shaped the outcome of the campaigns that followed. Both Abraham Lincoln and Jefferson Davis selected army leaders they felt would be acceptable to

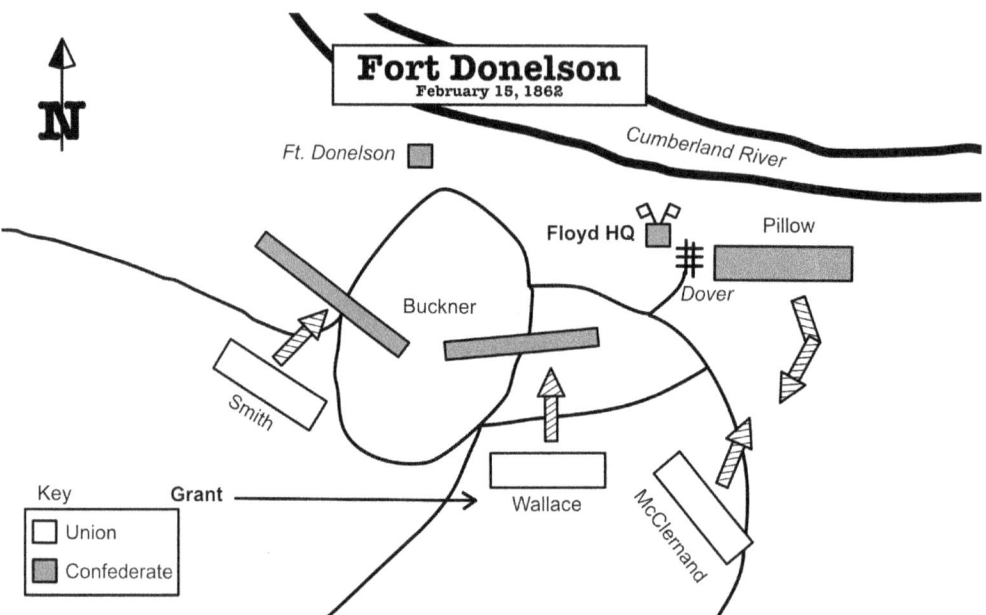

When Gideon Pillow led Confederate forces to attack the Federal division under McClernand, Grant was conferring with Flag Officer Foote on board a Union gunboat. Once Grant returned to the field, the North counterattacked while the Confederates withdrew into the Fort Donelson works (courtesy Margaret A. Zimmermann).

the western governors of the warring states, and we should look briefly at the ways in which these decisions played out. Once military commanders had been chosen, it was the responsibility of the political leaders to set objectives that could be achieved.

Once Lincoln's original choice of John Charles Fremont failed, he selected Henry Wager Halleck to lead Union forces in the Mississippi Valley. Halleck soon discovered that Fremont had already selected U.S. Grant as one of his leading officers, and while Grant was not Halleck's choice (Halleck would have preferred General Charles F. Smith), Fremont's decision was allowed to stand. Halleck is often censured for his occasional rough treatment of Grant in early 1862, but it is interesting to note his actual support of Grant when it really counted. On January 30, Halleck wrote to Grant: "You will organize your command ... precisely as you may deem best for the public service.... Don't let political applications ... trouble you a particle. All such applications & arrangements are sheer nonsense & will not be regarded."[20]

Halleck's chief of staff, Brigadier General George W. Cullem, also wrote to say much the same thing. By the time the expedition sailed, Halleck released Lieutenant-Colonel James McPherson, another West Pointer, to serve as Grant's chief engineer. Even though McPherson may have been sent by Halleck to spy on Grant, he soon became an enthusiastic devotee. These actions all strongly suggest that Grant had the active support of his immediate superior.[21]

Just after the fall of Fort Henry on February 7, Grant prepared for his move against Fort Donelson. His objective was both clear and attainable: capture Fort Donelson and open the Cumberland River to Union navigation. While Fort Henry had fallen, however, the rain also fell in sheets, and he was forced to delay any overland movement until February 12. Once Grant invested the fort and the Confederates prepared to attack him on the 15th, General Halleck urged General Sherman, who was returning to duty under Halleck in the West, to write Grant as follows: "I am just arrived here [Paducah, Kentucky] and by order of Gen. Halleck prepared to hasten all reinforcements & supplies." Providing logistical support for Grant, Sherman wrote further that he, along with Halleck's chief of staff and Halleck himself, all stood ready to help Grant in any way possible. At one point, Halleck was fearful that Grant might fail if the Confederates attacked him in force and did what he could to provide support. As he wrote these lines, reinforcements were flowing from Halleck to Grant to assist him. One might well ask how the Confederate strategic thinking compared at this time?[22]

On September 10, 1861, Jefferson Davis appointed Major General Albert Sidney Johnston to command all Confederate forces in Kentucky and Tennessee (called Department No. 2). Earlier, Davis followed the recommendations of Governor Isham Harris of Tennessee and appointed his fellow West Point friend Episcopal Bishop Leonidas Polk (June 25, 1861) as well as lawyer and Mexican War veteran Gideon Pillow (July 9, 1861) to major commands in western Tennessee. Earlier Pillow was instrumental in securing the Democratic nomination for presidential candidate James K. Polk. Still active in politics, Pillow secured the support of fellow Democrat Harris for his command. After Pillow and Polk arranged the invasion of Kentucky in the fall of 1861, Polk went on to command Confederate forces stationed mainly at Columbus, Kentucky. Appointed by theater commander Albert Sidney Johnston, former Secretary of War, John B. Floyd, was selected to command Fort Donelson after the fort's former commander, Lloyd Tilghman, surrendered at Fort Henry. Nevertheless, Gideon Pillow would re-emerge shortly to take charge of the Confederate attack on February 15. Compare the military credentials of this group with the men who would lead what would become the Army of Northern Virginia in 1862. Joseph E. Johnston, Robert E. Lee, James Longstreet and Stonewall Jackson were all highly regarded West Point professionals with substantial military experience. In the West, the command decisions of Davis, Harris and Johnston brought second-rate officers into leadership positions.[23]

While he might have sent other professionals, such as William Hardee, or gone himself to take command of this key location, Johnston chose the former U.S. Secretary of War, infamous for attempting to move small arms and artillery south before the start of the Civil War. As a politician, Floyd had only limited combat experience in western Virginia, but his resume showed extensive legal experience. One of Floyd's first communications with Johnston was to beg him to come personally to Fort Donelson and tell him what to do. Was he supposed to hold Fort Donelson or evacuate the place and withdraw to Nashville, Tennessee? Johnston failed to respond, and while the garrison was reinforced, Floyd had only Gideon Pillow for counsel along with Buckner. Floyd considered evacuation while Pillow urged him to hold the fort and then attack Grant. The Confederates at Fort Donelson did not have a clear objective in mind. Holding the fort against lengthening odds was a poor choice and waiting too long to retreat was a fatal decision.

Unfortunately for the Confederates, U.S. Grant held the initiative from the very beginning of the campaign. Grant planned the descent upon Fort Henry and worked cooperatively with Flag Officer Foote to capture the fort. Then both Foote and Grant agreed that the flag officer needed to steam downstream on the Tennessee River and then head upstream on the Cumberland River. Even though the gunboat attack on Fort Donelson failed, Grant was still able to move his army within striking distance of the fortifications as the bombardment took place.

Grant's personal leadership and forceful intervention during the battle on February 15 led to the Federal ability to take and hold the initiative for the entire operation. While the Confederates took the offensive at the beginning of the day, the Union army under Grant regained the initiative by early afternoon and never relinquished it. It was the final attack of the day, and not the first action at dawn, that decided the outcome of battle. When the Confederates surrendered *en masse* to the Federal force confronting them on February 16, the Union army clearly held the initiative.[24]

Under first one commander and then the next, the Confederates failed to confront the Union advance and gradually retired into their trenches. Even after General Pillow led an attack on the Union forces of McClernand, Grant was able to wrest the initiative away from the South after Pillow voluntarily retreated into his trenches. Floyd meekly allowed the initiative to pass out of his hands. Grant then launched his own counterattack, and the Confederates surrendered the next day.

As their first major campaign unfolded, Grant achieved command unity and enjoyed the cooperation of all three of his division commanders. Generals Charles F. Smith (originally Grant's instructor at West Point), Lew Wallace and John A. McClernand fought valiantly to hold back the Confederate onslaught. Without specific orders, Lew Wallace brought reinforcements to the hard-pressed McClernand.[25]

Through no fault of his own, Grant was in conference with the wounded Flag Officer Foote at the onset of battle, but his presence in the early afternoon galvanized his entire force into action and was clearly effective on the battlefield. Grant's active leadership versus Floyd's passive followership altered the outcome of the battle at Donelson and led to the surrender of the Confederate forces.[26]

With Floyd in command, his lieutenants included Gideon Pillow, Simon B. Buckner and Bushrod Johnson. Apparently, Johnson was not consulted during this time, and Pillow quarreled with Buckner. During the Mexican War, Pillow had authored a scurrilous article about the commander of the U.S. Army, Winfield Scott, and Buckner had taken it upon himself to vigorously counterattack Pillow. Now with his subordinates at loggerheads, Floyd acquiesced to Pillow's advice and remained in the fort originally to defend it. Then he launched a breakout assault to escape, and finally, on the advice of Buckner, surrendered everything to Grant. One looks in vain for evidence of Floyd's activity on the battlefield until he observed Pillow's forces retreating along with Buckner, and then once again, he assented to his subordinate's decision. This may have been his sole recorded appearance on the field. Both Floyd and Pillow would make their

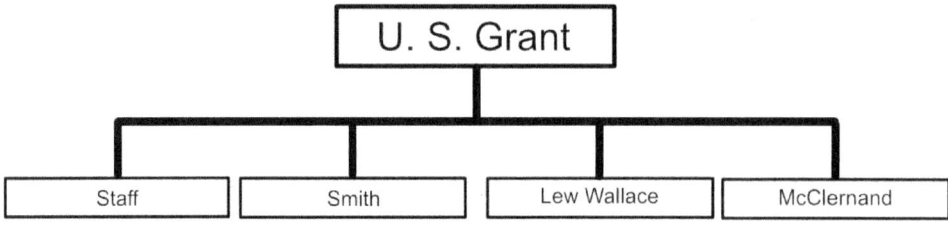

Army organization under Brigadier General U.S. Grant at Fort Donelson. West Pointers Grant and Charles F. Smith led the Union forces at Fort Donelson, and two political appointees, Lew Wallace and John A. McClernand, led two divisions in the army. As the Federal forces expanded in size, a variety of political appointees were thrown together with West Point regulars to command the new armies (courtesy Margaret A. Zimmermann).

ignominious escape and leave Buckner holding the command "bag." With the fall of Fort Henry and the capitulation at Donelson, A.S. Johnston was now forced to give up Columbus on the Mississippi River and Bowling Green in the center of Kentucky.

An interesting sidelight comes from William Preston Johnston. As his father, A.S. Johnston, was responsible for selecting the commanding officers at Fort Donelson, Johnston comments on Floyd as follows: "There is no need to pursue with unmerited blame any of the generals in command.... Floyd was of a bold and impetuous temper, but he was a mountaineer; and, except a few months' experience in warfare among the Alleghenies, a novice in military operations. The moment he felt himself cooped up within the intrenchments, his active spirit lost its spring."[27]

Even though U.S. Grant served as a quartermaster during the Mexican War, his staff officers, of course, supervised logistical arrangements and the actual distribution of food and ammunition during the Civil War. Fortunately for them, Grant's previous experience was beneficial in helping them organize their work. By this time, many of Grant's general staff officers had been with him since 1861 and discharged their duties very effectively. Major Joseph D. Webster, Grant's chief of staff, accompanied Grant upon his battlefield arrival and was quick to oversee the small arms ammunition re-supply for the men. Even though Grant's soldiers may have been cold and uncomfortable, they did not lack for ammunition or basic commissary provisions as the battle opened. It is instructive to note that on the day of battle, February 15, Grant's aide, Captain Hillyer, was writing to Grant's division commanders, "You will direct that each regimental quartermaster proceed to our transports on the river [about three miles north] and draw rations for the regiment receipting for them in gross.... Waggons [sic] will be furnished at the river for those who have not got them."[28]

Often overlooked by Civil War historians, staff officers who supported an army were ultimately responsible for providing food, ammunition and a host of critical supplies. These duties were usually performed by a group of officers known as a general

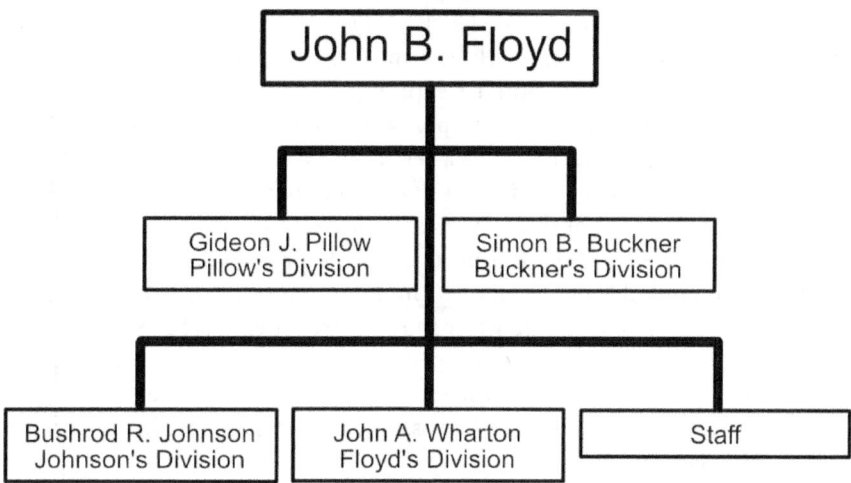

Confederate Army organization under Brigadier John B. Floyd at Fort Donelson. In like manner to Union practice, the immediate subordinates consisted of West Pointers Johnson and Buckner along with attorney Pillow. Unfortunately, Floyd was also new to his position and this group of officers did not work well together (courtesy Margaret A. Zimmermann).

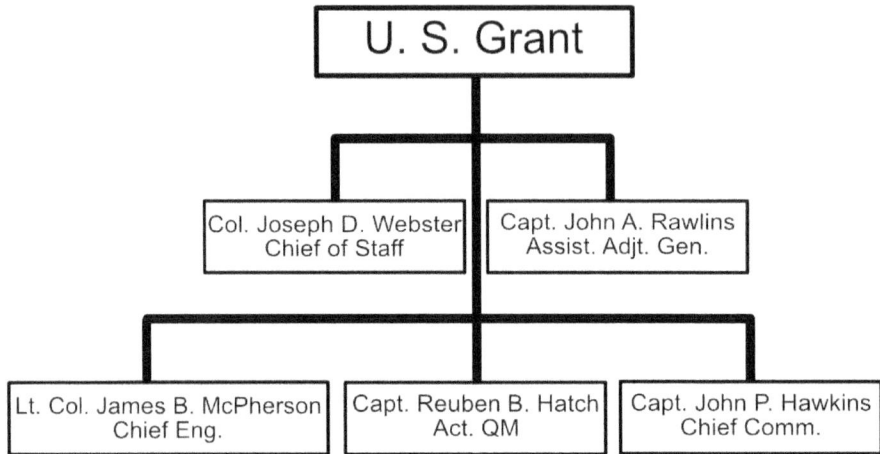

Selected Union staff members at Fort Donelson. Grant's staff included West Pointers and Regular Army officers Webster and McPherson, while Hawkins and Reuben Hatch brought merchandise experience as background for their responsibilities (courtesy Margaret A. Zimmermann).

staff, while other officers served as a general's personal staff by delivering important orders and acting as his eyes and ears while a battle was in progress.

Grant's staff may still have had much to learn, but they were both active and effective on his behalf. Grant also wrote telling comments on the Confederate logistics: "The amount of supplies captured here is very large, sufficient probably for twenty days for all my army.... Of rice I don't know that we will want any more during the war." And this: "The enemy had evidently prepared for a long siege. Their supplies of munitions of war and provisions were very large." And finally this: "If harness was sent for thirty or forty teams I could rig out that number from captured mules and wagons."[29]

By comparison, Floyd commanded Fort Donelson without a formal staff. He brought a handful of staff officers with him into the fort, and he retained the services of the few members of Lloyd Tilghman's staff who had not surrendered at Fort Henry. He relied heavily on staff officers accompanying his other subordinates, all of whom arrived at the fort at different times. As a result, the Confederate army at Fort Donelson was largely an *ad hoc* force, and the staff that supported them was a motley crew as well. The steamboat landing at the Dover Hotel served as the arrival point for soldiers and supplies. The Confederate staff proved unable to properly distribute the ammunition and food that landed there. Logistics and the failure of Confederate leadership to properly supply the army played a key role in the defeat at Fort Donelson. Excerpts from Confederate reports illustrate this phenomenon. Major W.H. Haynes, chief of commissary, later wrote, "It may be proper for me to say that I never met General Pillow before the morning of February 9. General Pillow assigned me to duty on his staff after arriving at Donelson, February 10."[30]

After the battle Pillow wrote Secretary of War Randolph: "I had kept up the fight with the forces under my immediate command for the last two hours by carrying ammunition in boxes upon the heads of details from the command for that purpose, my supply of 60 rounds having been exhausted in the long struggle, and no wagon could go to the battle-field on account of the thick undergrowth and want of road."[31]

Nathan Bedford Forrest included the following comment in his report: "On the night of the fight (15th) ... no rations were prepared or taken on the field; blankets and knapsacks were left behind; no order of retreat was prescribed; no quartermaster, commissary or ordnance stores were prepared ... I had again and again during the day sent portions of my command into the intrenchments [sic] and had ammunition brought out on horseback."[32]

Colonel William Baldwin's report contained two important comments on Confederate ammunition and the weapons they used. "Our ammunition had been so rapidly expended as to entirely exhaust the supply from some regiments. Numbers had provided themselves from the cartridges of the dead and wounded enemy." His second comment spoke to the performance of smoothbore muskets: "I would beg leave to remark here that the efficiency of the smoothbore musket and ball and buck-shot cartridges was fully demonstrated on this occasion, and ... our troops [must close] rapidly upon the enemy, when our rapid loading and firing proves immensely destructive and the long-range arms of the enemy lose their superiority."[33]

Confederate soldiers fighting in other western battles could have echoed Colonel Baldwin's comments as well. Flintlocks obviously did not work well in pouring rain, but if the men could close within 100 yards of their opponents these weapons were still very effective. Furthermore, a close examination of other battles from 1862 suggests that the ranges at which soldiers from both sides engaged one another in combat were often under 100 yards.[34]

Prior to the Union investment of Donelson, the Confederates failed to use their superior manpower resources and send anyone out to contest Grant's advance. Some sources suggest they apparently mustered around 17,000 men at one point, but confusion at the command level allowed Grant's force, without interference, over broken terrain and on two separate roads, to approach the fort. This was one opportunity that passed unnoticed at the time. While the Confederates committed all of Pillow's men

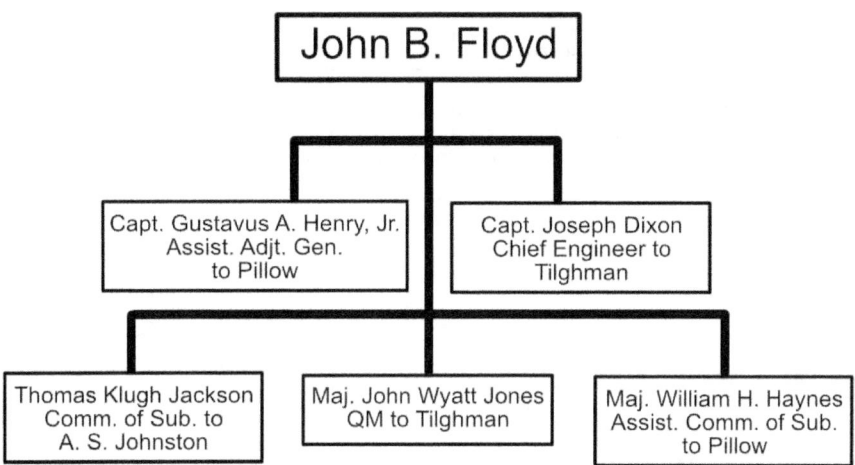

Selected Confederate staff officers at Fort Donelson. While Dixon, Jackson and Gilmer had West Point backgrounds, Henry, Jones and Haynes had legal or business experience. Unfortunately, they had never worked with one another before and had received ambiguous and conflicting instructions, and thus failed to provide necessary food or ammunition to the Confederate force at Donelson (courtesy Margaret A. Zimmermann).

and a portion of Buckner's as well for their assault on February 15, the entire garrison was apparently not fully mobilized for combat, as other men remained behind to man the defense works and garrison the fort. On the other hand, Grant committed his entire force as soon as he was able to re-supply his men with ammunition. All three Union divisions were ordered forward simultaneously.[35]

While the outcome of many Civil War battles seemed to achieve little strategically, this early campaign on Grant's part led to substantial strategic results. The Confederate position at Columbus, Kentucky, on the Mississippi River was outflanked, and the Confederates were forced to withdraw to positions farther south. Kentucky was lost to the Confederacy, and the Cumberland River was opened to Nashville, Tennessee. Perhaps most importantly, the Tennessee River was opened all the way from Fort Henry to Muscle Shoals in Alabama. Except for temporary forays, the Confederates failed to recover permanently their original possessions in Kentucky and Tennessee. Grant achieved strategic support for his effort; he formed a cohesive team from a group of individuals and finally demonstrated active, hands-on leadership during the critical moments of the battle. As other engagements for 1862 in the western theater are discussed, these six categories allow us to use observable variables of success, and as a result, one is better able to judge the effectiveness of Civil War leadership.

Six Elements of Victory at Fort Donelson

Donelson	*Clear, Attainable Objective*	*Operational Initiative*	*Command Unity*
Grant	Achieved	Achieved	Achieved
Floyd	Not Achieved	Not Achieved	Not Achieved
	Logistics/Staff	*Used All Resources*	*Strategic Outcome*
Grant	Achieved	Achieved	Achieved
Floyd	Not Achieved	Not Achieved	Not Achieved

By changing commanders too often and by (once again) allowing a subordinate to command a critical force, the Confederates failed to achieve success in any of the six determinants. Grant, on the other hand, was well along in developing a team of people (including naval elements) that successfully achieved a common goal.

Chapter 3

Pea Ridge

Arkansas Travelers

With the outbreak of war, a key question arose: Would Missouri remain a border state or would Confederate elements be able to seize it for the South? Current and former governors, Claiborne Jackson and Sterling Price, strained to raise Confederate forces. While a substantial German anti-slavery population controlled St. Louis, vocal slave supporters began organizing and training at Camp Jackson with an eye to seizing the nearby Federal arsenal. On May 10, 1861, however, Union Captain Nathaniel Lyon seized Camp Jackson in St. Louis and proceeded to hold the U.S. Armory and arsenal for the North.

Missouri was strategically critical for the Union. Advancing south along the Mississippi River, the Union army and armored gunboats needed a secure right flank. Without this protection, Confederate defenders supporting Vicksburg and points south would always be able to threaten Northern encroachments. Reinforcements from Texas and Arkansas, the movement of food supplies such as beef from west of the river, and even actions that would threaten attacks against major Northern supply depots at St. Louis were always possible. Northern armies could not win the war by conquering Arkansas, but the Federal cause could be damaged or delayed if the Union flank was successfully turned from this direction. Missouri, Kansas and Arkansas were all viewed as largely wilderness areas. Inhabited by Indians, bushwhackers and other anti–Union forces, the territory just west of the Mississippi River was truly the "Wild West." On August 10, 1861, Confederate forces under Sterling Price, the former governor of Missouri, and Ben McCulloch, the former Texas Ranger, defeated a small army of Union soldiers under Nathaniel Lyon at Wilson's Creek. They killed Lyon and temporarily neutered any Union attempt to move much beyond the confines of St. Louis. General John Fremont, the first Republican candidate for President in 1856, had been appointed earlier by Lincoln to take and hold Missouri for the Union. But after he failed to support Lyon, failed to retract his pronouncement freeing all the slaves in Missouri, and allowed widespread graft and corruption to permeate his forces, Lincoln removed him. Colonel Grenville Dodge summarized the feelings of some when he wrote, in a letter to his mother, "Fremont was a big enthusiastic man but had poor discipline and was very extravagant." The new commander was highly regarded as an accomplished soldier, although he had not seen any major combat. Now Major General Henry Wager Halleck needed someone to actively campaign in the field, secure Missouri, and wrest the initiative from the South in Arkansas. What to do? General Samuel Curtis had kept the city of St. Louis pacified and safe for the Union since the death of Lyon, and on December 25,

1861, here was Halleck's candidate, and Halleck chose him for the job.[1]

General Curtis graduated from West Point in 1831, ranked 27 of 33. Active in engineering and the law, Curtis saw action in the Mexican War as Colonel of the 2nd Ohio Volunteers. After the war, he lived in Iowa and served three terms in the U.S. Congress. As an early and prominent Republican, Curtis had also been considered for cabinet posts in the newly formed Lincoln administration. While serving in St. Louis, he reorganized the war effort there to redeem it from Fremont's ineptitude. It soon became the major supply depot for Union armies in the West. Recognizing competence when he saw it, Halleck appointed Curtis to command the army and gave him experienced subordinates to assist him in driving the Confederates out of Missouri.[2]

Brigadier General Curtis faced truly challenging circumstances. His mission: secure Missouri and begin an offensive into northwestern Arkansas. He was given command of the Army of the Southwest, about 12,000 men. His task was very straightforward. Clear Missouri of Sterling Price, advance into Arkansas, and attack any force that Price, Ben McCulloch, and the local Native Americans could raise. Then secure the Union right flank in the process. The Confederates raised approximately 16,500 men, threatened Missouri from northwest Arkansas, and even launched a forward movement into Missouri. Curtis began his march from Springfield, Missouri, a little over 200 miles from Elkhorn Tavern or Pea Ridge. Obviously, logistics would play an important role for both forces as they moved largely without rail or river transportation.[3]

In Missouri, Confederate General Sterling Price had been reinforced by

Major General Earl Van Dorn (courtesy The Civil War Museum, Kenosha, WI).

Brigadier General Samuel R. Curtis (Library of Congress).

another Confederate force under Ben McCulloch that marched north from Arkansas. By now the Confederates had reoccupied Springfield and were threatening to advance once again. Halleck determined to protect his right flank as he projected his own offensive against Confederate forces, located throughout Kentucky and Tennessee. Halleck ordered forces under John Pope to move south on the Mississippi River to capture Island No. 10 and sent U.S. Grant toward Forts Henry and Donelson. He needed another force to move through Springfield and into northwest Arkansas to protect his right flank. In early 1862, Halleck turned to General Curtis.

Having set the stage for combat in the far west, both North and South prepared for conflict. To secure Missouri for the Union, General Curtis needed to travel southwest out of St. Louis. The railroad reached from St. Louis to the little town of Rolla, deep in the center of the state. From the end of the rail line there, it was another 275 miles to the northwestern border of Arkansas. A Confederate force under Sterling Price occupied the town of Springfield, roughly midway between Rolla and the Arkansas border. The battlefield of Pea Ridge lies just over the border near the town of Bentonville, on the far western border of Arkansas. A dirt road by the name of Telegraph Road wound its way through the area. Curtis had to leave the railhead, secure wagons for his ordnance, and march the entire distance to Arkansas while supplying his army with food. Both Halleck and Curtis worked together to solve the problem.

Under General Curtis, the Army of the Southwest, as his force was now called, advanced in four divisions. Curtis's second in command was Franz Sigel, who was originally born in Germany and commanded the army's First Division. Sigel attended the Karlsruhe Military Academy before coming to the U.S. in 1852 and settling in St Louis. Grouping two divisions with their numerous German immigrants under Sigel, Curtis placed the First Division tactically under Colonel Peter J. Osterhaus, who had attended the Berlin Military Academy and settled in St. Louis in 1858. Brigadier General Alexander S. Asboth commanded the Second Division. Jefferson C. Davis commanded the Third Division. Colonel Eugene A. Carr, West Point Class of 1850, who would eventually rise to the rank of brevet major general, led the Fourth Division. All of them had seen action at Wilson's Creek, and while they were on the losing side, all of them had by now experienced Civil War combat. Of the three, Sigel is, of course, the most abused by historians, but he was to serve Curtis well during the actual battle at Pea Ridge.[4]

Once Halleck learned that Sterling Price had advanced tentatively north from Springfield, he quickly reinforced Curtis's little army near Rolla where the railroad ended. Halleck knew that Curtis would need logistical support to begin any campaign, let alone one commencing in mid-winter. As a result, Halleck sent West Point graduate Captain Philip Sheridan to Curtis as his quartermaster. "Little Phil," as he was called for his diminutive height, Sheridan was both feisty and a capable organizer. Sheridan and Curtis would later quarrel, Curtis and Sigel would maintain a strictly formal relationship, and yet Curtis was able to hold his command together and reach a successful conclusion in the coming campaign. Without rails or water, Curtis sustained his entire force logistically, employing only Captain Sheridan's wagons and ingenuity.

While Sheridan's memory may be at times challenged, he comments on his dual role of chief quartermaster and chief of commissary during the Pea Ridge campaign, and they are still worth perusing. "Having reported to General Curtis, … I labored day and night to remedy [the defects Sheridan believed he found] and … soon brought things into shape, putting the transportation in good working order, giving each regiment its proper quota of wagons, and turning the surplus into the general supply trains of the army." Later after Curtis had been successful at Pea Ridge, and despite the angry differences of opinion that would divide these two men, Sheridan would still write: "No matter what merit belonged to individual commanders, I was always convinced that Curtis was deserving of the highest commendation, not only for the skill displayed on the field, but for a zeal and daring in campaign which was not often exhibited at that early period of the war." Sheridan immediately ordered that regiments reduce their wagon support from 28 to two. Some officers protested or attempted to refuse. In the end, "He finally succeeded in reorganizing the trains."[5]

By February 13, 1862, Curtis marched his force south to Springfield, Missouri. Sheridan, in his memoirs, praises Colonel Grenville Dodge (one of the brigade commanders destined to rise to greater prominence as the war progressed) as an officer who was particularly helpful for him and assisted him ably in his efforts to supply the army. Dodge writes, "We had to feed and forage the command from a sparsely populated country with little in it and it has always been a wonder to me how he so successfully did it. During this campaign, Captain Sheridan tented with me. He had a great difficulty in getting the necessary details for running mills, foraging, etc…. He would come to me and at times he would have the entire 4th Iowa detailed at different mills and out upon foraging expeditions." This quote suggests once more that Curtis had a strong supporting cast as he began his Pea Ridge campaign. One can argue that Curtis was perhaps not the most famous or distinguished general serving the Union during the Civil War, but he clearly assembled an accomplished group of subordinates and staff officers to support his efforts.[6]

One other decision helped Curtis achieve success on his campaign. As they advanced, Curtis and Sheridan both agreed that the army would live off the countryside. Unlike the case with Don Carlos Buell's force in Tennessee, foraging was encouraged for the Army of the Southwest. Beginning in Missouri, Curtis authorized Sheridan to establish mills, obtain grain and move food supplies forward to the army.[7]

On the Confederate side, Sterling Price and Ben McCulloch argued vigorously with one another after their combined victory at Wilson's Creek, and now their army had separated into two parts, each commanded by one of the quarreling generals. Hoping to regain control of Missouri, 53-year-old former governor Sterling Price led the Missouri contingent of Confederates. Without formal military training, he saw action during the Mexican War as Colonel of the 2nd Missouri and as Brigadier General of volunteers. Born in 1811, Ben McCulloch fought at San Jacinto during the Texas War for Independence. He served during the Mexican War under Zachary Taylor and battled Indians as Captain of the Texas Rangers. McCulloch was particularly helpful for Taylor as he led a force of scouts that moved ahead of the army to identify enemy forces. As noted earlier in the prologue, McCulloch often scouted alone or with limited forces of his rangers and was most comfortable acting with these small groups of soldiers. Also without formal military training, McCulloch served as Brigadier General in the Provisional Confederate Army.[8]

At one point, McCulloch even traveled to Richmond to plead his case for army leadership directly with Jefferson Davis. On November 28, 1861, Missouri was accepted as a Confederate state, but Davis remained unsure of how to handle his quarreling duo. On January 16, 1862, Davis made his decision. He would appoint someone to command both McCulloch and Price. Enter Major General Earl Van Dorn. A friend of Davis, Van Dorn was appointed to command the new Department of Trans-Mississippi. As a great nephew of Andrew Jackson, he received an education at West Point and graduated in 1842. Bravely fighting in the Mexican War, he spent most of his time in the cavalry fighting Indians following the war's conclusion. Jefferson Davis believed Van Dorn would be an ideal choice to command a Confederate army west of the Mississippi River.[9]

Van Dorn was now 41 years old. After Van Dorn's murder in May of 1863 at the hands of a Dr. Peters who felt Van Dorn had violated his wife, history has not been kind to Van Dorn; besides losing at Pea Ridge, he later failed to march to the support of A.S. Johnston before Shiloh, and he is credited with losing the battle of Corinth. While he captured and destroyed Grant's supply base at Holly Springs, late in 1862, his detractors have not forgotten his other mistakes. At the Battle of Pea Ridge, however, Van Dorn would struggle against very difficult circumstances. Besides two quarreling sub-commanders, Van Dorn was not blessed with a centralized staff during the Pea Ridge campaign. Van Dorn arrived with only his chief of staff and an aide-de-camp.[10]

Brigadier General Benjamin McCulloch. His death early at the Battle of Pea Ridge led to confusion on the part of the Confederate right wing as the Confederate forces quickly ran through three commanders, all dead or captured. *Frank Leslie's History of the Civil War, 1895,* 86 (courtesy The Civil War Museum, Kenosha, WI).

On January 10, 1862, President Davis created the Trans Mississippi District of Department No. 2 and assigned Van Dorn to command it. When he appeared in Arkansas and took command, Van Dorn found about 5,700 men under McCulloch and another 8,000 men under Price along with some 65 artillery pieces. Van Dorn also hoped that Albert Pike, who had organized (very loosely) 2,500 Native Americans, would join him. From Little Rock, on the opposite side of the state, Van Dorn announced his new command on January 29; almost the entire state of Arkansas separated him from his army. Now, however, he chose not to move west and assume personal control. By February 7, Van Dorn was writing to Price with the hope that they might muster up to 25,000 men: "With these, can we not hope to take Saint Louis by rapid marches and assault?" On February 14, Van Dorn was still planning a march on St Louis. He also believed that in the dead of winter, "I have been informed ... that the counties around you are rich in everything in the way of provisions needed by an army." Van Dorn was dreaming.[11]

Meanwhile, after capturing Springfield, Missouri, Union General Samuel Curtis split his column in two to facilitate foraging from the countryside and pursue Price to the south. Price, caught by surprise, began pulling out under Federal pressure. While Price appeared to be well equipped with wagons and supplies at first, the rapid enemy advance and Price's loose logistical organization left his supply wagons straining to escape the oncoming Federal force. Price retreated to a point about 12 miles south of Elkhorn Tavern. On February 16, a message to General McCulloch announced that Price "had been fighting for two days without sleep or eating." A second message noted once again that Price was "short of rations and his men have not had sleep for two days and nights." Once they joined forces on the 17th, McCulloch realized that Price's force was largely exhausted and that he had abandoned many of his wagons during the retreat.[12]

By February 20, after considerable skirmishing, the Confederate forces under McCulloch and Price reached the town of Fayetteville, Arkansas, the major supply depot for Price's army. Unable to move everything during the retreat, the commanders opened the doors to the warehouses and allowed the army to loot everything portable as they retreated. Ammunition stored in an arsenal was burned. Without proper organization or enough wagons, the logistical support for Van Dorn's army was severely damaged at one stroke. As enlistments expired, Confederates also left the army to go home. Apparently, Price lost almost 1,200 men in this fashion during the retreat. On the Union side and realizing that he was well beyond his ability to fully supply his own force, General Curtis halted his army before the end of February to allow his men to rest and for additional supplies to reach him. This, of course, also allowed the Confederates to regroup.[13]

Major General Sterling Price. Besides quarreling with Ben McCulloch, the former Governor of Missouri and Mexican War veteran Sterling Price lost a good deal of his supply train during the earlier Confederate retreat from the Federal army under Curtis. Now at Pea Ridge, the commander of the army, Van Dorn, was forced to rely on Price for Confederate supplies and the use of Price's staff. When they finally discovered that Price's supply train was far distant from the battlefield, the Confederates knew they were defeated and must retreat from Elkhorn Tavern. After the battle, Price opted to create a new staff that accompanied him along with Van Dorn to another battle at Corinth (Library of Congress).

But the reader must pause for a moment. The commander of the combined Confederate force was Earl Van Dorn, and he was obviously not accompanying retreating forces of McCulloch and Price. He was, in fact, still in the little town of Pocahontas, on the Black River in eastern Arkansas. When he received word that the Federals were advancing into Arkansas on February 22, he was almost 250 miles from the scene of the real action. Traveling by steamboat, canoe and then horseback, Van Dorn was accompanied solely by his own chief of staff, Colonel Dabney Maury, two slaves, and an aide: "None of the gentlemen of my personal staff, with the exception of Colonel Maury, assistant adjutant general, and Lieut. C. Sulivane, my aide de-camp, accompanied me from Jacksonport." Crossing a river by canoe in the chill of winter, Van Dorn was thrown out and soon after developed a fever. He finally emerged from an ambulance at the little town of Van Buren near Fort Smith and ordered offensive action. On March 3, he met with McCulloch and Price to coordinate their operation against Curtis. On March 4, with over 16,500 men, they advanced to attack Curtis. Van Dorn appeared largely oblivious to the fact that Price's men had just traveled over 200 miles while poorly supplied. In fact, Van Dorn had never met either of his two subordinates before this battle, and he attempted to integrate green troops (many of them unarmed) and uncontrolled Native Americans into his force. Now he expected this entire assemblage to function with a sense of camaraderie and teamwork in desperate combat. He also ordered the entire army to force-march toward Pea Ridge. William Tunnard describes Van Dorn at this moment in time. "Impetuous, at times rash and reckless, brave and daring to a fault, with his usual spirit, he was about to hurl his army on the foe. The men felt that there was to be no retreating, no more waiting. The two forces having at length been united, he hesitated not a day as to his course. All extra clothing, baggage, tents, etc., were ordered to be left behind. Provisions (such as were on hand) were prepared."[14]

As described earlier, Brigadier General Curtis had reached the end of his supply tether and decided to pull back slightly to find better forage and to shorten his supply lines. On March 5, after the Confederates had been on the road for almost two days, Curtis learned of the Confederate proximity to his own army. Not knowing the specific direction of the Confederate advance, Curtis once again split his force in two (one for each possible enemy approach march) and prepared to meet them. Sending orders out to hasten the retreat, Curtis moved his forces north toward a defensive line he could establish on Pea Ridge and south of Elkhorn Tavern. Lagging behind with his own force and failing to follow his original orders, Franz Sigel provided a tempting target for Confederate forces, and on March 6, Union troops and Confederates spent time skirmishing. Van Dorn hoped to catch Sigel alone as Sigel hurried north: "It had evidently been his intention to cut Sigel off, capture his corps, and whip Curtis in detail, but that little Dutchman was equal to the emergency." Van Dorn's problem, however, was that the weather was awful, and his men were fatigued from their arduous trek and lacked supplies. Bravery cannot always compensate for hunger or exhaustion, and Sigel escaped.[15]

Van Dorn now faced the entire Union army, still divided in two, on high ground under Curtis. While Van Dorn outnumbered them, a stand-up fight would be a challenge. What to do? Meeting with McCulloch and Price, Van Dorn considered his options. A direct assault was not advised. A move around the Union flank was considered and adopted, although Van Dorn's subordinates apparently struggled to contain the general from marching along an even more ambitious route. As the Union Army originally faced south, Van Dorn proposed to attack one portion of it under Sigel and march around it to the north. After cutting off the Union retreat to the north, the Confederates would face south and destroy Curtis's outnumbered force. Poor staff performance again hindered the advance. As the nighttime march around the Union flank unfolded, the infantry and artillery preceded the cavalry and the movement ground to a halt as they came upon a bridgeless creek that needed crossing. The Confederate advance was delayed even further by felled trees and a frigid night, and by the next morning, the Confederate Army of the West was barely intact. The men were weary, hungry and broken from their rapid march and the loss of rest and want of food. Early on the morning of March 7, 1862, they approached the site known as Pea Ridge, near Elk Horn Tavern. Price's command was on one side of the Federal Army near Elkhorn Tavern and McCulloch's force was still marching toward the Federal rear. The Confederates began their journey to the battlefield on March 4 with only three days' cooked rations available. These were largely gone by March 7 and certainly exhausted by March 8. Despite the protests of both McCulloch and Price, however, Van Dorn persisted in his plan of attack.[16]

As the Confederates forged clear past the Federal defensive position and moved to the north, Curtis became aware of their movement, and he decided to fight it out with a counterattack. Van Dorn's pre-combat consultation had been contentious, but when Curtis met with his subordinates, he, too, discovered a range of opinion. When Curtis's orders were issued, however, he, at least, enjoyed the loyalty of his commanders. With their support he moved to discover the extent of the Confederate force gathering to the north and then engage them.

Battle of Leetown

The first force to confront the Confederates (in what became known as the Battle of Leetown) was the division commanded by Peter Osterhaus, under the command of Franz Sigel. Coming up against Ben McCulloch's Confederates and Albert Pike's Indians and heavily outnumbered by them, Osterhaus had the choice of pulling back and letting the Confederates reach the Union wagon train with its supplies and ammunition or attacking vigorously with a forlorn hope. Following Curtis's intentions, Osterhaus attacked and, facing overwhelming odds, was quickly routed and his guns captured. The Federals retreated and formed up once again to receive the Confederates, and McCulloch prepared to continue his attack. He neglected, however, to inform Van Dorn of his plan.[17]

As he was not willing to send skirmishers or staff officers to do his reconnaissance, McCulloch decided to investigate the Union position himself. Riding alone toward the Union position he was shot down and killed. His second in command, Brigadier General James McIntosh, then advanced with additional forces. Mounted and moving forward to the attack, he too was shot down and killed. The Confederate attack halted. B. Warren Stone, Colonel of the 6th Texas Cavalry wrote: "About the time of our second formation of line, our distinguished leader, the gallant, chivalrous McCulloch fell … but a short time after this … fell Brig. Gen. James McIntosh…. Several hours elapsed before I knew certainly of their sad fate, [and their deaths left] me in the most perplexed condition and mental anguish." Once informed of Osterhaus's plight, General Curtis ordered the Third Division to his aid.[18]

Now the third Confederate officer in line of command, General Louis Hébert led a brigade forward; his regiments became intermingled, and he was captured by Union troops. The Confederates were completely thwarted. Losing three commanders in one afternoon, McCulloch's force was stymied and then disintegrated. Once Albert Pike discovered (by midafternoon) that he was now actually in charge of McCulloch's entire force, he felt his best move would be to disengage and march to join Price near Elkhorn Tavern.[19]

Battle of Elkhorn Tavern, Day One

On the Confederate left (Union right near Elkhorn Tavern), Van Dorn and Price were slow to initiate their attack, and while the Union forces were hard-pressed to hold their ground, the Confederate forces failed to achieve a complete breakthrough in this area either. Outnumbering the Union forces almost two to one, they forced the Federal forces back from Elkhorn Tavern, but the Union lines never gave way entirely. Reinforcements from Sigel also made a timely appearance before the end of the day.

The Union army was still divided, but during the night, Curtis was able to unite his forces. The Confederates, on the other hand, remained divided. McCulloch's surviving force moved to join Price, but their trains (wagons containing what little food the army possessed and all the reserve ammunition) remained absent, miles from Van Dorn's main force. No orders were sent to them and they, in turn, did not communicate their separation from the main forces of Van Dorn's army. In fact, the train (with 3,000 men to guard it) was a full eight miles from the actual crossroads at Elkhorn Tavern. Van Dorn himself later alluded to the supply issue in his report: "In the course of the night I ascertained that the ammunition was almost exhausted, and that the officer in charge of the ordnance supplies could not find his wagons, which with the subsistence train, had been sent to Bentonville. Most of the troops had been without any food since the morning of the 6th and the artillery horses were beaten out." But the officer in charge of the ordnance train and other supplies later wrote that while he remained with his wagons, no one told him what to do or where to go.[20]

Brigadier General Martin Green of the Missouri State Guard, and the officer in charge, narrates: "On the morning of the 7th I was ordered to leave the baggage at camp, near Camp Stephens.... [Then] I received a message from Colonel Wood, General Price's aide to bring the baggage up to the army.... When within 1 mile of the battle ground ... I met my messenger, bringing an order to return with the baggage to Elm Springs."[21]

Battle of Elkhorn Tavern, Day Two

When March 8 dawned, and after a lengthy wait, Van Dorn accompanied Price and they wheeled their numerous guns forward to engage the Federals. They had advantages in numbers with both artillery and manpower in the early morning hours. They just didn't have enough ammunition, and Van Dorn only committed 2-3 batteries at a time against the North. On the Federal side, no one had convinced Curtis that he was badly outnumbered or outgunned, and he carefully stationed his infantry behind his guns near Elkhorn Tavern and prepared to engage the Confederates. On the left side of the line, Franz Sigel organized much of Curtis's artillery along with a force of infantry primed for an advance. Around 8 a.m. the two sides began hammering each other. The Union force was united. The Confederates had slept on their arms and had neither food nor additional ammunition for their guns. After their limbers had been emptied and under a brisk crossfire from the Union artillery, the Confederates realized that the day was lost. Van Dorn looked in vain for his supplies, but they were still miles from the battlefield near Bentonville. By 10 a.m. Van Dorn realized the Confederates had lost.

Left: Brigadier General Franz Sigel. While he did not have much success on other battlefields during the Civil War, Sigel managed to avert the destruction of his force early at Pea Ridge, then contributed significantly to the Union victory on the second day's action near Elkhorn Tavern (Library of Congress).

Below: At Pea Ridge, General Van Dorn divided his army as he marched around Big Mountain and fought two separate actions the first day. His lengthy march placed his army to the north of Federal forces and compelled General Curtis to face north in fighting the battle. His force under General McCulloch came to grief as the day wore on, and without supplies of food or ammunition, Van Dorn was forced to contend with the entire Union army under Curtis on the second day of battle (courtesy Margaret A. Zimmermann).

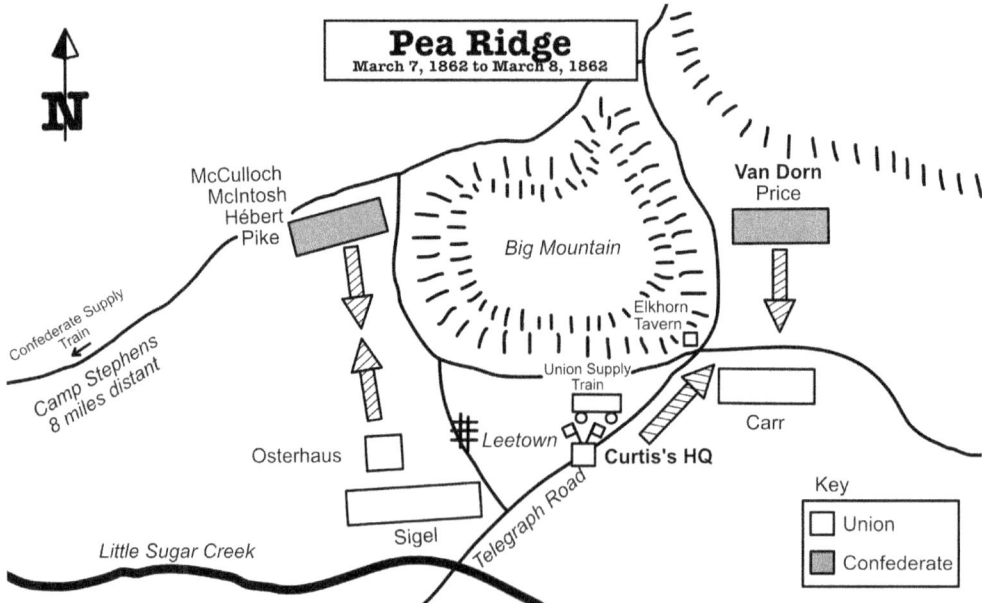

A hasty Confederate retreat followed, and Curtis remained in control of the entire battlefield. The Confederate army was badly damaged.[22]

* * *

While Van Dorn originally believed his objective was to lead an offensive on the east side of Arkansas and Missouri toward St. Louis, his true assignment was to defend Arkansas from a Union advance. Instead of defense, Van Dorn risked an attack. Curtis's objective was clear: Defend Missouri from Confederate attacks by marching into northwestern Arkansas and defeating the Confederates there. He proceeded to accomplish this goal.

For the Confederates, strategic support for armies west of the Mississippi River was absent. Jefferson Davis could appoint Earl Van Dorn to command an army there, but no reinforcements followed, and clear objectives for Van Dorn were not forthcoming. While they mustered more men and artillery pieces than their Union counterparts, the Confederates were unable to assemble their forces in a way that allowed them to use their superior numbers to advantage. Another major question dogged Van Dorn as well. Should he move his force to join A.S. Johnston before Shiloh, or should he move along the Mississippi River toward St. Louis? As January and February passed, the Union army under General Curtis answered the strategic question. While Van Dorn remained in eastern Arkansas, Curtis marched southwest toward a divided Confederate command.

The Union also faced challenging strategic and operational decisions. While Halleck is often faulted for a variety of reasons, he provided very able overall direction for the advance into Arkansas. Samuel Curtis was a fine choice as field commander and Philip Sheridan proved an able assistant in the critical role of quartermaster and commissary.

By seizing the initiative and advancing through Missouri into Arkansas, Curtis denied the Confederates any opportunity they might have sought for their own offensive operation. While Curtis was badly outnumbered as the battle opened, his subordinates proved to be a feisty bunch by attacking the Confederates and taking the initiative early in the battle. On the second day of battle, Curtis clearly seized the initiative by uniting his artillery and sending Sigel forward to the attack with his infantry. By doing so, he forced the Confederates into a precipitous retreat. Following the battle Curtis also retained the initiative.[23]

For the North, the issue of command unity became an open question. After the Battle of Wilson's Creek, Franz Sigel's participation in the battle and his actions following became controversial. Did he obey the orders of General Nathaniel Lyon, the army commander? Did he remain active and helpful after Lyon's death and the retreat of the Union army in defeat? Sigel was both attacked by other officers and defended by the German American press. There were some who wanted Sigel promoted to command the larger force now gathering under General Henry W. Halleck to reclaim Missouri for the Union. In the end, General Samuel R. Curtis received the command, and Sigel was asked to move his force of two divisions to join Curtis. Sigel decided to cooperate with this arrangement and, at times, served Curtis well during the expedition. While Curtis was placed in a potentially disastrous tactical situation at Pea Ridge, he was able to use his subordinates effectively to accomplish all the things that Van Dorn proved unwilling or unable to do on the other side of the hill.[24]

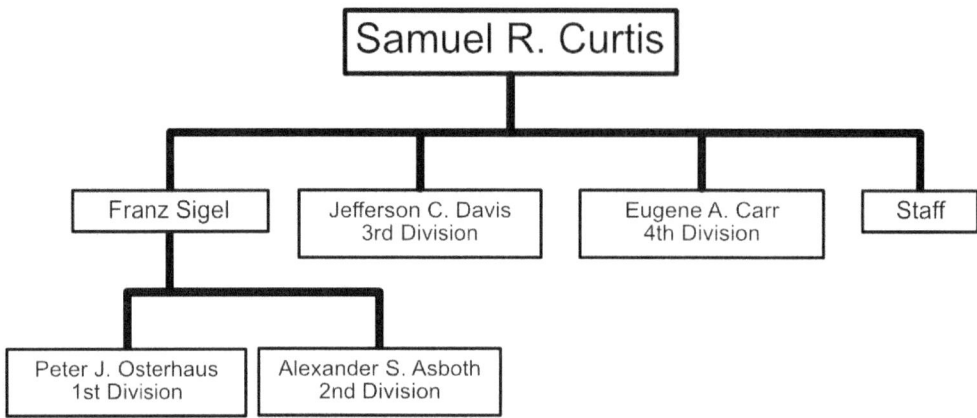

Organization of the Union Army under Brigadier General Samuel R. Curtis. These four divisions were all commanded by experienced soldiers. Osterhaus had graduated from the Berlin Military Academy, Asboth served as a wartime army officer during the Hungarian revolt (1847–1851), Jefferson Davis served with U.S. Army Regulars from 1847 on, and Carr was a West Point graduate who served on active duty upon graduation (courtesy Margaret A. Zimmermann).

During the battle, however, Curtis and Sigel became involved in a serious discussion. When Sigel had withdrawn in the face of Van Dorn's forced march, he was delayed when one of his units mistakenly detached itself from the main body. Sigel waited to reunite his force, and Curtis became concerned over the apparent danger that now seemed to confront them. As the Confederates closed in on March 7, Sigel and Curtis finally agreed on their tactical dispositions. Even though Sigel met with Curtis around 2 a.m. on the 8th and urged retreat, Curtis elected to stay and fight it out. Assisting Curtis overnight and in the early morning hours of the 8th, Sigel directed the placement of the Union artillery, which proved decisive during the next day's events. After the defeat of McCulloch's division, Sigel's men finally moved to help Curtis as he battled Price's force. The combination of Union artillery and Sigel's reinforcements helped win the day. While the two commanders would quarrel after the battle, and while Sheridan and other officers would join in attacks on Curtis, they were collectively able to agree on a battle-winning strategy after all.[25]

As a result, the question of command unity can be controversial. General Sigel was not known for his quiet obedience to orders, and yet at Pea Ridge he did his best to follow Curtis's directions. He was forceful in making suggestions, and Curtis was willing to give him freedom of action, particularly on the second day of battle. In the end, however, Sigel and the other Union generals provided solid support for Curtis. The Confederates originally had infantry, cavalry and especially artillery, more than anything the Union could bring to bear, over 16,000 men. Curtis was never able to bring more than about 10,500 men to the field, but the Federals provided a cooperative team for combat. The Confederates fielded colorful individualists, and the South paid heavily for this decision.[26]

Curtis moved actively around the Elkhorn Tavern battleground and directed his subordinates from horseback. His immediate reports, Sigel, Davis, Osterhaus and Carr, all performed well on the battlefield. They also followed orders. (After the battle, there was certainly squabbling enough to go around, but during the two days of combat under his direct supervision, his subordinates turned in a solid performance.) One might accuse

Curtis of getting too close to the firing line on occasion, but he spent most of his time commanding actively from a comfortable distance when the shooting was underway.[27]

The campaign and battle for Pea Ridge was a struggle for the South from the very beginning. Price and McCulloch quarreled all through the fall and into the winter. When Davis chose Van Dorn to break up the contentiousness, Van Dorn stayed far from his army for almost a full month. In the meantime, the Union forces advanced, and Price destroyed most of his own supplies. Finally, when Van Dorn did appear, his overly aggressive actions came near to causing the disintegration of his army.

As a result of his tardy appearance for the Confederate side, Van Dorn was not in a position to develop a cooperative team with his immediate subordinates. He failed to bring staff officers with him, failed to coordinate the staff he found to feed and arm his force, and finally he failed to provide clear direction once his forces approached the battlefield. During the battle, Confederate subordinate officers attempted to follow Van Dorn's directions, but the army dissolved into chaos as these men failed to work together effectively. McCulloch undertook his own reconnaissance and was killed. Speaking of Ben McCulloch, Tunnard notes, "It was his individuality, reliance on his own personal observations, regardless of extraneous assistance, which led him to needlessly expose himself at Elk Horn. Forbidding his staff to follow him, he departed to make personal observations and reconnoiter the enemy's position, ere ordering the mass of his troops into battle." McIntosh followed suit and was also killed. Hébert was captured, and no one gave Pike any directions at all. Under Van Dorn, a lack of staff officers meant he had to rely on Price for staff support, and after Price was wounded, no one apparently thought of bringing up additional ordnance wagons. Van Dorn's officers argued against his command to force march toward the Union lines without proper rest or food. When they failed to convince Van Dorn, however, the Confederate offense was badly damaged. While Curtis was willing to consider the advice of Sigel, Van Dorn was just as clearly not going to listen to his own officers.[28]

On the Confederate side, Van Dorn was ill when the battle opened, but he spent time with Price and actively directed the battle near Elkhorn Tavern. On the second day of battle, his fever had apparently broken and he could accompany the wounded Price as the battle opened.[29]

The Union army clearly had an advantage in providing effective staff for their

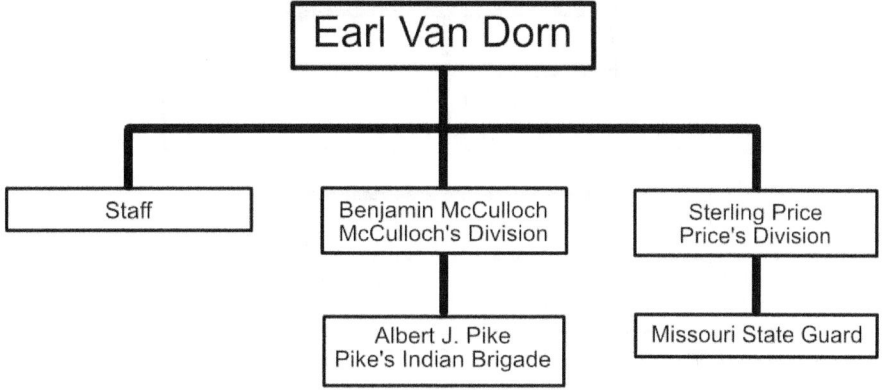

Organization of the Confederate Army under Major General Earl Van Dorn. While they could claim service in the war with Mexico, none of Earl Van Dorn's immediate subordinates had any formal military training (courtesy Margaret A. Zimmermann).

forces. Sheridan was an excellent quartermaster who provided active support for the logistical needs of the army. A corporal of Company G, 9th Iowa Infantry commented, "Following the engagement at Sugar Creek, Feb. 14, 1862, Price retreated. It was useless for Curtis to think of pursuing the rebels further.... Rest and recuperation were imperative.... Grist mills were seized, grain brought in, and in a few days the men were feasting on the fat of the land."[30]

As the Confederates approached Curtis's force and he was trying to buy time to reunite the army, Curtis called once more upon Colonel Dodge. The Colonel was asked to take his unit of 4th Iowa out and fell trees in the path of the oncoming Confederates. Taking his command, Dodge moved out and did just that. Here we see where the talents of soldiers raised in a different environment can make a difference: "We had a captain in our regiment, O.H.P. Scott who had been a railroad builder, and was always ready for a job of railroad building or timber cutting; and on the night of the 6th he was detailed, with a number of men to assist Colonel Dodge."[31]

Ordnance wagons were kept near the units in combat and at other times, logistical support was forthcoming. Curtis was careful to protect his wagons throughout the campaign and the battle.[32] He was stretched, but he organized his resources to successfully face his Confederate foe with confidence.[33]

As the Union army approached before the battle, Sterling Price was responsible for the large-scale destruction of his own wagons. Also, when Van Dorn made his original decision to force march into battle, his overzealousness led to incredible suffering on the part of the Confederates. By doing so, Van Dorn demanded forced marching from his men in the dead of winter, and then he failed to provide them with necessary food or ammunition. Tunnard reports: "Thus, as these fine and comfortable quarters melted away into ashes, it entailed on the regiment the loss of nearly everything they had, besides a large quantity of quartermaster and commissary stores and forage."[34]

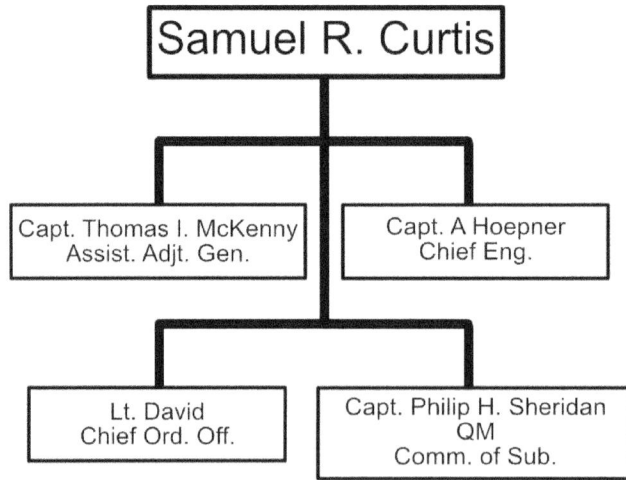

Selected Union Staff under Curtis. Phil Sheridan graduated from West Point in 1853 and served in the Regular Army, Thomas I. McKenny had pre-war railroad and construction experience, and Captain Hoepner had pre-war engineering experience. See note 33 (courtesy Margaret A. Zimmermann).

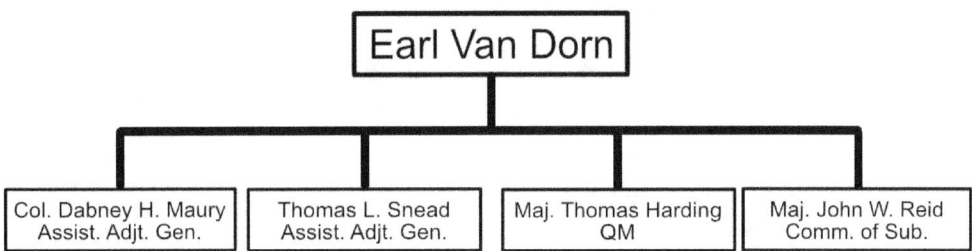

Selected Confederate staff under Van Dorn and Price. Maury was the sole staff officer (West Point 1846) serving with Van Dorn. Thomas Snead, pre-war attorney, Thomas Harding, pre-war business, and John Reid, pre-war lawyer, politician, and Mexican War veteran, all served under Sterling Price (courtesy Margaret A. Zimmermann).

Van Dorn failed to send any instructions to the officer in charge of the Confederate ordnance wagons and other supplies. Price's staff was also unable to make a difference in this area. When the contest opened, McCulloch eschewed the services of staff and scouts and was killed, but his failure to remain in touch with Van Dorn and other subordinates led directly to confusion and defeat on the Confederate right flank. Without clear communication between the staff and Confederate leadership, the staff work in general was below par, and the specific failure to bring up ammunition on the second day of combat was fatal to the Confederate cause.[35]

Both sides attempted to use all the resources they had for combat, but here, too, the Union was more successful. Curtis used every unit in his little army for some type of combat during the two-day engagement. On the Confederate side, the division of McCulloch was not used effectively. Attacks were launched in piecemeal fashion, and in the end, only some of his men were directly involved. Once the three division commanders were killed or captured, the unit dissolved and was no longer combat-worthy. As a result, the full division was never used on the first day of battle, and, apparently, they were unable to join their brethren near Elkhorn Tavern for the second day. Grenville Dodge writes, "and the fact that all of Generals McIntosh's and McCulloch's troops after the second days fight, when they were killed, ran off to Bentonville, only one or two regiments making round to the rear to join Price, leaving Gen. Van Dorn the third day with Price's men alone to whip an army, he had failed to move the day before with all his men. The third day the enemy's show of fight was for the purpose of getting off, nothing more."[36]

Although Curtis did not pursue the defeated Confederates, several strategic outcomes emerged from the Union victory. Consequently, there is disagreement over Curtis's actions following the battle. A full Confederate army that could take and hold the state never really threatened Missouri. Confederate forces from the Trans-Mississippi would not be involved in the battle for Shiloh. While Van Dorn's forces would eventually cross the Mississippi River and menace Corinth, he stripped Arkansas of any supplies that might have been useful for renewing the struggle later in the year. The Confederate army that eventually confronted the Federal forces at Prairie Grove lacked several essentials needed to ensure victory, e.g., ammunition for the artillery. The Union, however, could not claim any lasting strategic success following the battle either.

Six Elements of Victory at Pea Ridge

Pea Ridge	Clear, Attainable Objective	Operational Initiative	Command Unity
Curtis	Achieved	Achieved	Achieved
Van Dorn	Not Achieved	Not Achieved	Not Achieved
	Logistics/Staff	*Used All Resources*	*Strategic Outcome*
Curtis	Achieved	Achieved	*Not Achieved
Van Dorn	Not Achieved	Not Achieved	Not Achieved

As his men were starving and his army ran short of ammunition, Earl Van Dorn struggled to achieve any of his objectives. Without knowledge of or a working relationship with his immediate subordinates or staff, Van Dorn failed in his efforts. On the other hand, even though Curtis was faced with truculent subordinates at times, he succeeded in directing their efforts to a successful conclusion.

Chapter 4

Opening the Mississippi River

On the west side of Kentucky and Tennessee, the Mississippi River and the valley of the Mississippi became critical strategic areas for both sides. Columbus, Kentucky, was the northernmost available river defense position for the Confederates, but if the Union managed to outflank that position by capturing Forts Henry and Donelson, Island No. 10 was the next defensible point. Bordering the Gulf of Mexico, New Orleans guarded the mouth of the Mississippi River. In the swamps and bayous north of Vicksburg, the geography of Chickasaw Bayou and the surrounding terrain protected the town from attack. Yet if the Union expected to threaten this fortress town from the north after the fall of Corinth, this was a logical location to assault. Attacking any of these places would require a joint army/navy effort, and while none of these three locations led to consequential land battles, they all require attention.

By 1860, population centers were beginning to grow up around the rivers in the South. Budding industries sprang up in these towns, and if the South were to remain independent, cities such as New Orleans (the largest and most important port in the country), Nashville and Memphis needed protection. Vicksburg, Mississippi, also connected the eastern Confederacy with the Trans-Mississippi region. Even though there was no bridge across the river, goods could flow easily across the Mississippi at this point. Both Kentucky and Tennessee provided an enormous supply of horses, mules, hogs and food. Other goods flowed from the west side of the river to benefit the Confederacy as well. Whichever side occupied these two states also held the keys to victory in the West for both the North and South.

By 1861, rail links connected the entire region, and when the rivers, roads, telegraph and rail lines are connected, the major supply lines for the two sides become visible. These places mark the locations where the armies would be drawn inexorably together to do battle. Columbus, Kentucky, Forts Henry and Donelson, and the battlefield of Shiloh in Tennessee, as well as other battlegrounds in these states, did not exist in isolation from physical and geographic elements. In fact, the early battles of the Civil War in Tennessee and Kentucky occurred where these important elements were grouped together. If Columbus was lost, then Island No. 10 on the Mississippi River, well-armed with heavy artillery, protected Tennessee and the river valley stretching south. The Confederates also had to guard the mouth of the Mississippi River at New Orleans. In 1861, two forts and a small river fleet shielded the third largest city in the United States. The South needed to hold these locations, and the North needed to conquer them.

In the beginning of 1862, Lincoln pushed for action. Too much talk and too little real effort had defined the Union stance in 1861 and threatened to produce the same result for 1862. George B. McClellan, in charge of the largest Union army located in the

East, contracted malaria and was temporarily confined to his bed, but Lincoln needed to prosecute the war. He was about to get his wish fulfilled, but the action would take place in the West.

While the Confederates developed their defenses in a deliberate fashion, the Union war effort took giant strides forward strategically. Brigadier General John Pope commanded a force of almost 25,000 men and partnered with Flag Officer Foote and his squadron of warships to capture Island No. 10. Even earlier in the war, Secretary of the Navy Welles and the Lincoln administration brought 60-year-old David Farragut out of semi-retirement in Maine. Could he lead a squadron of ships past the Mississippi forts covering New Orleans, and take the town? He was willing to try. Scott's "Anaconda" was beginning to stir. The Atlantic and Gulf blockades were becoming more effective, but the North under Lincoln structured a strategic river plan to bear fruit in the West. Lincoln's often-derided Special Order #1 on January 27, 1862, which called for a simultaneous advance from all Union forces on February 22, 1862, led to snickering as McClellan and several other generals ignored it. However, in the West, a simultaneous thrust south along the Mississippi, Tennessee and Cumberland rivers, combined with another blow northward toward New Orleans, was to bear strategic fruit, and by June of 1862 the South would be on the ropes.

In the opening days of the Civil War, the South had no navy. On March 4, 1861, Stephen Mallory was appointed Secretary of the Confederate Navy, and it was under Mallory's leadership that the South assumed the burden of constructing armored warships for defense. Mallory brought a powerful vision for the creation of a national navy, a fleet of giant ships with heavier armor and larger guns than their Northern counterparts. Beyond the fortresses that ringed the South, the phoenix-like CSS *Virginia* emerged from the ooze of Norfolk, the CSS *Louisiana* had her keel laid in New Orleans, and the CSS *Arkansas* began building, first at Memphis and then on the Yazoo River near Vicksburg. Finally the CSS *Manassas* was built as well. Existing ship hulls were used, casemates were built of railroad track iron, and heavy guns came from Norfolk and the Tredegar Iron Works. Together they gave the Confederacy hope that they could both sweep the Federals off the Mississippi River and push them away from Southern port cities as well. The energetic Mallory also encouraged the production of entire warship squadrons at New Orleans and Memphis. Heavily armored ships, backed by rams and gunboats, chains and river mines, would protect the major ports in the West and South.[1]

Unfortunately for the South, too many ships were being constructed with too few resources and no coordination of effort. The *Manassas* and the *Arkansas* were the only two armored vessels to appear in the West. While Mallory was able to acquire several ships dedicated to commerce raiding, he experienced little success in building Confederate warships for home defense. Gideon Welles, the Union Secretary of the Navy, supervised and supported the construction of a large blockading fleet, a large transport fleet, and a large, armored warship force that utterly throttled the South's attempts at naval supremacy. He supported army/navy cooperation wherever he could and was largely successful in recommending superior naval leaders.

As Farragut gathered his ships for a blow at New Orleans, the Eads ironclads, the Ellet rams and the steamboat gunships all poured out of shipyards in Cincinnati, Pittsburgh and Cairo, Illinois. The Union planned to send them south to conquer the major rivers. In the Confederacy, workmen went on strike and weeks were lost as individuals and states acted out their individuality to slow the Southern defensive efforts.

Chapter 4. Opening the Mississippi River

Among the Confederate defeats in 1862, two major strategic disasters occurred that did not involve the consequential use of infantry: Island No. 10 and New Orleans. The South needed to hold both ends of the Mississippi River to keep the Confederacy unified. With Texas, Arkansas and Missouri all on the west bank of the river, military supplies and armed forces needed to move easily across the water. By the middle of April 1862, the South lost control over both ends of the river. While these actions were decided because of Southern strategic errors, they still demand some explanation. Then in December of 1862, an abortive Union thrust north of Vicksburg by way of the Chickasaw Bayou miscarried. At various times, the North would achieve great strategic success but also humiliating failures. For the South, their efforts would, for the most part, founder. These three actions were not the standard infantry, cavalry and artillery duels described elsewhere in this book, but a summary of events here will help connect all the threads of the story.

* * *

With Confederate defeats at Forts Henry and Donelson in mid–February of 1862, it became obvious to the Confederates that Columbus, Kentucky, was no longer tenable. The Confederates still wished to provide protection for Memphis, Tennessee, but they needed to find a point north of the city where a successful defense might be made. Island No. 10 was that spot, a little over 120 miles north of Memphis. On the Mississippi River, islands south of where the Ohio River flows into the Mississippi were numbered at that time. When it appeared at the end of March that Brigadier General John P. McCown's defense of the island was not as determined as the Confederates hoped, Brigadier General William W. Mackall replaced McCown. Both Johnston and his second-in-command, P.G.T. Beauregard, thought highly of his abilities based on his service with distinction in the Mexican War and as A. S. Johnston's chief of staff. Within the first week of Mackall's arrival, the Confederates in his little force were overwhelmed when they faced odds of over 9:1. He was without naval support at that time as well. The Confederate plan to construct numerous warships on the Mississippi had failed completely by that time. In attempting to construct a half dozen armored warships, the Confederates managed just one boat with one gun, and it was stationed in New Orleans. Strikes, delayed shipping and competing shipyards spelled doom for Confederate naval efforts in the West.[2]

Back in the fall of 1861, Flag Officer Foote spelled out the Northern army/navy relations on western waters: "You are fully aware that we are here for the purpose of cooperating with, and under the direction of, the commanding general of the Western army." No similar Confederate directives emerged to counter the planned Union buildup of heavy iron on the rivers. Bishop Leonidas Polk settled originally on Columbus, Kentucky, and by December of 1861 that place held 22,000 men and 140 guns. But as Forts Henry and Donelson fell to the North, soldiers were pulled away for Albert Sidney Johnston's army and many of the guns were moved to Island No. 10. By mid–March, McCown could count about 7,500 men (many of them ill) and 51 pieces of ordnance.[3]

Union General John Pope commanded over 25,000 men and Flag Officer Foote's squadron of six gunboats, several mortar boats and transport vessels for the affair. While the approach march was a complicated one through swamps and wet bottomlands, Pope was able to capture New Madrid across the river from Island No. 10 and send two of Foote's gunboats past the island. Hardworking Federal staff officers, an excellent unit of engineers, and combined efforts with U.S. naval gunboats made this all possible. Once the gunboats passed the island defenses, the Confederates could no longer retreat and save their garrison. On April 8, the Southern defense ended and Mackall surrendered. The Mississippi River was soon open to navigation all the way to Vicksburg, Mississippi, from the north.[4]

Following the battle, the Union vessels sailed farther south on the Mississippi and were involved in capturing Fort Pillow and Memphis, Tennessee, by June 6, 1862. For the river engagement in front of Memphis, the North mustered nine boats, five Eads gunboats and four Ellet rams. The Confederates countered with a group of eight converted steamboats, sent north from New Orleans. While both types of Federal warship "squadrons" had their own commander, each Confederate steamer was under an independent captain. When the brawl ended, the Confederate squadron was destroyed, and the one boat left fled downstream to the Yazoo River. Confederate operations on the western waters ended. The one exception is highlighted in the Chickasaw Bluffs section.[5]

Brigadier General John Pope. Pope commanded the overwhelming Union Army and accompanying naval forces that captured Island No. 10 and opened the Mississippi River all the way to Vicksburg, Mississippi (Library of Congress).

* * *

January 8, 1815, marked the first great battle for New Orleans. Of all the American generals available for the War of 1812, Andrew Jackson was most certainly made for the fight at New Orleans. Eight thousand British soldiers and sailors attacked a polyglot force of 4,732 Americans, pirates, Native Americans and Creoles under Jackson and failed miserably in their assault.

When hostilities erupted with Mexico in May of 1846, the United States was totally unprepared for the war militarily. New Orleans, however, became the logistical key for American victory. Thousands of wagons, draft animals and armed men prepared for an invasion of Mexico. In New Orleans over 163 vessels were chartered and assembled to supply General Scott's force. This was a remarkable achievement both for the army and for the city of New Orleans that provided outstanding logistical support. By 1860, New Orleans was the busiest port in the country, it generated the greatest revenue of any port city, and it was poised to do the same for the newborn Confederacy. But in the early months of the Civil War, Confederate strategic thinking had an eggshell effect of creating an all-around defense that was equally brittle throughout its outer edges. Every creek and inlet bred anxiety among the Confederate governors, and this attitude led to an attempt to hold everything. Once the outer shell was penetrated in any location, the more delicate insides of the Confederate homeland would be exposed. As the war unfolded, Jefferson Davis and the Richmond government appointed two commanders, one for Island No. 10 and one for New Orleans, who proved to be inept.[6]

Needing another Andrew Jackson, Davis bypassed P.G.T. Beauregard and Braxton Bragg, both from New Orleans at the time, and instead appointed General David E. Twiggs, age 71. He was described as "physically infirm and often unable to leave his quarters." From April of 1861 until September 25, Twiggs remained in command and then was replaced by Mansfield Lovell. Lovell brought energy to the task of defending the town, but he was unable to reverse the rising tide of defeat. At the inquest that followed the fall of the city, Lovell noted, for example, "Gen. Twiggs ... received from the Norfolk navy-yard more than 100 old navy guns ... so worn as to be unfit for friction tubes. Many of the guns had been cast more than forty years [ago]." The guns from Norfolk (Gosport Navy Yard), sprinkled along the east coast of the Confederacy from Virginia to Florida, were all in working order. The ones sent to New Orleans clearly were not.[7]

* * *

By April of 1862, U.S. Admiral David Farragut commanded 17 warships, 21 mortar schooners, four coal ships and seven steamers, a total of approximately 49 vessels. Having served actively and successfully in the U. S. Navy since the War of 1812, Farragut was originally recommended for this role by his foster brother, David Dixon Porter, commander of the mortar schooners. General Benjamin Butler also joined the expedition with 15,000 men. South of New Orleans along the Gulf coast stood Ship Island. Earlier the Confederates decided not to defend it and pulled back closer to the city. When the Federal invading force appeared, the island was used as a helpful staging area for the coming action. Butler's 15,000 men were landed, and the expedition's necessary supplies were housed there. Unknown to the Confederates, the Federal officer in charge of originally strengthening the fortifications now supplied Farragut with a complete set of plans for the two forts protecting New Orleans.[8]

On April 18, 21 mortar boats, each carrying one 13-inch mortar firing a 216-pound explosive charge and under the command of Commander David Dixon Porter, opened fire on Fort Jackson. About 3,000 rounds later, the bombardment ended for the day. Porter had originally boasted that he would reduce the forts within 48 hours with his mortars. While most of the Federal attention focused on Fort Jackson, St. Phillip received some attention as well. Days passed and the forts were still operational. Disappointed with the results and impatient to attack, on the night of April 23–24, Farragut ordered his fleet of 17 warships to drive past the forts and head upriver. Anxious to move ahead before the Confederates completed any more warships or strengthened their defense further, Farragut planned a night attack. As his squadron passed the forts, the Confederate ram *Manassas* appeared and joined the melee, but when it rammed one of the Union vessels, its lone gun was dismounted, and its captain ran it aground. After the crew abandoned ship and the boat was still under fire, the ram broke loose from the shoreline and drifted helplessly downstream. A few Confederate gunboats disputed the passage as well, but Farragut would not be denied. By morning, 14 ships of the Union fleet were anchored near the city, and Ben Butler's infantry were prepared to join the fray. Major General Lovell ordered Confederate forces to leave the city and retreat upstream. With 170,000 civilians present but only 3,000 militia available for their defense, he was not prepared to needlessly sacrifice lives. The two forts held out briefly until the 28th, but then surrendered to the inevitable. By April 29, the city formally surrendered, and Ben Butler approached to occupy the town.[9]

Two critical problems impeded Confederate defensive efforts. If the Confederates had constructed just one substantial ironclad vessel, all the wooden Union warships assembled in front of New Orleans would have been obsolete. Not content with constructing one ironclad warship, however, the Confederates over-reached and attempted the construction of five of these monsters along with a heavily armored gunboat, the *Eastport*, on the Tennessee River. As noted earlier, only one armored warship, the *Manassas* carrying a single gun, appeared. Displaying only one or two guns each, 11 other nondescript vessels were stationed nearby. When Farragut ordered his flotilla to sail past the forts guarding the city on April 24, they were able to steam all the way past the forts and proceed to the city docks of New Orleans, 70 miles upstream.[10]

Besides their failure to build sufficient warships, the Confederates at New Orleans also suffered from a lack of manpower. By the end of 1861, Louisiana raised almost 30,000 soldiers for the war effort. By April of 1862, however, only 3,500 were available for service in front of New Orleans. Where were the others? The remainder had been siphoned off to seemingly more critical locations, and their services were lost to Louisiana. Complicating matters, three different secretaries of war served the Confederacy from February of 1861 to March of 1862. It appears that the Confederacy had the ability to assemble greater

Admiral David Glasgow Farragut. Against a weak Confederate defense of a key Southern port, Farragut led the U.S. Navy to capture New Orleans (Library of Congress).

numbers of men and guns for the town's defense but simply failed to provide the necessary support. In fact, soldiers from all states west of the Appalachians were sent off to Virginia. From throughout the South, over 36 regiments, five battalions of infantry and four companies of artillery arrived in Virginia by April of 1862. States such as Louisiana were stripped of manpower (eight regiments, two battalions and four companies of artillery served Lee in the East) while other forces moved north to Tennessee. Using the *Staff Ride* regimental averages, approximately 20,000 Confederates moved from west to east as manpower for Lee's Army. Other units also manned fortifications along the Confederate coastline from Virginia to Alabama. In other words, the strategic decision to mass Southern troops from both western and eastern Confederate states, primarily in Virginia but also along the coast, led to critical shortages of soldiers in western states during major engagements. One can only imagine what another 20,000 available men in the West might have accomplished in early 1862.[11]

After the capture of New Orleans, inevitable finger-pointing occurred in the Confederacy, and a commission was duly arraigned to investigate the reason behind the loss. Yet the damage was done. Island No. 10 in the north and New Orleans in the south were the twin anchors that held the Confederacy together. West of the Mississippi River in Arkansas and Texas, crops and beef might still be gathered, and a few soldiers recruited for a Trans-Mississippi defense, but the Confederacy's hope for an independent nation with secure borders had been dashed. Only a small band of the river was open for the Confederates, and this stretch of the river kept merely a slender thread of communication open with the far western lands. And this was only April of 1862.

* * *

The third action recorded in this chapter takes the reader to Chickasaw Bluffs near Vicksburg. Once again this was not a meeting engagement between two different armies, but rather an attempt on the part of the Union to capture Vicksburg through a surprise movement. Vicksburg, sometimes called the "Gibraltar of the Confederacy," was located at a critical place on the Mississippi River. Island No. 10 to the north and New Orleans to the south had both fallen in April of 1862, and Vicksburg, heavily fortified by now, continued to support Confederate efforts east and west of the Mississippi while blocking Northern access to the sea. The Yazoo Bayou had already seen its share of action in the summer of 1862.

There the Confederates proved that just one armored boat could make a huge difference on the Mississippi River. The *Arkansas* was seen as just that type of war-winning vessel. The construction of the warship began in Memphis, and then under Union pressure, it was moved to the Yazoo Bayou where she could be completed. When she emerged on July 15, 1862, under the command of the now ubiquitous Isaac Brown, she ran through the assembled Federal river gunboat squadron and docked at Vicksburg. Five Federal gunboats and Farragut's wooden vessels all had the opportunity to fire on the *Arkansas* and did so with some accuracy. The *Arkansas*, however, was able to maneuver her way past the Federal squadrons and dock safely. Myron Smith estimates that over 18 Union vessels carrying 100 heavy guns opened fire on the Confederate vessel as it slipped away. Later, Vicksburg commander, Earl Van Dorn, sent it downriver without its captain, and the vessel was beached and destroyed.[12]

By the fall of 1862, Major General U.S. Grant was approaching Vicksburg from the north. As he moved along the Mobile and Ohio Railroad line, he traveled from LaGrange, Tennessee, through northern Mississippi toward Grenada. Major General John C. Pemberton, in charge of the Confederate army in Mississippi, faced two choices: Either allow Grant to approach Vicksburg from the north unopposed, or march out to confront Grant while leaving Vicksburg behind with a smaller garrison. To make Pemberton's choice more difficult, Grant proposed to send Major General William T. Sherman south on transports to threaten Vicksburg from the river.

In early December of 1862, Grant reached Oxford, Mississippi. Pemberton's force fell back to Grenada and waited for Grant's next move. On December 8, Grant ordered Sherman to assemble a force in Memphis and then launch an attack on Vicksburg from the water. By December 20, Sherman began sending transports with four divisions south on the Mississippi. By December 25, Sherman reached the mouth of the Yazoo River, north of Vicksburg with 32,000 men, and proposed landing his force upstream near a place called Chickasaw Bayou. Capture the heights above the bayou, approximately 12 miles upstream and his force would be within a short walking distance of Vicksburg. At the same time, however, the Confederates had other ideas.[13]

To halt Grant's advance, the Confederates employed two cavalry forces, one under Nathan Bedford Forrest and another one under Earl Van Dorn. In the middle of December, Forrest attacked a section of the Mobile and Ohio Railroad and endangered Grant's entire supply operation. Then on December 20, Van Dorn struck Grant's main supply depot at Holly Springs with 3,500 men and destroyed it. Van Dorn had struggled earlier in the year at both Pea Ridge and Corinth, but now in charge of cavalry, he was in his element. Grant's offensive ended immediately. On December 23, Grant would signal, "Raids made upon the railroad to my rear by Forrest ... and by Van Dorn ... have cut me off from supplies, so that farther advance by this route is perfectly impracticable." Grant's decision created a problem for Sherman at this point; Grant had no way of communicating the information to his lieutenant. Sherman wrote, "Not one word could I

Brigadier General William T. Sherman. While he achieved success under Grant at Shiloh, his efforts were unsuccessful at Chickasaw Bluffs. He found the terrain challenging, lost the element of surprise, and with the destruction of Holly Springs, Grant's army could no longer support him (Library of Congress).

hear from General Grant who was supposed to be pushing south." Sherman had one more problem: Pemberton knew that he was coming and where he would land.[14]

Sherman's men began spilling ashore on December 25 near Johnson's plantation, on the Yazoo. The Confederates were waiting. Earlier Pemberton had placed Major General Martin Smith in overall command at Vicksburg and sent Stephen D. Lee to occupy ground north of the city. General Smith had engineered the defenses at New Orleans prior to the Union attack and, while the Confederates systematically denuded the city of soldiers, he had greatly improved the defenses. He was well qualified to erect formidable barriers to fight off enemy movements along the bayou. Under Smith, Captain Wofford skillfully prepared the defenses on the Yazoo. Now as Sherman's forces disembarked, entrenchments, artillery and infantry were all waiting for Sherman as he moved inland.[15]

Sherman's attack was a failure from the start. Of his 32,000 men, Sherman was able to engage only about nine regiments during the action. There was delay in moving toward the Confederate defenses. December 27 and 28 both elapsed as Sherman moved forward. To make a successful attack on the Confederate position, the Union forces had to traverse difficult terrain, and finally they were forced to bring up a pontoon train to bridge a smaller bayou. Sherman wrote, "At the point where Morgan L. Smith's division reached the bayou was a narrow sand-pit, with abatis thrown down by the enemy on our side, with the same deep, boggy bayou, with a levee parapet and system of cross-batteries and rifle-pits on the other side." Again, he wrote, "Morgan's division had the pontoon bridge. The pontoon bridge was placed during the night across a bayou ... which turned out to be an inferior one, and it was therefore useless; but the natural crossing remained, and I ordered him to cross over with his division."[16]

There was delay once again as the Union generals failed to start the action until almost 11:00 on the morning of December 29. The result was a slaughter. Sherman records 1,776 casualties while Pemberton reports 204 Confederates killed, wounded and missing. Sherman had an objective, but the original plan evaporated with the burning of Grant's supply base at Holly Springs. Sherman's subordinates, particularly General Morgan, were less than supportive in their efforts. His army numbered 32,000 but only nine regiments participated actively in the engagement. Sherman himself did not closely supervise his own officers, and Sherman and his "team" violated several "Principles of War" for this action.[17]

Chapter 5

Shiloh

The War Comes of Age

The Battle of Shiloh was the largest and one of the most critical contests in the West during the spring of 1862. By taking Forts Henry and Donelson in February of 1862, the North had thrown the South back on defense. River lines were opened, and major southern cities such as Nashville were now threatened. But the South still had the resources and willpower to strike back. An energetic response was needed. A new Confederate figure now entered the story—one who took on a critical role that helped determine Confederate fortunes going forward, the very aggressive P.G.T. Beauregard.

General Albert Sidney Johnston faced a Union advance in the West along both the Tennessee River past Fort Henry and the Cumberland River past Fort Donelson. The defeat at Mill Springs led to the demise of the eastern end of his line, but he still contested the Mississippi River Valley at Columbus, Kentucky, and Island No. 10. The surrender at Fort Donelson and the Union occupation of Nashville, however, were disasters for the South. Hoping to buoy the hopes of Confederates in the West while removing a political problem in the East, Jefferson Davis now sent General Pierre Gustave Toutant Beauregard to Johnston's aid, leaving the East on February 2, 1862. The victor at Fort Sumter and First Bull Run arrived in Bowling Green, Kentucky, in time to confer with General Johnston one day after the fall of Fort Henry on February 7. As a result of earlier Confederate defeats there and at Mill Springs, Johnston was forced to cede all of Kentucky and a good part of Tennessee to the Union advance in February of 1862. Beauregard and Johnston met again in Nashville on February 14 to coordinate their efforts, and when they emerged the Southern strategy became offensive. Unfortunately, no record of the meeting survives, but we can see a united effort to pull Southern resources together shortly afterward.[1]

While Union General Don Carlos Buell occupied the Nashville area on the Cumberland River with his army, Ulysses S. Grant advanced from Fort Donelson with his reinforced army to Pittsburg Landing on the Tennessee River. General Halleck had temporarily placed General Charles F. Smith in command of the advancing Union army that encamped at Pittsburg Landing, but then reinstated Grant after Lincoln pressed him for specific reasons for his proposed change. If Buell joined Grant on the Tennessee, together they could march from Pittsburg Landing to Corinth, Mississippi, and cut the only direct east-west rail line available to the Confederacy. On March 13, Brigadier General Charles F. Smith wrote to Grant about the steamboat landing, "It is a good place to hold & from whence to operate." Just inland stood a little chapel known as Shiloh Church. Grant also saw the move to Pittsburgh Landing as a precursor to an offensive against Corinth to cut the Confederate rail lines there. At the same time, Beauregard

Major General U.S. Grant (Library of Congress).

Major General Albert S. Johnston. *Frank Leslie's Illustrated History of the Civil War* (courtesy The Civil War Museum, Kenosha, WI).

and Johnston saw a chance to retrieve the dire Confederate strategic situation. If they could field a force larger than Grant's, they might attack and crush him, and then threaten Buell. If they held the Cumberland River, they might even be able to defeat Buell or re-occupy Nashville—or perhaps achieve both goals. Before anything else, however, they had to assemble a mighty host and move offensively on Grant's army.[2]

On March 24, Johnston and Beauregard met once more, this time in Corinth. Their final decision: Unite Confederate forces from all over the western theater and beat back the northern offensive in detail—first Grant, then Buell. They agreed on their first objective: defeat and possibly destroy Grant's army. Under the circumstances, their goal was challenging but realistic. President Davis in Richmond was also on board. The challenge was to strike while the two Northern armies were separated. Letters and messages flowed from Beauregard to Southern governors pleading for recruits, and President Davis in turn authorized a general concentration at Corinth, Mississippi. While A.S. Johnston organized his force near Murfreesboro, Braxton Bragg at Pensacola, Florida, Mansfield Lovell at New Orleans, and Earl Van Dorn in Arkansas were pressed to send their forces to join Beauregard at Corinth. Under orders from General Beauregard, General Leonidas Polk also moved his force to Corinth from the Columbus, Kentucky, area. At one point, a dispirited A.S. Johnston offered command of his army to Beauregard, but he was turned down. It was apparent, however, that Johnston often treated Beauregard as a peer and not a subordinate. The two now determined to continue working together.[3]

A new army coalesced as Johnston

and Beauregard strove to unite these disparate forces into one army. One historian calls them an "unorganized multitude." Johnston needed to train and equip this new force, organize them into cohesive units, and complete his plans for an attack on Grant within a two-week timeframe. Many of these Southern soldiers had never seen real combat before.[4]

Three different army corps and a reserve corps assembled at Corinth from all over the South. The railroads worked under difficult circumstances to disgorge the entire force in Corinth by April 2. Logistical support was forthcoming as well. By rail came 50 wagons (some assembly required) and Johnston's force now had an ammunition train with 1,800,000 rounds of small arms ammunition and 3,000 artillery shells for support. The South was by this time all energy, and Corinth became the anchor for the entire Confederate war effort in the West. Johnston was in overall command with 45,000 men, versus Grant with 40,000. Between the loss of Fort Donelson in February and the arrival of early April, the Confederates lost almost 14,000 men and a month of time by retreating, gathering new forces, and uniting them at Corinth. Johnston even hoped to bring General Earl Van Dorn's army to Corinth from Arkansas. Van Dorn, however, was defeated at the Battle of Pea Ridge on March 7–8, 1862, and despite pleas from Johnston and his own efforts, was unable to travel closer than Memphis by April 7 with his 20,000 men.[5]

For the Federal forces, General Buell did not move quickly to support Grant. Two months elapsed as he conducted his leisurely march across 90 miles of Tennessee roads, swamps, rivers and bridges toward Grant. Along the way, he secured Nashville, and by early April, he was getting much closer to Grant's army. While Buell commanded 28,000 men, he wasn't on the ground yet, and the Confederate convocation was kept secret from the North. Twenty miles separated Johnston at Corinth from Grant's outposts. On April 3, Johnston ordered his forces forward. Union camps were strung out around little Shiloh Church and as late as April 4, Sherman was sending word back to Grant from his tent that "I do not apprehend anything like an attack on our position," and Grant telegraphed Halleck, "I have scarcely the faintest idea of an attack being made upon us, but will be prepared should such a thing take place." Grant was comfortably

Major General P. G. T. Beauregard. One of the victors at First Bull Run, Beauregard served loyally under Johnston as they planned their attack on the Union Army at Shiloh. During the battle, Beauregard took up positions near the Confederate center and left. At times he was near the Shiloh chapel. After Johnston's untimely death, Beauregard took command and received much of the blame afterward for losing the battle (Library of Congress).

situated to the north of his army, in the town of Savannah, Tennessee, nine miles downriver at the Cherry mansion. He was not alarmed by the skirmishing and hurrahing that was already occurring between the two forces just outside the Union lines.[6]

Now the Confederates needed a tactical plan to defeat Grant, and on several occasions Johnston and Beauregard met to coordinate their attack. Johnston envisioned a three-corps assault along one strong line. If he pushed in from his right, he could separate Grant's left from the Tennessee River and force him back into the swamps and away from his logistical base at Pittsburgh Landing. Over 100 steamboats kept Grant supplied, and separation from that lifeline would be fatal. Following another meeting on April 3, Johnston telegraphed his version of the plan to Davis: "On Pittsburg, Beauregard second in command; Polk, left; Hardee, center; Bragg, right wing; Breckinridge, reserve." At the same time, Beauregard discussed it with his own chief of staff, Thomas Jordan, and a new plan emerged by the next morning. As described by Johnston's son, William Preston Johnston, the attack formation was aligned as follows: "His front line ... was under Hardee ... and extended from Owl Creek to Lick Creek, more than three miles.... Bragg commanded the second line. The third line, or reserve, was composed of the First Corps under Polk, and three brigades under Breckinridge."[7]

After two days of marching, however, the Confederates realized that with a heavy rainstorm in progress and an army that had never marched anywhere together, the attack must be postponed. On the evening of April 5, a Confederate council of war with all major commanders participating, except for William J. Hardee, was held. Rain and gloom prevailed at first, but in the end, Johnston re-asserted his authority. The attack was on for April 6. Thomas Jordan wrote and disseminated orders based on Napoleon's own orders before Waterloo. They included the following: "The major-general commanding directs that you will prepare your division for a move early to-morrow morning, 6 a. m., taking five days cooked rations ... and 100 rounds of ammunition to each man." That may have been the plan, but there were still regiments without food or ammunition. The 2nd Texas, for example, reported the following: "Not having received the provisions ordered for the regiment, we left with a short two and a half days' rations." The 16th Louisiana reported that they had no food or rest since April 4, two days before the battle opened. Perhaps Jordan had forgotten the past: Napoleon lost the Battle of Waterloo![8]

* * *

During the night of April 5, Beauregard and Bragg approached him and suggested a retreat while they still could pull out. He responded, "Gentlemen, we shall attack at daylight tomorrow." Later to an aide he stated, "I would attack them if they were a million." As dawn broke on Sunday, April 6, Albert Sidney Johnston pressed his attack against Grant's force. This came after his immediate subordinate, Beauregard, once again urged a retreat instead. He felt that the element of surprise had been lost by a long march, some premature skirmishing, and the noise created as men test-fired their weapons. Beauregard had organized the army into three main lines, and now the Confederates advanced through Union skirmishers.[9] As they advanced, Confederate brigades and commanders quickly became hopelessly entangled.

Grant's army was organized in six divisions, five on the field at Pittsburgh Landing

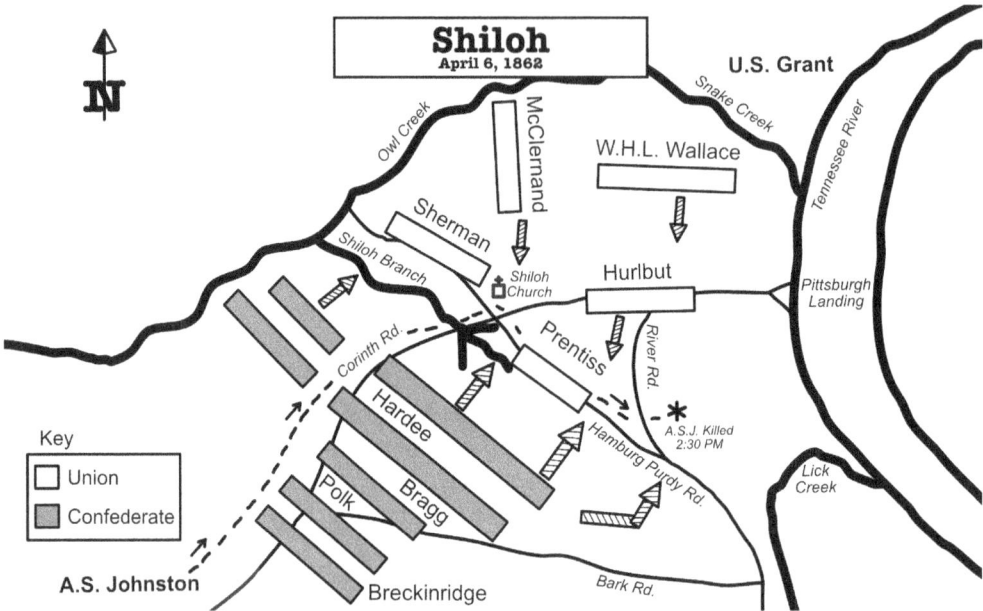

Johnston's original plan required the Confederate Army to push the Federals into Snake Creek. Beauregard's revised plan as dictated by Colonel Thomas Jordan (shown here in part) called for a frontal assault on Union camps near the Tennessee River. Consequently, Beauregard's plan from Jordan quickly led also to an immediate attack on the Union right under Sherman. Early in the day Johnston rode up the Corinth Road, spent time in Prentiss's camp and then moved to the right of the Confederate line where he was later killed. The battle raged along the entire front from left to right. Once Grant came ashore at Pittsburgh Landing, he rode about his lines meeting his division generals throughout the day (courtesy Margaret A. Zimmermann).

and one farther downstream with General Lew Wallace. At Shiloh, the first Confederate onslaught found Generals William T. Sherman and Benjamin Prentiss coming out of their tents to form lines of battle. Generals John McClernand, W.H.L. Wallace and Stephen A. Hurlbut would be engaged shortly. The North was surprised by the Confederate onslaught, but the Confederates did not find the Federals sleeping in their tents. Advancing across open fields, but also on steep inclines down to creek bottoms and then up toward heavily defended Union lines, the Confederates first pitched into Sherman. At the same time, McClernand formed a line of battle and moved to support him.

While they were both surprised, Sherman and McClernand had time to muster their men, form their lines and fight back. As General Hardee's force (at this point a brigade under General Patrick Cleburne) advanced, they ran into stiff opposition. He later wrote: "[Sherman's division] was very advantageously posted and overlapped my left flank by at least half a brigade.... Everywhere his musketry and artillery at short range swept the open spaces.... An almost impossible morass, jutting out from the foot of the height on which the enemy's tents stood, impeded the advance of my center, and finally caused a wide opening in my line.... My own horse got bogged down in it and threw me." The musket and artillery ranges were close and volleys were deadly, but the Union forces were forced back very slowly during the day as individual brigades fought fiercely or dissolved under pressure. While the Confederates had an advantage in the opening hours, the terrain and Union resolve held back their onslaught. Grant himself was just

Chapter 5. Shiloh

holding his first cup of coffee at the Cherry Mansion, nine miles downstream, when the fighting began.[10]

Sherman and McClernand held their own in the early going, but General Benjamin Prentiss struggled to hold the center of the Union line. With fewer men, fewer artillery pieces and terrain that was less forbidding, Prentiss was pushed back early on and his camp was occupied by victorious Confederates. As the rebels attacked by brigade only rather than launching a coordinated assault, the Federal army was given a chance to defend itself. Unfortunately for Prentiss, the Confederates moved around his right flank and pushed him back decisively. By 8:00 his original camp was taken and by 10:30 Sherman, McClernand and Prentiss had all fallen back to a second Union position.[11]

The Confederates launched brigade-level attacks that bore the opposing Union brigades back, but their three-line offensive forces quickly blended together and one command after another was intermingled in the woods, deep underbrush and undulating terrain. Visibility was limited, but early in the day it appeared that the Confederates had everything going for them. While Johnston hoped that his early maneuvers would break through Union resistance, he sent some Confederates northwest and then realized that there were more Union soldiers off to the northeast.[12]

After 9 a.m., following Grant's arrival from his headquarters downriver, he moved from one division to another along the entire Union side. Johnston rode from one Confederate brigade to another and eventually toward the right of the Confederate line. Now the second part of the battle took shape. Prentiss, along with help from W.H.L. Wallace (who was later mortally wounded), gathered his remnants along the Sunken Road (a shallow depression in the center of the Union line), but it provided enough of a gap in the wooded terrain to allow his infantry to form and the artillery to support him. General Hurlbut formed up on the Union left and confronted the right side of the Confederate advance. Sherman and McClernand might be forced back on their right, but the Union forces in the center were determined to hold where they were. The Confederates had a choice: Avoid the tough nut in the center of the line and work around the flanks, or plough through the middle. In the meantime, Johnston realized that he needed to push through from the right side of his line to fulfill his original plan. He forged ahead to provide the necessary leadership for the Confederates there.[13]

During the afternoon, the Confederates exercised all of their options. As the forces of Sherman and McClernand were pushed back on the Union right, so were the forces of Hurlbut on the left, leaving Prentiss with W.H.L. Wallace in the "Hornet's Nest" of Union resistance in the center. The Confederates could not resist the urge to hit it directly. As Confederate attacks lost their punch against the Sunken Road, General Ruggles, serving under Braxton Bragg, stepped up and by 3:30 p.m. had assembled a mass battery to pound the Federals. Approximately 59 guns rained shot and shell into the Hornet's Nest for an hour, and between 4:30 and 5:00 p.m. under renewed infantry assault, the trapped Federals, including General Prentiss, surrendered.[14]

On the same side of the Confederate line, Albert Sidney Johnston received his death wound by 2:00 and expired by 2:30. Beauregard was informed about 30 minutes later and took command. The Confederates re-formed briefly around 5:00 p.m. and moved prisoners to the rear; some exchanged old muskets for new Enfields, and they moved forward again. Under Colonel J.D. Webster of his staff, however, Grant had managed to cobble together one last line, and Buell's forces were coming onto the field. The gunboats *Lexington* and *Tyler* joined in from the river with their heavy naval guns, and by

6:00 p.m. Beauregard called off any further Confederate attack. Beauregard hoped to rest quietly overnight and finish the job in the morning. Grant now faced the choice of "fight or run," and as the rain poured down overnight, he made his decision. "I propose to attack," said Grant, and he was true to his word. Grant's force was reduced to maybe 18,000 men, but he was still determined to attack on Monday.[15]

After a heavy nighttime storm, Monday morning dawned with bright sunlight as first Grant and then Beauregard began pressing forward—once more in brigade-level piecemeal attacks. Grant and Buell had conferred. Lew Wallace appeared on the field to reinforce Grant's army directly, and Buell advanced three new divisions into action. From 7:00 until sometime after 10:00 in the morning, confused brigade-level fighting punctuated the day's progression. Between 10:00 and 10:30 a.m., Grant was able to pull together survivors and newcomers alike for one coordinated push forward. The evidence suggests that he wanted to send everyone in at once, and even though inevitable delays occurred, by 10:30 most of the Union force was gaining ground. This behavior, committing all of his available forces, stands in stark contrast to Confederate efforts to commit first one brigade and then another to combat.[16]

From 10:30–2:30 the battle raged but the direction was all the same—back toward the Confederate lines. By 2:30 Beauregard realized he was beaten and signaled retreat. Exhausted, shocked by the carnage, and buffeted by the storm, Grant chose not to pursue. On the day following the battle, Beauregard continued pulling his army back to Corinth and Bragg described its condition: "My Dear General: Our condition is horrible. Troops utterly disorganized and demoralized. Road almost impassable. No provisions and no forage; consequently everything is feeble." Bragg later wrote in his own report of the battle: "The arrival during the night [April 6–7] of a large and fresh army to reinforce the enemy ... and, after a long and bloody contest with superior forces, compelled us to retire from the field, leaving our killed, many of our wounded, and nearly all of the trophies of the previous day's victories." The Union was only slightly better off but now it could complete its assembly. Henry Wager Halleck appeared by April 11 and exercised personal command over a host that finally reached 120,000 men.[17]

Within just a few days, other Confederate dominoes tipped over. On April 8, Island No. 10 fell to the Union, Fort Pillow fell on June 4, Memphis surrendered after a river battle on June 6, and the Mississippi River was open to Vicksburg. April 29 saw New Orleans fall as well. The loss of both Memphis and Nashville effectively took much of Tennessee out of the Confederacy for the rest of the summer, and gloom descended on the South. Tactically, Grant secured victory at a huge cost, but strategically the South suffered greater manpower losses and huge territorial reductions at the same time. Donelson was gone with 13,000 prisoners, Island No. 10 yielded a further 7,000, and Shiloh took another 10,700 off the Southern ledgers. Further losses like these would doom the Confederacy. In the East, McClellan approached from the water, marched up the York Peninsula, and came within six miles of Richmond in May. When Joe Johnston set out to fight McClellan on May 31, he went down seriously wounded and his army was equally despondent.[18]

* * *

Grant's original objective was clear: Gather at Pittsburg Landing, march to Corinth and defeat A.S. Johnston. At Corinth, Confederate rail lines heading in any direction would be severed. A.S. Johnston's goal was also uncomplicated: Assemble a Confederate army and defeat Grant before Buell could reinforce him.

Reviewing the six questions raised at the beginning of this study, it seems reasonable to reach several conclusions. Both the North and the South provided as many men and supplies as they could muster. Lincoln was quite willing for General Halleck to unite the armies of both Grant and Buell as the Confederates were gathering their forces. The President also supported Grant as the commander of the Federal army. General Halleck pushed reinforcements and supplies forward as quickly as he could. The Richmond government supported Johnston and Beauregard by seconding their call to secure additional soldiers from the Confederate coastlines to help defend the Corinth area and launch a pre-emptive strike against the Federals at Shiloh. By including the governors of several Confederate states on his personal staff, Johnston was able to attract additional support. For the first time since organizing their forces in the East, the Confederacy tried to unite men from its periphery and attempt a concentration at Corinth, both to prevent a further Union advance and to amass the strength to challenge advancing Union forces. Both sides made good-faith strategic efforts to support their field armies.

During the battle, the operational initiative wavered between Union and Confederate offensive efforts. Before the battle, Grant initially suggested a push directly on Corinth, but Halleck demurred and ordered Grant to wait for Buell to join him. Much has been made of Grant's failure to entrench, but he was hoping Buell would arrive earlier. He was also hoping to advance quickly on Corinth and cut the Confederate rail lines crossing the state of Tennessee. Even though a portion of Buell's force under General Nelson was available on the evening of April 5, Grant felt secure with his own army. Buell's tardy approach and Grant's lack of information about Confederate intentions helped to create an offensive opportunity for the Confederates. Grant (with Sherman as his lieutenant) failed to send out scouting forces to find the Confederates, and both Grant and Sherman discounted early reports of a Confederate presence at Shiloh. Johnston and Beauregard worked together to prepare an early morning assault on the Union forces gathered at Pittsburg Landing. Even though the details of the plan were not clear, both men did their best to make their offensive succeed. By the second day of battle, however, Grant had effectively wrested the initiative away from the Confederates, and Grant's advance brought Union victory on the second day at Shiloh.

Grant was in sole command, and with one exception, achieved a large degree of command unity, while his subordinates, for the most part, carried out his commands. He faced and overcame several challenges, but in the end, his subordinates worked hard to secure a battlefield victory. General Sherman was the only West Point division commander on the field for Grant during the first day's action. Earlier on March 12, West Pointer General C.F. Smith slipped while moving into a small boat near shore, was badly injured, was unable to participate in the battle, and he later succumbed to an infection. As he was the second West Point officer commanding a division in Grant's army, this was a heavy blow for the Union. W.H.L. Wallace, another officer without a West Point degree, took command of Smith's division at Shiloh. Grant met several times with Sherman, and it appears that Sherman worked actively with General McClernand. Lieutenant Colonel Adolf Engelmann of the 43rd Illinois Volunteers wrote the following: "The men being cheered on by General McClernand, who was present in the thickest of the fight, for a long period maintained a fearful conflict." After the initial Confederate surprise attack, Sherman was clearly outstanding. McClernand followed orders and worked cooperatively with Sherman. General Prentiss may not have followed Grant's intentions entirely and may have remained in place too long on the Sunken Road, but his defense, along with that of W.H.L. Wallace, delayed the Confederate advance for much of the afternoon. Colonel Quinn of the 12th Michigan, one of Prentiss's units, wrote thus: "[General Prentiss] was a brave man and cheered his men to duty during the whole day. Where the fight was thickest and danger the greatest there was he found, and his presence gave renewed confidence." While he might be criticized for some of his decisions, he did his best to hold his position for as long as possible. General Hurlbut received the title: "the gallant Hurlbut" by General Benjamin Prentiss. These quotes serve to underline the fact that several Union officers during combat respected their division commanders or peers, and they indeed fought vigorously to defend the Union position at Shiloh. Lew Wallace was undoubtedly suspect in his performance on the first day but was far more effective on the second.[19]

Except for Sherman, amateurs commanded the divisions in Grant's army. Grant for the most part, however, still achieved unity of command, even with this group of lieutenants. His immediate subordinates and staff knew what they were supposed to do; he personally offered them encouragement throughout the day and, except for Lew Wallace, they performed well. On the second day, Grant secured the support of Generals Buell and Wallace for a unified advance. In maintaining unity of command, to what extent can it be said that Grant moved actively around the battlefield and communicated directly with his subordinates? Through this lens, many of the six questions posed in the introduction to this study may be answered.

During the first day of battle, Grant met with commanders individually on at least three occasions. He communicated clearly with all of them, yet he let them direct their own tactical battles. And yes, Grant was lucky. Grant's luck was also supported by grit when, finally, Grant decided to stick it out, bring up Buell and attack the next day.

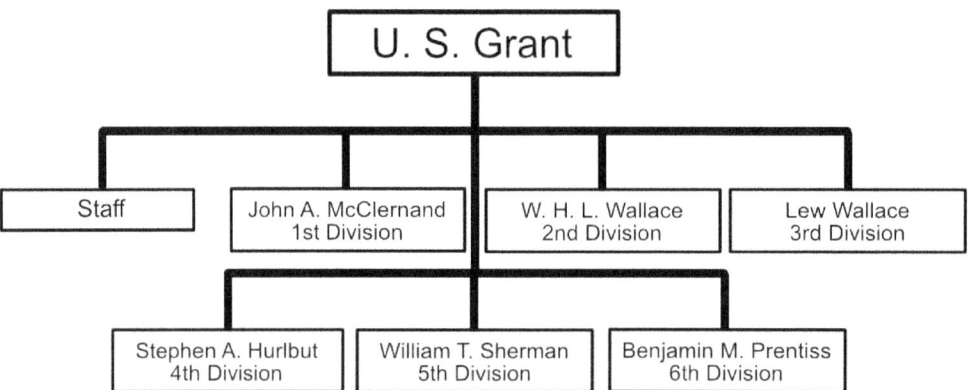

Army organization under Major General U.S. Grant at Shiloh. With the untimely injury to General Charles Smith, Grant was left with a single West Point officer (Sherman) as an immediate subordinate. Nevertheless, this group of men led a determined Federal effort that blunted the Confederate assaults on the first day. Joined by Buell's army and the division of Lew Wallace on the second day, Grant's army took the initiative and secured a victory (courtesy Margaret A. Zimmermann).

- At 7:00 a.m., Grant hears cannon fire, leaves his coffee, steps aboard his headquarters boat, the *Tigress,* and motors off. Afterward he and his subordinates are careful to cover their tracks, but the evidence here demonstrates that he, like Wellington in the past, has been "humbugged."
- At 7:30 approximately, Grant meets with Lew Wallace at Crump's Landing downstream and tells him to wait for additional orders.
- At 8:30, Grant meets with W.H.L. Wallace, is briefed by him, and orders up additional ordnance wagons for the infantry.
- From 9:00–10:00, Grant meets with Sherman, McClernand and Prentiss as they are under heavy pressure. Their units have already fallen back through their original camps.
- At 10:30 approximately, Grant meets with Hurlbut.
- From 11:00–12:00 p.m., Grant meets at least once more with Sherman and comes under fire.
- In the afternoon, Grant meets Buell on one of the steamboats and they confer.
- At 2:30 approximately, Grant returns to visit Sherman.
- From 3:00–4:30, Grant attempts to rally fugitives and rides his "last line" to review Union defenses.[20]

There is a method to all this activity. While Confederate commanders struggled to lead brigades or even regiments into combat, Grant met or communicated systematically with each of his subordinates. Other than with General Lew Wallace, who failed to march to the sound of the guns, Grant was in relatively close contact with the rest of his command during the battle. While he met only briefly with Buell in the afternoon, he perhaps felt awkward about giving the other officer specific direction.

By the end of the day, one can say with certainty that, while Grant had been forced back on the tactical defensive, he still succeeded in achieving some semblance of unity within his command structure. No division commander was unaware or uncertain of his role (except for Lew Wallace, who remained confused), because Grant stated his goals directly and unequivocally. While he was on crutches from an earlier fall from his horse, he was in good health, demonstrated excellent stamina, and remained personally active all over the field of battle. His staff did not always support him effectively, but he made up the difference with personal energy and a focused determination to hold out. They, in turn, worked arduously to support Grant during the day. Ammunition was generally distributed to all in need, messages were sent, and serious efforts were made to get Lew Wallace into the fight. This was in stark contrast to his Confederate counterparts. Beauregard remained near Sherman's headquarters on Sunday and seldom ventured out at any great distance to see the field for himself. Johnston saw portions of the field as a brigade commander might, but he was dead before he could traverse the whole field to see the bigger picture.

On the second day, Grant pressed the attack with every man he could muster. This, too, became his hallmark: Attack everywhere with everyone. As Brigadier General Dodge later wrote, "It was General Grant's determination in every battle to use against the enemy every gun at his command, and when his battles are studied it is wonderful to see how he marshaled his forces." This behavior replicated his decision on the battleground near Fort Donelson. Later he would attempt to expand on this idea as commander-in-chief during the 1864 Overland Campaign: Push every one of the Union armies forward at the same time.[21]

On the Confederate side, unity of command proved to be an elusive goal. Confusion was the order of the day as two different plans were at odds with one another. Johnston's subordinates, however, all sought to sustain him once the battle was joined. By ranging off to the right of the Confederate line, A.S. Johnston abdicated a portion of his role as army commander. His subordinates were loyal, but they were often forced to make command decisions without his guiding hand. Beauregard did his best to inspire Confederate victory, particularly on the second day of battle, but by then, the weight of Union forces became too great. Johnston commanded a diverse group of subordinates, and in the end, all of them were reasonably effective in supporting the Confederate efforts on both days of battle.

It appears that Johnston and Beauregard divided their widely separated forces between them for the purpose of command and control. Johnston led from the front and eventually, the right side of the line, while Beauregard was active in sending aides from the rear to control the rest of the battle. Beauregard later wrote the following: "General Johnston said that he should go to the front, leaving me in the general direction, as the exigencies of the battle might arise." The historian Charles Roland suggests that Johnston was more active on the left and center of the line early in the day. He notes that Johnston rallied one of Hardee's brigades that was repulsed in an early assault and directed Bragg's force to move up as well. General William J. Hardee led Johnston's attack on the left side of his line in the early hours of April 6. By 5:00 a.m. his men were in action. General Braxton Bragg provided active leadership throughout the

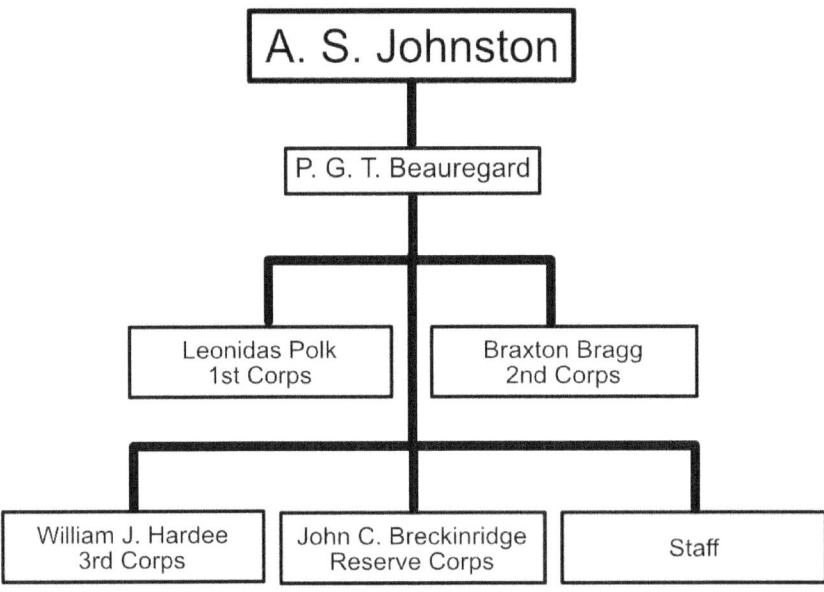

Army organization under Major General A. S. Johnston. Generals Beauregard, Hardee and Bragg had all graduated from West Point and had experienced combat before Shiloh. Polk was an appointee of President Davis and Breckinridge was the former Vice President of the United States. Polk, Hardee and Breckinridge all later played critical roles throughout 1862 in the West. As Johnston assembled a new army on the way to Shiloh, these men faced huge organizational challenges. While they supported Johnston's plan and did their best to carry out his wishes, their efforts fell short of success (courtesy Margaret A. Zimmermann).

day. Around 10:30 in the morning, Bragg met General Polk on the battlefield, and they agreed to divide specific portions of the battlefield between them. Hardee remained on the left, Polk took the center, and Bragg commanded the right-center of the line. Eventually Breckinridge would fill in the far right end of the Confederate advance and follow the direct orders of Johnston. While the Confederate high command struggled to reorganize their intermingled forces on the field, they at least did their best to support the general advance against the Federal lines. On the second day, Hardee, Bragg, Polk and Breckinridge served loyally under Beauregard and did everything they could to salvage the Confederate army after its defeat.[22]

Now it is important to ask the same question concerning General Johnston. In maintaining unity of command, to what extent can it be said that Johnston moved actively around the battlefield and communicated directly with his subordinates? How did he spend his time before he was killed on the first day?

- Between 5:30 and 6:00 a.m., Johnston rides onto the battlefield and, at about 6:00 a.m., watches a brigade attack from the left of the Confederate line. Helps rally a brigade under the command of General Shavers.
- Around 7:00, Johnston witnesses Patrick Cleburne's assault from the Confederate left. Orders a brigade under Confederate General Stewart to the right of his line.
- From 7:30 to 8:30, Johnston rides into one of Union General Prentiss's original camps, the camp of the 18th Wisconsin.
- Johnston determined to "order forward the reserve," under General Breckinridge and joins Bowen's Brigade. Johnston continues to move actively from one Confederate brigade to another on the right of his line.
- From 9:30 to 11:15, he remains in the camp and attempts to halt looting there. He continues to direct the Confederate attack from the right of his line.
- From 11:30 a.m. to 1:30 p.m. approximately, Johnston advances to higher ground with the Confederate right flank (Bowen's Brigade of Breckenridge).
- Around 2:00, Johnston advances with Breckenridge and is mortally wounded.[23]

As he inspired his troops, Johnston's personal bravery was remarkable. His command of the Confederate Army, however, largely ceased after the middle of the morning. Acting as a division and then brigade commander, he attempted to press the right side of the Confederate line forward, but at the same time, his subordinates commanded the remaining two-thirds of the Confederate line. With such a lengthy front, where communications were made more difficult by a lack of lateral roads, the Confederate command structure broke down.

For the Confederates, Johnston was active in the left and center of the Confederate army during the early hours of Sunday. Once he moved to the right flank of the Confederate army, he directed those forces to good effect as well. But battles require the effective coordination of the entire military force, and by moving off to the right flank, Johnston was unable to carry out that requirement. Beauregard, on the other hand, remained largely in one general area the first day and then failed to prepare either an attack or defense for the second day. Both generals relied on their subordinates to cooperate in moving the Confederate assault forward. While Beauregard led bravely on the second day, simple bravery was not enough. Grant was the more effective commander on both days.

Looking back to the prologue on the Mexican War, the reader can see that General Winfield Scott used over 30 staff officers to assist him in directing an army of around 10,000 men. The logistical challenge of marching from Veracruz to Mexico City presented multiple problems, and Scott was fortunate to direct a very able group of staff officers. In the early months of 1862, however, both North and South struggled to appoint competent staff officers in the western theater and far fewer officers were assigned to important staff duties. Staff officers themselves often preferred a line assignment where both quick promotion and fame were possible. A careful examination of the staff appointments for both sides shows the challenges they faced. While there are obviously other elements to good staff work beyond providing food for the soldiers, ammunition for the battle, and communications across the battlefield, only the efforts to provide these three necessities are reviewed here.

For the North, Henry Wager Halleck, U.S. Grant and Don Carlos Buell each appointed their own staff officers. In some ways, it was helpful for Grant to stand on the defensive the first day at Shiloh as food and ammunition were readily at hand for his units. The local terrain and divisional positions were well known to his officers, and messages could be more easily delivered as a result. The Union Army also relied heavily on divisional staff officers to provide for the needs of each unit. As early as March 15, Grant had John Rawlins issue General Orders No. 21 which specified job descriptions for each staff member: "The necessity for order, and regularity about Head Quarters, especially in keeping the records, makes it necessary to assign particular duties to each member of the Staff." This was largely the same group of men who served earlier under Grant at the Fort Henry and Donelson campaign. Several of them joined Grant even earlier during his Belmont expedition in late 1861. As a result, enough time had elapsed for them to work together cooperatively as a group, and we should remember that Grant had also served time as regimental quartermaster in the Mexican War and afterward.[24]

Except for a lack of modern weapons, Grant's army was well supplied and equipped. As the battle unfolded, his aides made certain to distribute ammunition to the hard-pressed soldiers. Artillery was also readily at hand and made a significant contribution to the Union effort. As noted earlier, Colonel Webster was able to amass over 50 guns in support of Grant's last line of defense, and the Confederates wisely decided not to attempt a final assault on this well-defended position.

By camping at Pittsburg Landing, the Union had time to amass the supplies needed to properly feed and supply the army. While there was some confusion arming new units as they appeared, there was no difficulty encountered in bringing tons of supplies by steamboat to the army. As for ammunition, Grant's army expended ammunition in the same prodigal fashion as the Confederates, but they enjoyed the presence of their own ordnance wagons in close proximity, and staff officers were active in bringing more to the front. Buell's forces were likewise well supplied as they crossed the Tennessee River for combat. In fact, we find occasional comments commending quartermasters for their efforts. From the Third Brigade of the First Division (McClernand) we read the following from Lieutenant Abram Ryan: "As I could do no further good remaining with the train, I rode forward to hurry up ammunition. Meeting with Lieut. C.C. Williams, brigade quartermaster, he gallantly volunteered to bring forward a train, designating a field where to meet the regiments.… Halting the advance, I eventually succeeded in getting the … regiments into line, when Quartermaster Williams returned with an ammunition train." Or from Brigadier General Alexander McD. McCook of Buell's army: "Three hours before, being convinced from the stubbornness with which the enemy was contending and the rapid discharges of my regiments that their 40 rounds of cartridges would soon be exhausted, I dispatched Lieutenant Campbell, my ordnance officer, for teams to bring up ammunition. He arrived at the opportune moment with three wagon loads."[25]

By the time the battle occurred, Grant enjoyed a more experienced staff following their work at Fort Donelson. R. Steven Jones, in his book on the use of staff officers during the Civil War, suggests that both Grant's general staff and personal staff "acted with speed, authority, and efficiency." Their performance at Shiloh, although still needing work, would significantly improve. While his personal aides might disappoint Grant at times, his general staff performed well. From a later date, Brigadier General Dodge shares his view of the relationship Grant enjoyed with members of his staff: "While at City Point [in 1864] I lived at headquarters, and for the first time came in continual contact with General Grant and General Rawlins.... It was their custom to sit out in front of the tent around the campfire of evenings until late in the night, and a free discussion of the battles and movements was held, which gave a better insight into the operations of the army than could possibly be obtained in any other way." Grant was already cultivating this relationship early in the war.[26]

General Grant's report after the close of battle at Shiloh summarizes the work of the staff during the action. "My personal staff are all deserving of particular mention, they having been engaged during the entire two days in conveying orders to every part of the field."[27]

Similar comments could not be advanced for Confederate staff efforts as they built, organized, and supplied their army from the ground up. There was simply too much to do in a very short time. Prior to the battle, Confederate staff members did their best to supply soldiers with weapons and ammunition. Unfortunately, untrained soldiers consumed several days of rations immediately, and when they stopped to loot Union camps, this extra-curricular activity delayed their advance. The major Confederate logistical problem appeared to be the re-supply of ammunition as their soldiers advanced. In some cases, this postponed offensive actions for over an hour as soldiers left the battle line to search for ammunition wagons. A review of the Confederate after-action

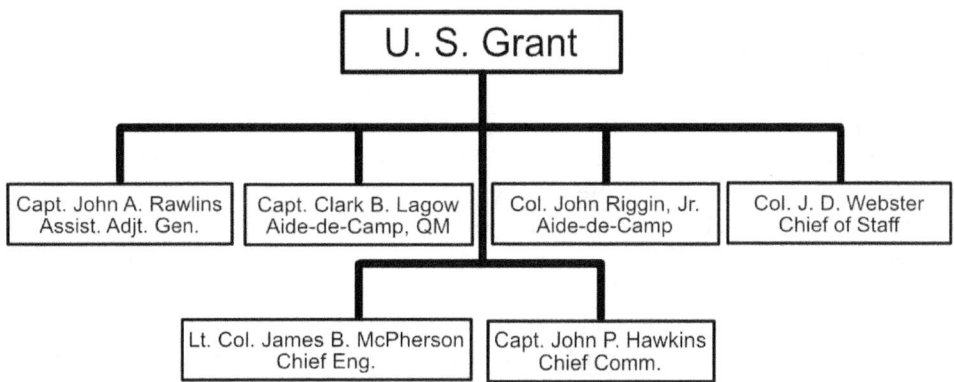

Selected Union staff under Grant. By the time the Battle of Shiloh was fought, Grant's staff had made good progress in working together and providing support for both Grant and the army (courtesy Margaret A. Zimmermann).

reports coming from the Shiloh battlefield suggests that at least 12 brigades (out of the 14 that reported) were delayed as they paused to find ammunition. A few regiments (four) apparently found their ordnance wagons close to them. Others paused to loot enemy camps (six) or were simply delayed (three) in searching for ammunition. Several regiments (seven) withdrew from combat for at least some time. Approximately 20 Confederate after-action reports from divisions, brigades and regiments attest to the problem. From Withers's Division we read: "After a sharp conflict they (the Union army) were dislodged and driven from their position, and Chalmers halted his command for a supply of ammunition." Later: "The division was then advanced … and halted for a supply of ammunition." Once again: "This division was moved promptly forward, although some regiments had not succeeded in getting a supply of ammunition, and had just entered a deep and precipitous ravine when the enemy opened a terrific fire upon it." And again: "After this fight our ammunition was exhausted, and, the wagons being some distance behind, we lost some time before I was replenished." The fact that it had rained heavily before the battle opened and during the night between Sunday and Monday, suggests that the poor roads and flooded fields disrupted wagon transportation, particularly wagons carrying large consignments of lead. Brigadier General Patrick Cleburne later wrote: "My men were out of ammunition. Owing to the nature of the ground my ammunition wagons could not follow, so I had to send a strong fatigue party back, and the men carried boxes of ammunition on their shoulders up and down the steep hills for more than a mile."[28]

Finally, the orders drawn up by Thomas Jordan and his staff led to inextricable confusion as the Confederates failed to coordinate their attacks as the first day wore on. From the report of the 9th Arkansas Battalion, we read the following: "Here we were ordered to remain by General Hardee … where we remained but a short time, when we were ordered forward by General Beauregard, and placed on the right of the line, commanded, I think, by Colonel Smith or General Stewart. This was about 10 a.m." Part of the communication challenge for staff members was the nature of the terrain. In his report, Major General William Hardee describes the problem: "From Mickey's 8 miles west from Pittsburg [Landing] rolling uplands, partially cultivated, interspersed with copses, thickets, and forests, with small fields, cultivated or abandoned, characterize the country from that point to the river."[29]

Braxton Bragg's report, however, summarizes the Confederate challenges quite well. We read the following: "But few regiments in my command had ever made a day's march…. Our organization had been most hasty with great deficiency in commanders, and was therefore very imperfect. The equipment was lamentably defective for field service, and our transportation, hastily impressed in the country, was deficient in quantity and very inferior in quality." While this is all quite true, it is also true that the Confederates had had almost a full year to address some of these needs, and they simply did not have enough time to do so effectively. As a result, critical training, organizational and logistical requirements had not been achieved. Later in his report, Bragg provided another damning summary when he wrote the following: "The want of proper organization and discipline, and the inferiority in many cases of our officers to the men they were expected to command, left us often without system or order." This statement suggests that Confederate staff officers were simply overwhelmed with their new responsibilities.[30]

Contributing to the staff challenges of organizing a new army, the changing roster of staff members themselves must have presented its own set of variables. For example,

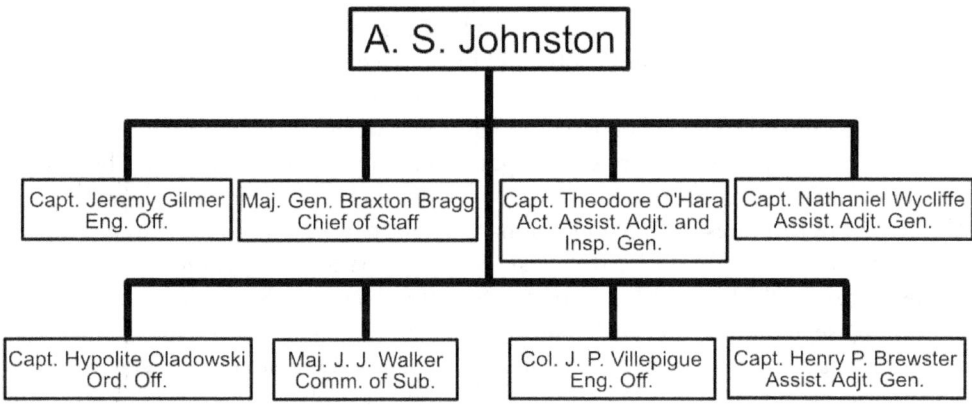

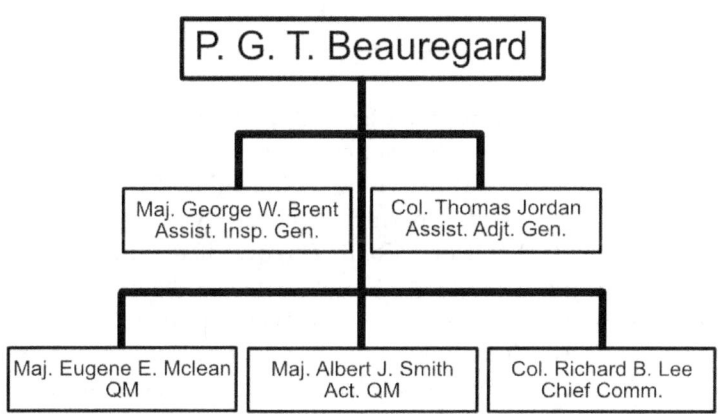

Selected Confederate staff under Johnston and Beauregard. Johnston and Beauregard each brought their own staff officers to Shiloh, and all played at least some role in supporting the Confederate efforts there. Unfortunately, the challenge of arming and feeding this new force, along with unceasing rain before the battle and the difficult terrain over which the inexperienced army fought, negated much of their work (courtesy Margaret A. Zimmermann).

on September 15, 1861, Colonel William Mackall was listed as Johnston's chief of staff and held this post until February 27, 1862. Then with Island No. 10 on the Mississippi River under threat of attack and under the command of a frightened Major General John P. McCown, newly promoted Brigadier General Mackall was detailed to command in his place. By March 4, 1862 (barely one month before Shiloh), General Braxton Bragg assumed the role of chief of staff for Johnston but also commanded one of Johnston's corps in the coming battle. By April 3, General Johnston used the services of Colonel Thomas Jordan (from Beauregard's staff), as his Assistant Adjutant General and some of his other staff officers as well. Under Beauregard's direction, Jordan issued the march orders and outlined the organizational structure of the Confederate Army for the day of battle. With a newly assembled force, an embryonic staff and inexperienced officers, the Confederate army faced a forbidding challenge at Shiloh.[31]

Except for Lew Wallace, Grant was able to employ his entire army the first day. One of Grant's hallmarks was his success in bringing all his resources to bear in combat. While Buell's army was not on the field in force on Sunday to face the Confederate onslaught, on the second day Grant was able to put every available man into action. The Confederates struggled to employ their entire army on the first day when three lines of men and a reserve force were each separated by hundreds of yards. On both days, attacks were seldom coordinated above a brigade or even at times a regimental level. While the Confederates had an edge in manpower, they were never able to use all of it at one time. Interestingly, both sides massed artillery batteries and used them at critical moments during the battle. The Confederates assembled over 50 guns to overcome the Union defense in the center of their lines, i.e., the Sunken Road. The Union army massed its artillery as part of Grant's last line of defense. Unified masses of artillery would not be seen in the West again until the Union Army of the Cumberland massed over 50 guns during the Battle of Stones River.

The Union army also possessed armed gunboats and used them effectively during the first day and night. The Confederates, of course, were unable to bring anything to bear on the river. It should be kept in mind, however, that the Confederates had 13 months to devise some form of naval presence on the western rivers and simply failed to build anything useful.

The strategic outcome of this battle favored the North. The road to the Southern heartland was wide open, the South had suffered irreplaceable casualties, and the North exploited this significant victory by marching on Corinth and the Confederate rail network. In the end, the rail lines were permanently cut. By losing 14,000 men at Henry and Donelson, another 8,000 at Island No. 10, and over 10,000 casualties at Shiloh, the South struggled afterward to match the North in raising the manpower in defense of their western states. Eventually in 1863, they would even bring reinforcements from the East to help even the odds. With vital economic resources denied to them after the fall of most of Tennessee in 1862, Confederate cavalry would be challenged to find enough horseflesh, and badly needed Confederate resources in food and raw materials would be lacking.

Bragg's later strategic and operational decisions in the summer of 1862 temporarily restored Southern fortunes in the West. After Beauregard retreated to Corinth and then abandoned the town, Braxton Bragg replaced him. Bragg reorganized the Confederate army at Tupelo, Mississippi, and then initiated a new campaign. After Grant's performance at Shiloh, he was temporarily shelved as Halleck stepped up to command the united Union host. Halleck would march slowly on Corinth, dashing any Union hopes of winning a complete victory in the West that summer. Only his promotion to the equivalent of chief of staff in Washington would bring Grant back to center stage in the West. Unfortunately, by then, Grant's once formidable army was largely scattered in defense of rail lines. In the meantime, Buell's efforts with the Army of the Ohio (eventually re-christened Army of the Cumberland) would remain the sole Union operation designed to push Bragg out of Tennessee altogether and take Chattanooga. Bragg had other ideas.

Summarizing the results of the battle in chart form, the evidence suggests that Grant successfully achieved the six goals necessary for a major victory in combat. While there may be disagreements over individual conclusions expressed below, the general pattern points out the extent of the Union victory at Shiloh. Similar summaries for other battles in 1862 point to similar conclusions and help us to better understand the reasons why the Confederates found themselves in such difficulty by the end of the year. Fortunately for them, Confederate armies in the East, with far greater resources and much stronger depth in leadership, had performed well enough to hold back Union advances in 1862.

Six Elements of Victory at Shiloh

Shiloh	Clear, Attainable Objective	Operational Initiative	Command Unity
Grant	Achieved	Not Achieved Day 1 Achieved Day 2	Achieved
Johnston	Achieved	Achieved Day 1	Achieved
Beauregard	Achieved Day 1 Not Achieved Day 2	Not Achieved Day 2	Achieved
	Logistics/Staff	*Used All Resources*	*Strategic Outcome*
Grant	Achieved	Achieved	Achieved
Johnston	Not Achieved	Not Achieved	Not Achieved
Beauregard	Not Achieved	Achieved	Not Achieved

While achieving their initial objective in surprising the Union army, the Confederates attempted more than they were able to accomplish on the first day of battle. Johnston's personal movement to the right of the Confederate line, the lack of timely ammunition resupply, Confederate delay in pursuing the attack, and then his demise left the Confederates without the victory they so badly needed. Grant was able to hold on the first day, supply his men with ammunition, and ultimately bring in the reinforcements needed to seize the initiative from the Confederates during the second day of combat.

Chapter 6

Richmond, Kentucky

Kirby Smith Wins for the Confederacy

On July 31, General Kirby Smith met with Braxton Bragg in Chattanooga and together the two men plotted strategy for a return to Kentucky. The Confederates hoped that a new campaign would result in recapturing the Bluegrass State, assist in raising new recruits, and breathe new life into their cause. Smith would lead off the movement, but he would advance from east to west through the Cumberland Gap while Bragg would march north from Chattanooga. Then, perhaps, but "perhaps" was the operative word, Smith would join Bragg for an attack on Buell followed by an invasion of Kentucky. By this time in the war, Kirby Smith had a solid record of achievement that supported his meteoric rise in the Confederate Army, and he was selected to lead a small invasion force westward. Also a West Point graduate, Smith had served bravely under both Taylor and Scott in the Mexican War. Commanding a brigade under Joseph Johnston at First Bull Run, Smith performed well but was badly wounded.[1]

The Battle of Richmond, Kentucky, demonstrates one example of where an exception can "prove the rule." The Confederate victory here compares favorably with the other seven victorious Union actions described elsewhere. In the case of Richmond, however, a Confederate force, similar in size to its Federal opponent when the battle opened, armed perhaps more poorly and not greatly supported in a strategic sense, was able to thoroughly defeat and even destroy the Union force it faced. A comparison of the commanders in this battle, their relations with staff and subordinates, and their behaviors on the battlefield, advance the argument that the six questions raised in the beginning of this book are indeed significant considerations for determining the outcome of a particular engagement.

In July of 1862, as Smith moved into Kentucky, the Union assembled a makeshift force under a former naval lieutenant now promoted suddenly to major general in the army, William "Bull" Nelson. As a Kentucky native, Nelson remained loyal to the Union and helped recruit soldiers for the Federal army. He also fought bravely at the Battle of Shiloh. Raw recruits from Indiana, Ohio and Kentucky were mustered in together under equally new (for the most part) commanders. On August 29 and 30, 1862, the action known as the Battle of Richmond occurred, and the Confederates won a complete victory over their Union opponents. Unfortunately for them, the small Confederate force was unable to reap any real strategic success from this engagement, and Kirby Smith determined to keep his army separate from that of Braxton Bragg. It was remarkable that the one Confederate victory in the West contained the same elements for victory that Union forces exhibited elsewhere throughout the year.[2]

When Smith moved into Kentucky beginning on August 13, General Buell was not able to send reinforcements from Nashville, and that meant that veteran troops would not be actively involved in halting Smith's invasion. Union Brigadier General George Morgan originally held the Cumberland Gap region and one of the four major passes through which Smith's little force had to pass to enter Kentucky. Lacking reinforcements, he was trapped, but at the same time compelled Kirby Smith to leave almost half his force to keep Morgan in place. Morgan was able to hold his position until September 17, over two weeks after the Battle of Richmond was fought, before retreating northward. Kirby Smith quickly moved his forces through the remaining gaps in the Cumberland Mountain range, and one Confederate option became painfully obvious; Bragg and Smith could unite and seize Kentucky.[3]

Major General Edmund Kirby Smith (Library of Congress).

In Nashville, General Buell sought to intervene by appointing Major General (as of July 1862) Nelson, and sent him to command a newly created scratch force. Buell hoped Nelson could hold off Kirby Smith until Buell himself had a chance to deal with Bragg. But Nelson, his staff and the brigadier generals who would command directly under him in eastern Kentucky were all at Nashville as late as August 19. The Northern governors and Brigadier General Boyle, in military command of Kentucky, were in a panic and they wanted something done immediately. The newly created Military Department of Ohio included five Midwestern states along with eastern Kentucky and was commanded by Major General Horatio Wright. While Buell could keep Nelson in motion, saying "You will continue the general direction of affairs in that state [Kentucky]," raw recruits from Indiana, Ohio and Kentucky were mustered in together under equally untested commanders.[4]

General Wright was hopeful that Nelson's force would keep the Kentucky River between his army of about 7,000 men and the approaching Confederate force of about the same number. The command structure, however, was wildly confused at this point. Governor Morton of Indiana placed Lew Wallace, of Shiloh fame, in command of Indiana troops and sent them south. In the meantime, Cassius Clay, former ambassador to Russia and a major general in the Mexican War, arrived in his home state to take charge. Leading five regiments of raw recruits and a few artillery pieces without all of their equipment present, he headed south as well. He planned to stay north of the Kentucky River. General Wright wrote Lew Wallace on August 23 and ordered him to stop his advance as well: "Stop your advance at Richmond until further orders." But Richmond, Kentucky, was south of the river, and Nelson arrived shortly thereafter to take command himself. The river could form a barrier so that a force numbering around 16,000 men could assemble as one group, use the river to create an obstacle for the Confederate army, and protect the towns of Lexington and Frankfort as well. When Nelson finally arrived with his immediate subordinates to take command, he promptly relieved Cassius Clay and proceeded to divide his force. Some men were marching to Richmond, Kentucky, and Nelson sent another force of similar size marching southwest into the Perryville area. Under Nelson's command, the two subordinate commanders at Richmond acted independently. Generals Charles Cruft and Mahlon Manson, possessing political rather than military connections, were placed in charge of the two brigades that Nelson met near Richmond, Kentucky. Manson had turned in an adequate performance earlier in the year at Mill Springs, but this time he was in over his head.[5]

Major General William "Bull" Nelson (Library of Congress).

* * *

Crossing the Kentucky River, Manson advanced and, by August 29, confronted the advanced guard of the Confederate forces under Kirby Smith. The day before, General Nelson had appeared nearby and ordered Manson to halt in place. Without leaving word of his whereabouts or further instructions, Nelson then departed Richmond for Lexington. These movements left Manson alone to face Smith's entire oncoming force. To further complicate matters, the Union forces lacked effective reconnaissance, and they had no idea where Kirby Smith's army was located. Aware of the Confederate advance somewhere in the area but not able to determine its size, Manson pushed his forces forward to occupy high ground on what would become the battlefield. At dawn on August 30, Manson faced General Patrick Cleburne's advanced force of veteran Confederates. After a desultory artillery duel, Confederate general Kirby Smith ordered Cleburne forward, and this action would become the first phase of the Battle of Richmond. Smith himself reached the battlefield around eight in the morning.⁶

General Cleburne's division included three brigades of infantry, and they joined Churchill's division. Cleburne deployed two of those brigades in his front line and sent the third brigade around to his left to outflank Manson's Union brigade. Around 10:00 in the morning, Cleburne's command, nicely aligned to overlap the Union brigade's right and left flanks, advanced and routed Manson. Cleburne himself was wounded, but that failed to halt the Confederate advance. A Confederate report stated, "By this time the infantry fire had become severe on the extreme right, and soon the enemy's line could be seen advancing rapidly in an effort to turn our right flank. This movement was skillfully foiled ... [and Confederate Preston Smith] 'in turn succeeded in turning the enemy's left, driving him

Brigadier General Patrick Cleburne. Cleburne's initial plan of attack went forward successfully despite the fact he was wounded early on. In 1862, he led a formidable striking force in several battles (Library of Congress).

from the field in great confusion.'" Cleburne fielded a force of about 3,000 men while Manson mustered about 3,500. Unfortunately for Manson, his men were all raw recruits, up against veterans. Lambert writes, "The lack of adequate preparation for the field was evident in every aspect of military organization and supply." Colonel William L. McMillen of the 95th Ohio noted that "little time or opportunity had been given to organize or drill the regiment."⁷

Following the defeat of Manson, the lead units of Cruft's brigade also appeared on the field after marching forward from Richmond. Manson ordered both brigades back to reform. Kirby Smith's Confederates followed closely and then

Brigadier General Charles Cruft. Cruft found himself in an untenable position at Richmond. Lacking timely direction from either Nelson or Manson, his men were finally routed off the field. A lack of communication and raw volunteers fatally damaged Union efforts at Richmond (Library of Congress).

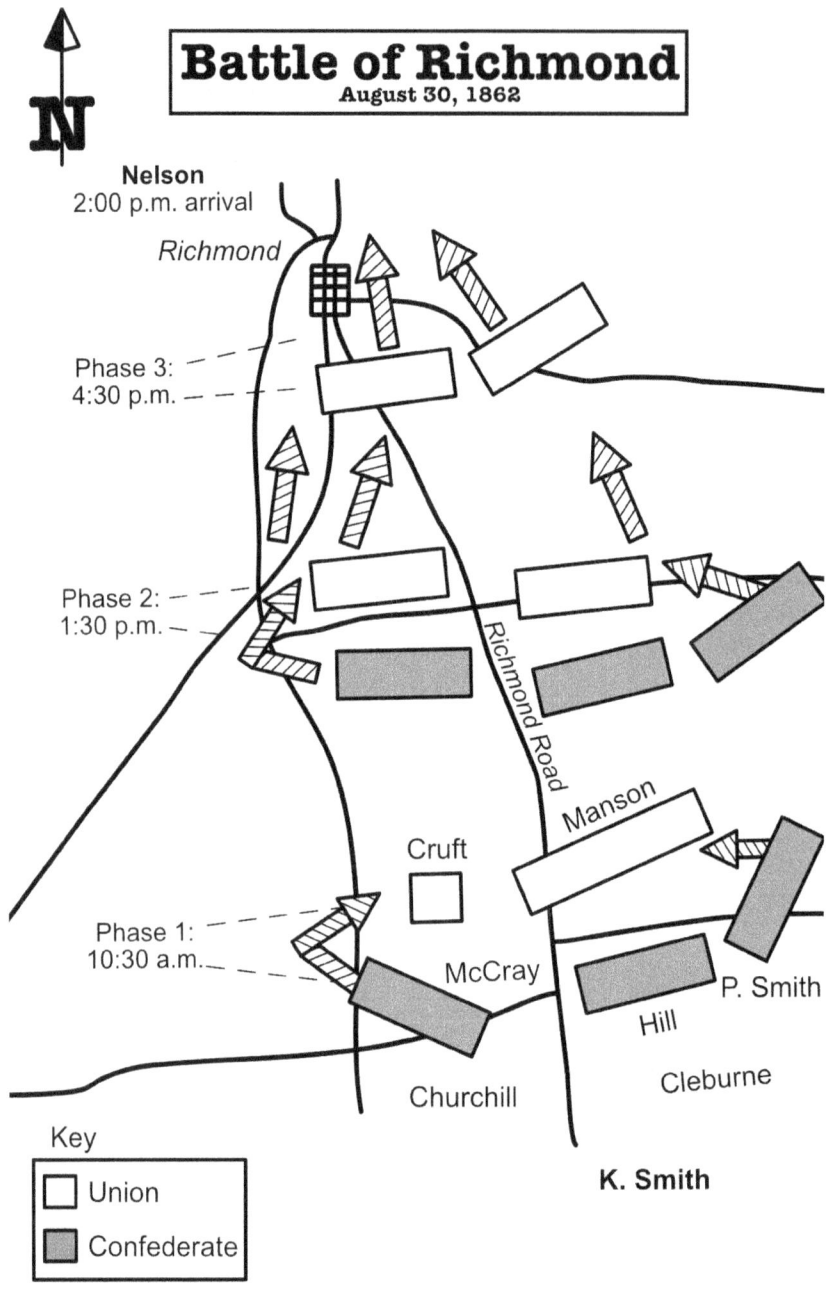

The Battle of Richmond occurred throughout the day in three separate actions. Before he was wounded, Confederate General Cleburne set the stage for a major Confederate victory with his brigades. Union generals Cruft and Manson were forced out of their advanced and exposed positions. During the second stage of combat, Kirby Smith personally directed the victorious advance against the poorly led and supplied Union Army. Even with the late arrival of Union commanding general William Nelson, the Federal Army was routed off the field. Not shown on the map was an advance by Confederate cavalry, and the resulting action, which cut off the Union retreat and led to the destruction of the entire Union force (courtesy Margaret A. Zimmermann).

paused to regroup. Paul Hammond writes, "The artillery of this [Preston Smith's] division had exhausted its ammunition, and some delay occurred in bringing up the ordnance train." Forming a line together around 1:30 p.m., Union forces attempted to hold back the Confederates, and the second phase of the battle was launched. As Cleburne's brigades moved forward, another Confederate brigade joined them, and 18 Confederate regiments completed the envelopment and defeat of the Union force. Cruft's brigade even advanced at first on the Union right, but the Confederates were ready for them. A Confederate brigade on the left of their line countered the Federal advance and "as the smoke lifted, the enemy could be seen within less than a hundred paces of where we stood, but in full flight, broken." Of the original 12 Federal fieldpieces, all but two had been withdrawn to search for additional ammunition.[8]

Retreating once more, the Union army tried to regroup around the town of Richmond. Around 2:00 p.m. General Nelson appeared and, in a peripatetic fashion, tried to rally the Union forces. It was no use. The third phase of the battle opened around 4:30 p.m. as Confederates, now in greatly superior numbers, attacked both Union flanks. The Confederates were rested and brought up fresh ammunition and water. While the Federals resisted fiercely for a short time, by 5:00 p.m. they were once again routed off the field. Hammond states "[their] army, now no longer an army but a mob, cavalry, infantry, artillery, and wagons, mingled together in complete confusion, rushed along the road for Lexington. All their trains and artillery and a large number of prisoners fell into our hands." Confederate cavalry under Colonel John Scott cut off the retreat of the Union forces as well and captured many of the fleeing Union soldiers, artillery and wagons. The Battle of Richmond was possibly the most complete Confederate victory of the war, certainly of 1862. When it ended, the Union had lost approximately 75 percent of their original force of 7,000, including about 5,000 captured. Smith accomplished what other Confederate forces utterly failed to do in the West in 1862. What would he do next?[9]

After his victory at Richmond, Kirby Smith marched quickly to Lexington, Kentucky, and there he waited for Bragg to appear. He was also anxious that his force from the Cumberland Gap would join him, he embarked on a recruiting campaign for willing Kentuckians, and divided his force into several smaller groups to occupy central Kentucky. Smith's army occupied the area, but Kentuckians were unwilling to join either Smith or the oncoming forces under Bragg. The recruiting mission was a failure. Finally, Smith wrote Bragg: "Unless ... you can move your column in this direction or make with me a combined attack on Louisville, ... I shall be compelled to fall back upon you for support."[10]

*   *   *

A clear Federal objective was lacking here, and no single commander was in charge. Some leaders thought that the Federal army should remain north of the Kentucky River, others thought it could advance and hold Richmond, and General Manson marched boldly to the attack. In the case of the Federals, strategic support for their efforts at Richmond, Kentucky, was meager at best. General Buell in Nashville was left to make his own decisions about who could manage the Federal response to the Confederate incursion under Kirby Smith. Buell selected Nelson, probably a poor choice. While the governor of Indiana exercised his own preference and placed Lew Wallace in charge of reinforcements, a politician and friend of Lincoln, Cassius Clay, appeared on the scene to muddy the waters still further. At the same time, however, the Washington authorities placed General Wright in charge of the operation but when the two Union brigades ostensibly under General Nelson, acting independently, advanced across the Kentucky River to confront Kirby Smith, they were defeated. President Lincoln, Governor Morton of Indiana and General Wright in Cincinnati all played a role in confusing the Union strategic response to the Confederate challenge. Before the battle occurred, command confusion created a major problem; there was seemingly no one in charge and no commonly agreed-upon objective for Union forces. William Nelson divided his force in the face of an enemy offensive, and General Manson fought a battle he was ordered to avoid.

On the Confederate side, the Richmond government supported the creation of Kirby Smith's army, and when it advanced it had acquired an additional division from Bragg to make it a solid force. By not placing someone in overall charge of the operation and by creating confusion within the "Department of East Tennessee," President Davis unnecessarily complicated relations between Bragg and Kirby Smith. Bragg, the senior officer present, now operated in Smith's department, and while Smith eventually won the battle of Richmond, few tangible results emerged. Smith unilaterally changed his original object, and instead of cooperating with Bragg against Buell, he decided to seize Lexington, Kentucky, and operate independently. What was Smith's objective? He could have joined Bragg after the battle, or he could have threatened Louisville, or he could have kept his force more unified to be able to help Bragg when necessary. He chose instead to remain quietly separate from Bragg, divided his force, and took no more aggressive action. Consequently, neither the Union nor the Confederate forces enjoyed the strategic relationship needed to profit from the ensuing action in Kentucky.[11]

Both sides took the offensive and tried to hold the initiative, but in this case only the Confederates were prepared to profit from their advance. The Battle of Richmond became a rare "meeting engagement" on the part of two advancing forces. While Kirby Smith failed to rally Kentuckians to the Confederate cause, he was able to open the Cumberland Gap and apply enough pressure against Nelson's Federal army to eliminate it. Throughout the battle, Smith's force seized and held the initiative. He was left in a position where he could have joined Bragg for an even more punishing attack after

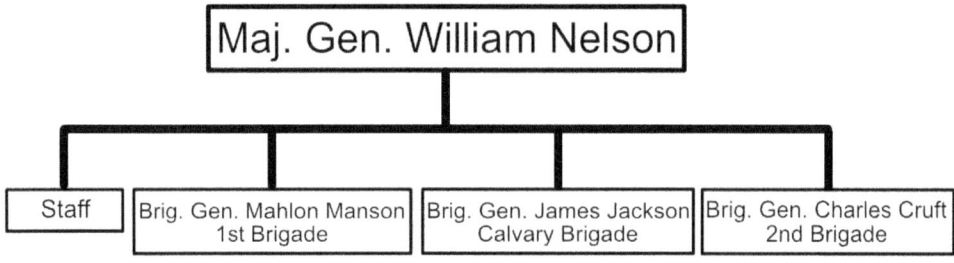

Army organization under Major General William Nelson. While this appears to be a simple organizational chart, the principal Union commanders never actually spoke directly to one another or set a plan of action for the battle. General Manson proceeded to advance toward the Confederate force on his own, General Cruft was drawn into the battle as the day proceeded, and General Nelson arrived on the battlefield too late to make a difference (courtesy Margaret A. Zimmermann).

Chapter 6. Richmond, Kentucky

the battle ended. Only after Nelson's force was destroyed did Smith's army fail to retain any real initiative. Even though he needed to bring his remaining force forward from the Cumberland Gap, and he needed to gather additional supplies for his army, Smith dispersed his men throughout the area.[12]

The Union army failed miserably after General Nelson failed to appear until later in the day and failed to communicate his location for his subordinates. General Manson marched forward on his own and failed to inform Cruft of his intentions, and no one bothered to locate the Confederate army until too late. When Nelson remained out of touch with his immediate commanders, and they in turn failed to inform him fully of events in the front lines, coordination ceased to exist. The pages of Civil War history may be searched diligently and still, it would be difficult to find another example of such egregious mismanagement and incompetence.[13]

The Confederates demonstrated a model of command unity during the battle. Smith collaborated carefully with his lieutenants. By first holding Cleburne back until Cleburne's soldiers were fully assembled on the battlefield, by feeding in reinforcements as needed, and then sending Confederate cavalry off to the Federal rear with clear orders to pursue at the close of the battle, Smith made this victory the most decisive in western Confederate history.[14]

Nelson arrived late to the battle. While not entirely to blame for this turn of events, he also failed to coordinate any helpful defensive action to hold off the Confederates and finally was wounded. Apparently, he had little or no communication with his subordinates, even after he arrived on the field of battle. This outcome suggests that Nelson rode from a distance too far removed to a position where it was too dangerous for him

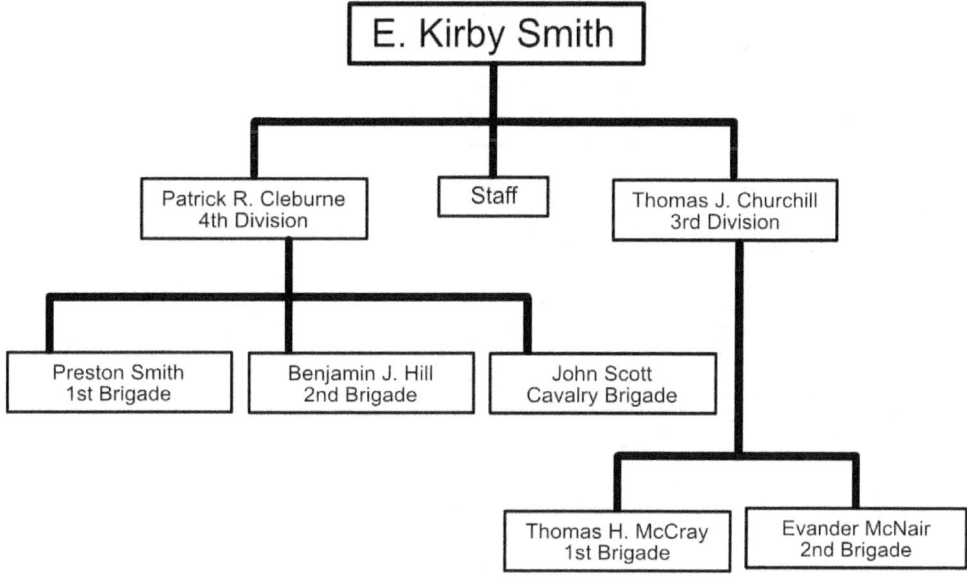

Army organization under Major General Kirby Smith. Veteran soldiers under a veteran commander (Cleburne) made all the difference. At each step of the way, the Confederate Army paused to regroup and resupply its ammunition before proceeding. After Cleburne was wounded, Kirby Smith continued the successful advance and never relinquished the initiative (courtesy Margaret A. Zimmermann).

to exercise overall command. He also lost his composure and began striking out at his own men and swearing uncontrollably. When he rode too close to the front lines, he was wounded in the thigh and forced to leave the field.[15]

The Confederate Kirby Smith, on the other hand, appeared to be exactly in the right place at the right time. He conferred early in the day with his lieutenants, he was active in bringing up reinforcements, and he directed the second and decisive attack of the day. Only at the end does McDonough suggest that he became excited himself and had to be restrained from leading the pursuit. By following his little army closely across the field of battle throughout the day, Smith appeared wherever needed to give necessary orders and direction for the Confederate effort.[16]

While not attempting to cover all aspects of supply and communication, this book has tracked issues of communication along with supplies of food and ammunition. Although not the fault of staff officers, Union generals Nelson, Manson and Cruft failed to communicate with one another on most occasions before and during the battle where some correspondence or instruction might have been useful. Most importantly for this action, the failure of the Union army to provide the appropriate ammunition for Union artillery is particularly telling. During one phase of the battle, as Union caissons finally appeared on the field, they arrived just in time to be captured by the advancing Confederates. While the original Union maneuvers might have precluded a Union victory under almost any circumstances, the fact that the Federals were forced to withdraw ten of their 12 artillery pieces before the second phase of the battle made defeat almost a certainty. Lambert writes, "The lack of adequate preparation for the field was evident in every aspect of military organization and supply."[17]

Kirby Smith's staff did their best to support his men on the march. While the entire area was short on food and water, Smith was able to supply his troops, just barely, but

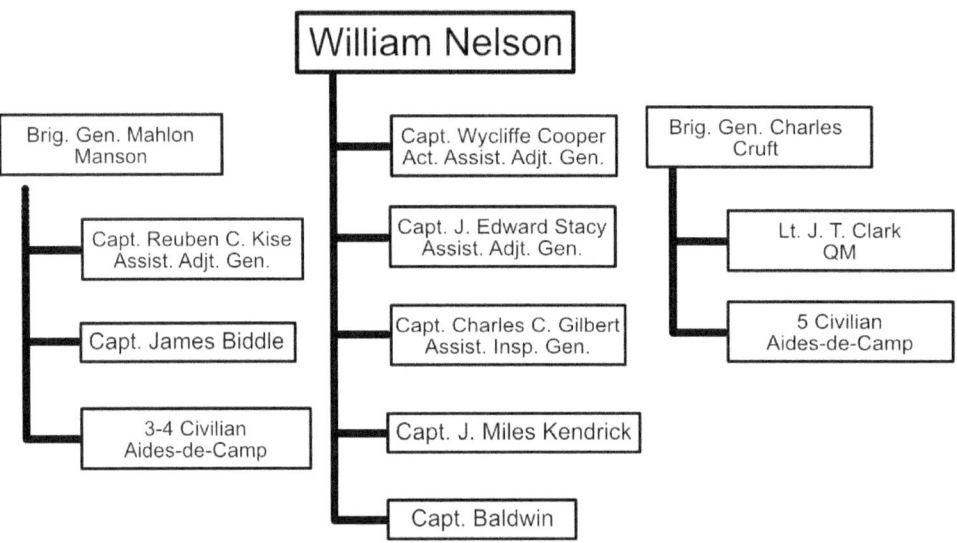

Selected Union staff officers. A host of staff officers received no clear instruction from the commanding generals, and the Union Army, including the artillery, ran short of ammunition at key moments. This diagram highlights the fragmented approach taken by Union commanders in directing the battle (courtesy Margaret A. Zimmermann).

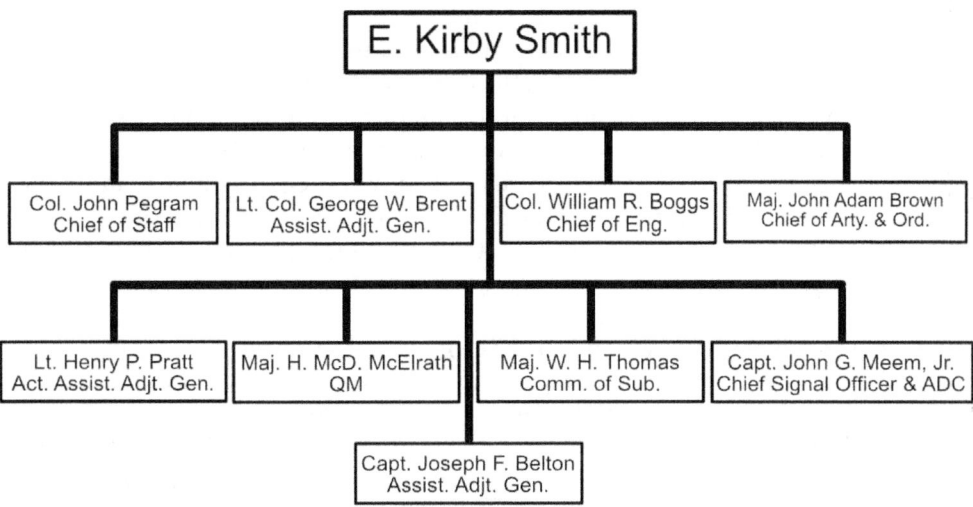

Selected Confederate staff officers. This diagram suggests that Kirby Smith developed a staff that functioned well throughout his campaign, and this staff organization compared favorably with the Union staff outlined earlier (courtesy Margaret A. Zimmermann).

during the battle his infantry and artillery were well supplied with ammunition. As the battle unfolded, he also took the time to rest his men and re-supply them with water and ammunition. Smith also did his best to acquire Federal supplies throughout his early campaign in Kentucky. As early as August 17, Colonel John Scott's cavalry captured "40 or 50 wagons." On August 23, while on the march, Confederate cavalry swallowed up 27 Union wagons. On August 25, another 15 wagons were captured and on August 28, Scott's Confederate cavalry picked up 137 wagons with supplies of all kinds. After the battle, Smith was able to seize all the remaining Union wagons, ambulances, caissons and nine artillery pieces left on the field. This formed the basis for his note to Braxton Bragg offering to share food and wagons with Bragg's force.[18]

A note on Confederate weapons seems appropriate here. At the Battle of Richmond, it appears that Cleburne's Confederates may have been armed in much the same fashion as other Confederates earlier in the year. At least one source suggests that weapons such as shotguns, squirrel rifles and flintlock muzzleloaders may still have been in use along with buck and ball muskets during the battle. At Richmond they proved very effective.[19]

The Union commanders committed only half of their available force to combat as the day opened. A second brigade under Cruft began to appear just as Manson's brigade crumbled. After both units had been mauled and retreated, the Confederates had secured an advantage in numbers. As the third and final Union defensive effort developed, the Federal force was badly outnumbered and without artillery support. Given the fact that the Union forces remained separated until later in the day, and the fact that additional artillery ammunition was not made available on the front lines, these two events probably doomed the Federal efforts. On the other hand, the Confederates used all the men they could feed into the battle. While the two forces were roughly equal at the beginning of the battle, the Confederates managed to secure a substantial advantage as the day wore on.[20]

Fortunately for the North, the loss of the battle caused no real strategic damage.

After President Davis ordered Smith to simply cooperate with Bragg, Smith chose to remain separated from him altogether. Partly because of Smith's decision as well as Bragg's reticence in pressing the matter, the Confederates suffered a strategic reverse at Perryville. By failing to entice Kentuckians to join them, the original object of the expedition also eluded the Confederates. With the outcome of this battle having such limited effects, neither side profited nor was damaged in any strategically significant fashion. Once again the six-point template shows the extent of the victory for one side and defeat for the other. In this case, the lack of a strategic outcome for the Confederates limited the extent of the victory.

Six Elements of Victory at Richmond

Richmond	Clear, Attainable Objective	Operational Initiative	Command Unity
Nelson	Not Achieved	Not Achieved	Not Achieved
Smith	Not Achieved	Achieved	Achieved
	Logistics/ Staff	*Used All Resources*	*Strategic Outcome*
Nelson	Not Achieved	Not Achieved	Not Achieved
Smith	Achieved	Achieved	Not Achieved

Against raw amateurs, Kirby Smith was able to win a decisive victory for the South with his little army. Unfortunately, he was unable to reap positive strategic results from the battle, and when he failed to join Bragg at Perryville, the two generals were forced to retreat in the face of a united Federal army.

CHAPTER 7

Perryville, Kentucky

Strategic Failures for Both Sides

As he rode into the little town of Perryville, Kentucky, on the morning of October 8, 1862, General Braxton Bragg watched a campaign that had begun in such high hopes disintegrate in front of him. Jefferson Davis had failed to appoint one theater commander for the Kentucky campaign. As a result, any hope Bragg might have held for combining up to four Confederate armies in Kentucky (his own Army of Mississippi numbered approximately 27,000 men, General Kirby Smith's Army of Kentucky contained 12,000 men, General Earl Van Dorn's force perhaps 16,000, and Humphrey Marshall's force around 3,000) failed to materialize. For a variety of reasons, Price, Van Dorn and Marshall failed to make the journey. Even Bragg himself was unable to bring more than about 16,000 men into Perryville for the day's action. Earlier, Bragg had ordered his second in command, Bishop Polk, to attack a lone Union army corps that presented itself in front of town. Instead of musketry and cannon fire that morning, however, Bragg could discern only birds chirping merrily as he rode into the village. Without strategic support and the active assistance of his subordinate, Bragg faced a bloody and frustrating day. Finally, as he sorted out the mess in front of him, he also discovered that the soldiers he hoped would lead the assault on the Union lines from the north side of Perryville remained in the town with its right flank in the air pointing to the northwest. How did this all happen?[1]

The Battles of Richmond and Perryville represent two strikingly different stories of combat for 1862. The battle at Richmond, Kentucky, provides the one clear Confederate victory for 1862 in the West. Yet while Confederates might claim an overwhelming tactical success here, they found that any strategic gain was sadly absent. At Perryville, a portion of Bragg's army won a marginal victory against a single Union corps under Buell, but here too, the Confederate withdrawal following the battle was a bitter end to a once-promising invasion. Neither Bragg nor Buell experienced success with any of the six criteria identified for this book. If all the other engagements of 1862 in the West had ended with similar frustrations on both sides, the Confederates would probably have achieved their independence. Applying these criteria to these battles provides an opportunity to review the question of how this came to be.

Corinth, Mississippi, June 15, 1862: Following the Battle of Shiloh, the combined Federal army, now under Halleck and over 100,000 strong, was in position to exert a crushing blow seemingly anywhere he chose. Halleck decided that it was time to remain in Corinth, disperse his force to protect railroad lines, and reorganize. Confederate General Basil Duke, often a fierce critic of Braxton Bragg, summarized this movement when he wrote, "As early as the 3rd of June, he [Halleck] began such dispersion of the army collected at Corinth and demonstrated his purpose of inaction, at least for the summer." As he began to do so, President Lincoln had other ideas. Leaving Grant on the Mississippi River to guard Corinth and Memphis and perhaps crack the Vicksburg nut from the north, on July 23, Lincoln named Halleck General-in-Chief of the Federal armies. Major General Don Carlos Buell remained in central Tennessee with his four divisions and was ordered south to Chattanooga. Knoxville was also named as a possible target. Before Bragg beat him to the prize, Buell moved haltingly toward Chattanooga from Nashville and even marched within about 12 miles of the city. Writing again, Basil Duke notes, "It was General Buell's policy to keep his forces widely distributed, rather than concentrated. This was expedient from the necessity of placing the troops in position where they could be most conveniently subsisted, and where by their labor the repairs of the roads could be effected." Earl Hess notes that the Deep South was logistically more difficult to manage than the states of Tennessee and Kentucky. Regardless of whether we blame Buell or understand Hess, the result was the same. Union armies were now more dispersed and unable to maintain a vigorous offensive.[2]

Short on time, manpower and supplies, the Confederates needed positive action to stay in the western war. On June 20, General Beauregard, then commanding the Army of Mississippi, traveled to a spa near Mobile, Alabama, seeking a rest and additional time to cure his physical ailments. With Albert S. Johnston

Major General Braxton Bragg. *The Century War Book* **(courtesy The Civil War Museum, Kenosha, WI).**

Major General Don Carlos Buell. *The Century War Book* **(courtesy The Civil War Museum, Kenosha, WI).**

dead and P.G.T. Beauregard ill after the battle at Shiloh and fall of Corinth, President Davis wanted new leadership immediately. Dissatisfied with Beauregard for what Davis believed was a lackluster performance and concerned that huge quantities of supplies had gone up in flames with Beauregard's botched departure from Corinth, he notified Beauregard that he was dismissed as the western theater commander. Braxton Bragg, a Mexican War veteran, hard-working Shiloh participant, and otherwise experienced soldier, was now placed in command. He had his army, but now what would he do?[3]

On June 27, Bragg assumed command of the Western Department of the Confederacy. On that same day from Tupelo, Mississippi, he wrote to Samuel Cooper in Richmond that Halleck had "divided his army.... This [Bragg's] army is rapidly improving in health and spirits. It should strike enemy's center [Buell] as soon as possible. Limited transportation presents bar to movement, but I am hopeful." Other Confederates also saw a promising strategic opportunity. As John Hunt Morgan led a cavalry force of raiders under Kirby Smith, he wrote from Kentucky, "The whole country [Kentucky] can be secured, and 25,000 to 30,000 men will join you at once." Confederate General Basil Duke, writing after the war, summarized his thoughts when he wrote the following: "In the second summer of the war, the Confederate banners, after having been driven far to the south, advanced again and were suddenly seen waving in the heart of Kentucky. If at such a time the Confederate arms had been triumphant from The Ohio [River] to the Potomac, if Northern territory had been threatened with general invasion, is there not some reason for believing that a conviction of the impossibility of subjugating the South might have taken hold of the Northern mind?"[4]

Unfortunately, Bragg would have to contend with other Confederate forces and the Richmond government itself for sustenance. From Richmond on June 28, Secretary of War Randolph confirmed Davis's telegram to Bragg, "assigning you permanently to the command of the department," and then writing, "General [E. Kirby] Smith is in great need of re-enforcements.... Aid him if you can." Smith could use another division of soldiers. The people responsible for strategy from Richmond and the generals in operational charge of matters in Tennessee were on different pages. Bragg had originally proposed to attack Buell's army in Tennessee, but as Kenneth Noe suggests, President Davis in Richmond had more aggressive ideas. He hoped that Bragg might defeat Buell in Tennessee but also move on Kentucky.[5]

On June 30, Bragg alerted Richmond to the fact that Buell, with 25,000 men now operating out of Nashville, threatened Chattanooga. Confederate General Kirby Smith, operating from Knoxville, Tennessee, and Bragg both felt they could contain the threat and mount their own offensive. They had plenty of cavalry and now they would use it. On July 14, Smith wrote to Jefferson Davis, outlining goals for cavalry raids by Morgan and Forrest: "Col. Morgan was sent by me with 1300 cavalry into Kentucky; the disorders in that state are extremely propitious for operations. Colonel Forrest with three regiments of cavalry was sent into Middle Tennessee. He will, I trust, delay Buell's movement until Bragg's columns make their appearance."[6]

He was right. Confederate cavalry caused massive disruptions to the Union forces, and Buell's threat to Chattanooga dissolved as he hunkered down to repair broken track and feed his own men. Much has been made of overwhelming Federal numbers as a determining factor in winning the Civil War, but in 1862, the South brought a larger mounted force to bear in these raids and often provided their cavalry with superlative leadership. Large numbers of Union soldiers also guarded vulnerable rail lines. It was now time for Bragg to complete his plans and set them in motion.

Bragg's advance to Perryville commenced with a series of cavalry actions that successfully screened his preparations. As the depth of the Tennessee and Cumberland Rivers fell and eliminated steamboat traffic as a result, the Union forces (particularly in Nashville) would naturally depend almost exclusively on rail traffic for logistical support. When Bragg cut that support, Buell was forced to rely on wagons. John Hunt Morgan, operating under Kirby Smith's direction, Nathan Bedford Forrest, and Bragg's own cavalry forces under General Wheeler led three columns at varying times across both Tennessee and Kentucky, and a clear pattern emerges from these raids. Absent effective Union cavalry and capable defenders, the Union rail system collapsed and forced Buell's army to rely on wagons for logistical support.[7]

On July 11, 1862, Forrest was able to capture Murfreesboro, about 30 miles away from Nashville. Finally, in one last successful burst of activity on August 10, Morgan's cavalry erupted on the Louisville and Nashville rail line north of Nashville and destroyed the Gallatin Tunnel, the only rail link from Nashville north to Kentucky. Deep in Confederate territory, Buell was without rail support, the Cumberland River was too dry for river traffic, and he was forced to use only wagons to supply his soldiers. In like manner, General Grant, in Memphis, was left with his forces scattered in small garrisons throughout Tennessee and unable to undertake offensive action. The initiative passed to the Confederates.[8]

Bragg's plan included several offensive elements. Bragg would gather his army of 27,000 men in Chattanooga and head north. With reinforcements sent from Bragg, Kirby Smith could bring 18,000 men from Knoxville west through the Cumberland Gap and unite with Bragg. Humphrey Marshall, then in western Virginia, might transfer his small force west as well. Finally, Bragg hoped to find a way to add either or both Sterling Price (16,000 men) and Earl Van Dorn (another 16,000 men) from southwest Tennessee, if they could find a way to elude and outmarch Grant. Bragg wrote hopefully, "Van Dorn and Price will advance simultaneously with us from Mississippi on West Tennessee, and I trust, we may all unite in Ohio."[9]

The challenges facing Bragg were enormous: Feed and clothe his men, train his raw recruits, find a way to move his army out of a Mississippi backwater and fend off the Federal juggernaut. At Tupelo, Mississippi, William Hardee, author of Hardee's Tactics, ably supported Bragg. Hardee would help train Bragg's men. Bishop Leonidas Polk also commanded another major portion of Bragg's force. While these changes could not overcome all the challenges facing the army after Shiloh, Bragg had addressed the most serious ones with some success.[10]

When Bragg and Edmund Kirby Smith met in the Chattanooga hotel room on July 29, they designed a joint offensive into Kentucky. Before the meeting, Bragg considered either a movement against Buell at Nashville or an offensive into Kentucky as possibilities. On August 1, Bragg wrote a more detailed description of his plan to Samuel Cooper. Smith would move on Cumberland Gap from Knoxville, and then following Smith's anticipated success against the Union General George Morgan, Bragg would move to Middle Tennessee. Together they would cut off General Buell from Louisville and reinforcements. If Buell was reinforced from Grant's army, then Van Dorn and Price could occupy West Tennessee. (Van Dorn, Price and even Humphrey Marshall would later prove unable to help Bragg.) It wasn't until August 27 that Bragg's chief ordnance officer wrote to a Captain H. McMain ordering him "to establish a depot of ordnance and ordnance stores at Dalton, Georgia." This was only one day before Bragg was to begin his campaign. Bragg also hoped that Kentucky would rise in support of the Confederacy. By July, the entire force was gathered in Chattanooga, but only after some additional delays were the requisite wagons assembled and Bragg was finally ready for action.[11]

On August 28, Bragg's army of 27,320 effective soldiers began its movement north from Chattanooga. Even at this time, logistical concerns plagued the army. On the 29th, Polk communicated with Bragg: "In consequence of the necessity of using the steamboats for foraging they [his wing of the army] have been restricted to the use of the flats in crossing the trains [wagons] [over the river]." On the same day, General Withers, one of Polk's division commanders, received this news: "General: Out of 231 four-horse wagons ordered for your division for subsistence stores I hope to get loaded and started tomorrow night 110.... Major Mason is buying and pressing mules and wagons all the time, but it is impossible to procure the requisite number (231) without waiting here at least ten days." Finally, Polk summarized his problems for Bragg: "No wagons can pass back [for forage] until all the trains connected with this command have come up." And "his teams are in too weak and starved condition. This will be two days that our animals will have been without forage. P.S. I shall not move forward tomorrow unless so instructed."[12]

Eventually Bragg acquired enough wagons to carry his ammunition and supplies north, and Doctor Quintard, a physician and minister accompanying the expedition, could write, "So we ... started off at 10 a.m. on the 28th of August, and following the route of our immense wagon train, which stretched out for miles along the road, we supposed we were all right, even though drinking water became the limiting factor at one point." After the Battle of Richmond, a victorious Kirby Smith wrote Bragg from Lexington on September 15: "We have captured 11,000 muskets ... and 2,000,000 rounds of ammunition. The other stores here are sufficient to subsist a large army for some time." On September 19, Kirby Smith began sending additional supplies to Bragg's army: "I have today ordered 50 wagons for you; 30 will be loaded with flour and hard bread." Bragg's plan was not only solid, but it also had a reasonable chance of success.[13]

Between September 7 and 10, Bragg reached and crossed the Cumberland River to enter the Bluegrass State. High heat and severe drought continued to plague his army. On September 7, his chief engineer wrote to Bragg and carefully outlined all the water "courses and Springs" to be found on the route from Sparta to Carthage, Kentucky. Now driving toward the Ohio River, Bragg advanced on Munfordville. Approaching the town, Bragg's advance force under Brigadier General James R. Chalmers attacked but failed to prevail in his assault. Then Bragg brought his entire force to bear and the Federals, under Colonel John T. Wilder, surrendered. Bragg stood between Buell and Louisville, but he hesitated. Perhaps he was waiting for Buell to recklessly attack him. Bragg's quartermaster now informed him that with the drought continuing and forage no longer available in the area picked clean by Colonel Wilder's men, the Confederate Army faced logistic ruin. Bragg decided to move on. Writing to the Adjutant General Samuel Cooper in Richmond on September 25, Bragg stated simply, "For want of provisions it was impossible for me to follow or even stay where I was, the population being nearly all hostile and the country barren and destitute." After this campaign and even after the close of the war, many Southerners viewed this decision as one of Bragg's biggest mistakes, and this action has been debated down to the present day.[14]

C.C. Gilbert, in his history of the campaign, writes: "By the 18th [of September] the movements of the Confederates showed that they were becoming uneasy. The difficulties of collecting subsistence were now pressing upon them. They had brought no supplies in their wagons, and they were now coming face to face with the problem of gathering them as they marched through a thinly inhabited country. Had General Bragg stopped to fight in the vicinity of Bowling Green [after Munfordville] with well-filled wagons, he would, in the event of a reverse, have still possessed his line of retreat; but he lacked subsistence." Buell estimated Bragg's force at 40–50,000 men and clung publicly to this story for the rest of his life. As Bragg moved northward, Buell fell behind the advancing Confederates. Forced to cut loose from his water-borne supplies, then compelled to do without railroad support, Buell took to his wagons as he marched slowly north to pursue Bragg.[15]

Earlier in the summer, General Buell had hoped to move deliberately but with insurmountable force on Chattanooga, but now that Bragg had eluded him, would Buell's objective be offensive or defensive? The Lincoln administration wanted offensive action, but Buell had other ideas, and as a result, neither Buell nor his superiors were acting in concert. First there was Chattanooga. As Buell's supply through Nashville dried up, he was reluctant to move on Chattanooga, even when urged by Lincoln and Halleck. On August 6, Halleck wrote Buell saying, "There is great dissatisfaction here at the slow movement of your army toward Chattanooga. It is feared the enemy will have time to concentrate his entire army against you." Buell responded on the 7th that Bragg might have already assembled up to 90,000 (!) men in preparation for his own offensive. Unconvinced that Buell was in peril, Halleck sent a rejoinder on August 12. "The administration is greatly dissatisfied with the slowness of your operations.… So strong is this dissatisfaction that I have several times been asked to recommend some officer to take your place." How did Don Carlos Buell find himself in this predicament?[16]

When Bragg advanced in late August, Buell, whose force was scattered in at least five locations, was uncertain of the direction of the offensive: Was Bragg moving to retake Nashville or marching north to Kentucky? What should Buell's objective be at this point: Should he move to intercept Bragg (offensive) or merely follow him north into Kentucky (defensive)? After Bragg's force of over 23,000 marched past Buell's force of over 45,000 at the end of August, one of Buell's staff members later recalled that a Confederate letter from Isham Harris, Confederate governor of Tennessee, outlining Bragg's entire plan for the invasion of Kentucky, was intercepted. Buell had been torn with indecision before this point, but now he still decided to assume a defensive posture. He would follow Bragg into Kentucky, protect Louisville, get reinforcements, and then perhaps he could face Bragg directly. After the surrender of the Federal garrison at Munfordville, Buell approached within 30 miles of Bragg's force. Patiently Buell waited for Bragg to move on. When Bragg finally did so, Buell continued to follow him quietly. The Northern newspapers, Northern governors, the Lincoln administration, and even some of his own soldiers, condemned him.[17]

With his own army on half rations, Buell faced a storm of criticism. A Confederate force only about half the size of his had stolen a march on Buell, and that general had now tamely given up all of Tennessee except for Nashville to the Confederates. Kentucky was threatened both by Bragg and by the second force under General Kirby Smith.

Bragg was calling for Kentucky to rise and join the Confederates; Northern governors in Illinois, Indiana and Ohio were frantic with worry. Buell appeared to march quietly and raggedly (men on half rations with worn shoes and uniforms) back to Louisville.[18]

As the Lincoln administration sought to replace General Buell, he arrived in Louisville, re-supplied his army and prepared to confront Bragg. But September 29 was a key date for his army's descent into chaos. General Halleck in Washington sent orders to General George Thomas to replace Buell and take charge, and the change was announced publicly, but to the embarrassment of the administration, Thomas refused the opportunity. On the same day, General Jefferson C. Davis (yes, he fought for the North) confronted General Nelson in the lobby of the Galt Hotel, Buell's headquarters, and after a fierce argument, Nelson was shot dead. Buell needed another corps commander, and he chose Charles Gilbert, a man with very limited ability, for this vital position. Buell's army proceeded to advance cautiously from Louisville to engage Bragg.[19]

Adding to Buell's problems was the size of his supply train. On October 3, 1862, Colonel Lewis Zahm of the 2nd Cavalry Brigade reported to Colonel Fry, Chief of Staff, that Buell's wagon train included 1,700 teams advancing behind Buell in three columns: "At 50 feet to the team, … it made a column of over 17 miles in length besides the brigade of [protecting] cavalry occupying nearly another mile."[20]

* * *

Writing about the battle itself, Confederate Sam Watkins said, "I was in every battle, skirmish and march that was made by the First Tennessee Regiment during the war, and I do not remember of a harder contest and more evenly fought battle than that of Perryville." Bragg understood Buell was reorganizing in Louisville preparatory to a march against him. Bragg reached Bardstown on September 23 and stayed in the area to rest and refit: "In this interval General Bragg selected a place near Bryantsville, behind Duck River, to serve as a general depot, and ordered the supplies which had been collected at Lexington to be transferred to it." While he inaugurated a Confederate governor in Kentucky and tried raising recruits, his hopes of success in Kentucky were dashed. As his army moved toward Harrodsburg, south of Frankfort, Bragg rode into the capitol to inaugurate a new governor of Kentucky, listen to speeches, and have a pleasant lunch. When shots rang out nearby, they signaled that unwelcome guests from the Union army approached! Without ceremony, Bragg left to rally his forces. But his men were scattered at that moment; for example, one force was stationed near Perryville and his supply train halted near Bryantsville. Furthermore, his cavalry was unable to give him a clear picture of Union movements. Kirby Smith announced that he believed the Federals were approaching him, while Polk thought the Union army threatened his force. Three large Federal columns were moving southeast from Louisville at the same time.[21]

On October 6, Hardee at Perryville signaled that he was facing a large Union force. General Cheatham's division from Polk's corps was available to join Hardee at Perryville, and Bragg ordered Polk there to take command. Bragg had hoped to unite his forces at Bardstown nearby, but now he was forced to change plans. By October 7, Bragg had all of Hardee's men (two divisions) in Perryville and Cheatham's division approaching as well. Cavalry reported that a Union force (under Alexander McDowell McCook) was moving in from the northwest. Bragg determined to use his entire force at Perryville to isolate what appeared to be a lone Union corps. While he galloped toward the town, he ordered Polk to attack early on October 8. If McCook's forces were assailed immediately, they might collapse under the pressure. But Polk decided that an attack was not something he wished to undertake. As Union forces marched toward Perryville in an arc from the northwest to the southwest, Polk placed his force in Perryville itself with a largely open right flank facing northwest. General Joseph Wheeler, screening the army at Perryville, failed to communicate any information to Bragg at this time. So much for unity of command![22]

October 8 dawned hot and clear. Bragg had ordered a dawn attack, but when he rode into Perryville, he discovered a new and discordant note. Everything was quiet. Bragg's plan called for a Confederate attack north and west of Perryville by Cheatham. Beginning at sunup, however, Union forces under Brigadier General Phil Sheridan approached from due west to find pools of water at Doctor's Creek, controlled by Hardee's men. Sheridan authorized a Union attack, and the battle began—at 3:15 a.m. on the southern end of the field. He wrote, "In accordance with the instructions of the general commanding I directed Col. Daniel McCook, … to occupy the heights in front of Doctor's Creek, so as to secure that water for our men." Sheridan pushed the Confederates back and occupied the creek bed, but then his corps commander, General Gilbert, ordered him to pull out of contact with the Confederates.[23]

As Buell approached Perryville, he too faced command challenges. One day prior to the battle, Buell's horse reared up and fell backward on the general. Buell was injured and moved gingerly into his command tent. Unfortunately for Buell, as he then moved from his tent to the John Dorsey house, he remained far behind the lines throughout the battle, and because of an acoustical shadow, never knew a battle was underway. In addition to the acoustical problem, as Buell dined graciously and took his three meals that day, no messenger appeared to inform him of combat. To make matters worse, his III Corps commander, Gilbert, remained at Buell's headquarters throughout the battle as well and failed to come to the aid of his embattled colleague McCook on the northern end of the battlefield. Some of Gilbert's men were also engaged during the day, but Gilbert never intervened directly.[24]

When October 8 dawned, Buell had already sent out his orders the previous evening around 8:00, and he expected everyone to move forward by 10:00 in the morning. After Buell's messengers took six and one half hours to deliver orders ten miles down the road, and once McCook finally got the orders, and gave his men both breakfast and water, another two and one half hours passed before he was ready to move. Other officers had failed to receive timely information, or they failed to communicate information to one another, with the result that Buell decided to wait in place one more day, bring all three corps together, and then attack Bragg. The heat and lack of water plagued both armies. The offensive initiative passed to Bragg.[25]

Bragg still believed it was safe for him to attack the isolated corps he believed was in his front. For his diary entry of October 8, George Brent confided, "We left Harrodsburg at 7 A.M. and reached the battlefield about 9:30 A.M. Genl Polk had formed his line of Battle crossing the Harrodsburg Pike and … It was a concave line…. The position was not so good. Genl Bragg changed the line, carrying the command of Cheatham to the extreme right…. Genl Polk's line was weak. His right inf [infantry] outflanked by the enemy." As a result, Frank Cheatham's division of Polk was pulled out from the south, rerouted to the north and prepared for combat. Cheatham wrote,

Chapter 7. Perryville, Kentucky

"On my arrival at Perryville, late in the night, I [was] placed ... in line of battle on the extreme left of his [Hardee's] corps to the left and beyond Perryville.... About 10 o'clock on the 8th, I was ordered by General Polk to move my division from the extreme left [south end] to the extreme right [north end] of the Confederate lines.... I had my division, three brigades, formed in column of brigades." Cheatham would attack first, then Hardee, *en echelon*, and the Confederates hoped to destroy McCook's isolated (they thought) corps.[26]

In an angry confrontation with Polk, Bragg ordered him forward along with Hardee—toward McCook, north and west of town. Damage to the relationship of the commanding officers had been done once again. Earlier in the campaign, Bragg had made several negative comments about Polk that became known to him, and now Polk's unsatisfactory performance near Perryville, at least in Bragg's mind, doomed their relationship. While Bragg insisted on a drive to crush McCook's corps, this was not his day. Neither was October 8 Buell's day as Buell had hoped to attack Bragg, and his plans were also doomed to failure.

Major General Leonidas Polk. Bragg and Polk never worked well together. Although Polk was a West Point graduate, he resigned from the army shortly after graduation and served the church instead. Bragg had little respect for Polk and made his opinion known publicly. Consequently, Polk never became part of a Confederate team under Bragg (Library of Congress).

Time marched on as Cheatham marched north. Detecting Union forces even farther north and west than originally thought, Cheatham's men were re-routed once more. By 1:30 p.m., after dispatching aides in a vain attempt to find out what was going on, Bragg rode forward himself from the Crawford House onto the battlefield to press the attack.[27]

While the original assault on McCook did not destroy him, enormous pressure was brought to bear on his force, and McCook had his hands full. Cheatham sent in one brigade under Brigadier General Daniel Donelson and a second under Brigadier General Alexander Stewart. These initial attacks faltered. Again, we hear from General Cheatham: "As soon as I had put Donelson and Stewart in position, I in person moved Maney's brigade by the right flank several hundred yards ... where he advanced up the bluff upon what I understand to have been Jackson's brigade, which formed the left of McCook's corps. Before dark, my command had possession of all the ground twelve or fifteen hundred yards to the front of where we found the enemy and held it until withdrawn during the night by orders of General Bragg." Confederate M.B. M'Farland comments further: "In the battle of Perryville, our regiment, the 9th Tennessee Infantry, and the other regiments of the brigade, were confronting, in close proximity, Jackson's eight-piece brass battery [under Lieutenant Parsons]. Captain Malone, ordered: 'Up and charge the battery.' We sprang to the attack, he leading and we charged and took the whole battery, killing General Jackson and routing the infantry supporting the battery." On the Union side, however, the defense was maintained stubbornly. Once the original position fell, the Union forces retreated and took up a second line. During another costly effort, fresh attacks across cornfields and uphill failed again. Union Surgeon Solon Marks comments: "It was found that the enemy had massed on our extreme left, and were preparing to charge on [our] batteries, but fortunately the First and Twenty-first Wisconsin and Seventy-ninth Pennsylvania Regiments were supporting those batteries, and poured such volleys into the advancing foe that they soon retreated with thinned ranks. Again and again, they charged on those guns to meet the same fate." Later he noted, "Our men were pushed back by force and numbers, but contested every inch of ground."[28]

General Alexander McCook. McCook would turn in disappointing performances both here and at Stones River. Surprised by the Confederate onslaught at Perryville, McCook would repeat this performance in future battles (Library of Congress).

Then it was Hardee's turn. While Hardee had also been ordered to attack *en echelon*, the maneuver was simply too complicated for the Confederates to deliver to perfection. At 3:00 p.m. his first attack under Brigadier General Patton Anderson went in. As an interim division commander, Anderson began his first large-scale action. Two of his brigades, operating separately, both failed in their assaults. The first brigade simply attacked independently. Brigadier General Simon Bolivar Buckner's division now struck along with another one of Anderson's brigades, also operating independently; these piecemeal attacks were repulsed with

General William Hardee. While General Hardee fought effectively for the South throughout the war, he, too, came to resent Bragg's leadership, and the Confederates failed to develop the necessary teamwork to succeed in battle (courtesy The Civil War Museum, Kenosha, WI).

Chapter 7. Perryville, Kentucky

heavy casualties on both sides. Another attack by General Cleburne's brigade followed, and finally another brigade attack led by Confederate General Johnson broke through. Between 3:45 and 4:30 p.m., additional Confederate attacks pressed McCook's Union corps back almost a mile in some places, but it had not been destroyed. Bragg himself rode forward again to observe at one point but McCook still held. Bragg's attempt at an *echelon* attack (Cheatham first, then Hardee) failed.[29]

South of McCook stood Gilbert's corps, but McCook's messages to Gilbert for help went unanswered. Late in the afternoon, McCook's messengers finally rode all the way back to Buell's headquarters but no one there, including Gilbert, believed that a battle was in progress. Much time was wasted as messengers crisscrossed the battlefield, but for most of the afternoon, McCook had to do without any assistance. Even General Thomas L. Crittenden to the far south under Thomas could have joined the battle, but he was without orders to do so. Buell would not issue orders, corps commanders would not act on their own, and no one communicated with anyone else. Finally, around 4:00 p.m., a member of McCook's staff appeared at Buell's headquarters and pleaded for help, and finally Buell ordered two brigades from Gilbert's III Corps to assist. These brigades helped stabilize the situation and by 6:30 in the evening, the battle became a bloody stalemate. While Bragg's forces failed to capture the battlefield, they badly damaged McCook's corps. Dr. Quintard summarized the entire day of battle when he wrote, "With the advance of Cheatham's division the battle of Perryville began in good earnest. Generals Cleburne and Bushrod Johnson supported General Cheatham, but it was not long before the whole Confederate line from right to left was advancing steadily, driving back the enemy. It was a fierce struggle." Michael Fitch in the 21st Wisconsin Infantry wrote, "[At Perryville] the large percentage of killed compared with the number wounded shows how close and deadly the fighting was."[30]

By 4:30 in the afternoon as the battle continued, both sides were running out of ammunition and energy. Earlier, around

Attack *En Echelon*

This tactical maneuver was designed to begin a series of attacks on an enemy position. Units would advance from right to left (1–4) at slightly different times or left to right. Enemy reserves could be drawn off to weaken one side or the other of the defending force. General Bragg used this tactic at Perryville and Stones River. General Van Dorn attempted the same maneuver at Corinth (courtesy Margaret A. Zimmermann).

3:00 p.m., Wheeler finally informed Bragg that he faced a very strong force south of town (Crittenden's II Corps), and Bragg now knew that he faced most of Buell's army. While Bragg's attacks continued beyond 3:30 p.m., his men were exhausted and largely out of ammunition. John Headley, a Confederate soldier in the battle, writes: "But our whole army was driving the enemy to the right and left and General Adams ordered a charge.... The enemy gave way in disorder, ... They were in a drove now like a flock of sheep, and we could not miss such a dense crowd.... The battle, in the mean while, was a perfect storm the sound of musketry never ceasing and the roar of cannon rolling without a break.... The sun had gone down and there was a lull all along the line." With both sides suffering major casualties and running out of ammunition, and with darkness falling around 4:30 p.m., the battle gradually petered out. Had the Confederates pushed through Union resistance and captured Federal supply wagons at the Dixville Crossroads, the battle might have ended far more favorably for them, but they were unable to make the final thrust and achieve success.[31]

Gathering his commanders at Crawford House around 9:00 p.m., Bragg ordered his force to disengage and then retreat. The army's supplies were at Camp Dick Robinson 19 miles away, and he knew Buell was present in full force. Buell gathered with some of his officers for supper at his headquarters, but it was only much later that he fully realized that a major battle had taken place without his knowledge or presence. Between two and three in the morning of October 9, the Confederate retreat got underway. Buell, finally waking to full knowledge of the situation, sent out plans for an attack, but as the sun rose, the Federals discovered that the Confederates were gone. The Union pursuit was slow and inept. Now at last, Kirby Smith united his force with Bragg, and together they made a slow and painful return to Chattanooga. In his report Bragg wrote, "For want of

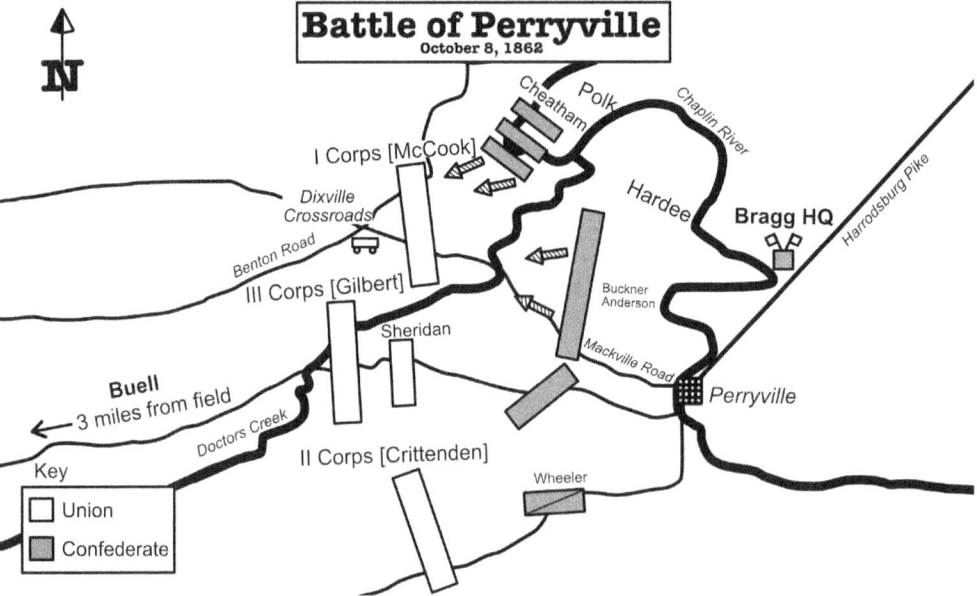

After Bragg reached Perryville, he ordered General Cheatham to march to the north end of the battlefield and begin the attack. Thus delayed, the Confederates fell just short of capturing the vital Dixville Crossroads before darkness ended the battle (courtesy Margaret A. Zimmermann).

provisions it was impossible for me to follow or even stay where I was. Kentucky would not rise. We have 15,000 stand of arms and no one to use them." The Confederate invasion of Kentucky was over. Few men joined the Confederate Army, Smith failed to unite with Bragg until the action ended, and Marshall, Van Dorn and Price were never available. The criticism of Bragg was not all one-sided. Ignoring the battle entirely, Dr. Quintard sides with Bragg in stating, "And it being clear that the two great objects of our invasion of Kentucky—the evacuation of Nashville [by the Union] and the inducement of Kentucky to join the Confederacy—would fail, Bragg decided only to gain time to effect a retreat with his spoils."[32]

Bragg was heavily criticized throughout the Confederacy for his retreat, but he had done the right thing. While he had prepared a sound plan for an offensive into Kentucky, he remained unsupported by Richmond, his peers and his immediate subordinates. In the end, the North held all of Kentucky and most of Tennessee and the war moved back to Nashville.[33]

* * *

For the North, Don Carlos Buell struggled with his superiors, including Lincoln, to define and secure a clear objective. Following George Thomas's victory at Mill Springs, Lincoln, and McClellan, as general in chief, originally wanted Buell to move east toward Knoxville. Buell marched south to Nashville instead. After reinforcing Grant at Shiloh, Buell's Army of the Cumberland was combined with the huge force assembled by Halleck, and together they all marched on Corinth. Following the siege and fall of Corinth, Buell was left on his own as Halleck travelled east to take the reins as general in chief. Buell was told to hold Nashville, hold the Cumberland Gap in East Tennessee, and attack Chattanooga, all simultaneously. His entire force was tied to a single railroad line for sustenance. Then he was faced with Confederate cavalry raids on his supply line, Kirby Smith's invasion of Kentucky, and Braxton Bragg's offensive through Tennessee. What to do? He decided to send one subordinate, William Nelson, to Kentucky while he marched after Bragg. He decided not to attack Bragg outside of Munfordville, but he did march to Louisville to defend Kentucky against both Bragg and Kirby Smith. But what was his true objective? Defeat Bragg and Smith while destroying their armies, or simply push them out of Kentucky? In the meantime, Northern governors were crying for help, he was faced with new recruits expected to fight within days of their enlistment, and the Lincoln government wanted quick action. In the area of strategic support, Buell received limited assistance. After failing to vigorously pursue and attack Bragg and just as he reached Louisville, Buell was fired by the Lincoln administration. Then he was reinstated shortly thereafter. Buell knew that the Lincoln administration did not support his original command decisions, and he was finally and permanently relieved after failing to pursue Bragg following the Battle of Perryville.

Buell repeatedly clashed with Lincoln and Halleck over his true objective. Why did he assume a defensive posture? Horace Fisher offers one explanation: "Our policy was clearly to act as an army of observation, marching parallel to Bragg's main Army and keeping in constant touch but avoiding a general engagement; that as we marched north, we should constantly be gaining strength by picking up our bridge and train guards, averaging 300 men to the mile,—the relative condition of the two Armies would be reversed, so that a Confederate victory would be fruitless to them and an indecisive battle would compel Bragg to retreat into Tennessee."[34]

After his arrival in St. Louis, Buell's posture changed immediately as he gathered his force for offensive action, but after the battle, his pursuit of Bragg lagged once again. After Buell's removal, the Buell Commission was formed to examine the failed campaign. During one hearing, George Thomas supplied the correct and necessary professional objective for Buell's army: "The object was to overtake the enemy, fight, and destroy him if possible, either by a disastrous defeat or by cutting off his retreat if he succeeded in getting off in considerable force from the battle-field." From Washington at the moment of crisis, Halleck supplied another goad for Buell. On September 27, he wrote, "It is hoped that your force is now strong enough to enable you to immediately advance upon the enemy. There are many reasons—some of them personal to yourself—why there should be as little delay as possible." Then Buell marched off to Perryville. But after the battle when everyone felt Buell should move decisively against Bragg, the pursuit lagged. Bragg moved first toward Knoxville and Buell moved ever so slowly back to Nashville. Buell's objectives throughout the campaign were attainable, but he never conformed to the hopes of President Lincoln, Halleck, his own subordinates, and many of his own men.[35]

For the South, Bragg received little support from the Richmond government as well. No one was ever placed in complete charge during the Kentucky campaign. Generals Kirby Smith, Humphrey Marshall, Sterling Price and Earl Van Dorn all operated separately. Even when Bragg sought to feed his army, he was forced to negotiate with Richmond over supplies that Lee wanted for his own army in Virginia. Bragg was not even allowed to select his own quartermaster: "Gen. Orders just received appoint Lieut Col. Eugene E. Lann (?) as Chief Q. Master to this command.... I must express my surprise and regret at this action of the Department without consulting me." Bragg expressed the "utter inefficiency" of this officer. Bragg also faced conflicting objectives. Should he unite with Kirby Smith in Tennessee, attack Buell and retake Nashville? But when Smith headed northwest toward Lexington, Kentucky, Bragg followed in Kentucky as well. Could he combine forces with Smith in Kentucky to defeat Buell outside of Louisville? But Bragg and Smith failed to unite their forces in Kentucky either. How long should Bragg wait in Kentucky trying to recruit Kentuckians for the Confederacy? He carried arms for 15,000 men but attracted only about 1,500. As Buell advanced with a much larger army, Bragg faced another choice: Should he attack a portion of Buell's army and then retreat, or should he simply leave Kentucky altogether? By leaving Bragg with limited authority, the Richmond government failed to support him. Then he chose a new objective, the defeat of one portion of Buell's army, and he failed to achieve this goal either.[36]

Within the "Principles of War," the idea of seizing, retaining and exploiting the initiative holds an important place. In the case of Perryville, neither side achieved this goal. Buell was slow to take the initiative in the summer of 1862 and even slower to pursue Bragg. When he finally reached Louisville in September, Buell moved forward to confront Bragg, but then after failing to achieve success at Perryville, Buell was even slower in following Bragg back into Tennessee. Buell held the initiative by virtue of his superior numbers, but he never used this opportunity to his advantage. His performance failed to secure the clear objective set for him and he failed to seize the initiative as well.

Bragg was equally unsuccessful in holding onto the initiative. Once he marched aggressively into Kentucky, he was unable to unite the force necessary to confront Buell, and in saving his army from destruction, was compelled to retreat. Bragg may have had an offensive opportunity after the Union surrender at Munfordville. If Kirby Smith had joined Bragg, they might have successfully confronted Buell at this point. Bragg also had an opportunity to march directly on Louisville, but he chose to march north and join Kirby Smith instead. Their failure to cooperate, and their misplaced faith in Kentuckian zeal for the rebellion, were decisive in leading to a Confederate withdrawal from Kentucky. While Buell technically retained operational initiative at the close of the battle, he simply failed to do more than recover lost territory.[37]

Neither commander achieved unity of command through the constructive support from their immediate subordinates. For the North, Buell was not well supported by his commanders. Acrimonious relations at Buell's headquarters led, in part, to the death of General Nelson. Buell made a poor choice in appointing Gilbert to corps command. Buell failed to secure the active support of George Thomas at critical moments during the campaign. More importantly, however, no other Union commander on the battlefield moved to assist McCook's corps. The *New York Times* correspondent summarized this acidly when he wrote, "While our forces were so fiercely fighting the enemy's superior numbers, the divisions of Gens. Smith, Van Cleve and Ward, of Crittenden's Corps, with their artillery, were standing in line of battle not more than two miles off.... Our subordinate officers and men were panting to be led forward. Yet there they stood for four mortal hours, in hearing of the guns that were answering the enemy, and theirs that were mowing down our comrades. We had overtaken the enemy, but were held back, and not allowed to fight."[38]

Buell was obviously not active at all during the battle, and as a result, he failed to achieve any unity of command within his army. As he never moved from the Dorsey House and apparently encouraged Gilbert, his II Corps commander, to stay with him for much of the day, Buell was detached from the battle and remained completely ineffective as a leader. It is unclear whether he was physically incapacitated on the day of battle or not, but his behavior at Perryville was substantially different from his demonstrated

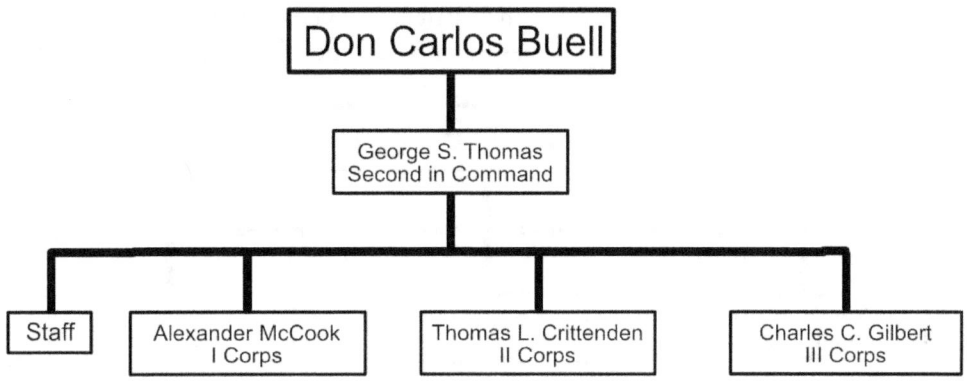

Army organization under Major General Don Carlos Buell. While both McCook and Gilbert were West Point graduates and Regular Army men, Crittenden had served during the Mexican War in a volunteer capacity and had a background of political activity. George Thomas (with his Regular Army experience) spent much of his time during the Perryville campaign with Crittenden (courtesy Margaret A. Zimmermann).

actions earlier at Shiloh. Yet he was able to rise from his bed the next day and begin moving about once more. Michael Fitch, a Union soldier from Wisconsin's 21st Volunteer Infantry, summarized his feelings this way: "I think that if the Union forces had been skillfully handled, the rebel army should have been crushed. But instead, Bragg got away.... General Buell seemed to lack the most essential quality of a commander. He hesitated. He was not prompt and aggressive ... he ought to have been up to the front with his staff ... the fact is, a general who does not crush the enemy when thus in his power, is not competent."[39]

Bragg failed utterly to achieve unity of command for his Confederates as General Polk marched to his own drummer. Polk was ordered to attack on October 8 at Perryville, and he refused to do so. Then once Bragg was on the scene, Polk delayed his troop movements until Bragg was forced to intervene personally and initiate the assault on McCook's corps. Not only did Bragg find fault with Polk's unwillingness to obey orders, but he also struggled with Polk's choice of tactics. Hardee, while not as obstinate as Polk, certainly did Bragg no favors by supporting Polk at critical times before and after the battle. Wheeler failed to inform Bragg that he faced a major Union force until very late in the day of battle. John Headley summarized the feelings of many Confederates toward Bragg when he wrote, after the retreat to Murfreesboro, "our exalted ideas in the beginning, of generals commanding armies had changed. The commanders at Fort Donelson, Beauregard at Shiloh, and Bragg and Smith in Kentucky had taxed our patience."[40]

Braxton Bragg's decisions and some of his actions brought on a storm of criticism, and while he was not solely to blame for Confederate misfortunes, he failed to mitigate them. Marcus Toney, a Confederate private at the time, wrote after the battle describing Bragg's decision to halt and personally inaugurate the new governor of Kentucky: "[We] went into camp at Bardstown, Ky. While here Governor Hawes was inaugurated General Bragg issued a proclamation calling on the Kentuckians to flock to his standard and fired a few volleys from the artillery, which broke all the glass in the windows of the courthouse.... General Buell's army marched to Louisville; and while we were playing soldier and living high in the blue grass country and losing men, General Buell was recruiting his army."[41]

Bragg was more active than Buell during the battle. While he had a headquarters location, at times he also moved about the battlefield. Even though several historians have criticized his behavior later at Stones River, and some of his decisions were clearly

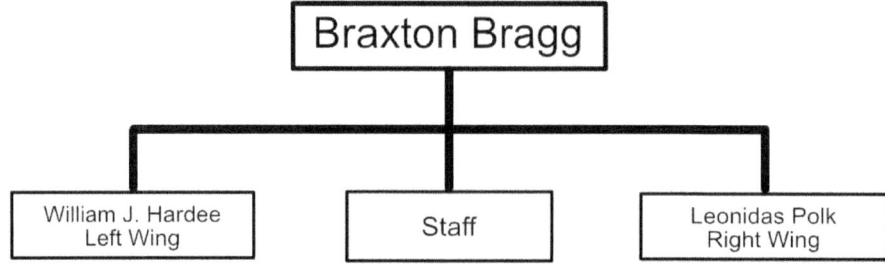

Confederate Army organization under Major General Braxton Bragg. Bragg's failure to win the effective support of his subordinates contributed to more than one Confederate defeat in 1862. By delaying the Confederate attack until almost 2:00 in the afternoon, Polk's tardy responses and Benjamin Cheatham's long march to the northern edge of the battlefield almost ensured that the sun would set before a decision could be reached on the battlefield (courtesy Margaret A. Zimmermann).

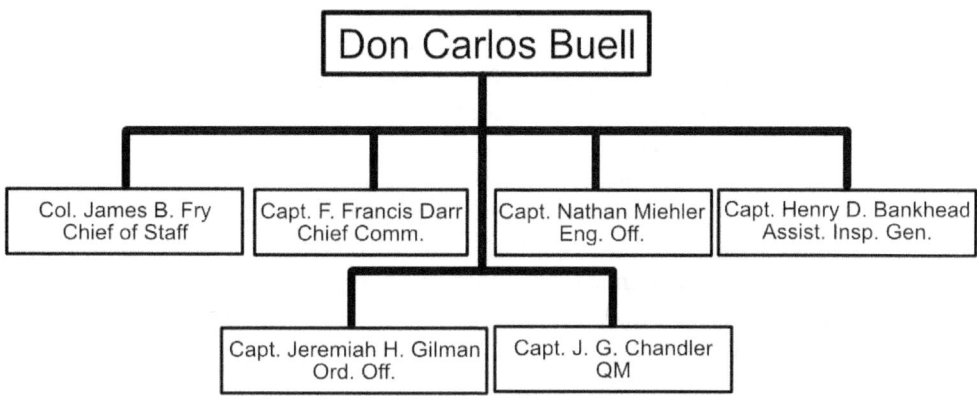

Selected Union staff officers under Don Carlos Buell. Buell's staff at Perryville included five West Pointers with extensive experience. As Buell himself remained absent from the battlefield, his staff was also removed from any effective role they might have played in the battle. Messages were also delayed on the fateful day, and corps commanders found themselves fighting in a vacuum (courtesy Margaret A. Zimmermann).

questionable, he was actively in command during this battle. Sam Watkins also commented after the battle, "Now citizen let me tell you what you never heard before, and that is this—there were many men with the rank and pay of General, who were not Generals; ... 'I know today many a private who would have made a good General.'"[42]

Northern logistical support was also sadly lacking at this stage of the war. The Northerners had not discovered a way to protect rail lines around Nashville, and this failure led in part to the dispersion of Northern forces and the end of Buell's offensive movements. As Bragg took advantage of Buell's discomfiture, Buell's men marched on half rations, barefoot and in rags on their way to Louisville. On the battlefield, the situation worsened. Combat began with a Union search for water! At Perryville, some Northern regiments ran out of ammunition as some ordnance officers failed to supply Union regiments as needed. Ordnance wagons apparently did not accompany all the men closely enough to provide additional ammunition. Buell's staff system did not function well at all. The simple inability of his staff officers to deliver messages accounted in large measure for the continuing Union confusion throughout the battle.

Despite many challenges, Bragg was able to mount a respectable campaign. His commissary and quartermaster departments did their best to supply him with the necessary food and clothing for his campaign. Hypolite Oladowski, as Bragg's chief ordnance officer throughout his tenure with the Army of Tennessee, turned in a remarkable performance supplying arms and ammunition for the fledgling force. In fact, careful study of Bragg's staff from this time reveals a few hard-working and efficient men such as George Brent, former Virginia attorney, and Oladowski. It is interesting to note, however, that staff officers and Oladowski often were the butt of crude jokes by soldiers who viewed them as noncombatant busybodies. Sam Watkins even takes the time to give him the name "Sheneral Owleydowsky." Bragg identified Oladowski as early as their days in New Orleans when this Polish immigrant with military experience was working in a New Orleans U.S. ordnance depot. Already in August Oladowski wrote forcefully to a Major W.R. Hunt: "I ... expect great help from you. Maybe I am too hasty to trouble you again; but supplies for

60,000 infantry, 5000 cavalry and 100 pieces of field pieces are not so easy to collect, ... My idea to prosecute this war is, never to rest, never to delay, from morning to night.... I trust in God, but keep powder dry and plenty of it.... Respectfully, H. OLADOWSKI. P.S.—Please order your clerk to spell my name correctly." Unfortunately, however, the heroic efforts of some staff officers were negated through the poor performance of others.[43]

In one egregious case for the Confederates, the ordnance officer for Brigadier General Brown (under Hardee) was reported drunk and failed to bring up any ammunition at all. But the lack of ammunition plagued the entire Confederate force by this time late in the day. Bragg's trains remained on the road to Harrodsburg, and it should be noted that Bragg's main supply base was located at Camp Dick Robinson, 19 miles down the road. While this problem plagued the Union forces as well, they had shorter distances to travel as they were often forced to retreat in the direction of the ordnance wagons. As a result, Bragg's staff proved incapable of providing the necessary food and ammunition to the Confederate army.[44]

Including one more logistical note, Sam Watkins commented as the Confederate army retreated, "From Perryville we went to Camp Dick Robinson and drew three days' rations, and then set fire to and destroyed all those great deposits of army stores which would have supplied the South for a year. We ate those rations and commenced our retreat out of Kentucky with empty haversacks and still emptier stomachs."[45] It appears that while some plunder was obtained and then moved south, other supplies were indeed destroyed. As a result, it is difficult to simply declare a decision in this area. Staff efforts seemed to compete with decisions made by the commanding generals, and of all the wagons Bragg collected, only about 300 made the return journey from Kentucky. Bragg's staff worked diligently to support him and yet their efforts did not seem to pay off when appropriate supplies needed to be obtained, retained or distributed.[46]

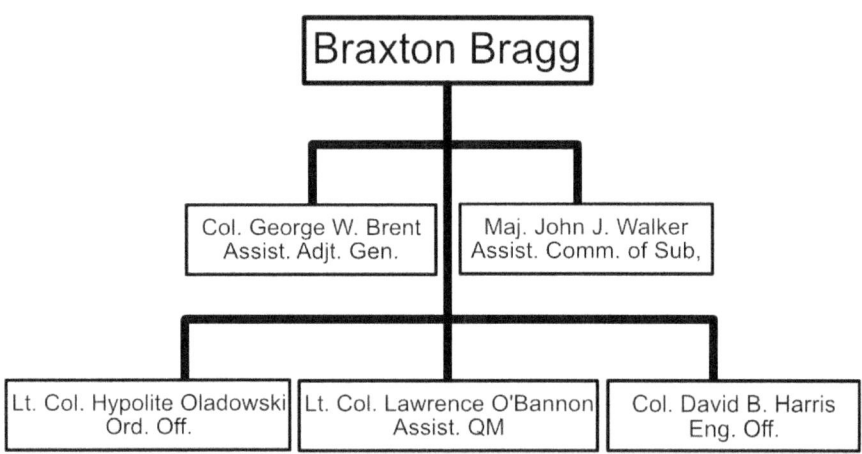

Selected Confederate staff officers under Bragg. As Bragg acted for a time as his own chief of staff, he was engrossed in the details of managing his army and appeared to leave several of the early battlefield decisions to his immediate subordinates. Before Bragg's physical appearance at Perryville, he left both Polk and Hardee to make their own way. Also on his staff, for example, George Brent helped as best he could, but with only legal and political experience in civilian life, he did not possess the expertise that Bragg apparently sought. See note 46 (courtesy Margaret A. Zimmermann).

Unaware that a battle was in progress, Buell failed utterly to commit his reserves and therefore did not use resources available to him. Further, his subordinates never seemed to move units larger than brigades from one part of the field to another for combat purposes. Both Gilbert and Rousseau failed to support McCook when it counted. At the height of the battle, Buell committed only two brigades to reinforce McCook, but prior to this time, his other corps commanders failed to provide any support at all. While we might make allowances for the technical argument that Buell did not specifically order reinforcements in a timely fashion, there is also the idea that, when a battle is in progress, good soldiers should "march to the sound of the guns."[47]

On the other hand, Bragg committed most of his resources to combat during the course of the day. It can be said, however, that by committing his soldiers *en echelon*, he was, in essence, attacking in piecemeal fashion, and therefore failing to commit his entire force. Contrasting Bragg's unsuccessful assaults, largely by brigade, to those of General Longstreet, for instance, who committed his entire corps at one time for combat, the western Confederates had not yet learned how to mass guns or infantry at critical points along the battle line. The larger question of why Bragg and Smith failed to unite their separate forces and commit more men to a unified attack on Buell's army also hovers in the background. While Bragg committed his available soldiers on the actual battlefield, he and Smith failed to unite their forces until after the battle ended and failed to use the resources available for them.

While Bragg could argue that his Confederate forces had achieved a tactical victory by pushing McCook's corps to the rear, he failed to drive the Union army off the field or achieve positive strategic results. Buell, for his part, failed completely in his attempt to bring Bragg to battle on favorable terms for the Union or even to challenge the Confederates tactically for much of the time. Even the *New York Times* commented, "Now, you ask was the battle of the 8th a victory? We answer that we do not regard it so. Our fearful loss of life the loss of a battery, and the lives of so many valuable officers, is hardly remunerated by the capture of a barren hill, the killing of five or six hundred wretched rebels, and the taking of a lot of guns and prisoners.... We were certainly not defeated; [and] the enemy was forced to abandon their positions." When the engagement ended, it was Bragg who needed to retreat from Kentucky. By default, Buell recovered the state for the Union and most of Tennessee as well. Strategically, the North was successful in recovering territory it had already secured once before. That he could have accomplished so much more never seemed to have crossed Buell's mind. As he relieved Buell, though, Lincoln was certainly aware of chances missed. For the Confederates, when the six criteria are applied to this engagement, even the minor tactical success at Perryville would result in diminishing Confederate hopes in the West. At Perryville, as with the engagements described earlier, the six factors discussed form a template that helps the student of history better understand why one side or the other was victorious and also shows the extent of the victory or defeat. At Perryville both sides failed to achieve success with any of the six factors associated with victory conditions.[48]

What lessons can be drawn from this campaign in which both sides failed to succeed? Neither commander lacked personal courage. Both commanders were intelligent, well-trained professionals. Yet neither commander experienced success in any of the six areas that have been examined for this study. Neither commander was able to set a clear goal for his campaign. Neither commander was able to harness the efforts of his immediate subordinates or staff to provide the collaboration or support needed for victory and, partly as a result, failed to take the necessary initiative to achieve victory. Neither commander found himself in a position to employ the full strength of his own army, and neither commander could exploit any possible success (strategic or tactical) that might have occurred before, during or after the battle. Leadership, teamwork, and an effective logistical foundation were lacking for both sides. Yet each of these six elements played a significant role in defining the reasons for failure during this engagement. The same can be said in defining the reasons for either triumph or defeat for other battles described in the book.

Six Elements of Victory at Perryville

Perryville	Clear, Attainable Objective	Operational Initiative	Command Unity
Buell	Not Achieved	Not Achieved	Not Achieved
Bragg	Not Achieved	Not Achieved	Not Achieved
	Logistics/Staff	Used All Resources	Strategic Outcome
Buell	Not Achieved	Not Achieved	Not Achieved
Bragg	Not Achieved	Not Achieved	Not Achieved

Neither Buell nor Bragg achieved any of the six objectives that victorious commanders sought. While Bragg's forces advanced during the day of battle, by the next morning, it was clear to Bragg that he must retreat.

Chapter 8

Corinth

The Confederacy Strikes Back

Now that the Union had been victorious at Shiloh, they faced a major question: what to do next? Corinth was the next critical and logical objective. By capturing Corinth, the North would damage Confederate rail transportation across the entire Confederacy. Almost all the military leaders on both sides believed that this was a critical junction. As one example, in his memoirs, U.S. Grant stated, "We ought to have seized it immediately," after Donelson, Nashville or Shiloh, but "it should have been taken, without delay, ... after the battle of Shiloh." But Grant was not in charge of the strategic decision-making at this point. Believing that Grant had perhaps been surprised at Shiloh, Major General Henry W. Halleck arrived there on April 11 and took personal control of the Army of the Tennessee. Then suspecting that the Confederates were still strong in numbers, Halleck consolidated no less than three Union armies totaling 100,000 men for his move. Capturing the railroad junction of Corinth, Mississippi, was his goal. He combined the Army of the Tennessee, now placed under the command of General Thomas, with the Army of the Ohio, coming off the Shiloh battlefield under Buell. Together with the Army of the Mississippi, fresh from its victory at Island No. 10 under Pope, Halleck believed that Corinth was well within his reach.[1]

As Halleck planned his advance on Corinth, Beauregard sought to improve the defenses of the town. Reinforcements came in regularly, the largest group from the Trans-Mississippi force of General Earl Van Dorn. Approximately 15,000 of his men arrived by rail from Memphis, and other reinforcements appeared to help Beauregard recoup his losses from Shiloh. Eventually raising a force of over 50,000 men, he rebuilt the Army of the Mississippi. Along with gratefully accepting reinforcements, Beauregard also laid out and prepared over seven miles of entrenchments for defense of the town.[2]

Once he united all three Union armies, Halleck reorganized them under his personal command and began planning for a methodical march toward Corinth. He needed to march 22 miles to accomplish his goal, and between April 27 and 29, his huge army began its march. Halleck's force needed to use several roads and found that the actual road network was poor; these dirt traces passed through deep woods, over numerous hills and, in many cases, swollen creeks along the way. Assuming the Confederate forces under Major General P.G.T. Beauregard were still extremely dangerous, Halleck proceeded with great caution. One of Halleck's warnings to Grant before Shiloh included a comment that Grant should entrench his position. Approaching Corinth and leaving nothing to chance, Halleck entrenched regularly. March and dig were the orders of the day. Following these instructions, the three armies found that they could move two to three miles per day before entrenching. Halleck would not be surprised. The Confederates, easily outnumbered by more than three to one, fell back on Corinth. Beauregard was not about to risk his badly damaged army in a fight against overwhelming odds.[3]

As the Union army neared the town, however, Corinth became an entrenched fortress, and prepared for a siege. Whenever possible, citizens fled the vicinity, and Beauregard called in reinforcements wherever they could be found. Finally, the Union armies completed their inexorable march and confronted the Confederates. In the meantime, Beauregard and the Confederates found an even more deadly enemy at work against them. While they assembled in Corinth, the Southerners found that the water supply was inadequate and foul. In the heavy heat of the day, operating with reduced rations, and laboring under very poor conditions, the Confederate army began to sicken and wither away. The casualty count, men dead, deserted or ill rivaled the battlefield damage caused by the Battle of Shiloh. For example, on May 15, General Beauregard's field return showed an aggregate total of 110,845 men present and absent, but only 51,218 present. Between May 7 and 9, the combined Union force reached the outer edges of Beauregard's defenses, and he began a stout resistance. At one point on May 9, Beauregard even sent out a sizeable force to attack the Federal troops. The skirmish at Farmington was hard-fought, and Halleck immediately slowed the pace of the Union advance. Between May 10 and May 28, the Union armies skirmished with Confederates, or in a few cases,

Major General William S. Rosecrans (Library of Congress).

Major General Earl Van Dorn (courtesy The Civil War Museum, Kenosha, WI).

advanced only at a snail's pace. Yet the Union offensive proceeded and the Confederates soon found themselves besieged in Corinth. The Union army also brought heavy siege artillery forward. Under these circumstances, Beauregard summoned his immediate subordinates to a council of war on May 25, 1862. Their advice: retreat! On May 25, General Hardee wrote to Beauregard, "The only remaining question is, whether the place should be evacuated before, or after, or during its defense.... I think the evacuation, if it be determined upon, should be made before the enemy opens fire.... I think our situation critical, and whatever is resolved on should be carried promptly into execution." Beauregard's response on May 26: "I concur fully in the above views, and already all needful preparations are being made for a proper and prompt evacuation of this place."[4]

Quietly assembling his forces for a silent and secret evacuation, Beauregard selected Tupelo, Mississippi, 45 miles to the south, as his next base. As early as May 24, General Orders specified that "All newspaper and other correspondents are hereby ordered to leave this post by the first train." Far enough away from the advancing Union forces, he hoped to rebuild the Confederate army and at least hold the Deep South, Mississippi, Alabama and parts of Louisiana. Moving stealthily, the Confederates abandoned Corinth on the 29th and 30th of May. The Union forces occupied the town immediately after. Then Halleck faced his next question: where to advance now? Vicksburg in Mississippi was attractive as well as Chattanooga, Tennessee, gateway to Georgia.[5]

General Halleck, however, decided that to feed his force and protect his supply lines, he must disperse, and beginning on June 10, he reorganized his three armies once again and began moving them in several different directions. This strategic mistake may have unnecessarily prolonged the war in the West for another full year. The Federal offensive movements had largely ended. For the time being, Vicksburg in Mississippi and Chattanooga in Tennessee were safe. As the Union army strengthened the defenses of Corinth, there was a feeling in the North that the war was progressing very well in the West. But Corinth would become a Confederate target once more when, later in the year, another army threatened Union control in northern Mississippi.[6]

Throughout the summer of 1862, the Confederacy tried its best to regain the initiative in the West. When Major General Henry Halleck carefully dissipated the enormous Union host, his men were scattered throughout the South, guarding railroad lines, important towns, bridges and other geographic areas that required vigilant attention. Now operating under Halleck's command, Don Carlos Buell also struggled to supply his far-flung divisions. But as Martin Van Creveld explained in *Supplying War*, an army on the march could forage for its supplies, keeping in mind that horses consumed about ten times as much food per capita as men did. Once that army halted to occupy territory or besiege defenders, however, they consumed food and forage, and the matter of supply became far more difficult. Unfortunately for the North, Buell was not overly aggressive in his movements, and the Federal advance ground to a halt.[7]

Closer to the Mississippi River, General U.S. Grant also faced the challenge of both holding territory and giving up the initiative to the rebel raiders as he attempted to consolidate gains made in his department. That left the Confederates with options. General Bragg reasoned that he could move his army to Chattanooga and then head north to Kentucky, dragging Buell along in pursuit. If he could unite his forces with those of Kirby Smith and any other available Confederate forces, he might undo the earlier Union gains of the spring. Two other small Confederate armies became part of this master plan as well. Earl Van Dorn had crossed the Mississippi River from Arkansas with the remains of his defeated army of Arkansans after the Battle of Pea Ridge, and Sterling Price brought his force from Missouri. If they operated separately, they could still be an annoyance for Grant, but they could not prevent him from reinforcing Buell when necessary. If they operated together, however, they could be formidable opponents. What would they do?

As Bragg's Confederates confronted Buell in Kentucky, Bragg expected Price and Van Dorn to operate together in keeping Grant occupied. If Van Dorn and Price were fortunate, they might even be able to join Bragg whenever Grant tried to reinforce Buell. Price saw the virtue in this and encouraged Van Dorn to join forces with him. At first Van Dorn was reluctant to do so, and Tim Smith suggests that neither Van Dorn nor Price were very close. After Van Dorn delayed on September 19, however, orders arrived from Jefferson Davis placing Van Dorn in charge of the combined force. The idea of command unity did not seem to be a priority on anyone's agenda at the time. While Price's force of two divisions, called the Army of the West, reported through Price to Van Dorn, Mansfield Lovell's division, sometimes termed the Army of West Tennessee, reported directly to Van Dorn. As paroled prisoners from Fort Donelson and Island No. 10 were released and Price suggested that they wait for additional reinforcements, Van Dorn disagreed and ordered an immediate advance on Corinth. Before uniting with Van Dorn, however, on September 19, Price marched through the town of Iuka. Hoping to catch the Confederates between two forces, Grant ordered an army under William Rosecrans and another three divisions under Major General E.O.C. Ord to converge on Price. When the two forces failed to act in concert, a bloody but inconclusive engagement ensued, and Price escaped.[8]

Van Dorn and Price now joined forces. Van Dorn took charge and decided that his attack on the rail center at Corinth would prove a distraction to Grant and would shield Bragg from facing forces other than those of Buell. While Van Dorn marched at first from the south, he determined that the Federals would expect an attack from that direction, and therefore an attack on the northern side of Corinth was his best option. He knew that the town was protected from attack by the trenches and gun positions that Beauregard had prepared earlier in the year, but he was not fully aware of everything else the North had done to secure the town. On the Union side, Grant ordered Rosecrans into Corinth to defend it against any Confederate assault. Following his graduation from West Point, Rosecrans became a skilled engineer and inventor. Although he did not serve in the Mexican War, he volunteered his services in the Civil War and won two skirmishes in western Virginia. Rosecrans was happy to oblige and quickly rode over to Corinth. While he wasn't certain at first that the town was indeed the next rebel target, he felt confident that he could repel any attack if necessary. On October 2, Earl Van Dorn approached Corinth with about 22,000 men while Rosecrans attempted to gather his forces of 21,147. The stage was set for the next action in the west.[9]

After uniting with Price, Van Dorn's force was an interesting, and at times quarrelsome, amalgam of men. In fact, Price's chief of staff, Thomas Snead, averred he would not serve under Van Dorn, and Price needed to smooth over this problem. Price's immediate subordinates, Brigadier General Dabney H. Maury and Brigadier General Louis Hébert, both commanded divisions under him. Maury had served as Van Dorn's chief of staff and adjutant general during the Pea Ridge campaign, and Hébert graduated third in his class of 1845 from West Point. In effect, both division generals were new commanders under Price, and Hébert would not perform well at Corinth. Now reassigned following the debacle at New Orleans, Mansfield Lovell was Van Dorn's other subordinate. His questionable performance during the battle harmed the Confederates as well. In essence, two of the three division commanders under Van Dorn would not support him effectively during the battle. As Sterling Price would be wounded once again, Van Dorn would struggle with his subordinates.[10]

On the Union side, Grant and Rosecrans had come to dislike one another after Rosecrans had failed to pursue and destroy Price earlier that summer at Iuka, but Grant was still determined to support the Federal effort to hold Corinth and destroy Van Dorn's army. Rosecrans's immediate subordinates offered a wide range of ability and experience. Within his Army of the Mississippi, Brigadier General David S. Stanley commanded one of his divisions and Brigadier General Charles S. Hamilton another. The Army of West Tennessee provided two divisions, one commanded by Brigadier General Thomas A. Davies and the other division under Brigadier General Thomas J. McKean. While all of these men had West Point preparation, this was not a distinguished group. For the Battle of Corinth, however, these men would provide competent and helpful support for Rosecrans as he struggled to hold the town.[11]

As Rosecrans's chief of staff, Colonel Arthur C. Ducat joined him before the battle. Later accounts of the battle are filled with examples of his energy and bravery as he traveled the battlefield on Rosecrans's behalf, bringing orders and explanations for movements that occasionally baffled Rosecrans's generals. As he moved to defend Corinth, Rosecrans made other improvements that included the establishment of a corps of spies, scouts, and the addition of topographical engineers for each of his brigades. Brigadier General Charles Hamilton commanded this group, and they were responsible for providing mapping information and news concerning enemy movements in the area.[12]

Following the unsuccessful battle at Pea Ridge, Sterling Price appointed a new group of staff officers to support his efforts, and Van Dorn himself now brought his own men. After the battle at Corinth, however, controversy broke out concerning Van Dorn's efforts to supply his army on the march, and these heated disagreements led to a court of inquiry afterward. While Van Dorn was cleared of wrongdoing, this war of words continued long after the battle.[13]

* * *

Eleven miles northwest of Corinth is the smaller town of Chewalla. As Van Dorn made his way into camp there on the evening of October 2, he brought his commanders together to inform them that Corinth was the object of his campaign. His subordinates immediately registered their concern and, in some cases, downright opposition. Maury favored Van Dorn's plan. Lovell suggested attacking elsewhere. Price counseled delay. By resting at Chewalla, Van Dorn also made it clear to the Federals that Corinth was his goal as well. Rosecrans gathered his forces in Corinth as Van Dorn approached. During the night of October 2, Rosecrans ordered his men to be ready for combat at sunrise on October 3, and he gave each division commander verbal orders before battle. In short, he expected to meet the Confederates outside of Corinth, hold them at bay for as long as possible, and then gradually draw them into the heavier defense lines closer to the town. Stanley's post-war speech in New York spelled out the details: "Accordingly, five redoubts were constructed, practically covering the approaches to Corinth from all directions. These redoubts had 4 guns each, 24 pounders, old style, or Parrotts of 20-pound caliber. The regulars of the 1st U.S. Infantry were drilled to work these guns." Unfortunately for the Confederates, while Van Dorn had excellent maps for his approach march, he neglected to gather information on the recently constructed Union fortifications in Corinth. He also failed to conduct a careful reconnaissance of the Union lines for combat on October 3 or October 4. Why no one bothered to contact Confederate sympathizers in the area about this large-scale Union construction project is unknown, but it does not speak well for Van Dorn's campaign preparations.[14]

Leaving Chewalla on the morning of October 3, the Confederates advanced on Corinth. Three miles short of their goal, they were forced to deploy and fight the first of several actions against the Federal forces that day. Van Dorn ordered an attack by *echelon*. Lovell's division advanced on Van Dorn's right against McKean's division of Union soldiers. After McKean's men buckled quickly, Lovell halted to reorganize. On Van Dorn's left, Brigadier General Hébert under Price then pressed ahead against General Davies of the Union, forcing him back. General Davies ordered up artillery, and they gained time for the Union defenders to regroup. During the course of the afternoon, the Union army successfully retreated to a series of defensive positions.[15]

Following his success against several Federal defensive positions, Van Dorn believed the battle was won, but the Union forces had simply retreated repeatedly to their next defensive location. Between 2:00 and 3:00 in the afternoon, the Confederates attacked once again in piecemeal fashion, and, failing to dislodge the Union soldiers completely, continued their attacks with Van Dorn riding among his men to encourage them. Without any fresh reserves to reinforce their gains, however, the Confederate attacks petered out. A shell fragment wounded Price, his men were exhausted, hungry and thirsty, and he believed they could attack no longer. Lovell continued to halt in place.[16]

On the other side of the hill, Rosecrans ordered General Stanley's division and other reinforcements to the front. The Confederates had marched 11 miles into combat under a 90°F sun without any available water and no food, and they simply ran out of steam as they pressed through three separate Union lines of defense. Once the firing stopped, both Union and Confederate armies loaded wagons with barrels of water and delivered them to the front lines. Then the Union forces quietly retired to their inner line, still largely unknown to the Confederates. Van Dorn suggested one more assault to finish the job, but Sterling Price demurred. Once again the Confederate leadership disagreed about the right course of action. There would be no final assault, and the Union forces would have the entire night to strengthen their defenses. In the meantime, food and water for the Confederates went largely missing.[17]

Overnight, both sides attempted to prepare for the next day's combat. Van Dorn planned a final blow by launching an attack from his left first. He, too, was enamored of an *echelon* attack. Accordingly, he sent orders to Brigadier General Hébert to lead the attack on October 4 once the artillery signaled the start of the attack. Smith, however, believes that the courier never reached Hébert, and that he stopped to sleep on the way. Then Maury's division would join in from his right side, and finally Lovell would attack. Time to launch the attack was set for 4:00 a.m. On the Union side, African Americans worked the night through to dig more extensive defense lines. Rosecrans met with his division commanders and outlined his plan of defense for the next day.[18]

Promptly at 4:00 a.m., three Confederate batteries opened fire, but then silence reigned over the battlefield. Where was Hébert? Three hours elapsed and Van Dorn,

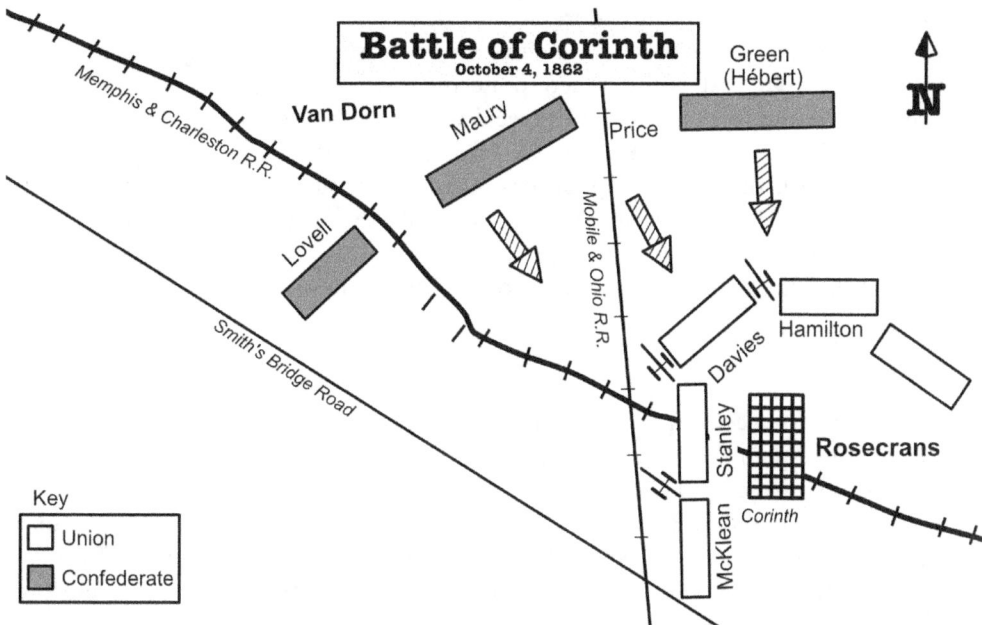

After achieving some success a day earlier, on October 4, Van Dorn attempted to attack Union forces in their defensive positions in front of Corinth. His *en echelon* attack failed when General Hébert reported in ill and delayed the entire battle. While Generals Green and Maury delivered spirited attacks that penetrated the town of Corinth itself, General Lovell failed to advance. Rosecrans was able to recover the initiative and defeat the Confederates (courtesy Margaret A. Zimmermann).

Price, Maury and Lovell all waited. As Van Dorn wrote after the battle, "Daylight came and there was no attack on the left. A staff officer was sent to Hébert to inquire the cause. That officer could not be found. Another messenger was sent and a third; and about 7 o'clock General Hébert came to my headquarters and reported sick." Now Brigadier General Green replaced him, but Green had no idea what he was supposed to do, and the Confederates experienced further delays while he received his instructions. On the Union side, Rosecrans could only ride his lines wondering what was happening. Finally, around 9:30 a.m., the Confederates attacked. As Price wrote later in his report, "It was after 9 o'clock when my line became generally and furiously engaged.... Here, as in previous actions, my artillery could not be effectively brought into action and but few of the guns were engaged." Against heavy Union resistance, the Confederates under Green forced the Federals back and, for a time, portions of two of Maury's brigades even penetrated the town of Corinth. Now at this point, a fatal hitch ruined the Confederate chances for victory.[19]

Away on the Confederate right flank, Brigadier General Mansfield Lovell, of New Orleans fame, was expected to attack. But Lovell's attack did not occur. Lovell sent Brigadier General John Bowen forward with his brigade to test the Union lines, but under heavy fire, and with Lovell's other brigades watching, Bowen was quickly forced back. Over one-third of the Confederate army sat quietly while the battle raged around them and then concluded around 11:00 a.m.. Out of touch and out of sight from much of the field, Van Dorn remained close to Price at the center of his line. In the meantime, Rosecrans rode among his front lines to steady his men and make defensive adjustments along with his division commanders. Rosecrans recovered Corinth, counterattacks drove the Confederates back, and Union reinforcements filled their lines once more.[20]

Without food or rest, without reconnoitering the Union defenses at Corinth, without the effective support of two of his three division commanders (Hébert and Lovell), Van Dorn's efforts were fruitless. On the other hand, Rosecrans had a clear plan for defending Corinth and had the support of his immediate subordinates. After the battle, Rosecrans did not launch a pursuit of Van Dorn until the next day, but the actual battle was a clear Union victory. Van Dorn was ruined as an army commander, and Rosecrans found himself promoted to lead the Army of the Cumberland in its next journey south.

* * *

Operating from central and western Mississippi, Generals Earl Van Dorn and Sterling Price united their forces with Corinth as their objective. If their attack on the town proved successful, General Grant and the Army of the Tennessee would be prevented from reinforcing General Buell. Buell, in his turn, would face Braxton Bragg alone as Bragg sought either to retake Nashville or the entire state of Kentucky. If Van Dorn failed to capture Corinth and break the rail connections there, Grant could reinforce Buell and march toward Vicksburg, Mississippi. Van Dorn's original assignment was both clear and attainable. He also had a formidable force to use in capturing the town. Once October 3 had passed, however, Van Dorn had a very limited chance to win the battle. Without a thorough reconnaissance and facing a determined defender behind secure fortifications, his task was not realistic.

As Rosecrans took command at Corinth, he was ordered to defend it against Van Dorn. If he achieved a major victory, he had the chance to destroy the only significant Confederate force preventing Grant from capturing Vicksburg in 1862. He, too, had a clear objective, and with the secure and improving defense lines around the town, Rosecrans could anticipate combat optimistically.

For the Union, strategic support came from U.S. Grant. While he was not physically located near Rosecrans, he was timely in sending reinforcements to assist in the defense of Corinth and the pursuit of the Confederates after the battle ended. On the Southern side, Jefferson Davis directed Van Dorn and Price to unite their forces so that their combined army would be a more formidable opponent for the North. On September 29, Secretary of War Randolph, writing to Van Dorn, ordered the following: "Assume forthwith the command of all the troops left in Mississippi, including General Price's column." In both cases, Rosecrans and Van Dorn received the backing of their superior officers or their political leadership. Rosecrans was somewhat prickly when dealing with Grant, and he appeared slow to pursue after the battle but then was adamant that he be allowed to chase Van Dorn. By then, Grant wanted the pursuit to cease, and Rosecrans confronted his superior by writing, "I most deeply dissent from your views." Nevertheless, Rosecrans had received additional reinforcements from Grant and received support throughout the battle.[21]

Grant as the theater commander and Rosecrans, his immediate subordinate, were forced to remain on the defensive as the Confederates regained the initiative. Would Van Dorn and Price unite their forces? Once they did, where would they go? Would they move toward Iuka or Corinth or strike at some other target? Grant was also ordered to send reinforcements to other theaters while this was being determined. Once Corinth became a more obvious target, Grant could send Rosecrans there and begin funneling additional troops in his direction as well. It wasn't until the close of the battle for Corinth that Rosecrans was able to fully exploit the initiative, and then his pursuit was neither vigorous nor successful.

While Van Dorn retained the overall initiative almost all of the way through the two days of combat at Corinth, Rosecrans regained it during the second day of battle on October 4 and began his pursuit following the battle. Van Dorn's attempts at an *echelon* attack once again demonstrated the potential pitfalls of such a complicated maneuver.

For the most part, the four Union division commanders responded effectively to Confederate attacks and helped Rosecrans achieve unity of command. Confederates broke through Union lines and even battled in the town of Corinth for a time, but the Union division commanders were active and often quite successful in carrying out Rosecrans's orders. On occasion, Rosecrans criticized his own generals. For example, he recorded this comment about the men serving General Davies the first day: "The enemy have ... come in on the Chewalla Road and have driven in Davies' left. Our men did not act or fight well." At other times, his subordinates fired back at him. General Davies responded heatedly to Rosecrans: "I would most respectfully ask, for the benefit of the service and for the honor of the division, that if you have changed your opinions you would as publicly give a refutation to these charges." Then Rosecrans relented: "General, In reply to your note just received, I will say that having read your ... report, ... I am satisfied they fought nobly the first day."[22]

While these examples indicate that the effectiveness of Rosecrans's generals was occasionally in question, they still fought well. At other times, his communications lacked clarity and his subordinates were completely confused. In response to one Rosecrans message, General Hamilton responded on October 3, "Respectfully returned. I cannot understand it." In the end, however, despite some confusion, Rosecrans's officers

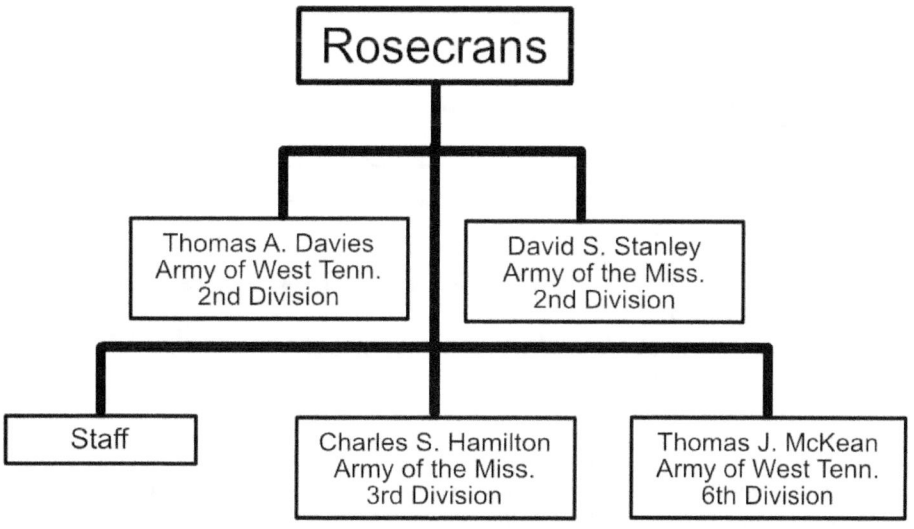

Army organization under Major General William S. Rosecrans. All four of the division commanders serving under Rosecrans were West Point regulars. While the relationships were not always friendly, these men responded professionally and worked together for victory at Corinth (courtesy Margaret A. Zimmermann).

acted for the common good and gave their best efforts to win the battle. General Davies, for example, was seen actively engaged in commanding his soldiers personally in support of the Union defense. Smith suggests that he was observed at one point stopping panicking artillery horses and again leading his men personally in combat. General Stanley was also observed encouraging individual regiments in combat. The same could not be said for several of Van Dorn's officers, particularly on October 4.[23]

By making a maximum effort, Rosecrans and his subordinates successfully defended Corinth, and Rosecrans along with his staff moved actively about the field to ensure victory. Rosecrans has been accused of peripatetic behaviors on the battlefield and sending orders that confused his subordinates. While this may have been true to a certain extent, it might be possible that historians who accuse him of these behaviors are trying to set the stage for his later mistake on the Chickamauga battlefield. Rosecrans confused at least one of his commanders and insulted at least two others in the heat of the moment, but his actions did not in themselves lead to any disasters. Rosecrans moved actively around the battlefield and provided hands-on direction for the combat that followed on the second day as well. The supportive actions of Rosecrans's staff and immediate subordinates seemed to compensate for any of his errors. Also, he met with all his senior officers each night of the action.

The Confederates labored with their command structure. While reporting to Earl Van Dorn, Sterling Price directly commanded both Martin Green and Dabney Maury. Mansfield Lovell's division was not technically connected to Price's Army of the West. Nevertheless, when Van Dorn issued orders, they traveled through Sterling Price and then went to all three division commanders. Green took over from Hébert who called in sick, and his division was hours late in assaulting the Union lines. Except for Bowen's brigade, Lovell's division saw little action on October 4. In the end, two out of three

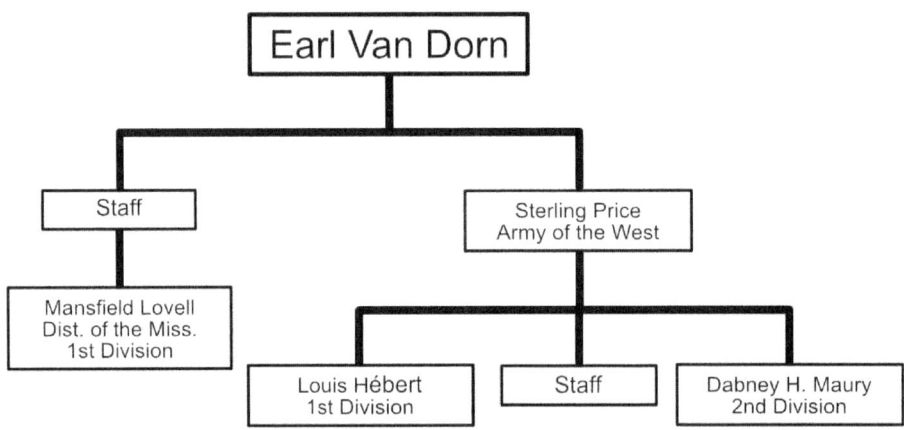

Army organization under Major General Earl Van Dorn. Apart from Sterling Price, Van Dorn's organization at Corinth included three West Point graduates who had served with the Regular Army. Unfortunately, they brought unnecessary baggage with them that would complicate relationships. Price and Van Dorn functioned together professionally but without warmth. Lovell had been in charge when New Orleans fell to the Union and did not work well with Van Dorn. Hébert had already served under Van Dorn at Pea Ridge and had not performed well there. Maury had served as Van Dorn's chief of staff, but now assumed a combat command (courtesy Margaret A. Zimmermann).

division commanders either failed to move promptly or didn't attack at all. Van Dorn was not well served by his immediate subordinates. Sterling Price was on the field of battle, but his role in the second day's action was limited. Van Dorn himself seemed to manage the battle by sending messengers on October 4. This appears to repeat the pattern set at Pea Ridge where coordination among the immediate subordinates was missing.

Did Van Dorn avail himself of engineer officers and other members of his command staff to plan carefully for his attack on the second day at Corinth, October 4? Did he have the full agreement of most of his officers for that attack? A Court of Inquiry was held to seek the answers to those questions, and a summary of the first part of that inquiry is enlightening. Beginning on November 10, 1862, the Court met to determine whether Brigadier General John Bowen's charges against General Earl Van Dorn had merit. At the close of the Corinth battle, Bowen was obviously upset after observing Van Dorn's actions during the Corinth campaign. His concerns strike at the heart of any study of generalship and the ability of commanding officers to work effectively with their subordinates.

Arguing that Van Dorn failed to make a proper reconnaissance of the Union lines, that he failed to properly supply his own army, that he failed to attack the Union inner works until the second day of battle, and that he failed to properly care for his wounded men, Bowen preferred a series of charges. Witnesses were called and Van Dorn was ultimately cleared of any wrongdoing but, divided into two areas, the charges warrant closer attention.

First to General Bowen and the issue of command unity. Born in 1830, Bowen graduated from West Point in 1853. After the Civil War broke out, he commanded an infantry regiment (1st Missouri) at Columbus, Kentucky, under General Polk and then a brigade under John C. Breckinridge at Shiloh where he was seriously wounded. Wiley Sword said of him at Shiloh: "Throughout the army, Bowen was known as a highly competent fighter." Philip Thomas Tucker in his biography gives numerous details supporting Bowen's competency and leadership abilities. By October of 1862, Bowen ably commanded a brigade within the division of General Mansfield Lovell. What had General Van Dorn done that so angered John Bowen?[24]

Brigadier General Albert Rust: "I think without doubt it would have been better to have continued the attack the same evening [October 3rd, rather than waiting overnight].... I was furnished with no plan or chart of the defenses the enemy had constructed and was not informed orally of their position and character."[25]

General Bowen testified: "On the night of the 3d, ... Gen. Lovell summoned Generals Villepique, Rust and myself to his headquarters for orders. He showed us a crude sketch of the works supposed to be in front of us; also in front of General Price's wing.... Maj. Manning M. Kimmel, [Assistant Adjutant General] of General Van Dorn's staff, who was also present, expressed his ignorance of the same fact to me. The works that were indicated for us to take in the morning were alleged to be one or two redoubts with three guns each ... probabilities expressed ... being in favor of but one of these."[26]

"In the morning (the 4th) we found a large and formidable force in our front, showing that, whether they had an accession of troops in the town or not, their left wing at least had been materially strengthened. No orders were given to me notifying me or the troops of Lovell's division of these re-enforcements. No preparation seemed to have been made to ascertain their character or extent."[27]

"My brigade was detailed as the storming party.... Satisfied that the information of the night before was not correct, I ordered up the Watson Battery, of my brigade.... It was responded to by eight or ten heavy guns from the front and as many from either flank from two other forts, which I had not before seen. I should think there were about twenty-four pieces of heavy artillery instead of three."[28]

When General Price was called to testify, he answered as follows: "Question. Should the attack have been continued? [After October 3.] Answer. Not necessarily. But: We could probably have won if General Lovell's troops had come up in time on the 3rd. They didn't."

Aside from the inquiry, there was one more question of command unity. On October 4, General Hébert failed to attack on time and then declared himself too ill to continue. The entire battle was delayed for over three hours. His second in command, General Green, needed to be brought up to speed on the attack plans before proceeding. Then General Lovell failed to launch his attack and also turned in a poor performance. He sent Brigadier General Bowen forward to reconnoiter the strong Union position, but then he recalled Bowen and failed to attack at all. This was clearly not a performance that exemplified command unity.[29]

For the most part, the four Union division commanders responded effectively to Confederate attacks. Confederates broke through Union lines and even battled in the town of Corinth for a time, but the division commanders were active and often quite successful in carrying out Rosecrans's orders. Price actively supported Van Dorn, but the division commanders failed to perform their assigned tasks.

As for Van Dorn, he was active on the field with his men during the early course of battle. For Van Dorn, neither he nor his staff responded adequately to the failure of his two division commanders to carry out his orders on the second day, and he remained ineffective in leading them. Tim Smith also suggests that he failed to provide for additional ammunition when needed and failed to undertake an earlier reconnaissance of the Union defenses. Perhaps both Van Dorn and Rosecrans were guilty of less than stellar performances during the two days of battle; however, it can also be suggested that because Rosecrans received more effective support from his staff and subordinates, the Union triumphed.

Rosecrans's staff officers were particularly active in moving about the battlefield, providing logistical support, and communicating their commander's orders. Lieutenant Colonel Ducat is lauded for his services at numerous times during the two days of combat, and he braved death on several occasions to deliver orders and provide clarity for the divisional generals working under Rosecrans. Several entries in the Official Records bear witness to the fact that additional water was provided in wagons, additional ammunition was provided as needed, and the staff organized the preparation of trenches and fortifications on the night of October 3. For example, Captain Frederick Prime had previously served as General Grant's chief engineer. He took the responsibility of laying out the fortifications of Corinth for General Rosecrans and the Union Army. These stout defenses were key in delaying the Confederate attack, and the artillery placed inside these works played havoc with the Confederate offensive. In general, these staff officers provided energetic and professional support for Rosecrans throughout the time of crisis at Corinth.[30]

When the Court of Inquiry opened and General Bowen outlined his charges, the area of logistics, particularly with an emphasis on food and ammunition, received a

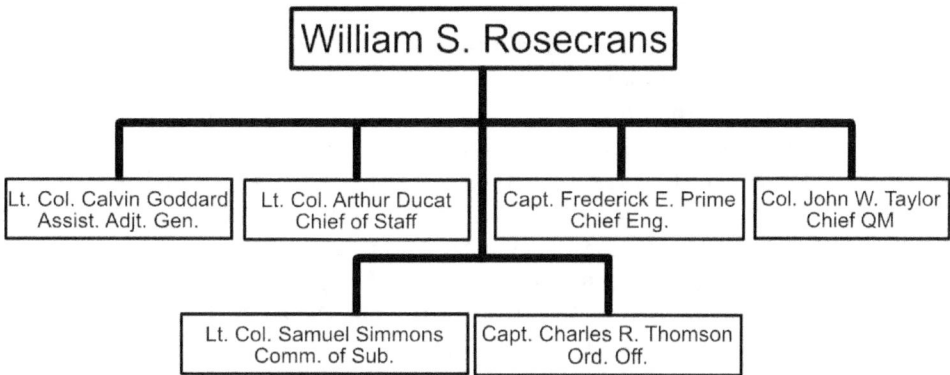

Selected Union staff officers. Of Rosecrans's staff officers, all had served in pre-war engineering or business. Captain Prime was a West Point graduate. All performed their duties effectively (courtesy Margaret A. Zimmermann).

great deal of attention. After his initial testimony, additional statements were made by a variety of officers that supported or refuted Bowen's claims. In the end, several telling comments described a failure of logistical support for the army. Brigadier General Albert Rust, commanding a brigade in Lovell's division, testified as follows: With respect to supplies, "in Lovell's division the attack [w]as made on the morning [of] the 3d, when the men had not more than one-half day's rations in their haversacks and their supply train too far in the rear to reach them in time to prepare more."[31]

On the retreat after the battle, Bowen commented: "Lovell's division [including Bowen's brigade] arrived at Holly Springs on the 10th. Having no wagons I could draw nothing that night (from the commissary).... I had not transportation enough for a commissary train, and had to divide ... rations issued immediately among regiments."[32]

Even when Sterling Price, a staunch supporter of Van Dorn, was questioned about supplies, he testified as follows: "Question. Was your supply of commissary stores insufficient when you marched to the attack? Answer. Yes, and I so informed General Van Dorn. General Van Dorn replied to me that he would spare me some rations on the way to Corinth, which he did." They came from Bowen's brigade.

When Colonel Robert Lowry of the Sixth Mississippi Regiment was questioned, the exchange went as follows: "Question. Were your supplies of commissary stores insufficient when you marched to Corinth or on the retreat? Answer. Yes, they were insufficient. Question. After encamping at Holly Springs, did your troops suffer by reason of the non-issue of breadstuffs? Answer. After getting encamped at Coldwater, (near Holly Springs) we were without rations, I think, for two days."[33]

A question arose about the treatment of the wounded after the battle. If an army is to remain whole and morale steady, assisting wounded soldiers is naturally a staff function that needs attention. A Lieutenant L.B. Hutchinson took the stand and testified that at least one train was used by wounded soldiers on the retreat, wounds went undressed, neither blankets nor food were available, doctors and medical personnel were not present, and no one appeared to be in charge.[34]

Captain L.H. Kennerly, 1st Missouri, confirmed that wounded were crowded in railroad cars, and wounded soldiers informed him they were without provisions. He was told that there was no surgeon, officer, nurse or attendant with them.[35]

When General Van Dorn's staff was questioned about supplies or wounded soldiers, however, their responses, not surprisingly, were quite different. Brigadier General D.H. Maury, Van Dorn's chief of staff before Corinth, and Major Edward Dillon, chief commissary of the army, both swore under oath that they had plenty of rations available. Maury blamed subordinate officers for not attending to their duties and thereby creating the issue. Dr. J.W.C. Smith, surgeon for the provisional army, stated that the wounded were properly cared for: "His [Van Dorn's] attention has been prompt and kind."[36]

The evidence, summarized, strongly suggests that under Van Dorn's leadership, his staff, their objections notwithstanding, failed to make appropriate provisions for supplying the army on its march to Corinth and its retreat after the battle. Even though Brigadier General Bowen's allegations were dismissed, he had made a very strong case that all was not well in Van Dorn's army. Consequently, one can reach the conclusion that at least a major portion of Van Dorn's army, probably under Lovell, was without appropriate foodstuffs. At least one trainload of the wounded went without basic care. It would appear that General Van Dorn repeated a pattern that was begun at Pea Ridge. While the Court of Inquiry cleared Van Dorn of any wrongdoing, he never commanded anything more than cavalry following this action.[37]

While Van Dorn's staff, along with those of Sterling Price, sought to provide necessary food and ammunition for the expedition, Smith notes that by October 4, many Confederate units were out of ammunition and the men had no food. Van Dorn's and Price's staff officers also proved to be ineffective during the action itself, particularly on the second day. Neither Van Dorn nor his staff officers could find Hébert until he himself reported in sick. Then another delay followed as Van Dorn sent word to Brigadier General Green that he was now in charge of Hébert's division. Both sides suffered greatly from the lack of water, but they used wagons to haul barrels of water forward for their fighting men. Small arms ammunition ran short, but both sides addressed the problem during lulls in the battle.[38]

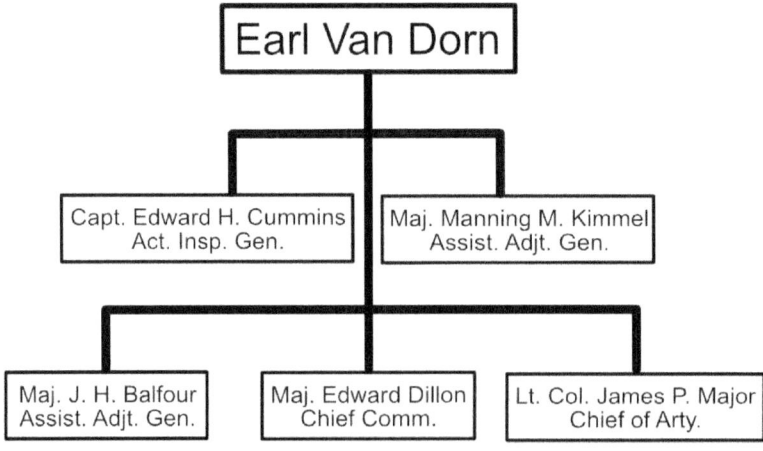

Selected Confederate staff officers. Even though Van Dorn had two West Pointers on his staff, this group struggled to supply the newly organized Confederate Army. Like the Confederate force at Shiloh, this force had been assembled recently, and the staff struggled to support both Van Dorn and Price. The Court of Inquiry highlighted those concerns. See note 38 (courtesy Margaret A. Zimmermann).

Van Dorn and Price failed to use their resources effectively. Neither cavalry nor scouts or spies identified the Union reserve lines and heavy artillery. On at least one occasion, Price sent his men forward into heavy resistance without artillery support. Piecemeal attacks seemed to dog the Confederate efforts throughout the battle. Tim Smith suggests that Van Dorn may have used only 9,000 men in his assault on October 4. While at times Rosecrans found it challenging to coordinate all the resources at his disposal, he was able to bring his heavy artillery to bear with solid results. He sent in reinforcements as needed, and he even used local freed slaves to strengthen his works between the days of battle. Despite some miscues on his part, Rosecrans brought his entire force to fight the Confederates.[39]

For both sides, the strategic outcome was somewhat limited. Van Dorn lost the battle, and as a result he failed to achieve any strategic success. Rosecrans won the battle and a promotion to command an army in his own right. Beyond this, however, the North proved unable to destroy the forces of Van Dorn. Neither side achieved any significant strategic gain because of the battle.

Six Elements of Victory at Corinth

Corinth	Clear, Attainable Objective	Operational Initiative	Command Unity
Rosecrans	Achieved	Not Achieved	Achieved
Van Dorn	Not Achieved	Not Achieved	Not Achieved
	Logistics/Staff	Used All Resources	Strategic Outcome
Rosecrans	Achieved	Achieved	Not Achieved
Van Dorn	Not Achieved	Not Achieved	Not Achieved

While Rosecrans failed to pursue immediately and Van Dorn escaped to Mississippi, Rosecrans had defeated the Confederate attempt to compromise Union gains in Tennessee.

Chapter 9

Prairie Grove

Arkansas Once More

By now, a pattern has emerged from several battles that seemed, on the surface, to be quite disparate. A variety of engagements that occurred under different weather conditions in contrasting geographic locations, and under diverse military leaders, began to have similar results. A commanding general usually set an objective and was supported in some fashion, either by his theater commander or the political leadership of his country. The army commander then faced a series of decisions. Take the initiative or give it up and simply defend a position? What should he do with supplies? Should he bring them within striking range of the battlefield to re-supply soldiers in need or keep wagons safely in the rear? Was the commander able to create a team with his subordinates and staff members, or would several of these people act as independent agents and entrepreneurs? Should the commander lead from the front and risk instant death, or lead from the rear and risk being uninvolved, or move about and lead from an area that affords him some visibility and immediate contact with his subordinates without placing him in too much personal danger? Some writers of history would suggest that the outcome of each battle is simply a matter of luck. Others would argue that all battle plans "go out the window" when the first shot is fired, and that as a result, many of these contests are just soldiers' battles. All the questions posed above can be asked in each of the battles shown in 1862, and the answers to these questions are often very clear.

The Battle of Prairie Grove offers enlightening instruction in each of these areas. Generals without any reputation or West Point training crossed swords, and the results are clearly delineated by asking the same questions for this battle that we have for all the others. For the Union side, two generals played a major role in the Battle of Prairie Grove. Brigadier General James G. Blunt was an officer largely without military experience, who at best was an average commander, probably with serious personal flaws. Likewise on the Confederate side, Thomas C. Hindman was personally brave but, like his Union adversaries, was without a West Point education and largely unknown in the Confederate pantheon of commanding generals. His army was larger than the Federal force, and substantially stronger than the portion of the Union army he faced early on the day of battle; he had reasonably modern small arms, and a competent, supporting cavalry arm. While his artillery was deficient, he was positioned to employ his guns effectively if he chose to do so. If he consumed his supplies carefully, he possessed enough ammunition and food to supply his force. Yet by the end of the day, December 7, 1862, Hindman's army was unable to achieve the victory he so badly sought. He was compelled to evacuate the battlefield in the night, and by the following day, the Confederates experienced one more loss in the Trans-Mississippi region. Missouri was now under Northern control for the remainder of the war, and Arkansas was no longer able to make a significant military contribution to Southern independence. How all that came to be is the subject of this chapter.

Several lessons can be drawn from the earlier battle at Pea Ridge and applied with reference to the contest at Prairie Grove on December 7, 1862. Following Pea Ridge on March 7 and 8, 1862, Earl Van Dorn left Arkansas with his army and all the supplies he could gather. Wagons, weapons, soldiers, and anything else at all portable that might help an army prepare for battle, crossed the Mississippi River with him and headed into Mississippi, and later, Tennessee. The defenses of Arkansas had been picked clean. While Van Dorn and Sterling Price were able to mount a serious threat to Union forces in northern Mississippi for a time, their actions left Arkansas largely without any means of defense. All of this was done without the prior knowledge of anyone in Arkansas. In losing the battle, Van Dorn experienced all the challenges facing a commander in Arkansas. When he first arrived, he brought only a single staff officer with him and was forced to rely on staff officers already present with the army. Partly as a result, his supply and ordnance wagons were parked miles from the battlefield and largely forgotten. He attempted to use a poorly armed and trained group of men comprising many new recruits and Native Americans. Prior to the days of battle, he initiated a forced march to the battlefield that led to hunger and suffering on the part of his army. Finally, he divided his force to entrap and

Major General Thomas C. Hindman (Library of Congress).

Brigadier General James G. Blunt (Library of Congress).

defeat the Union army. Following the battle, his men withdrew in disorder from the field, and he eventually left the state altogether. Now Prairie Grove would repeat this result.

On the Union side, General Samuel Curtis likewise withdrew his force following the action. While Missouri was protected from Confederate incursions, western Arkansas remained a backwater for both Union and Confederate interests. Curtis later attempted an advance toward Little Rock in eastern Arkansas in July of 1862, but when the supporting Union gunboats were recalled for more important duties, his march into Arkansas foundered over supply issues.[1]

Searching for Van Dorn's replacement, Jefferson Davis first tried Thomas C. Hindman, and then when that choice became controversial, he hit upon Major General Theophilus Holmes. Born in North Carolina and graduating from West Point in 1829, the 58-year-old Holmes had served in the Mexican War. At the First Battle of Bull Run, Holmes commanded a brigade, and Douglas Southall Freeman mentions Holmes in a chapter titled "Subordinates of Promise." Under Lee, however, Holmes's performance was not remarkable during the Seven Days battles in the East, and he was reassigned. He was described as a general from the "Old Army" who was both stiff and deaf. Freeman and Steven E. Woodworth write that Holmes was also a "close friend" of Jefferson Davis. Once again, this achievement led to a more responsible assignment, commander of the Trans-Mississippi Department. He replaced a leader who was considered by some to be too abrasive, Major General Hindman. As he reorganized the department into three districts, however, Holmes retained Hindman and asked him to raise an army for service in northwest Arkansas. They would be named the First Corps of the Army of Trans-Mississippi.[2]

Major General Thomas C. Hindman was born in 1828 and turned 34 in 1862. Growing up originally in Tennessee, then moving to Mississippi and finally to Arkansas in 1854, he appeared to be an ideal candidate for a president struggling to find talent among his commanding generals. He was without West Point experience, but he had seen action during the Mexican War, led a brigade at Shiloh, and in a time of peace before the war, he had even been wounded seriously fighting bravely alongside Patrick Cleburne to fend off attackers in Little Rock. Elected to the House of Representatives in 1858 and again in 1860, he was popular in Arkansas and had a reputation for bravery. Except for his brief stint during the Mexican War, however, Hindman brought little military expertise to his new job; but according to his son, he was also known as a friend of Jefferson Davis. He was both a spellbinding orator and leader of the Democratic Party. Beginning in May of 1862, Hindman took just 70 days to achieve results. Raising 20,000 men and obtaining equipment for a new army, he enlisted a force that grew to 40 regiments and 12 batteries of artillery. While his actions were militarily sound, they raised the political ire of the local politicians, and this explains Davis's decision to appoint Theophilus Holmes to manage the political affairs of Arkansas from Little Rock. Hindman stayed with the army. If Arkansas was to remain independent in the new Confederacy, stern measures must be adopted and Hindman was the man to do it. Hindman and Holmes would express divergent views later on, but in the beginning, all went well for their partnership. Holmes was able to soothe the feelings of the local politicos, and Hindman went to work. But the logistical damage that Van Dorn had wrought would haunt Hindman throughout his short time in Arkansas. For the citizens of Arkansas, the Confederacy proved adept and generous at appointing army commanders but exceptionally parsimonious at providing the means of defense. In return, Arkansas had already sent the flower of their manhood east to fight in other Confederate armies—a now familiar story.³

Following the Battle of Pea Ridge, politics played an equally important role for the North. Although Samuel Curtis retained his overall responsibilities for Missouri, he appointed Brigadier General John Schofield to lead an army in the field. Curtis's health had not fully recovered from the arduous Pea Ridge affair, and he suggested that someone else should take the field under his direction. He had also attracted a bevy of jealous Union officers and was in the process of stirring up political difficulty in his District of Missouri. On October 12, 1862, Curtis appointed Brigadier General John Schofield (West Point, 7th in the Class of 1853) to lead the Army of the Frontier. Schofield divided the force into three divisions. Then Schofield fell ill during the Union army's fall campaign to Springfield in October and November. As he began a return trip to St. Louis to recuperate, his lieutenant, Brigadier General Totten, was the only West Pointer left in the field. He took command of Missouri troops on November 14 while Schofield was ill, but he was then called to St. Louis as a witness in a court martial. With the approach of winter, his withdrawal left Brigadier General James G. Blunt in command of his division and field commander of the entire force.

An early ally of Senator James K. Lane from Kansas, who advocated for his appointment, Blunt did not have a West Point pedigree. At one point, Schofield commanded Blunt's division and his own. By November 20, as Schofield headed to St. Louis for recuperation, Brigadier General Blunt now assumed command of the entire force, subject to the orders of Curtis in St. Louis. When Totten left, Brigadier General Francis J. Herron, former bank clerk and militia captain, was appointed under Blunt's overall command to direct the movements of the two Missouri divisions. Herron had fought bravely at Wilson's Creek and won a Medal of Honor; he also fought at Pea Ridge. With the West Pointers out of commission, the Union Army would labor on with two brave, well-meaning volunteers.⁴

If all of this has the appearance of shifting sand,

Brigadier General Francis Herron. His remarkable march before the battle saved Blunt's force from destruction and made the Union victory at Prairie Grove possible (Library of Congress).

the description demonstrates that army commanders for both sides came and went with great frequency. As a result, new army commanders needed to work exceptionally hard to mold their staff officers and immediate subordinates into a fighting team. All the commanding officers involved on both sides were political appointees. None of these men were West Pointers and all of them had limited command experience before their rapid promotions in 1862. Yet they were all called upon for extraordinary efforts at the spur of the moment. For the Union army, however, all of these changes meant that a unified and controlling direction for a campaign was missing. The Army of the Frontier was broken into two groups: one division under Blunt was located just over the northwestern Arkansas border, while the other two divisions, commanded by Herron, returned to Springfield. What was their objective or goal?[5]

Pause for a moment to set the stage for this action. Hindman commanded a Confederate force located near Fort Smith in northwestern Arkansas. Two Union forces faced him at this time. Brigadier General Blunt's force from Kansas approached from the northwest, and Herron's force was about 100 miles northeast and still in Missouri. In some ways, this positioning of forces could be viewed as an inverted triangle. Hindman, with 11,000 active soldiers and 26 guns at the southern point, faced two widely separated, hostile forces. Blunt, with 5,000 men, 16 guns and a train guard, was the closer of the two Union forces. Herron, with 4,200 men, 24 guns and his train guard, was still located at Springfield. If Hindman, located about 35 miles south of Blunt, could get between the Union forces and annihilate first one and then the other, the campaign would be his.[6]

After Brigadier General Samuel R. Curtis aborted his advance on Little Rock, General Blunt and his division paid damaging visits to northwestern Arkansas. On September 29–30, one of Blunt's brigades had defeated a small Confederate force at a place called Newtonia, and by November 28, Blunt had pushed the Confederates back from Old Fort Wayne and won another skirmish at Cane Hill. This was located southwest of both Prairie Grove and Schofield's force at Fayetteville. Earlier on October 4, John Schofield had also appeared and united the Union Army of the Frontier in that same location. By October 18, Schofield moved into northwestern Arkansas, but between October 27 and November 4, Schofield's force, now headed by Totten, withdrew to Lexington, Missouri. After a telegraph conversation with Major General Curtis, they were ordered to undertake a scorched-earth withdrawal to discourage Confederate offensive action. Schofield returned to St. Louis; his successor, Totten, followed shortly thereafter, and Brigadier General Herron took command of the Missouri troops, now widely separated from Blunt. There had been a flurry of activity but relatively little had been accomplished. Missouri was militarily protected from Confederate invasion, and except for Blunt's small force near Prairie Grove, Arkansas, remained outside the sphere of Union control.[7]

On the other side, Hindman was hoping to find an opportunity to strike back after the Confederates had suffered so many losses over the spring and summer. After being appointed commander of the First Corps of the Trans-Mississippi and joining his army permanently around October 15, Hindman had relatively little time to acclimate to his new situation. But as Herron marched off to the east and Blunt hung on in the area, Hindman saw his chance. Short on supplies, thanks to Earl Van Dorn's earlier evacuation of Arkansas, Hindman reorganized his force, named it the Trans-Mississippi Army, and prepared to move against Blunt. Three infantry commanders served directly under

Hindman: Brigadier Generals John S. Roane, politician and Mexican War veteran, Francis A. Shoup, West Point Class of 1855, and Daniel M. Frost, West Point Class of 1844. General John S. Marmaduke, West Point Class of 1857, commanded a fourth (cavalry) division. Almost 15,000 men gathered at Fort Smith, but only about 12,000 had weapons that worked. As Hindman reorganized his force, Marmaduke reported from his reconnaissance that Blunt had 7,000–8,000 men and was vulnerable to surprise attack.[8]

The operational situation was complicated. The force being entrusted to Hindman in northwestern Arkansas was hardly ready to take the field. On October 26, Holmes sent a message to Samuel Cooper in Richmond that read in part, "[my men] are a crude mass of undisciplined material, 7,000 of whom are without arms of any kind, and a large part of the remainder have only the shot-guns and rifles of the country. At present the only generals I have are Major-General Hindman and Brigadier-Generals Roane and McCulloch, with two Missouri brigadier-generals . . Roane is useless as a commander.... All the brigades are now commanded by colonels, most of whom are not qualified to command a regiment."[9]

Nevertheless, on November 2, Holmes received a message from Samuel Cooper in Richmond: "The President directs me to say that if the state of your command will enable you to do so he thinks it advisable that you should throw re-enforcements, say to the extent of 10,000 men, across the river at Vicksburg, to aid General Pemberton." Cooper pressed Holmes to reinforce Vicksburg; Holmes wanted Hindman to take defensive action, while Hindman planned his attack. As the two generals sparred by telegraph, the Confederates in the Trans-Mississippi Department operated without a clear objective.[10]

It was Hindman's cavalry commander, Marmaduke, who helped decide the issue. His commissary train was located at a place called Cane Hill; Blunt became aware of his proximity and decided to take the initiative. While the remainder of the Union forces in Missouri under General Curtis planned their winter hiatus, Blunt prepared his own offensive. From Fort Smith came a Union commissary train to support Blunt—two miles long. On Thanksgiving Day, Blunt's force left for Cane Hill and on November 28, his force met Marmaduke's men at Cane Hill itself. After a 90-minute skirmish, the Confederates fled once again. Attempting to hold two different defensive positions, they were soundly defeated. Blunt, leading from the very front lines, was ecstatic. But it was at this point that he was separated from Herron's Missouri troops by over 100 miles of barren territory. As Marmaduke retreated and informed Hindman of the action, Hindman, 35 miles from Blunt's location, now believed that this was his chance to seize the initiative. On December 1, he crossed the Arkansas River with 12,000 men and on December 3, his formal advance began. But by the next day, during a bitter winter storm, he realized that his journey would be quite challenging. On December 2, Union general Blunt realized he was facing a major force and telegraphed for help. Could the two Missouri divisions, now under Herron, move up and help? Would Hindman reach Blunt before Herron could reinforce him?

Blunt sent an imperative message to Totten on December 2: "I desire you to move as much of your force as possible, especially the infantry, to my support, as I do not intend to leave this position without a fight." Blunt to Curtis, December 2, 1862: "My scouts ... report Hindman and Marmaduke concentrating their forces, 25,000 strong.... I have requested General Totten to re-enforce me by forced marches, ... but I have no knowledge of his present locality, and have got to hunt him up."[11]

In still another telegram that emphasized the Federal needs on the Mississippi River itself, as opposed to southwestern Missouri or northwestern Arkansas, Henry W. Halleck, now General-in-Chief of the Union armies, wrote to Curtis, December 2, 1862: "Telegraph in round numbers the forces which can be detached from your department by the 15th instant, ... for an expedition down the Mississippi."[12]

Hindman's telegraphic exchange with Holmes is also instructive. On November 3, he wrote thanking Holmes for additional arms, ammunition and other supplies, and then requested more men and artillery: "That would enable me to maintain myself during the winter and to push forward in the spring." On November 10, Holmes wrote Hindman and noted that Union troops threatened Arkansas, stating: "Whether they intend to invade or resist invasion I cannot tell. If the former can you sustain yourself? If the latter, you certainly will not be able to attack them, ... which, ... will make them double your strength. I am in great doubt what to do." On November 11, Holmes asked him to consider sending the 10,000 men requested by Davis to Vicksburg. Again, while Hindman was thinking offensively, Holmes was exploring defensive alternatives. On November 14, Holmes wrote, "you are not strong enough to fight him if he comes down in force. I am greatly alarmed about the small-pox; if it gets among the troops it will be fatal to us." Then on the 15th, Holmes again wrote, "Please write to me whether you think it possible this winter to <u>hold</u> the Indian country and Northwestern Arkansas and concentrate enough force to take Helena, the object being to <u>hold</u> and fortify it" (author's underlining). But eventually Holmes gave in to Hindman's insistence that he be allowed to attack.[13]

Unfortunately for Hindman, his advance moved more slowly than he would have liked. His march toward Blunt took three full days to cover the distance, but by December 6 he was much closer. While he waited for Hindman to appear, Blunt needed to decide the next question: Would he wait for Hindman where he was or move back toward Herron to make their junction an easier one? He elected to wait. By December 6, Hindman was drawing near. By December 6, following a truly remarkable feat, Herron was also approaching the area—marching 100 miles in three days, when the normal march rate was about 12 miles a day. Some writers have suggested that Blunt was simply lucky in winning this battle, but Brigadier General Herron was clearly the ideal subordinate for this particular occasion. He pressed his men to force march over 30 miles a day for three full days in order to support his commanding general. While Herron might have been simply "average" in his role on the battlefield, he outdid himself supporting Blunt through his exceptional trek. As his supporting artillery accompanied him, Herron's appearance was even more advantageous.[14]

Apprised of Herron's approach to Prairie Grove, Hindman now changed the direction of his offensive. Instead of attacking Blunt in his exposed position, he would march past him and attack Herron first and then return to finish off the remainder of the Union force. Gathering his generals together on the evening of December 6, Hindman changed his orders to them. Instead of marching northwest for Blunt, he would shift directions and march northeast for Herron. In his report he wrote, "the several commanders of divisions were assembled on the night of the 6th, to receive final instructions.... It now seemed evident that that plan [the original plan of attacking Blunt alone] would simply cause the retirement of Blunt upon his reinforcements, without accepting battle.... I might by adopting a different plan, destroy the re-enforcements and afterward fight the main body on equal terms. To withdraw without fighting at all, would discourage my own troops…. Influenced by these considerations, I determined to risk an engagement."[15]

On December 6, Blunt asked Herron to send his cavalry over to Blunt's command as soon as possible. In the meantime, Hindman decided to use one division to face Blunt and occupy his attention and send his other three against Herron. Blunt's wagon train of 400 vehicles with additional supplies and ammunition remained at Rhea's Mill, close at hand, while Hindman's wagon train with additional food and ammunition would eventually occupy the quaintly named but more distant village of Hogeye. Leaving a small cavalry force to occupy Blunt's attention, Hindman advanced on Herron.[16]

* * *

The morning of December 7 dawned, and Hindman stayed for a time with Shoup's division in the rear of the army. They had marched nearly 15 miles the previous day without food and were sadly drained. Hindman later wrote, "It was painful to observe the exhaustion of the men. They had marched nearly 15 miles. None of them had eaten since the preceding day. The rations of all had been insufficient for over thirty days. Many, overcome with fatigue, had been left on the roadside." Captain S.T. Buffner, recalling the action after the war stated, "General Hindman's plan was to engage and defeat Blunt before Herron could come up, but the roughness of the road over Boston Mountains and the rawness of troops delayed his march and he failed in this. This was literally an open-field battle, and a desperate one. There was no place of shelter upon any portion." By 10:00 a.m., however, Hindman set up his headquarters at the little village of Prairie Grove, some distance back from the battlefield. He felt his division commanders could manage the assault he had ordered, but they chose a different course of action. In the opening skirmish, cavalrymen of Marmaduke's mounted division attacked and routed a small force of Federal cavalry. As Herron's main force approached, the Confederate cavalry withdrew, but before Hindman arrived, General Shoup, one of the West Pointers commanding the Second Division, decided to deploy on a ridge near Prairie Grove itself to await Herron's attack. When Hindman appeared, he agreed with Shoup's decision.[17]

Now, instead of attacking, the Confederates gave up the initiative and waited for an attack on their position. General Herron would oblige. As he arrived on the battlefield, Herron was alerted to the presence of Confederates manning a battery of artillery in front of him and decided to attack. First the artillery from both sides came into play. Herron commanded 20 guns, 16 of them rifled, and they opened on the Confederate position. The Confederates with only ten guns available at first, smoothbores and howitzers, returned fire ineffectually. After the noisy but largely harmless bombardment, Herron began his assault on the waiting Confederate force.[18]

The initiative passed to the Federals as first one Union regiment and then another surged across the battlefield. Herron commanded six regiments divided creatively among four brigade commanders, and he now launched piecemeal attacks against what he supposed was an exposed Confederate battery. Two regiments attacked, were repulsed by an entire brigade of Confederates, and retreated. One of the units was the 20th Wisconsin, and after the battle, "P," a soldier of the 20th, shared his thoughts with *The Madison Journal* in Wisconsin: "From the time our first man fell in the terrible charge until we withdrew was not more than fifteen minutes, and we lost 50 killed and 130 wounded—nearly half the command. We did not again participate in the fight except to fire a few rounds at very long range."[19]

The Confederate soldiers, without the intervention of their own division commanders, began a disorganized pursuit that immediately ran into the hot fire of Herron's 24 guns, and they retreated in their turn. Now two more Union regiments advanced and were badly damaged. "P" wrote, "Next the Illinois 37th and the 26th Indiana prepared to make a charge. They had seen war at Pea Ridge and are the crack regiments of the Army of the Frontier, so that much was expected of them. They advanced up the hill in magnificent style but like the 19th and 20th were repulsed. Things looked to me very much like a defeat, and had it not been for our great superiority in artillery we should have been badly beaten." As the day advanced, Herron's force was now stretched to its fighting limit. Where was Blunt?[20]

Southwest of the Prairie Grove battlefield, Blunt had spent a fruitless morning being entertained by Confederates forming up in front of his defensive position but never quite moving to the attack. By 10:00 a.m. he was out of patience and, hearing gunfire from Herron's force near Prairie Grove, realized that the real battle was elsewhere. Moving as quickly as he could with his force, he marched first northwest toward little Rhea's Mill where his supply train was parked, then on the only available road, and finally across open farmland toward the battlefield. Shortly after 3:00 p.m. Blunt arrived at a hill overlooking the battlefield. After the battle, a disgusted Confederate, W.L. Morrison from Texas, wrote, "We had Blount [sic] completely cut off from Herron, and we stood there half the day.... For some mysterious reason the impatiently wished-for command was not given. Blount was permitted unmolested to make a circuit around our

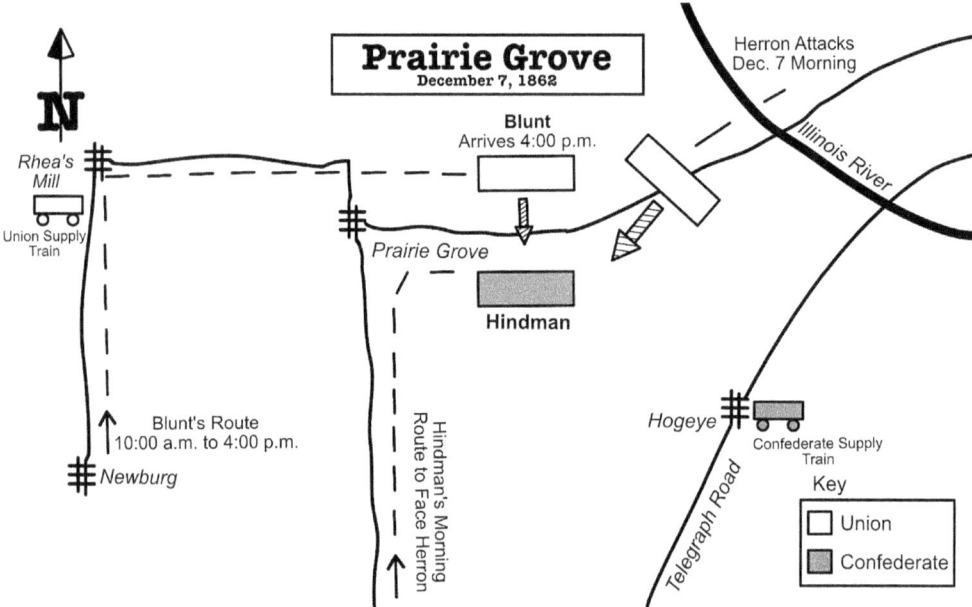

During the first phase of the battle, Union General Herron confronted and attacked Hindman's approaching Confederates, but he was hard-pressed to hold his position. General Blunt completed his march from the Newburg area around 4:00 in the afternoon and attacked as well. While Hindman held off Federal attacks, he realized his reserve ammunition and supplies were in far-off Hogeye, and he retreated the following day (courtesy Margaret A. Zimmermann).

right wing to the west and to join Herron.... Imagine our chagrin when ... we were ordered to fall in and retrace our steps toward Van Buren."[21]

Once Blunt was in place, he took enough time to prepare all his available men for an assault. His 16 guns opened fire and, around 4:00 p.m., he advanced with his entire force. While Hindman fed troops onto the Confederate left flank, Blunt went in with his men. The Confederates, however, were able to hold. As the sun sank by 5:00 p.m., the battle ended. A stalemate! Now the Confederate leadership realized that they were low on ammunition. F.M. Knox encapsulated the entire battle this way: "After we left Elm Springs we went south and camped a while and then went north and fought the battle of Prairie Grove under General Hindman. We camped on the battlefield that night. Three of us had a chicken and plenty of frozen apples for supper; no bread or salt."[22]

* * *

Samuel Curtis and the original field commander, John Schofield, planned a comparatively quiet winter in Arkansas and Missouri. General Blunt, however, sought to entice the Confederates into one last battle. Given the fact that both Curtis and Herron supported his objective in the end, and victory followed Herron's heroic march, it becomes apparent that his objective became both clear and attainable.

On the other hand, the Confederates had no such success. Holmes, the overall Trans-Mississippi commander, desired a defensive posture, and the Richmond government supported this desire. His immediate subordinate, Hindman, in charge of the army's First Corps, determined to achieve the opposite—an offensive. It is apparent that this force was not prepared for serious combat in the winter and, once Herron appeared on the Union side, the object of defeating the larger Federal force became unrealistic.

Under Blunt, the Union army held the initiative throughout and immediately following the battle. Herron mistakenly attacked Confederate forces with single regiments, and Blunt marched to the sound of the guns. Even though the Confederates held off several Union assaults, by the end of the day, they were ready to withdraw. Originally Hindman hoped to attack and defeat each of the smaller Union forces he faced, but he was unable to seize and hold the initiative at any time. Without food or ammunition, Hindman's force retreated precipitously, leaking deserters and leaving bandits and chaos in its wake. While Kirby Smith arrived later to assume control over the entire Trans-Mississippi area, the Confederates would never be able to fully recover Arkansas or effectively threaten Missouri. Hindman's effort ended in failure.[23]

Blunt and Herron had steadfast support from their subordinates. As Blunt's second-in-command, Herron made a remarkable march, but his performance on the battlefield was less than stellar. He failed to scout the Confederate battle line thoroughly before ordering his original charge, and then, after it was repulsed, he tried the same tactic once more with similar results. Fortunately for Herron, his artillerymen held the position for him until Blunt could appear.

A report from Battery F, 1st Missouri Light Artillery, Captain Murphy commanding, reinforces this impression: "the battery did superb execution, and, in conjunction with the other battery in my command ... silenced all those the enemy brought forward, as soon as their position could be ascertained." Herron writes, "Two [Confederate] batteries were so much damaged by the firing from Foust's and Murphy's guns as to be entirely worthless, and several guns were hauled off in wagons. All of their artillery

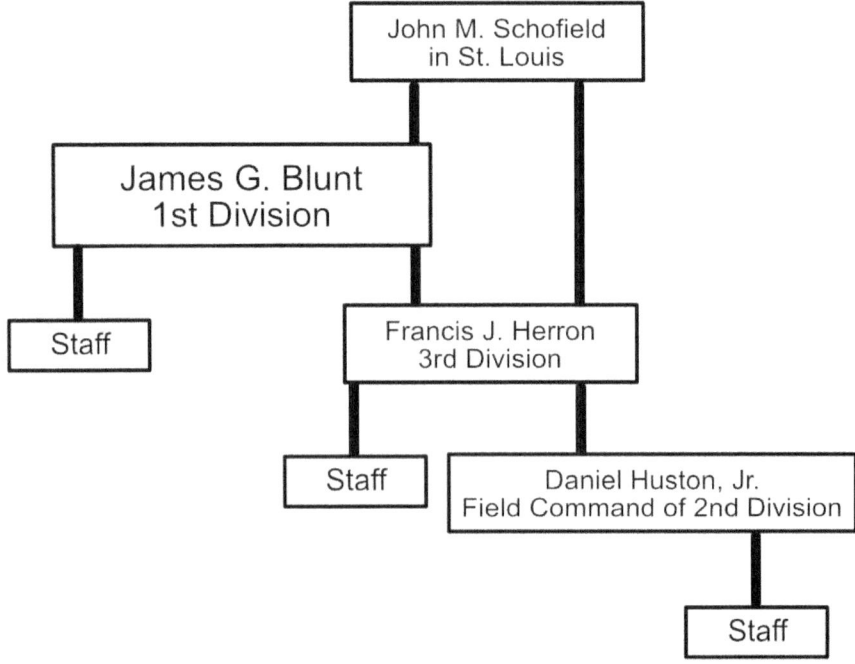

Army organization under Brigadier General Blunt. Brigadier General James G. Blunt was senior to the new 3rd Division commander, Francis J. Herron. While Blunt remained in a dangerous position, Herron marched over 100 miles in three days to reach him with reinforcements (courtesy Margaret A. Zimmermann).

horses were left dead on the field and the caissons taken away by mules in the night." Confederate Captain S.T. Buffner agreed: "The enemy greatly outnumbered us and outranked us in the character of cannon, having the most improved rifle guns, and handled them with remarkable skill."[24]

After Hindman reached the Prairie Grove battlefield, he lost the initiative he once held. His division commanders had simply not followed his original orders and failed to launch any meaningful attacks on the badly outnumbered Federals. All the West Point officers, Shoup in particular, encouraged Hindman to stand on the defense. With only regimental and brigade leadership experience, Hindman let his division commanders act cautiously, and by taking only conservative actions at first, the Confederates relinquished any opportunity they might have had for crushing Herron and then turning on Blunt.

On the Union side, Blunt, Herron and their subordinates had been active all over Prairie Grove. Blunt and Herron had both made egregious mistakes as part of the campaign. Blunt expected Herron to do all the marching and come to him. Herron launched piecemeal attacks throughout the morning of December 7. But by staying on the field, both men could see what needed to be done and take steps to accomplish their goals.

For the Union, staff officers provided solid logistical support. Herron brought all of his ordnance to the battlefield, and Blunt kept his train within a close distance from the field as well. The Union army was able to rearm and prepare for additional combat if that had become necessary. Both Blunt and Herron appear to have acquired the necessary food for their men during a winter campaign. After the battle, Blunt's force calmly

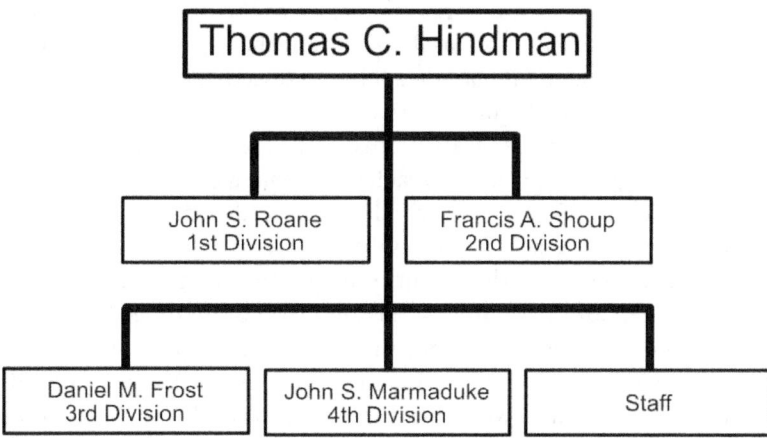

Army organization under Major General Hindman. Even though Hindman originally ordered his officers to attack Herron near Prairie Grove, they instead preferred to defend their position (courtesy Margaret A. Zimmermann).

reloaded cartridge boxes and caissons and prepared for action the next day. Their supplies were easily available. Blunt enjoyed the firm support of both staff and immediate subordinates during the day and all through the night. Their aides kept both Blunt and Herron informed once the battle opened, and additional food and ammunition were readily available.[25]

The Confederates suffered from the lack of both food and ammunition. When Hindman changed direction for his force and sent it off to fight Herron, he left his trains well in the rear. Afterward, Hindman reported that his wagons were 30 miles behind his

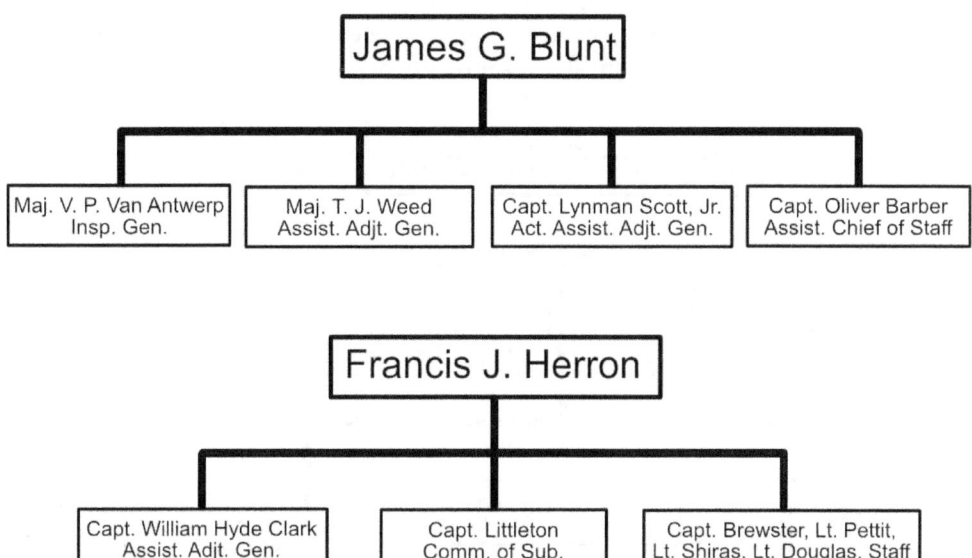

Selected Union staff officers. Each Federal division commander employed his own staff. Fortunately for Blunt, his train was kept nearby throughout the contest. See note 25 (courtesy Margaret A. Zimmermann).

force and that he had neither food nor ammunition as the day ended. To avoid capture, they perhaps had begun an early trek back to Fort Smith, or perhaps Hindman had other reasons for making this statement, but in fact he possessed neither food nor ammunition anywhere close to his army. His men had not eaten for days as they marched through bitter weather to confront the Federals. In his post-battle report, Hindman writes, "In the midst of this struggle information reached me that a considerable body of Federal cavalry was approaching Hog-eye, to which place I ordered my trains. I directed the wagons retired on the Telegraph Road to Oliver's. This was done without loss."[26] Captain Buffner also commented, "That night General Hindman withdrew his army. I did not understand it then and with others censured the commander for drawing off. We did not … know that our supply of ammunition was not sufficient for another day's fight, and we did not consider that our men and horses had been without a full ration for two days. One of the wonders is how we ever got ammunition and how we obtained sufficient supplies of food and forage from the desolate country through which we passed." Union soldier J.F. Benton also noted, "I saw in the haversacks on a number of their dead bodies at Prairie Grove nothing but a kind of meal made of parched corn, a piece of bacon, and a piece of black-looking bread, which we could not eat unless we felt the pinch of hunger more keenly than we have at any time in the past."[27]

By marching overland and combining his forces with those of Herron, Blunt committed everything he had readily available to the battle. The Federal artillery was a superior weapon on the battlefield of Prairie Grove, and with the close of 1862, it was becoming apparent that the North was beginning to achieve supremacy in both numbers and quality of artillery.

The Confederates had originally gathered a large force near Fort Smith, and they had armed many of them with modern Enfields. It had proven impossible to recover from Earl Van Dorn's predatory removal from Arkansas anything of value for his own army. Hindman was unable to bring all the men recruited over the past few months, but he armed and brought everyone he could. As 1862 ended for the Confederates, the Union was indeed able to bring greater resources to bear in several areas. For example,

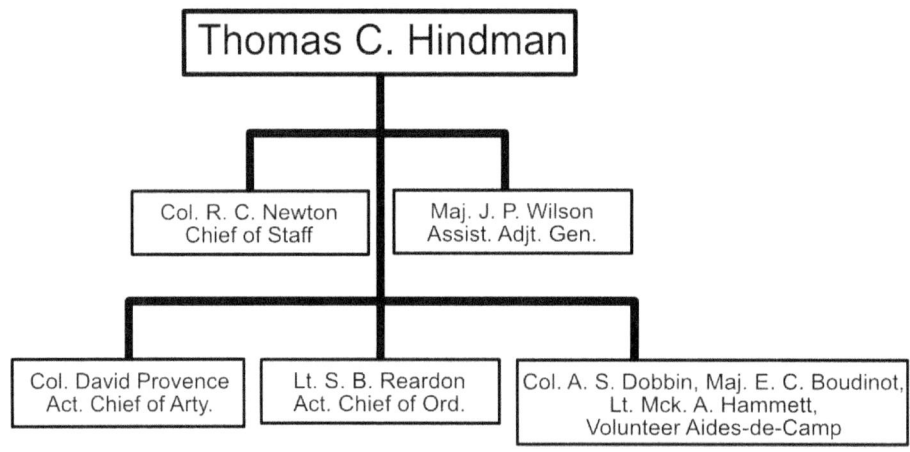

Selected Confederate staff officers. Unfortunately for Hindman, the location of his supply train negated their efforts to support him logistically. See note 27 (courtesy Margaret A. Zimmermann).

the Union brought 40 pieces of artillery onto the field, including 18 rifled guns; the Confederates could only muster 26 guns, only two of them rifled. Their 11, 6-lb guns and 13 howitzers had served the U.S. Army well in the Mexican War, but times had changed.[28]

This was an interesting strategic moment for the Union forces. After the battle and as Hindman was retreating, John Schofield in St. Louis, the actual army commander, ordered no pursuit. Generals Blunt and Herron, however, decided to stalk the Confederates, reaching Van Buren, Arkansas, by December 28 when they raided the town. In the end, however, the question of logistics came to the surface once again, and they were forced to retreat. Schofield was livid and wanted disciplinary action taken, but his superiors decided that a battlefield victory and a safe return of the army did not warrant a court martial. The Union held the initiative, and yet they proved unable to exercise it effectively.

As night fell, Hindman understood that the Union forces were now united. On December 8, Blunt and Hindman paused to parlay. Hindman bought time for his retreat, and Blunt was not eager to pursue at this time. For the Confederates, the Battle of Prairie Grove was a limited strategic defeat. Their army had been badly handled, Missouri was no longer a viable option for a Confederate offensive, and even a key portion of northwest Arkansas had been lost. Hindman later admitted to Theophilus Holmes, his superior, that he failed to press the enemy and, as time went on, the two of them had a falling out. Hindman had reluctant support from Holmes in the beginning, but by the end of his time in Arkansas, he lost even that reluctant support. Interestingly, however, the Trans-Mississippi territory would undergo one more revival in the months ahead. Kirby Smith arrived, refused to send men or materials east to help anyone else, and he rebuilt the army of Trans-Mississippi one more time into a formidable force. With this new army, he defeated a major Union expedition under Nathaniel Banks in 1864. He had the same resource base available to Hindman and Holmes, but he used it far differently.[29]

Hindman's battle report summarized the Confederate situation as he saw it: "Considering that my men were destitute of food, their wagons 30 miles in rear, and not to be brought forward without imminent danger of being lost; that my small supply of ammunition was reduced far below what would be necessary for another day's fighting, and that my battery animals were literally dying of starvation, and could not be foraged in the presence of a superior force of the enemy, I determined to retire."[30]

In March of 1863, Hindman asked for a transfer out of Arkansas to serve Bragg, and his wish was granted. He would go on to serve the Confederacy until the end of the war. In 1868, when he returned home to Arkansas, he was murdered. Blunt and Herron were both promoted to major generalships after the battle, but their achievements would differ greatly after this engagement. Eventually Blunt would bring a force to capture Fort Smith in Arkansas and expel the Confederates, but he would achieve little after this expedition. He died in 1881. Herron would go on to command a division under Grant at Vicksburg and be promoted to command a corps.

By now, Henry Wager Halleck settled into his role as commander in chief of the Union armies, and he commented on the limited strategic value of military action in northwestern Arkansas. His summation is worth reviewing. On February 17, 1863, approximately two months after the battle at Prairie Grove, he had this to say: "To operate ... [in] Western Arkansas is bad strategy at any time, and almost an impossibility in the winter season … we may defeat the enemy a dozen times on the western border of the two States, and our victories, like those of Pea Ridge and Prairie Grove, be without important results."[31]

Six Elements of Victory at Prairie Grove

Prairie Grove	Clear, Attainable Objective	Operational Initiative	Command Unity
Blunt	Achieved	Achieved*	Achieved
Hindman	Not Achieved	Not Achieved	Not Achieved
	Logistics/Staff	Used All Resources	Strategic Outcome
Blunt	Achieved	Achieved	Not Achieved
Hindman	Not Achieved	Not Achieved	Not Achieved

Despite placing his division originally in a dangerous position, Blunt was reinforced in a timely fashion by Herron. Hindman, however, failed to attack either Blunt or Herron individually and was ultimately forced to retreat. Neither side gained strategically after the battle.

Chapter 10

Stones River

Fatal Flaws in Confederate Strategy and Leadership

We come now to the climax of our story. In southeast Tennessee, the Confederates had one final opportunity to halt any Union advance from Nashville into the last Confederate-held space of this critically important state. A victory here would protect Chattanooga and the state of Georgia for future Confederate operations. By December 15, 1862, the Union General Ambrose E. Burnside in the East had been decisively defeated at Fredericksburg. Another Confederate victory in the West might revive hopes of foreign intervention. It would certainly prolong the war, perhaps leading to the exhaustion of the United States. Into this uncertain conflict came two commanding generals with somewhat questionable skills as commanders. Braxton Bragg had expertly reorganized and trained the Army of Tennessee in earlier months, but his campaign for Perryville and occupation of Kentucky had failed. William S. Rosecrans had been a solid fighter at Iuka and Corinth. In the process, he managed to antagonize his superiors and some of his lieutenants. Two commanders, with perhaps limited skills, would face off for this crucial contest to decide the fate of Tennessee. Who would prevail? The fate of Tennessee and the war in the West also hung in the balance. Serious questions needed resolution. To what extent had army organization matured in the North and South so that subordinates and staff members would collaborate and work effectively with the commander? Which side would succeed in providing ample food and ammunition for their men? Finally, would one side or the other hold the initiative for strategic success at the close of the contest? To what extent would these factors determine the degree of victory or defeat for either side?

After the Battle of Shiloh in April, the Union had gone without a major success in the West. It was true that several strategic places had been captured, and it was also true that the South's second largest state, in terms of economic vitality, had been severely damaged, but the South was just as determined to gain its independence and retain slavery as ever before. Lincoln had already issued a preliminary Emancipation Proclamation, but for the edict to have any real effect and to keep European nations out of the contest, the North needed to demonstrate that its armies were able to accomplish more than occupying hostile space. Rosecrans had demonstrated at Iuka and Corinth that he was more than willing to engage the Confederates in battle, and now he had his opportunity. George Thomas, the only other viable candidate, had publicly refused army leadership earlier in the year. As a result, when another command opportunity arose, Abraham Lincoln selected Rosecrans. The official announcement was publicized on October 24, and Rosecrans, based in Nashville, set his sights on Chattanooga, only 30 miles away and the gateway to Atlanta, Georgia.[1]

As he planned his new offensive, Rosecrans utilized the services of George H. Thomas, Thomas L. Crittenden and Alexander M. McCook. George Thomas had enjoyed complete success as a brigade commander during the Battle of Mill Springs, Kentucky, in January of 1862. He served under General Don Carlos Buell at Perryville, and now he was asked to serve under William S. Rosecrans. As the Federal government had re-ordered the seniority of Rosecrans so his commission predated that of Thomas, Thomas at first protested Rosecrans's appointment. After exchanging further telegrams with Washington and speaking directly with Rosecrans, however, Thomas acquiesced to the new command arrangement. He would serve Rosecrans loyally in the Stones River campaign.

McCook's corps had been badly damaged at Perryville, and he did not enjoy a solid reputation within the army. He had graduated from West Point, and he was part of the influential McCook family that sent 14 members to fight in the Civil War. Graduating from West Point in 1852, he ranked 30 out of a class of 45. A famous quote from General John Beatty, who called McCook a "chucklehead," suggested that he was not perhaps the brightest of officers, and this assertion has often been used to suggest McCook's limitations. Thomas L. Crittenden also served as a corps commander. He was the son of a U.S. senator, had served as a volunteer aide to Zachary Taylor during the Mexican War, and became a prominent Kentucky attorney before the Civil War.

None of these three men had worked exceptionally well under Buell, but Rosecrans retained all of them. As a result, Rosecrans enjoyed the dependability of George Thomas, a fine commander, but he also retained two other corps commanders with more modest credentials. Rosecrans was determined to reorganize his mounted arm and appointed Major General David Stanley, West Point Class of 1852, following his solid performance at the Battle of Corinth. Previously scattered mounted units were now fused into one solid division. Rosecrans also merged the regular army regiments into a single brigade and created a separate pioneer brigade for engineering support. Rosecrans further took the time to reorganize his general staff, and consequently his staff officers performed more professionally during this campaign than ever before.[2]

Pressures rose in Washington for a victory. Between December 11 and 15, the Union Army of the

Major General Braxton Bragg (courtesy The Civil War Museum, Kenosha, WI).

Potomac under Ambrose Burnside suffered a stunning defeat at Fredericksburg. The Emancipation Proclamation was due to go into force by January 1, a proclamation that changed the nature of the struggle to a war on slavery, and Lincoln hoped thereby to keep the British and French out of the conflict. Sherman was blocked at Vicksburg, Grant's supplies were burned at Holly Springs, and Burnside's army was defeated at Fredericksburg. Lincoln, along with Secretary of War Edwin Stanton and General in Chief Henry Wager Halleck, hoped that Rosecrans would be able to do something in Tennessee to reverse the tide of Union defeats. Another loss could mean catastrophe. Any kind of victory would mean a strategic reprieve for the fortunes of the North. Stanton and Halleck applied pressure on Rosecrans to advance and achieve a victory in December to alter the course of Union fortunes. Rosecrans, obviously,

Major General William S. Rosecrans (Library of Congress).

was reluctant to proceed until he had repaired his damaged army. Although still technically the XIV Corps, this fighting force would eventually assume the title of the Army of the Cumberland. Both North and South had a great deal riding on the fortunes of the two armies camped just 30 miles apart—at Nashville and Murfreesboro, Tennessee.³

Bragg was determined to deny Union access to Georgia. Both Bragg and Rosecrans retained officers who had been with their respective forces for some time. The same two corps commanders who fought previously with Bragg at Perryville, William Hardee and Leonidas Polk, assisted him once again. Serving under Hardee as a division commander was John C. Breckinridge. Former vice-presidential candidate and son of Kentucky, he would also play a prominent role. None of these three commanders enjoyed a positive working relationship with Bragg. Following the disastrous Perryville campaign, Polk visited Richmond on November 4 with a blunt message. Fire Bragg! Hardee sent his own letter to Preston Johnston, an aide to President Jefferson Davis, with a similar message. Hardee's junior officers were infected with their commander's anti–Bragg stance as well. Joe Wheeler, a Bragg supporter, directed Bragg's cavalry force, although his performance would be a mixed one during this campaign. Bragg openly blamed John C. Breckinridge for not joining him at Perryville, and Breckinridge was averse to serving under him any longer. While his absence at Perryville was not his fault, Breckinridge was still not in Bragg's good graces. Now Davis faced a difficult choice. Should he replace Bragg or Bragg's subordinates? Davis then tried his own creative solution; he would keep everyone. Bragg remained in command of the army. Hardee and Polk continued to serve directly under him, and Breckinridge would command a division under

Hardee. Finally, Davis ordered that Confederate forces in Tennessee be united into one army (Bragg's) and then in early December, Davis visited the Army of Tennessee personally to see for himself what else might be done. In this manner, the strategic dimension of Davis's decisions served to undercut the Confederate war effort in Tennessee.[4]

On December 12, President Davis arrived at Murfreesboro to visit with Bragg and evaluate the condition of Bragg's army. Earlier on November 24, Davis appointed Joseph E. Johnston to lead the entire department. Johnston, however, decided to treat this assignment as an advisory arrangement. Now Davis ordered Bragg to send an entire division (8,776 men under Carter Stevenson) to Vicksburg to aid in its defense. Confederates were concerned that Grant was threatening Vicksburg, on the Mississippi River, and sought reinforcements for John Pemberton, the commander. Johnston had earlier asked Davis to order General Theophilus Holmes in Arkansas to send reinforcements. Johnston later wrote, "In a friendly note to General Holmes, Mr. Davis pointed out to him that he would benefit the service by sending twenty thousand men into Mississippi, but gave him no order; consequently no troops came." Holmes, of course, was engaged in the Prairie Grove campaign and his troops were not readily available. Stevenson's men constituted almost one quarter of Bragg's available force. When Bragg later ordered John Hunt Morgan (3,900 men) and Nathan Bedford Forrest (2,000 men) on raids, he reduced his strength by over 14,000 soldiers. It appears that Bragg was not on good terms with either Morgan or Forrest, and so he detached commanders he thought might be troublesome. On December 14, Murfreesboro and the Confederate Army were in a festive mood. This was Morgan's wedding day. President Davis was present as well and left Murfreesboro later that day. A major dance followed on the 15th. Bragg was not expecting a Federal advance any longer in 1862. The year was almost over, and winter quarters beckoned.[5]

While most men on the Confederate side believed that a Union offensive from Nashville toward Murfreesboro was unlikely at this late time of the year, a forward movement was certainly feasible. It appears that President Davis and General Bragg viewed this prospect from different angles. Larry Daniel notes that Davis was probably more fearful about possible developments in Mississippi and wanted reinforcements sent there immediately (Stevenson's division). He was willing to let General Bragg trade space for time in Tennessee, and perhaps even withdraw if Rosecrans moved forward aggressively. While Bragg also viewed an advance by Rosecrans as a possibility, he appeared more optimistic about confronting, and perhaps even counterattacking, a Federal movement.[6]

Before Christmas Day, Rosecrans learned about Stevenson's relocation to Vicksburg and the raids of Forrest and Morgan. He knew this was the time to move. Even though his relations with Secretary of War Stanton were brittle currently, Lincoln, Halleck, and Quartermaster General Montgomery Meigs nonetheless supported Rosecrans. Recruits, weapons and horses all flowed into his army. The night before he moved forward, he met in conference with his commanders and outlined plans verbally. Written orders followed. On December 26, he was finally satisfied with his army's preparations and began his advance from Nashville. For his part, Bragg had dispersed his army over a 36-mile arc and awaited developments. As Rosecrans neared Murfreesboro, Bragg straddled Stones River, but as a result of both President Davis's decisions and Bragg's actions, strategic support was in fact lacking for his army. A clear objective was also missing: Was Bragg expected to hold his ground or retreat? Or, if an opportunity presented itself, should he consider an attack?[7]

Chapter 10. Stones River

Also lacking effective cavalry reconnaissance at times, Bragg was at first surprised when Rosecrans advanced. Surprised, but still optimistic. On the 27th, Bragg sent off orders for his army to concentrate around Murfreesboro. On Sunday, December 28, Bragg held a council of war to determine his options and met with all of his corps, division and brigade commanders. Orders were then issued. On December 29 and 30, both armies continued to maneuver and skirmish. Although Bragg had initially erected breastworks along the banks of Stones River, he now decided to launch an attack and began massing troops on his left flank. Union General Crittenden had marched as far as Stones River itself and had been ordered by Rosecrans to cross when his skirmishers came under heavy fire. Crittenden then pulled everyone back and avoided disaster. Bragg spent time on the potential battleground and confirmed his decision to seize the initiative and strike. At first Bragg planned his attack to thrust through the center of the Federal line and seize McFadden's Hill, but General Polk suggested that Hardee on the left might have greater success. As a result, Bragg ordered Hardee, his most competent commander, to prepare his assault there. It looked to some Confederates as though Rosecrans was weakest on his right flank, the Confederate left. Bragg even added John P. McCown's division (from Kirby Smith's force) to extend Hardee's wing, and Breckinridge, commanding one of Hardee's divisions, deployed on the right flank of Bragg's force. Bragg was troubled about a possible Union thrust around his right flank and into his rear. Orders were issued at 1:50 a.m. on the morning of December 31. In the meantime, Rosecrans planned an attack on the right side of Bragg's line.[8]

* * *

As night fell, various Union commanders began to have doubts about the right flank. During a 9 o'clock meeting with his generals, Rosecrans ordered McCook to give the appearance of extending his line further to the right and fool the Confederates by lighting fires far off on that flank. During the night, two of McCook's officers, Brigadier General Phil Sheridan and Colonel Joshua Sill, went to McCook and expressed their concerns. General Stanley of the cavalry also paid him a visit and warned of enemy activity on his right flank. Rosecrans, however, simply trusted McCook to do "the right thing." While McCook was somewhat concerned about his role, he was also apparently lulled by the quiet of the night and slept soundly. No one in the Confederate Army seemed fooled by the Union fires. No defensive works were raised on the Union side and no special precautions guarded the right flank. Some historians have likened this atmosphere to the one that preceded the Battle of Shiloh.[9]

Beginning at 6:30 in the morning, Hardee's attack swept in against McCook. By contrast, Rosecrans's plan required extra maneuvering across Stones River and additional time to form up to attack the Confederate forces there. Rosecrans moved too slowly, and McCown's Confederate division attacked first. As the entire division moved forward during the initial assault, it began shifting to its left, and a gap opened in the Confederate front line. As the division veered off to the west, a supporting line consisting of Cleburne's Division was ordered into the gap. As a result, an important reserve unit was committed early in the battle. Beyond Cleburne's line, Major General Benjamin Cheatham of Polk was expected to drive forward. It appears, however, that Cheatham may have been in his cups early that morning, and he slid off his horse to lay prostrate on the ground rather than lead his men into battle. An hour elapsed before he was able to contribute to the attack. Several Union brigades dissolved under the weight of Hardee's assault, McCook's wagon train of reserve and commissary stores was threatened, and his force was pushed back. The Confederates advanced, much like a swinging door into the Federal right flank. Bragg's plan of advance *en echelon* called for careful timing and precision marching in the middle of battle. As the Confederate attack developed, Rosecrans cancelled his own planned attack against the Confederates and struggled to regain control on his right. While Bragg remained for much of the day at his headquarters, Rosecrans rode actively about his lines, summoning reinforcements in an effort to hold back the Confederate flood. Now events began conspiring against the Confederates.[10]

As they advanced, the Confederate line needed to be lengthened as a result, and Hardee was forced to feed additional reinforcements from his reserve force into his front line. Consequently, the Confederates lost their impetus during the advance. The Confederates sought to reach the Nashville Pike and cut off Rosecrans from his base at Nashville. Once again, Larry Daniel makes the point that if Bragg had pushed on through the center to McFadden's Hill, he might have been able to push Rosecrans away from the Pike altogether. Even though ammunition wagons moved along with Hardee, his lines were forced to pause, regroup and delay their advance. He needed additional resources to complete the Confederate victory. Enter Polk once again.[11]

The Fighting Bishop was deployed next to Hardee, and Bragg now ordered this force forward toward the center of the Union line. The Union army used limestone outcroppings and wooded areas to help bolster their defense. As earlier reported, Cheatham of Polk was an hour late, and Polk decided to attack this day with individual brigades, one after another. When Cheatham finally succeeded in advancing, his drive came intermittently also, one brigade attack following the last one. The rest of Polk's corps eventually found itself following suit. By noon, the Federal position was desperate, but the Confederates proved unable to push through the final portion of the stoutly defended line. When Polk's force west of Stones River began to run short of men, Breckinridge, on the east side of the river, was ordered by Bragg to send three brigades to assist. But this maneuver would not occur as quickly as it might sound on paper. Messages and movements went back and forth for the better part of three hours, from 10:00 in the morning until 1:00 in the afternoon. Within ten minutes of starting his movement toward Polk's position, Breckinridge determined that the Union forces on his front were moving to attack him, and he asked Bragg to let him retain those men. Bragg faced a challenging decision: attack at McFadden's Ford, his original thought, or reinforce Polk or even Hardee. Finally, Breckinridge and Bragg, after further confusion, decided that the three brigades could proceed to Polk's aid after all. Off they marched. Once again, they crossed the river, marched west, and headed into battle. How would Polk employ them?[12]

One brigade at a time! In they went and finally succeeded in capturing a densely wooded area known as the Round Forest. By this time, however, the Confederate offensive force was spent. In the face of heavy Union artillery positioned by George Thomas, at least 18 pieces massed on the Union right and another eight facing south, the forces of Hardee on the far left and Polk in the center were forced to a halt. Even so, by 4:00 p.m. Bragg thought he had won the day and just needed a little more daylight to finish the job. In some places, the Confederates had advanced up to two or three miles. The Union forces had been forced back across the entire right side of the Union line, wagons had been captured and some destroyed. Rosecrans appeared to be on the ropes, and the Confederates saw victory coming the next morning. Telegrams went flying off announcing the victory, but Rosecrans wasn't finished. He spent the day of battle moving purposefully from one unit to another, placing infantry and artillery in strong defensive positions. As G.C. Kniffin writes in his article, "Rosecrans seemed ubiquitous. All these dispositions [changes in the Union defense posture] had been made under his personal supervision." His men had been pushed all the way back to the Nashville Pike, but he was still hopeful of survival. Around noon, Rosecrans, Thomas and Crittenden, together with their staff officers, observed the action on the Union right, and a Confederate shell decapitated Julius Garesché, Rosecrans's chief of staff. Rosecrans was unmoved, however, and continued to direct the Federal efforts. The end of the day brought the Union commanders together for a nighttime conference. Hold in place or retreat? Rosecrans asked for opinions, then rode about his lines and returned to order the army to persevere exactly where it was on the battlefield.[13]

The next morning, New Year's Day, found Rosecrans with his Army of the Cumberland still in position. The Confederates were shocked. Rather than commit his men to the major attack the previous day, Joe Wheeler and his cavalry had raided the Federal rear, capturing and burning wagons, and Union supplies of food were low. Rosecrans's army, however, had enough to live on, and by the evening of December 31, two more brigades of infantry moved in to join the army. As January 1 wore on, Bragg realized that the Union Army was not withdrawing. While he appeared on the battlefield during the first morning of the battle, Bragg also spent much of the remaining time in his headquarters. January 1 passed with little action on either side, and January 2 dawned with both sides gazing at each other once more. Confederate batteries opened on Union artillery near the center of the Union line. The two sides dueled, and then around noon, Bragg made a remarkable decision.[14]

Crossing Stones River to the east on January 1, a Union force of around 4,000 men had occupied an elevated piece of land. Altogether Rosecrans moved a full division across, and now on January 2, Bragg could either retreat after his earlier victory of December 31 or attack. He had already declared victory on December 31, and a retreat was not an option for him. Summoning Major General John C. Breckinridge to his headquarters, Bragg ordered his general to advance. He was told to drive his battered division toward the hill in possession of the Federals on the Confederate right, take the high ground, and push over the river toward the Federal left flank. If he could capture McFadden Hill, he would overlook the Nashville Pike and finally defeat the Federals. Seeing Federal artillery in large numbers with supporting infantry, Breckinridge was appalled and protested. But Bragg insisted, and Breckinridge gave the appropriate orders. Over 5,000 Confederates prepared to advance. When they did, they were able to capture the original hill on their right flank and east of the river, but as they tried crossing to the other side, the 57 Union guns, supported by accompanying musketry, destroyed the attack. Then Union infantry counterattacked and drove the Confederates back as well. Smaller than Pickett's Charge in size, Breckinridge's onslaught met the same fate. His force sustained heavy casualties.[15]

By 10:00 the next morning, Bragg determined to retreat. He had suffered around 10,000 casualties while the Union Army lost almost 13,000 men, killed, wounded and captured. Rosecrans failed to counterattack, but Bragg knew he must leave. His active force consisted of less than one-third of the men he had brought to Stones River. His subordinates agreed and by midnight of January 3 the retreat began. A stubbornly fought battle, Stones River had been almost another Shiloh in its intensity. At one point, Bragg's force came close to crushing Rosecrans's right flank, and had they reached the Nashville Pike in force, Bragg might have won the entire affair. But while one might argue that this was almost a tactical draw and Rosecrans was too battered to pursue, strategically this was a Union victory of major proportions.[16]

Except for Chattanooga and Knoxville, all of Kentucky and Tennessee were firmly in Union hands. The Emancipation Proclamation came into being on a positive note. The British and French had no reason to intervene, and after 1862, the Confederacy was indeed faced with much longer odds and significant manpower and material shortages that could not be restored any longer. In 1862, the Confederacy might have hoped for a military victory or even an impressive stalemate. By January 3, 1863, they were finished militarily in the West. They could only reach a stalemate with the North by introducing major reinforcements from another theater of action. They might win an occasional tactical engagement or succeed in raiding behind Union lines, but the flower of their army was gone.[17]

Major General John C. Breckinridge. His final attack against Rosecrans proved disastrous for the Confederates, and Breckinridge blamed Bragg for forcing the issue. This was the final act for the Confederates at Stones River. The two men had never gotten on well together (Library of Congress).

Any hope the Confederacy had for naval construction also vanished by the summer of 1862. The Northern blockade was becoming increasingly effective, and with the decline of the Confederate rail system (wrecked by overuse in 1862) the Confederates were unable to transport the necessary goods to their armies in the West. Inflation was beginning to work against the Confederacy, and now, if they converted areas used for cotton production into additional croplands, great swaths of land for planting crops or supporting animals were irretrievably lost to them. Even if the Confederates had recaptured a small piece of Tennessee, there was no time to plant and harvest crops; it was a hopeless task to rebuild their ruined rail lines or build ships to re-inhabit their rivers. The year 1862 was clearly THE turning point in the western war. Some might argue that this outcome had been reached when Bragg retreated from Perryville. Perhaps so, but the Battle of Stones River terminated

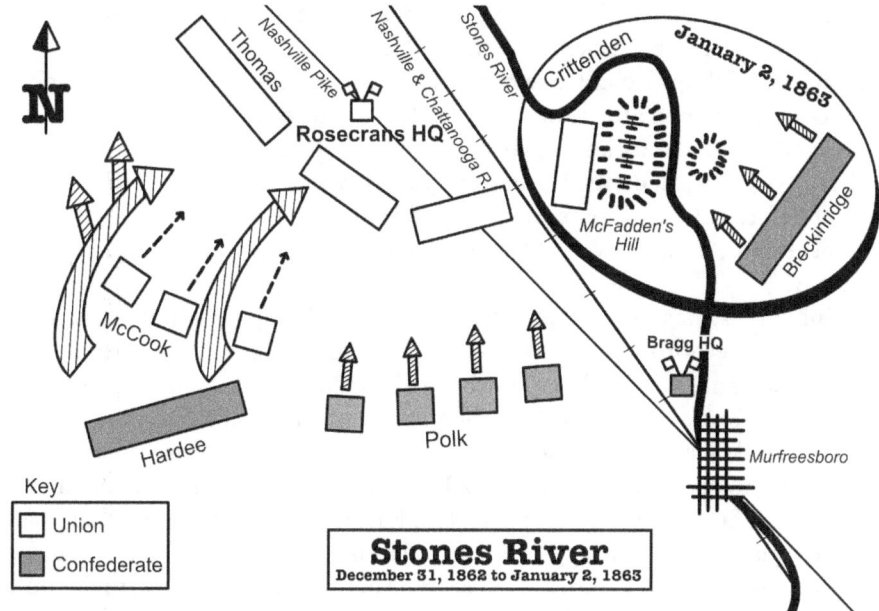

On the first day of battle, Hardee's initial attack pressed the Federals back to the Nashville Pike, but Polk's brigade-sized attacks were ultimately unsuccessful. The key position on McFadden's Hill remained in Union hands throughout the battle (courtesy Margaret A. Zimmermann).

realistic Confederate hopes in the West. In 1864, John Bell Hood would discover this truth during his campaign.

* * *

For the North, Rosecrans had the strategic support of his military and political superiors in Washington. Both the general and his superiors in Washington had full agreement on the objective to be achieved. He needed to attack and defeat Bragg's Confederate army and open the road to Chattanooga, Tennessee. While Halleck and Secretary of War Stanton fussed about his tardiness in moving, the military and political leadership in Washington clearly supported his efforts. He obtained his cavalry commander, he received bounteous supplies, and he could restructure his force as he wished.

On the other hand, the political and military leadership in Richmond damaged Bragg, and he in turn, harmed his own cause. As noted earlier, Davis feared for Vicksburg in Mississippi and was willing to allow Bragg to surrender space in Tennessee if needed. Bragg wanted to fight on but, to confront Rosecrans, he needed more soldiers. His goal of defeating Rosecrans was obviously a different objective than Davis suggested. Bragg also needed subordinates who would sustain his efforts. Davis's decision to keep both Bragg and his detractors (Polk, Hardee and Breckinridge) together in the Army of Tennessee created major command and control problems for Bragg.[18]

Bragg needed to review the odds he faced as well. His force numbered around 37,700 and Rosecrans fielded a force of over 55,000 men. Bragg may not have known the precise number in Rosecrans's army, but based on Joe Johnston's estimate of Rosecrans's strength of 65,000 men on December 6, he had a reasonably good estimate in hand. Having faced Buell's army in Kentucky, Bragg knew he was heavily outnumbered at that point. When Bragg attacked at Stones River, an observer might have raised this question: Was Bragg's objective both clear and *attainable*?[19]

The final part of Bragg's challenge concerned the direction of the attack itself. At one point, Bragg considered attacking with Hardee on the left, and at another time, he considered an attack on the Union center with Polk's corps. At one time or another, he reinforced each of his lieutenants. Daniel suggests that this indecision continued late into the night before battle. In some ways it is a fair question to ask: What was Bragg's objective? These concerns suggest that General Bragg was hardly in a position to attack the Union army.[20]

Following Christmas Day, when Rosecrans took the operational initiative by advancing on Murfreesboro, Bragg seized the tactical advantage with his attack on the right flank of Rosecrans. Bragg held the initiative throughout the first day of battle with both infantry attacks and cavalry raids. Even on the final day of combat, Bragg pressed Breckinridge's attack against the Federals in the face of daunting odds. Through Confederate strategic and operational decisions, a Federal army that had grown much larger than his own was, surprisingly, almost defeated. His initiative ended, however, by the close of the first day of battle. Bragg's efforts on January 2 had no chance for success. Once action was begun on December 31, Rosecrans never attempted to seize the initiative from Bragg either. Even after driving off Breckinridge, the Union army never followed the retreating Confederate force.

Bragg was ill served by his subordinates. Wheeler, like Stuart in the east, galloped off and, while he succeeded in disrupting Union supply efforts, he failed to thoroughly damage Rosecrans's supply trains or to intervene meaningfully on either day of the battle. Polk and Breckinridge both failed to support Bragg in any consequential way. Following his damaging efforts at Perryville, Bishop Polk simply did not provide professional support for Bragg's attack. Breckinridge, for his part, was slow to reinforce Bragg when he was needed on the first day of battle. He may have been acting prudently rather than willfully disobeying orders, but his inability to provide timely reinforcements for Bragg was troublesome. Hours slid past while Bragg and Breckinridge miscommunicated. Breckinridge was not disloyal to Bragg, but the two officers failed to communicate

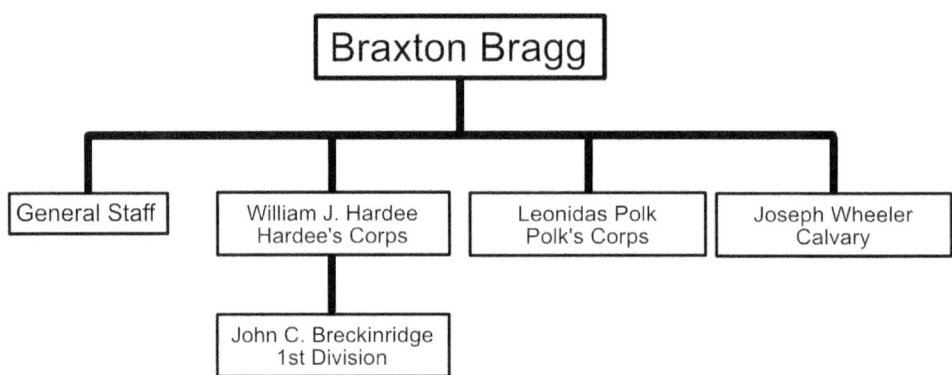

Partial Army organization under Major General Bragg. While other divisions besides Breckinridge's were engaged during the contest, these officers experienced most of the direct contact with Bragg during the battle. Although Joe Wheeler continued to support Bragg, none of his other senior officers were content to serve under him (courtesy Margaret A. Zimmermann).

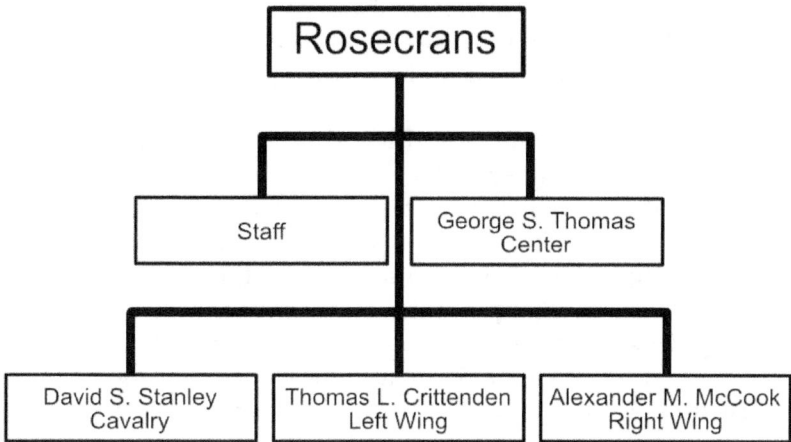

Army organization under Major General Rosecrans. Except for General Alexander McCook, Rosecrans had the professional support of all his senior officers, and they worked together effectively to stem the Confederate attack at Stones River (courtesy Margaret A. Zimmermann).

effectively. Hardee was perhaps the only immediate subordinate who came close to winning the battle for Bragg.[21]

Rosecrans enjoyed the loyalty of his immediate corps commanders. Except for McCook, the other officers provided substantial support for him while the cavalry performed capably under Stanley. Thomas and Crittenden have gone largely without criticism for the roles they played during the battle. Thomas was most helpful in holding the right side of Rosecrans's line and assembling a solid array of artillery in support. Mendenhall, in charge of the Union artillery under Crittenden on the left, did splendid service on the final day of battle.

Rosecrans moved actively about the field throughout the battle. One might argue that on occasion he was too peripatetic in his efforts, but if he was in danger from time to time, he often appeared at the right place and gave intelligent direction to the battle. Even though he lost the services of his chief of staff, Garesché, and put other staff members in danger, he was effective in mounting a sound defense. In the end, even if Rosecrans had gone down, George Thomas was there to provide leadership. Rosecrans's decision to remain on the battlefield after the first day was the right one.

Bragg was far less effective. He remained for hours in his headquarters and then intervened at the wrong moments during the battle. Even before the fighting began, he may have picked the wrong location for his army by straddling Stones River. At no point did he actively intervene to order attacks larger than brigade-level from Polk. This was Bragg's third major battle of the year, and by this time he should have realized that Bishop Polk was unable to direct a competent attack on his own. Apparently, no one took the time to oversee his deployment for battle or contest his decision to attack by brigades, *en echelon*. At Perryville, Bragg had intervened to correct the bishop's faulty alignment and failure to move before the battle, but at Stones River, there was apparently no oversight. Even though Bragg spent time with Polk on the first day of battle, Polk had already reorganized his force in the middle of the night prior to launching his men and then assaulted in piecemeal fashion on December 31.

One more issue appears here. While Bragg was active on the field of battle at various times, the question arises once more: Should he have offered battle in the first place? If the answer is yes, then perhaps he needed to take a much more active role in directly supervising the Confederate attacks. If the answer is no, then perhaps any amount of activity on Bragg's part became pointless. Consequently, there is no simple answer to the question of whether his activity on the battlefield was sufficient in meeting the needs of his army. While we might fault Bragg for being less active on the battlefield than necessary, one should also consider the question of whether he needed to engage in battle at all. As a result, an asterisk has been placed in the summary box closing this chapter. While simple numeric answers may seem satisfying at times, it can be a more complicated matter to determine the proper course of action for an army commander.

Even though Union wagon trains were occasionally captured and burnt, Rosecrans was still given the resources with which to fight the battle. Fitch, for example, notes the following: "Some of the subsistence trains which had been ordered back to Nashville, to be out of our way and of danger, had been destroyed by rebel cavalry." It is interesting to note that on both sides respective staff sizes had grown significantly, and staff officers were becoming more professional. Gone were some of the personal relatives, friends and hangers-on seen earlier in 1862. For example, Bragg's staff had swelled to 36 men on the day of battle.[22]

Bragg's staff had indeed expanded by the time Stones River was fought. The issue, however, is this: Did this expanded staff properly sustain Bragg and the Army of Tennessee? This study has focused almost exclusively on questions of food, ammunition and communications for the army. On the one hand, the Confederate Army of Tennessee was located directly on the Nashville and Chattanooga Railroad line and had been camped in a productive agricultural area for some time. This permitted sufficient food and ammunition to be delivered to the army. During the battle itself, we have evidence of additional ammunition being distributed to the men in the ranks. On the other hand, nagging questions remain. Bragg's unofficial chief of staff was still George Brent, who while obviously competent, still lacked any formal training for this role. Earlier Bragg had acted for a time as his own chief of staff on the march to Perryville, and while the army did not perish, it certainly struggled, and Bragg was compelled to spend many hours managing a paper trail. Now at Stones River, his staff was called upon to deliver messages, provide food, secure ammunition, and keep the commanding general properly informed of events occurring on and near the battlefield. Christopher Kolakowski notes that as Hardee advanced on the battlefield, he had largely outrun his supply of ammunition.[23]

Other staff issues arose as well. Larry Daniel notes that Lieutenant Colonel Lawrence O'Bannon of the Quartermaster Department (who had served in a similar capacity at Perryville) did not do well at Stones River and his replacement, Lieutenant Colonel J.B. McMicken was an alcoholic and ineffective. Daniel's conclusions are not very complimentary. He notes that the general staff was "undistinguished," apparently did not cooperate well with one another, and failed to assist Bragg in any substantive manner. Finally, while Rosecrans's quartermaster, commissary and artillery staff leaders continued their roles after Stones River, several of their Confederate counterparts did not.[24]

By splitting Hardee's corps and placing his men on the far left and far right of his line, Bragg also made communications more challenging during the battle. Breckinridge, who reported to Hardee, found himself in immediate contact with both Bragg and

Polk, but Hardee was left out of the process. Cavalry also appeared ineffective in providing information that Bragg could have used. Bragg's decision to reinforce Polk's failure rather than Hardee's success was also unproductive.[25]

As Wheeler's cavalry was off attacking Union wagons, and while both Morgan and Forest were off raiding, staff officers failed to apprise Bragg of Union movements near the field of battle. Neither Breckinridge nor his aides were able to locate his own cavalry supports under Brigadier Generals John Pegram and John Wharton when needed on January 2. There appears to be little evidence that the staff was fully active in providing accurate or timely information for Bragg as the battle unfolded. While he apparently did not move about the battlefield to see things for himself, the staff apparently failed to do so either. Larry Daniel concludes that "the staff's role in preparing for the retreat from Kentucky and later for the Battle of Murfreesboro proved minimal to nonexistent." They were apparently present in greater numbers than before, but they failed to be an effective team acting in support of the commanding general.[26]

Finally, the issue of McFadden's Hill reappears. While Bragg may have been torn between attacking Rosecrans's right or left flank, no one on his staff apparently pointed out the importance of this terrain feature on the battlefield. As Battlefield Stop #6 today, most visitors to the Stones River National Battlefield Park look out across the river, viewing the hill from the Union perspective.[27] Turning the other way, however, one can see how dominant this hill could be in overlooking both the Nashville Pike and the railroad line. As Bragg and his staff had an opportunity to visit and scout the entire battlefield area before the battle occurred, one must ask another question: Why did no one suggest the importance of this piece of terrain to Bragg?[28]

For the Battle of Stones River, Rosecrans assembled a large and competent group. While his staff was not filled with West Point graduates, they performed a valuable task

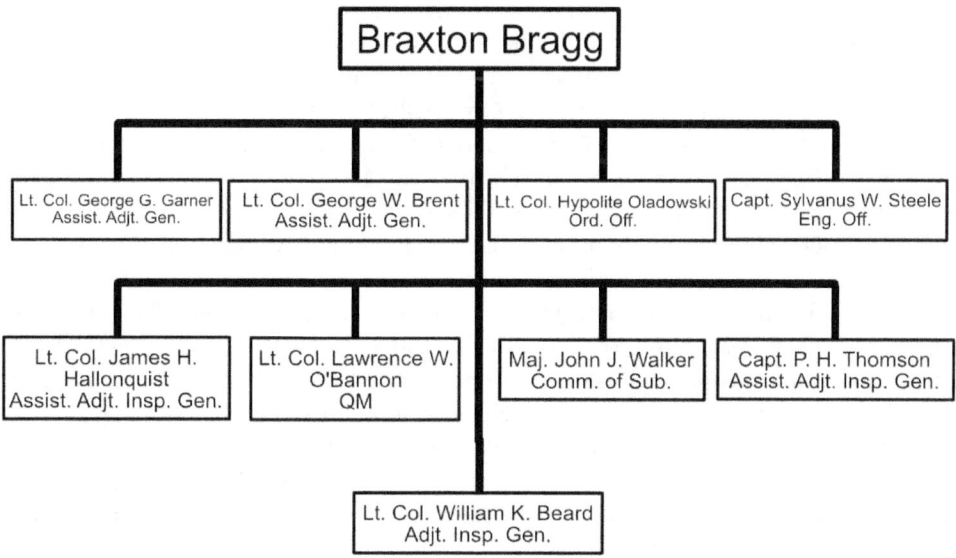

Selected Confederate staff officers. By the time Stones River was fought, Bragg had taken steps to improve the quality of his staff. However, this group of officers still retained several men with limited experience in managing military affairs. See note 28 (courtesy Margaret A. Zimmermann).

in supporting their commander for this campaign. Quartermasters were able to assemble large quantities of supplies prior to the Union movement out of Nashville.

Logistically, the XIV Corps (or the Army of the Cumberland, as they were named after the battle) overcame several hurdles during the campaign. Rosecrans handpicked his new chief of staff, Julius Garesché. Colonel Garesché graduated from West Point in 1841, was a personal acquaintance of Rosecrans, shared the same religion, and held similar political beliefs. The newly created Pioneer Brigade was designed to improve roads and bridges on the army's march forward. Topographical engineers were also needed. From Garesché: "The commanding officer of every corps, division, and brigade in this army will collect all the information accessible to him in relation to the roads, fords, ferries, bridges, mountain passes, defiles, the general configuration of the country, its resources, &c, and prepare sketches of the same." While short of trained engineers, Rosecrans energetically expanded his support staff by deliberately drafting men from each major unit of his army.[29]

Rosecrans bombarded Washington for supplies, horses and weapons for his army. Telegraphic exchanges with Henry Halleck in Washington were a regular occurrence. Telegram from Halleck to Rosecrans, November 27, 1862: "I have approved your requisition on the Engineer Department for more carts drays, &c, but I must warn you against this piling up of impediments…. If you remain long at Nashville you will disappoint the wishes of the Government."

Telegram from Rosecrans to Halleck, November 27, 1862: "The carts are for engineer work about Nashville."

Telegram to Halleck, December 3, 1862: "Cavalry arms arriving slowly: they are indispensable to an effectual and steady advance, which is the only one that will avail us anything worth the cost."

Halleck to Rosecrans, December 4, 1862: "If you remain one more week in Nashville, I cannot prevent your removal…. The Government demands action, and if you cannot respond to that demand some one else will be tried."

Rosecrans to Halleck, December 4, 1862: "To threats of removal or the like I must be permitted to say that I am insensible." Obviously, Rosecrans was not removed.[30]

By Christmas Eve, Rosecrans had amassed supplies for a 20-day campaign away from Nashville and was ready to march. By early 1863, the Quartermaster Department required the services of almost 3,000 wagons, most with six-mule teams along with about 600 ambulances. Fitch estimated that at Stones River about 1,500 horses were killed, and of course these would need to be replaced. This was done before Rosecrans began the Tullahoma Campaign in 1863. The army also required about 50 trainloads of supplies (300 tons) brought to the front by the Louisville and Nashville Railroad. Fitch enumerated the cords of wood (18,000), along with tons of coal and other supplies consumed by the Army of the Cumberland. He noted that the Quartermaster's Department in Nashville consisted of over 3,000 men. While his estimates covered the period following the Battle of Stones River, it is a fair assumption to say that the army required similar amounts prior to the battle as well. By late 1862, these were astonishing numbers that the Confederacy could not match.[31]

Chief Quartermaster, John Taylor, had previously served under John Fremont and then John Pope at the time Pope's army captured Island No. 10, earlier in the year. As Rosecrans commanded the force that successfully defended Corinth from Earl Van Dorn's attack in October, Rosecrans had requested Taylor (along with several other staff officers) to join him from Pope's Army of the Mississippi. Serving directly under Taylor in Rosecrans's headquarters was Captain Simon Perkins, and Lenette S. Taylor has described his quartermaster responsibilities in detail. She notes that on each day, trains of 100 wagons or more came out of Nashville to secure forage for the army. During and after the battle, she describes the efforts of Perkins and other quartermasters to keep the army supplied with food and ammunition. While Wheeler's raid threatened Rosecrans's supply lines, they failed to disrupt them.[32]

The Commissary Department, under the leadership of Lieutenant Colonel Samuel Simmons, provided food for the army. He served under Generals Nathaniel Lyon, John Charles Fremont, U.S. Grant, and finally in Rosecrans's army. This suggests that he served, as Fitch suggests, to the "universal satisfaction" of the army. The Provost Marshal-General of the army, Major William Wiles, was responsible for keeping order within the army by supervising the legal aspects of military life, appointing a provost-judge (unique to the Army of the Cumberland), and managing business relationships with sutlers and other civilians. Along with other Federal armies, this general staff provided the necessary technical support required by a commanding general. While general staff officers served with the Confederacy and their numbers increased as the war matured, the South never managed to appoint such an experienced and fully qualified group of people to manage the complexities of mid-nineteenth-century war. Although not directly connected to the general staff, other staff officers controlled a secret service contingent for spying and suppression of smuggling, and the army Signal Corps and Telegraph Department provided comprehensive telegraphic communication throughout the various military commands under Rosecrans.[33]

The result of all this preparation was that Rosecrans's force was well supplied when it moved southeast. Even though over 200 wagonloads of supplies were captured and destroyed by Wheeler's cavalry before and during the battle itself, the Army of the Cumberland was able to continue fighting on for an additional two days (January 1 and 2). The destruction of the wagons caused Rosecrans to pause and reflect on whether he should remain in place after December 31, but his decision to remain included the fact that his supplies were still sufficient for combat. Finally, it should be noted that Rosecrans was able to construct a supply center at Murfreesboro (Fortress Rosecrans) immediately following the battle, and over the next seven months, this supply center provided the means for Rosecrans's brilliant Tullahoma Campaign which followed. Jim Lewis notes that the facility and fortifications covered "nearly 200 acres" and provided three-months' worth of supplies for 65,000 men in the field. Fitch concludes his Quartermaster summary with the following: "When General Rosecrans assumed command of the Army of the Cumberland, it was destitute of nearly everything. Now it is abundantly supplied,—better, perhaps, than any other in the field."[34]

Several members of Rosecrans's staff were accomplished professionals serving in a variety of active business positions before the war. While West Point officers were few in numbers for the North as well as the South, their civilian counterparts in the Union brought an array of useful talents and experiences with them.[35] Careers in civil engineering, hardware store ownership, railroads and mining were common experiences for staff members. As a result, the complexities of arming, clothing, feeding and moving large forces of men were not unknown to these staff officers. The Confederacy seemed to lack this more urban and industrialized management experience, and the staff work in Confederate armies probably suffered as a result.[36]

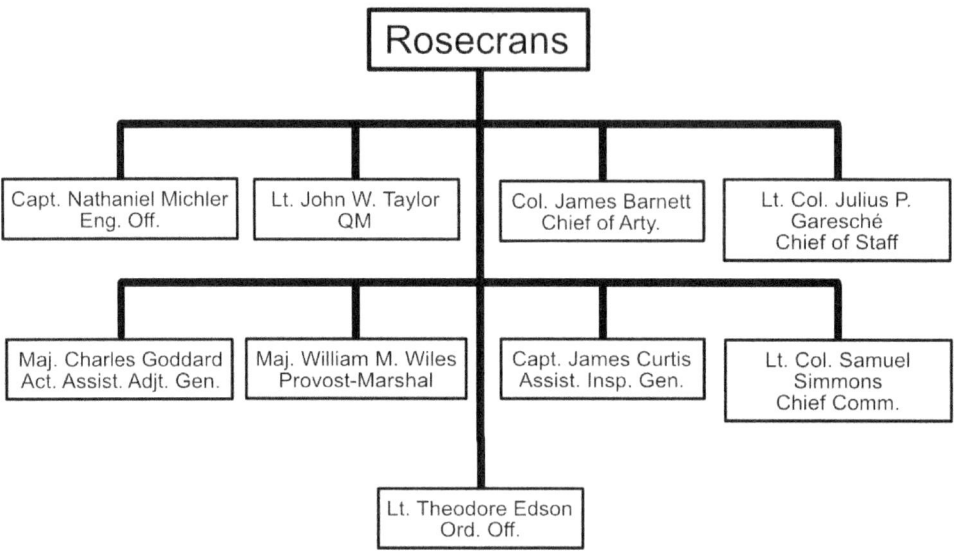

Selected Union staff officers. Upon taking command of the army, Rosecrans took steps to develop a fully professional staff. At Stones River, he was able to continue the contest even after the destruction of some of his supply wagons. See note 36 (courtesy Margaret A. Zimmermann).

While Rosecrans utilized all his available men and resources, the narrative for Stones River becomes complicated when discussing the ability of the Confederates to use all the resources originally available to them. An entire division left Bragg's army before the battle began, and while Bragg can be faulted for sending so many cavalrymen far afield, there is also evidence showing that he expected Morgan to return in time for combat duty. In fact, Bragg called up and employed all his remaining force, except for a token guard in his rear. One can reasonably conclude that Bragg used his available resources to the best of his ability. Consequently, the summary category at the end of the chapter contains an asterisk that points to this complexity.

The Confederate government may be faulted, however, for failing to provide Bragg with sufficient resources to defend a vital area in middle Tennessee against Rosecrans. It wasn't until the fall of 1863 that Davis and Lee consented to move additional resources west to help Bragg at Chickamauga. While one can make an argument for reinforcing Vicksburg in 1862, a similar argument could be made for maintaining the overall strength of Bragg's Army of Tennessee and drawing resources from other parts of the Confederacy to do so. To further complicate matters, Bragg really failed to mount an all-out assault on the first day of battle. While Hardee was completely engaged, Polk sent only brigade-sized packets into combat, one after the other in piecemeal fashion. Polk's artillery was concentrated briefly at one point, but in general, Bragg's artillery was spread evenly around the field. On January 2, Mendenhall's Union concentration on or near McFadden's Hill proved decisive in breaking Breckinridge's attack and, at other times, Union artillery was assembled for maximum effect as well. Union artillery at Stones River was clustered in larger groups tactically and consisted of pieces that were both numerous and more modern than their Southern opponents. As the war moved into 1863, their Federal forces would heavily overmatch Southern artillery in the West.

In a strategic sense, Bragg was unsuccessful, and Rosecrans was victorious. As mentioned earlier, the battle might be considered a tactical draw, but clearly this was a strategic success for the North. Abraham Lincoln certainly thought so. As he was an excellent strategist politically, and as Lincoln had become a very capable strategic thinker in the military sphere, he emphatically telegraphed Rosecrans at a later time, "I can never forget … you gave us a hard earned victory, which, had there been a defeat instead, the nation could scarcely have lived over." Bragg quit the field, knowing that he could not hold his ground after January 2. Unfortunately, he left many wounded men behind and could not afford their loss. Even though Rosecrans did not pursue with his battered army, he held the ground, and the Union was victorious in a strategic western battle.[37]

Six Elements of Victory at Stones River

Stones River	Clear, Attainable Objective	Operational Initiative	Command Unity
Rosecrans	Achieved	Not Achieved	Achieved
Bragg	Not Achieved*	Not Achieved	Not Achieved
	Logistics/Staff	Used All Resources	Strategic Outcome
Rosecrans	Achieved	Achieved	Achieved
Bragg	Not Achieved	Not Achieved*	Not Achieved

Fortunately for Rosecrans, his immediate subordinates and staff provided valuable support and enabled him to overcome the initial shock of the Confederate onslaught. At this late date, despite his best efforts, the Confederate army under Bragg was unable to reverse the Union advance through Tennessee.

Chapter 11

Reflections on Civil War Leadership

Now at this juncture, the evidence suggests that at least six determinants affected the outcome of combat in the Civil War. Reviewing each action, shown in the tables summarizing each chapter, several conclusions can be drawn. When a general won a clear victory, such as Thomas at Mill Springs, Grant at Fort Donelson, Grant on the second day of Shiloh, Smith at Richmond, and Curtis at Pea Ridge, they also achieved a clear preponderance of successes in the six categories outlined on the list. In other words, Thomas, Grant, Smith and Curtis all experienced success in almost every category. Generals who opposed them experienced an absence of events operating in their favor. Even if a student of history wishes to dispute any single category, the overall result is so lopsided that the winning side still achieved a significant victory.

1. Clear and Attainable Objective: The successful general receives the support of the political leadership as they prepare clear and attainable objectives for his army.

Twelve actions are described in the book and nine of them involved tactical infantry engagements. The fall of Island No. 10, New Orleans, and the Union failure at the Yazoo River were primarily the result of poor strategic decisions taken by the Confederacy or poor communications and leadership on the part of the North. Of the remaining nine engagements reviewed in detail, all seven Union victories included strategic support from either President Abraham Lincoln or Henry Halleck as theater commander. The U.S. Army assigned the area of "objective" as one of its Principles of War for many years, and we can see this concern borne out in several Civil War battles of 1862. In some cases for the North, both the army commander and his superiors agreed on a clear objective or set of objectives. The one battle lost by the North involved wildly varying sets of objectives.

For the Union, U.S. Grant obviously did not have the trust or friendship of Henry Halleck, and yet Halleck arranged for reinforcements when he needed to do so. Between the end of the Fort Donelson campaign and the onset of the Shiloh campaign, their relationship deteriorated again. In the end, however, Halleck sustained Grant strategically as he commanded the army that fought at Shiloh in April of 1862. Halleck assisted Grant's movement against Fort Henry and encouraged Grant at Fort Donelson. The North made its share of strategic mistakes in 1862, and these mistakes served to prolong the war. The Yazoo expedition was another example of both strategic and operational mistakes. In two other cases, Halleck had the opportunity to keep his army more united than he did, and Don Carlos Buell had an excellent chance to capture Chattanooga by mid-year.

On occasion, the Union failed to connect battlefield victories with later strategic advances, and this delayed the prosecution of the war in the West. For example, Thomas was unable to gain any true strategic advantage after Mill Springs by capturing Knoxville, Tennessee. The two Union victories in Arkansas safeguarded Missouri from Confederate incursions (although not from guerrilla warfare). After Rosecrans's victory at Corinth, the North proved unable to follow through with a successful advance to Vicksburg. After Grant's offensive ended with the Confederate raid at Holly Springs, Sherman was left all alone for his abortive assault at Chickasaw Bluffs. Except for the Battle of Richmond, the North did not make the kinds of strategic or operational mistakes that cost them entire battles during this time.

In selecting objectives that at times were neither clear nor realistic, the Confederacy stumbled at first. Zollicoffer had no reason for crossing the Cumberland in January of 1862 and confronting Thomas. Van Dorn pushed his army mercilessly forward to defeat Curtis at Pea Ridge, and Hindman appeared to take similar risks later in the year. They both did so without proper logistical support. What were John B. Floyd and Gideon Pillow trying to accomplish at Fort Donelson? After receiving instructions from A.S. Johnston to withdraw toward Nashville, Pillow led an assault on the Union lines, but then withdrew after opening a path to safety.

At no point in either the Perryville or Stones River campaign did President Davis and Braxton Bragg fully agree on Confederate strategy. Bragg never received authorization to lead the armies gathering in Tennessee and Mississippi for the late summer campaign, and Davis refused to allow Bragg to choose his subordinates, or even some key staff officers. While Davis supported Bragg by keeping him in command of the Army of Tennessee, Davis also accommodated the anti–Bragg faction within his army by retaining Bishop Polk and other disloyal officers. Critical foodstuffs and supplies were also withheld from Bragg throughout his time in Tennessee and sent to Lee's army instead. Bragg may have brought on many of his own problems, but from a strategic view, he often went unsupported in the West. Neither the South as an aspiring nation nor Confederate leaders in the West encountered the same luxury of time that the Union enjoyed in gathering and applying its resources to the conflict.[1]

The selection of professional commanding officers also played an important role in securing clear objectives for winning the war. Both sides struggled in this area. On more than one occasion, Lincoln hoped to combine political popularity with military direction and failed. When John C. Fremont came to grief by trying to emancipate slaves in his district, he was removed. Lincoln and Fremont were clearly at odds in setting objectives for the North. The same fate befell Don Carlos Buell as he failed to confront his Confederate adversaries with energy and decision. The appointment of William Nelson before the battle at Richmond led to a Federal disaster. With the selection of Thomas, Grant and Rosecrans, the North experienced much greater success in this area.

In the South as well, President Davis struggled to find common cause with many of his political/military appointees. Without informing the President, Polk and Pillow set a goal to invade Kentucky and left Davis with a *fait accompli*. But both remained in command of important Confederate forces. Davis and Beauregard were never comfortably paired, and Davis failed to unite with Bragg in determining goals and army leadership for recapturing or even holding Kentucky and Tennessee. The inability of the Confederates to set clear strategic or operational goals hampered their military effectiveness throughout 1862.

2. Operational Initiative: The successful general seizes the initiative at the close of battle.

In this study, the term initiative has been used to examine a general's battlefield efforts at the close of battle. Later, the question of strategic value is raised to ask whether a battle had lasting, positive effects for one side. This can be another challenging area to examine. Any army might seize the initiative and attack its opponent early in the day or throughout the first day of battle. But the side that took the offensive at the close of the battle, even if this occurred on the second day of combat, can be said to have finally seized the initiative and carried the day. For example, although Grant has been criticized for leaving his army unattended at both Donelson and Shiloh, once he returned, both of his armies were able to seize the initiative by the close of each action.

It was the army commander's responsibility to seize the initiative and hold onto it throughout a campaign and ensuing combat. Even if offensive movement, operationally, following a battle, did not always occur for the North, on several occasions Union commanders were advancing with their forces and were able to exercise offensive movements at the immediate close of combat (Mill Springs, Donelson, Pea Ridge, Shiloh and Prairie Grove). Corinth and Stones River remain question marks in some respects. Rosecrans chose not to undertake any offensive maneuvers at the close of combat on either occasion, and indeed for a full six months after Stones River, but Bragg was still forced to retreat and give up all but a small sliver of Tennessee after the battle.

Buell was acting on the defensive by the close of the day at Perryville, and it appears that strategically he wished to return to his "war of geography" by retaking Nashville. Neither Curtis nor Blunt could successfully pursue Confederate forces even though they were experiencing success on the battlefield at the close of those actions. In like manner, Rosecrans proved unable to follow up his two victories energetically during the close of battle at Corinth and Stones River. Although Rosecrans was quiescent at the end of the day, Stones River proceeded to be strategically important for the North, and therefore while Rosecrans proved unable to exploit victory on the day of battle, the outcome that followed was strategically important.

3. Command Unity: The successful general enjoys the effective support of his subordinates.

In seven of the nine engagements described in this book, the Union commander received his lieutenants' professional support. With the exceptions of Richmond, Kentucky, and Perryville, every Federal army commander succeeded in working acceptably with his subordinates. While one might question Lew Wallace's contributions on the first day of Shiloh, he was more effective on the second day. The other division commanders, amateur and professional, appeared to do their best for the cause on both days. Even Don Carlos Buell performed well on the second day in support of Grant's forward movement, and it can therefore be said that Grant received substantial assistance from his subordinates.

While Union generals, such as Grant, may have turned in a less-than-stellar performance at places such as Shiloh, Grant's subordinates, such as Sherman, helped Grant reach the end of the day and become famous for ordering an attack on the following morning. In the West, Union commanding generals appeared to assemble staff officers and/or acquire subordinates who truly helped even mediocre commanders perform well. An excellent example of this support comes from General James G. Blunt at Prairie Grove, Arkansas. Even though Blunt refused to withdraw his small force in the face of heavy odds, his subordinate, General Herron, completed an astonishing march to reach Blunt's exposed force. Then, together, while their piecemeal attacks were inadequate in producing clear-cut victory in battle, the performance of their artillery officers helped them hold out until the Confederate General Thomas Hindman retreated. Once again, the actions of competent subordinates for the Union forces helped bring victory to their cause.

For the Union forces, their commanding officers were also active on the fields of battle in seven of nine engagements, all clear Union victories, while their Confederate counterparts were active during their victory at Richmond, Kentucky, and in three different actions. This would suggest that lack of command activity contributed on several other occasions to Confederate defeat. Once again, if a commander or key lieutenant was active on the day of battle but rode too close to the front lines for too long a time, this action could lead to disaster. Unfortunately, if a battle should probably not have been undertaken in the first place (Mill Springs or Stones River comes to mind for the Confederates), a general's activity on the battlefield may have been perfectly appropriate, but the army could still lose the battle regardless of his personal activity.

On the Confederate side, the lieutenants failed to cooperate effectively in all but two engagements. This was a critical component if one wishes to understand Southern failures. Albert Sidney Johnston had his subordinates' active support at Shiloh, and Kirby Smith likewise had his lieutenants' complete support. Yet earlier in the year, even Johnston failed to impress William J. Hardee as they worked together following the Fort Donelson debacle. We can also point to numerous examples of egregious behavior when we follow other Confederate commanders. If a key subordinate pressed too close to the scene of action (e.g., Zollicoffer at Mill Springs or McCulloch at Pea Ridge) their early demise in combat was clearly detrimental to the Confederate cause, even if their actions in moving forward were well-intentioned. As the campaigning season wore on, Braxton Bragg failed to work effectively with peers, such as Kirby Smith, or immediate subordinates, such as Polk. Although originally he was energetic enough in helping to gather resources for the war, Bishop Polk appeared to exercise a pernicious influence throughout 1861 and 1862.

4. Effective Staff/Logistics: The successful general enjoys the support of a competent staff. The staff generally succeeds in providing good communications across the battlefield and supervises logistical support (e.g., distribution of ammunition and food).

This area remains a difficult one to quantify, and this topic does not appear in the Nine Principles written for the U.S. Army. Nevertheless, good communication on the battlefield was essential and the appropriate distribution of food and ammunition were similarly critical components to victory in the Civil War. Generals, as well as their staff officers (often personal staff), might fail on some occasions or succeed in others to communicate clearly during a battle. On some occasions, reaching a firm conclusion here is admittedly challenging. For the Union army, staff work and logistical success appeared to support their efforts in seven of nine engagements (with Buell at Perryville and

Nelson at Richmond being the exceptions). At Perryville, Buell was out of touch with many of his subordinates and they with him. Aides apparently failed to provide senior officers with timely information for much of the day as well.

Confederate staff work was less effective, and only one occasion—Richmond, Kentucky—marked successful staff efforts. Looking closely at the staff work supporting Van Dorn at Corinth, one can see a real question about its effectiveness. Although disputed by Van Dorn afterward, logistical support was missing, and the results also suggest that staff communication across the battlefield on the second day was lacking as well. Earlier at Pea Ridge, he failed to bring his staff with him, and Price's staff also failed to assist in a meaningful way. Someone simply forgot to bring up ammunition for the second day of battle, and this mistake was a critical one.

While this book does not attempt to treat logistics in its entirety, the proper distribution of food and ammunition challenged both sides, and on several occasions the Confederates failed in the task of parceling out the supplies of ammunition or food that were available to them. Before the battle at Pea Ridge, Van Dorn ordered a forced march and apparently failed to feed his men adequately in the three days leading up to the battle. At Shiloh, the Confederate army struggled to support the brigades leading the attack, and it was often difficult to bring ordnance wagons within easy supporting distance of the advancing army. While some of the looting done by Confederates in the Union camp took place because many of the Confederates were green soldiers, some of the delay they experienced during their attack was caused when men paused to feed empty stomachs or hunt for replacement weapons or ammunition.

The critical subject of useful staff work is explored further in Appendix I. The North had been undergoing a significant industrial revolution for some time, and the Civil War facilitated this economic development. While in 1862 these newly developed industrial capabilities had a positive impact on Northern efforts, the lack of a strong industrial base in following years would witness a more complete and devastating impact on the South. Without a cadre of experienced men who understood that a hierarchical and more organized approach to war approximated similar technical skills in business and engineering, the South often struggled to fill key staff positions effectively.

5. Full Use of Resources: The successful general commits all of his resources in a timely fashion for battle.

Employing all available resources, all at once, played a major role in determining victory or defeat. Bragg (and Van Dorn at Corinth) insisted on piecemeal assaults. These unsuccessful attacks have acquired the term, attack *en echelon*, that is, an attack by one brigade or division at a time along the enemy's line. Bragg pursued this tactic doggedly each time he led his army into battle. Given the complicated nature of this type of offensive, it seemed to break down in its execution every time it was employed. Some attacking units were late to engage and, on occasion, others moved off in the wrong direction or stopped moving forward altogether as the battle progressed. Grant, Thomas, Curtis, and Kirby Smith all pressed an attack with as many soldiers as they possibly could. For each of these commanders, their assaults brought solid results. Witness Lincoln's admonition to General Joseph Hooker, "Put in all of your men." In the West, only Albert Sidney Johnston attempted to engage all of his men at once, but by adopting Thomas Jordan's battle plan and stacking his formations several divisions deep, Johnston's army was also deprived of bringing his entire strength to bear at one time. By allowing command

and control issues to fester throughout the army, the Confederates were unable to coordinate their assaults and bring their entire force to bear.[2]

With the exceptions of Richmond and Perryville, the Union army appeared to apply all its resources in the other seven engagements. On the other hand, the Confederate army appeared to bring all its resources to bear solely at the Battle of Richmond. For other engagements in 1862, forces were committed in piecemeal fashion through *en echelon* attacks or simply left out of the action. The Richmond government finally sent Longstreet's corps west in 1863, but many would argue that the Confederate military defeat in the West had been largely determined by then.

6. Strategic Outcome: After the battle, the successful general achieves strategic success.

After April of 1862, the Union continued to win mostly technical or minor victories, but the Confederates began to achieve greater success in several categories. At Perryville, Bragg was unable to remain on the battlefield after initial success during the first day's contest, and he stymied Buell's attempt to bring about a clear Confederate defeat. By retreating from Kentucky, Bragg failed to achieve any of his strategic goals, and Buell was at least able to recover lost territory within the state. By failing to defeat Bragg or pursue him, however, Buell reaped few strategic accomplishments afterward. At Corinth, Rosecrans won a clear-cut, if difficult, victory over Van Dorn, but when he failed to pursue Van Dorn vigorously after the close of battle, a true strategic victory eluded him. Prairie Grove was another closely fought battle, but when the Confederates retreated at the end of the day, this meant that the battle brought an end to their ability to threaten Missouri or even hold important areas of Arkansas. Even though Bragg came close to destroying Rosecrans at Stones River, his retreat from the battlefield on the third day left the field to the Federal army, causing a major crisis in morale for people of the South.

Stalemates in campaigns sometimes came about when both sides recorded a number of failures within these six categories, and only the physical occupation of the battlefield spelled a narrow victory for one side and defeat for the other. At Perryville, Bragg scored a minor tactical success, but then in the face of overwhelming numbers withdrew from the field. Buell's slow movements negated any opportunity the Union might have had for claiming victory here. As a result, the outcome of Perryville would suggest that the Union had achieved a very minor success with a high casualty rate. But there was no corresponding strategic gain. The same can be said for Kirby Smith's clear victory in Kentucky. Although his casualties were not crippling, he proved unable to wring any strategic advantage out of his victory.

Are some of these traits more important than others? For this study, limited to only nine actions, the author did not feel that the limited data itself (absent a good deal of speculation) provided a clear answer, and therefore he did not attempt the guesswork associated with suggesting an answer.

As 1862 receded into bloody memory, what new requirements for waging war emerged? As commanders struggled to make sense of the widespread carnage, one conclusion became more obvious. With the increasingly complex nature of the conflict and the large-scale armies that were called into being, much more was required from a leader than just bravery. While the commander of the army remained a lonely figure, the truly effective commander needed to rely on the trust and encouragement from the leaders, political and military, who placed him in command. He needed to rely on his team of subordinates and staff to both understand and execute his wishes. He also required from his team original and constructive ideas as he formulated his own plans and responded to crises. This may seem obvious to the serious student of military history and leadership, but it is a fundamental, and perhaps indispensable, truth often missing from the accounts we are given to study.

Appendix I
Distribution of Food and Ammunition

Of the six questions raised in the beginning of the book, the area of logistics was arguably a key component in determining battlefield success and, as the war progressed, the Union army became increasingly successful in supporting its armies. During the Mexican War, the U.S. Army was well staffed with West Point officers. Major General Winfield Scott set a high standard for staff support with his able assistants. During the Civil War, however, neither North nor South could rely on the very limited supply of West Point graduates available to fill all their staff positions. The South tried a variety of ad-hoc staff experiments in the West while the North relied on men who brought a wide variety of business experiences with them. Both sides also relied on brigade and divisional staff members to manage logistical challenges. As the year progressed, both sides increased the number of staff officers at the army level. Consequently, when we read about the Battle of Stones River, both sides employed a robust logistics staff in comparison to earlier actions in the West.

Earlier in the war, as West Point graduates and former army officers returned to commands in the North and South, almost all these officers desired combat duty. With the huge number of recruits flocking to the colors, both sides used former regulars and West Point graduates in leadership positions. Both North and South searched for men who could fill remaining staff positions competently. The South turned to a variety of attorneys and men who possessed the willingness to help organize the food, arms and ammunition needed by the soldiers. As railroads, the telegraph and steamboats also played a critical role in the war, both sides attempted to recruit men with experience in these areas as well. The North, however, excelled in finding experienced individuals who could support the logistical needs of their armies.

As mentioned earlier, from 1840 to 1860, the United States had undergone an industrial revolution. North of the Ohio River this meant that railroads were growing exponentially, and steamboats filled the need for moving large quantities of goods on rivers west of the Appalachians. This economic growth largely bypassed the South. Demographics from the period suggest strongly that population growth occurred mainly in urban areas, and immigrants from overseas also moved in large numbers to join this swelling urban population. Except for New Orleans, most of these urban centers were in the North such as Boston, Philadelphia, New York, Cincinnati, Chicago and St. Louis. Throughout the war, the South could not build locomotives, produce telegraph wire or railroad tracks. The North, on the other hand, experienced great success in all of these areas. For example, one inventor in the North created a machine capable of producing a new horseshoe every second and had people fully capable of distributing this output throughout the entire armed forces network. On a more local level, it would appear that Southern inability to distribute resources (specifically food and ammunition) during several campaigns suggests that staff and line officers failed to coordinate their efforts. In his book *Engineering Victory*, Thomas Army, Jr., suggests that the North had implemented effective educational reforms and had developed a system of labor that prized "mechanical ability, ingenuity, and imagination." Except for a handful of locations in the South, an agricultural system built on slavery could not compete.[1]

For seven Northern victories, a review of the actual staff officers finds one statistic that stands out. The North used several men who were familiar with business practices that were developing during the industrial revolution. In the battles described here, 44 key staff officers were identified by name. Eight of them fought in at least two battles with Grant or Rosecrans. Nineteen of them had a West Point or regular army background. An additional 12 men had backgrounds as merchants or businessmen. Twenty-seven of these men were promoted after serving in combat.

For the Confederates, a similar review suggests the following: Forty-eight officers were identified by name, and 17 former West Point or regular army officers served in staff positions. Only two merchants, or anyone with business experience, were identified as staff officers. At least nine lawyers or newspaper editors served in staff positions. While almost half of these officers were promoted after the battles they fought, another substantial group was never heard from again in staff or leadership positions. For example, after the Battle of Pea Ridge, Sterling Price replaced his entire staff as he crossed the Mississippi River to fight in Tennessee and Mississippi. It is also noteworthy that the Confederate staff at the Battle of Corinth did not perform well, either. The high turnover of staff members may have affected their performance. Interestingly, for the one Confederate victory at Richmond, the South employed West Point officers almost exclusively in both field and staff commands, while the North employed none. For the other eight battles, however, the evidence suggests that 70 percent of the Union staff members were either West Pointers or had extensive business, engineering or railroad experience. For the South only 43 percent could make the same claim.[2]

If we broaden the scope and include a larger group of staff officers serving in the West, we find similar statistics. Of 139 Union officers who served on staffs during the war in the West, merchants made up 42 percent of the total, West Point officers made up 24 percent, and lawyers made up 20 percent of the whole. These were the top three categories. For the most part, pre-war lawyers served as adjutants or aides-de-camp in Union forces. For the 151 Confederate officers identified, 34 percent consisted of pre-war lawyers, 18 percent came from West Point graduates, and 17 percent came from farms and plantations, a striking difference. Only 14 percent listed business experience. These statistics do not speak to the competence or intelligence of the officers involved, but they do serve to suggest that a larger percentage of Union staff officers appeared more able to support the heavy demands that a commanding general might need to place upon them.[3]

Confederate inability to distribute food and ammunition for their armies proved to be a major failing. At Mill Springs, Donelson, Shiloh, Pea Ridge, Perryville, Prairie Grove, Corinth and even Stones River, the failure of Confederate officers to distribute food or ammunition played a role in the Confederate defeat, and this failure occurred more often than any of the other identified factors.

At the most basic level, Northern recruits often possessed skills that were useful for the logistical needs of the army. Two examples serve to illustrate this point. As part of the industrial revolution occurring in the North, large numbers of immigrants appeared, particularly from the German states. Between 1840 and 1860, over 1,500,000 German immigrants came to the United States. Of these, approximately 200,000 German immigrants served in the Union Army. Both Don Tolzman and Bruce Levine further cite the presence of German Americans who were carpenters, cabinetmakers, tanners, weavers, bakers, butchers, foundry men, millers, coopers, coppersmiths, blacksmiths, and tailors.[4]

At the next level of operation, we are introduced to Captain Simon Perkins, Jr. Lenette Taylor writes that by February of 1862, Perkins, at age 23, was appointed captain and assistant quartermaster, serving at first in Louisville and then in Nashville. His pre-war education included work in his father's railroad office and then in his uncle's iron company. He also spent time in Cleveland working as a bank teller and learning accounting. After his assignment to Nashville in 1862, we learn that he supervised the hiring of 93 new workers in his first month there and supervised steamboat, rail, and wagon transportation primarily for General Buell. By late April of 1862, he supervised the delivery of 11 million pounds of forage on 27 steamboats to Pittsburgh Landing in Tennessee. The South was unable to call on many men with this type of immigrant background or other men with the experience of working for railroad, commercial and other industrial concerns.[5]

In summary it is fair to say this: At the tactical level, many individual Union soldiers had the education and "know-how" to provide support for the more complicated logistics requirements of the mid-nineteenth century. Consequently, staff officers in the North, assigned to distributing the necessary food and ammunition for the troops, usually functioned effectively as part of a larger team supporting the commanding general. For the Confederates, their staff officers were not incompetent, but they appeared less capable of making up for the commanding officer's limitations when it came to distributing the necessary quantities of food and ammunition.[6]

As a result of the industrial revolution in the North, their armies contained large numbers of men with business, engineering and commercial experience that would properly support the needs of any army. Once again, the South might claim a rough parity in arms and manpower on the field of battle throughout most of 1862, but with the passage of time, the South lost the opportunity to win the war militarily.[7]

Appendix II
Artillery Improvements

One of the enduring myths of the Civil War suggested that the Confederates were badly outnumbered and outgunned in almost every engagement with the North. With artillery, however, the differences between the two sides can be compared and clarified. The comparison at Shiloh in April of 1862 and Stones River in December suggests that almost a rough parity in arms existed in the beginning of the year. The Confederates had but a short time to take advantage of that equivalence before the North mustered overwhelming resources, and they were unable to do so. The "long arm" of artillery illustrates that time frame. A summary of artillery pieces used by both sides would suggest the following conclusions:

At Shiloh, the number of pieces available to both sides on the first day was approximately equal: Union = 117, Confederate = 113. Six-pound smoothbore guns and 12-pound howitzers used by the Union (43 percent of the whole) made up much of the Union armament. Another 25 percent consisted of the inferior James Rifle, a brass gun bored for rifling. As some have suggested, while the James Rifle was technically a rifled piece, this gun failed to give Union soldiers a significant battlefield advantage. After firing for a time, the rifling was worn down and the piece reverted to a smoothbore, where extra windage reduced accuracy. A careful study of the James Rifle also noted that the early production of the sabot, a lead device used around the exterior of the shell that adhered to the rifled grooves of the gun, tended to disintegrate and fly off the shell as close as 50 feet from the weapon. As the report reads, "The lead sabots were prone to break up on exiting the gun, subjecting close by troops to the detriments of friendly fire. The shell is generally believed to have been relatively unstable in flight." In other words, the possession of this fieldpiece gave the Union no real advantage on the battlefield. Only about 11 percent of the Union guns were more modern rifles.[1]

For the Confederates, two types of pieces (6-pound smoothbores and 12-pound howitzers) made up about 82 percent of available pieces at Shiloh. Another 18 percent of their guns were rifled. The 6-pound, 1841 smoothbore gun and 12-pound howitzer were two weapons left over from the Mexican War. The United States began introducing the 10-pound Parrott Rifle, 6" Ordnance Rifle, and the 12-pound gun-howitzer (the Napoleon) into front line units when the war began. At Shiloh, neither side had a significant advantage or disadvantage in the artillery. Given the broken nature of the terrain and limited visibility, the more modern rifles would be even less effective.[2]

By the time of Stones River, however, the Union XIV Corps had acquired a somewhat different set of guns. The Union Army could boast of 147 guns versus the

Confederate's 100. Unfortunately for the Confederates, the Union used their numerical and qualitative advantage on two occasions during the battle to achieve a defensive success. This occurred when Thomas and Rosecrans worked together to defend the Nashville Pike and when Mendenhall assembled his batteries to drive back the offensive undertaken by Breckinridge's division on the third day of action. Roughly the same percentage of Union guns consisted of 6-pound smoothbores and 12-pound howitzers (43 percent at Shiloh and 37 percent at Stones River). Now 27 percent of the Union weapons consisted of modern rifled pieces, and another 8.5 percent of their guns were the more modern 12-pound Napoleons. James Rifles (only 8 percent of the Union inventory) were beginning to disappear.[3]

For the Confederates, 64 percent of the known artillery inventory still used 6-pound guns or 12-pound howitzers, only an 18 percent reduction in the percentage of these inferior weapons used since Shiloh. This suggested that the Confederates were not able to modernize their collection very effectively in 1862. This would also suggest that the North was already pulling ahead in both numbers and quality of artillery pieces. Given the fact that Bragg continued to divide his artillery evenly throughout his command, the tactical use of these weapons was not changing dramatically either.[4]

A summary of Stones River artillery would suggest that by December of 1862, Confederate artillery in the West was falling behind that of the North in both quality and quantity. The battle at Prairie Grove produced a similar outcome in the same month. Given the fact that Lee's artillery underwent a makeover at the Tredegar Iron Works during the winter months of 1862–1863 and Bragg's artillery had no such advantage, this meant that barring some type of miracle or a significant change in Confederate strategy or operations, 1863 would not end well in the West for the Confederates.

By 1863, the Confederates would certainly be heavily outgunned in the West. On a par with the Union early in 1862, this rough parity would disappear by 1863. The developments in artillery comprise just one aspect of the evolving Union superiority in most areas after 1862. Once again, this illustrates why the Confederates needed to win on the battlefield early in the war or seek foreign intervention.

Chapter Notes

Introduction

1. Richard M. McMurry, *Two Great Rebel Armies: An Essay in Confederate Military History* (Chapel Hill: University of North Carolina Press, 1989) 19–21, 34.

2. Peter G. Northouse, *Leadership: Theory and Practice*, 6th Edition (Los Angeles: Sage Publications, Inc., 2013) 20–23, 75–97; John Keegan, *The American Civil War* (New York: Alfred A. Knopf, 2009) 331; See also, Edgar F. Puryear, *American Generalship: Character is Everything: The Art of Command* (New York: Ballantine Books, 2003) 338–361; Robert L. Taylor, William E. Rosenbach and Eric B. Rosenbach, eds., *Military Leadership: In Pursuit of Excellence* (Philadelphia: Westview Press, 2009) 32–33, 150; T. Harry Williams, "The Military Leadership of the North and the South: The Harmon Memorial Lectures in Military History Number Two" (Colorado: United States Air Force Academy, 1960) 6, 7, 9, 20; B. H. Liddell Hart, *Thoughts on War* (London: Spellmount Publishers Ltd., 1998) 123; Roger H. Nye, *The Challenge of Command: Reading for Military Excellence* (Wayne, NJ: Avery Publishing Group Inc., 1986) 62, 136; Martin Van Creveld, *Command in War* (Cambridge: Harvard University Press, 1985) 5–7, 12, 16; Trevor N. Dupuy, *Numbers, Predictions and War* (New York: The Bobbs-Merrill Company, Inc., 1979) 6–10; Trevor N. Dupuy, *The Evolution of Weapons and Warfare* (New York: The Bobbs-Merrill Company, Inc., 1980) 286–294, 312; For a more recent perspective, see Jim Mattis and Bing West, *Call Sign Chaos* (New York: Random House, 2019) 87, 88, 103, 198, 210, 235, 237, 239, 240, 241.

3. *Field Manual 3-0: Operations* (Washington, D.C.: Department of the Army, 2008) A-1, A-2. The manual uses the following nine principles: 1) Objective; 2) Offensive; 3) Mass; 4) Economy of Force; 5) Maneuver; 6) Unity of Command; 7) Security; 8) Surprise; 9) Simplicity; In 1902, G. F. R. Henderson outlined the original eight principles, like those used later by the U.S. Army; G. F. R. Henderson, "Strategy," *Encyclopedia Britannica* Vol. 9 of 33 (New York: The Encyclopedia Britannica Company, 1902) 4–7; Sun Tzu, *The Art of War* (numerous editions); J. F. C. Fuller, *The Foundations of the Science of War* (London: Hutchinson and Company, 1926) 220–21; Nine principles were described. John I. Alger, *The Quest for Victory: The History of the Principles of War* (Westport: Greenwood Press, 1982) 197, 232, 240, 241, 244, 253–55; Air Marshal David Evans, *War: A Matter of Principles* (Fairbairn, Australia: Aerospace Centre, 2000) 5–10.

4. George R. Agassiz, ed., *Meade's Headquarters 1863–1865: Letters of Colonel Theodore Lyman* (Boston: The Atlantic Monthly Press, 1922) 81.

5. Grenville M. Dodge, *Personal Recollections of President Abraham Lincoln, General Ulysses S. Grant, General William T. Sherman* (Glendale, California: The Arthur H. Clark Company, 1914) 129.

6. Adam Badeau, *Military History of Ulysses S. Grant, From April 1861 to April 1865*, 1 (New York: D. Appleton and Company, 1885) 85.

7. *Field Manual 3-0: Operations* (Washington, D.C.: Department of the Army, 2008) A1-A2. "Direct every operation toward a clearly defined, decisive and attainable objective."

8. *Ibid.* "Seize, retain, and exploit the initiative."

9. *Ibid.* "Unity of Command. For every objective, seek unity of command and unity of effort."

10. Martin Van Creveld, *Command in War* (Cambridge, MA: Harvard University Press, 1985) 103–111; McMurray, *ibid.*: 35. McMurray defines the four elements that he believes necessary for successful command; *Field Manual 3-0* (Washington, D.C.: Department of the Army, 2008) A1-A2. One critical need is indeed covered by the "Principles" statement: "Prepare clear, uncomplicated plans and concise orders to ensure thorough understanding." Still another concern is referenced in the British manual described in an earlier note; Evans, 10.

11. Field Manual 3-0 (Washington, D.C.: Department of the Army, 2008) "Mass and Economy of Force."

Prologue

1. Ezra J. Warner, *Generals in Blue: Lives of the Union Commanders* (Baton Rouge: Louisiana State University, 1964) George H. Thomas (500–01),

U.S. Grant (183–86), Samuel R. Curtis 107–08), William Nelson (343–44), Don Carlos Buell (51–2), William S. Rosecrans (410–11), James G. Blunt (37–8); Ezra J. Warner, *Generals in Gray: Lives of the Confederate Commanders* (Baton Rouge: Louisiana State University Press, 1959) George B. Crittenden (65–6), John B. Floyd (89–90), Earl Van Dorn, 314–15), A.S. Johnston, 159–60), Edmund K. Smith (279–80), Braxton Bragg (30–1), Thomas C. Hindman (137–38).

2. David A. Clary, *Eagle and Empire: The United States, Mexico, and the Struggle for a Continent* (New York: Bantam Books, 2009) 68; K. Jack Bauer, *The Mexican War 1846-1848* (New York: Macmillan Publishing Company, 1974) 395.

3. Clary, 104–105.

4. 29th Congress, 1st Session. House Executive Documents Numbers 197, 207, 209; *Dispatches from General Taylor;* 29th Congress, 2nd Session; Senate Document 4.

5. Timothy D. Johnson, ed., *Memoirs of Lieut-General Winfield Scott* (Knoxville: University of Tennessee Press, 2015) 195–196.

6. Ulysses S. Grant, *Personal Memoirs of U.S. Grant* (New York: Charles L. Webster & Company, 1885–1886) 47, 66.

7. Justin Harvey Smith, *The War with Mexico*, 2 (New York: Macmillan Publishing Co., 1919) 26.

8. Erna Risch, *Quartermaster Support of the Army: 1775-1939* (Washington, D.C.: Center of Military History, 1989) 245; Russell F. Weigley, *The American Way of War: A History of United States Military Strategy and Policy* (New York: MacMillan Publishing Company, 1973) 73. Weigley carefully summarizes Taylor's challenges and faults. He concludes that Taylor's campaign was "a throwback to the amateurishness of the War of 1812."

9. Allan Peskin, *Winfield Scott and the Profession of Arms* (Kent: The Kent State University Press, 2003) 147, 149; Bauer, 73, 322.

10. 30th Congress, 1st Session. House Executive Document 59; *Correspondence between the Secretary of War and General Scott.* Major-General Winfield Scott to William L. Marcy, Secretary of War. Dispatch communicating the capitulation of Vera Cruz. March 29, 1847. Major-General Winfield Scott to William L. Marcy, Secretary of War. Dispatch communicating Scott's official report of the Battle of Cerro Gordo. April 19, 1847; Major-General Winfield Scott, to William L. Marcy, Secretary of War. Dispatch communicating Scott's official report of the Battle of Molino del Rey. September 11, 1846. Major-General Winfield Scott to William L. Marcy, Secretary of War. Dispatch communicating Scott's report of the battles for, and occupation of, Mexico City.

11. Johnson, 204; John S. D. Eisenhower, *So Far From God: The U.S. War With Mexico 1846-1848* (New York: Random House, 1989) 91–95, 363–364.

12. Eisenhower, 62; Clary, 118, 119, 130–131, 143.

13. Taylor's Orders No. 124. October 1, 1846, House Executive Document No. 60, Thirtieth Congress, First Session, p. 508, Serial No. 520; Walter Prescott Webb, *The Texas Rangers: A Century of Frontier Defense* (New York: Harper & Brothers, Publishers, 1935) 110.

14. Samuel E. Chamberlain, *My Confession: Recollections of a Rogue* (New York: Harper and Brothers, 1956) 110–111.

15. Chamberlain, 121.

16. Chamberlain, 126–127.

17. Chamberlain, 139.

18. Bauer, 322, 371–374.

19. Smith, II, 48, 49, 147.

20. Smith, II, 143.

21. Clary, 97, 143, 162.

22. Risch, 267–270; Annual Report of the Secretary of War, 1847.

23. Chamberlain, 175; Stephen A. Carney, *The U.S. Army Campaigns of the Mexican War: The Occupation of Mexico, May 1846-July 1848* (U.S. Army Center of Military History, Publication 73-3) 42–45; Clary, 282.

24. Selected Staff Officers with Zachary Taylor; Johnson, 233–236; Captain William W. S. Bliss, Assistant Adjutant General. West Point, Class of 1833. Cullum I, 542; Lieutenant Colonel Mathew Mountjoy Payne, Inspector General; Regular Army (20th Infantry) beginning in 1812; Theo. F. Rodenbaugh, ed., *Journal of the Military Service Institution of the United States,* 11 (New York: Governor's Island, 1890) 847; Captain George G. Waggaman, Commissary of Subsistence. West Point, Class of 1835, Cullum I, 608. *House Documents,* Vol. 33, p. 29. May 29, 1846; 29th Congress, 2nd Session; Letter from Zachary Taylor to Adjutant General (Brigadier General R. Jones) of the Army. In May of 1846, Captain Waggaman was relieved of duty as a result of health issues; 30th Congress, 1st Session, 302. Lieutenant Jeremiah M. Scarritt, Chief Engineer. West Point, Class of 1838. Cullum I, 699; Lieutenant Jacob E. Blake, Topographical Engineer. West Point Class of 1833, Cullum I, 558. Killed at Palo Alto; Lieutenant George G. Meade, Topographical Engineer. West Point, Class of 1835, Cullum I, 601; Major Craig, Ordnance Department; Captain George H. Crossman, Quartermasters Department. West Point, Class of 1823. Cullum I, 315; Captain Abraham C. Myers, Quartermasters Department. West Point, Class of 1833, Cullum, I, 562; Major John Munroe: Chief of Artillery. West Point 1814. Cullum I, 113; Additional staff officers were utilized from the staff of General John Wool. Colonel Sylvester Churchill: Inspector General. Regular Army; Captain Amos B. Eaton: Chief of the Subsistence Department. West Point, Class of 1826, Cullum I, 381; Captain Ebenezer S. Sibley, Assistant-Quartermaster. West Point, Class of 1827, Cullum I, 386.

25. Johnson, ed., 214.

26. Bauer, 272; Risch, 290–292.

27. Smith, II, 73, NB 362; Dr. Alvin P. Stauffer, "Supply of the First American Overseas Expeditionary Force: The Quartermaster's

Department and the Mexican War." *Quartermaster Review* (May-June, 1950) 1–6.

28. Johnson, 214, 233–235. For staff members of commanding officers, I have included individuals normally termed "General Staff" along with other critical and professional staff members from departments such as Ordnance, Quartermaster and Commissary. I have omitted aid-de-camps and other volunteer or ancillary aides. In this fashion, within Scott's Memoirs and contained in his reports to the War Department, Scott's General Staff included the following people who served from the original landing at Vera Cruz to the conquest of Mexico City: Captain H. L. Scott, Acting Assistant Adjutant General. West Point. See above. Lieutenant-Colonel Ethan Allen Hitchcock, acting Inspector General. West Point. See above, Major John L. Smith, Chief Engineer. Regular Army; Captain Benjamin Huger, Ordnance Department. West Point, Class of 1825, Cullum 1, 343; Captain James R. Irwin, Chief Quartermaster. West Point, Class of 1825, Cullum 1, 353; Captain John B. Grayson, Commissarial Department. West Point, Class of 1826, Cullum 1, 376; Surgeon General Thomas Lawson, Regimental Surgeon, beginning in War of 1812. Surgeon General of U.S. Regular Army beginning in 1836; Scott's General Staff consisted of Scott's Inspector General and 5 aides-de-camp. Four topographical engineers were on his staff. Three officers were in his Ordnance Dept. His Pay Dept. consisted of three officers. The Quartermaster's Department included the Chief Quartermaster and eight subordinates. The Subsistence Department included two officers. The Medical Department included the Surgeon General and 30 medical officers and volunteers. For Civil War engagements described later, aides-de-camp and subordinate officers are not listed either. The Pay and Medical Departments have not been included. The Little Cabinet included the following: Colonel Joseph G. Totten, Chief Engineer. West Point Class of 1805, Cullum 1, 63; Colonel Hitchcock, Acting Inspector General. West Point Class of 1817, Cullum 1, 167; Captain Robert E. Lee, Engineer. West Point, Class of 1829, Cullum 1, 420; First Lieutenant Henry L. Scot, acting Adjutant General. West Point, Class of 1833, Cullum 1, 565.

29. Smith, II, 149.
30. Smith, II, 154.
31. Clary, 212.

Chapter 1

1. Charles P. Roland, *Albert Sidney Johnston: Soldier of Three Republics* (Austin: University of Texas Press, 1964) 253, 260–261, 268–269, 271–274; Richard M. McMurray, *Two Great Rebel Armies: An Essay in Confederate Military History* (Chapel Hill: University of North Carolina Press, 1989) 119–121; Roland Dunbar, ed., *Jefferson Davis Constitutionalist: His Letters, Papers and Speeches,* 5. Jackson, MS: Dept. of Archives and History, 1923) 329; Ezra J. Warner, *Generals in Gray: Lives of the Confederate Commanders* (Baton Rouge: Louisiana State University Press: 1959) 159–60; Thomas Lawrence Connelly, *Army of the Heartland: The Army of Tennessee 1861–1862* (Baton Rouge: Louisiana State University Press, 1967) 96–99.

2. Warner, 349–350.
3. Connelly, 86–87, 49, 94–95; John W. Simpson, "A Boy's Story of the Battle of Mill Springs." *Confederate Veteran* 18, 335.
4. Connelly, 52, 97–98; Warner, 65–66; Robert E. L. Krick, *Staff Officers in Gray: A Biographical Register of the Staff Officers in the Army of Northern Virginia* (Chapel Hill: University of North Carolina Press, 2003) 319.
5. *War of the Rebellion: A Compilation of the Official Records of the Union and Confederate Armies* (Washington, D.C.: U.S. Government Printing Office, 1880–1901) 7 (part 1): 79. Hereafter cited as *OR* with volume and part afterward. Francis F. McKinney, *Education in Violence: The Life of George H. Thomas and the History of the Army of the Cumberland* (Chicago: Americana House, 1991) 127–128.
6. *OR* 7(1): 80, 82, 84–86, 87, 91, 111.
7. *OR*, 1, 7(1): 102–103, 111–114, 115.
8. McKinney, 485; *OR Ibid.*: 86, 108; Joseph R. Reinhart, trans. and ed., *A German Hurrah!: Civil War Letters of Friedrich Bertsch and Wilhelm Stängel, 9th Ohio Infantry* (Kent: The Kent State University Press, 2010) 206.
9. Connelly, 99; *OR Ibid.*: 112.
10. McKinney, 127. *OR*, 1, 7(1): 81.
11. William Preston Johnston, *The Life of Albert Sidney Johnston* (Austin: State House Press, 1997) 394–395.
12. *OR*, 1, 7(1): 91; *Weekly Pioneer,* Jan. 31, 1862.
13. *OR*, 1, 7(1): 815; *Weekly Pioneer.*
14. Reinhart, 212. *OR*, 1, 7:79–82.
15. McKinney, 109, 125; *Confederate Veteran* 6, 128; Johnston, 395.
16. Krick, 319, 333; *OR* 7(1): 109.
17. Warner, 44–45.
18. R. M. Kelly, "Holding Kentucky for the Union," *Battles and Leaders,* Vol. 1, 392 (New York: Castle Books, 1956).
19. *OR* 1, 7: 91.
20. *OR* 1, 7: 815. "The Kentucky Victory: Scenes on the Battle Field," *The Weekly Pioneer & Democrat* (Friday, February 14, 1862) 1.
21. Reinhart, 212. "Our Army Correspondence. The Kentucky Battle. Letter from the Second Regiment [Minnesota]." *The Weekly Pioneer & Democrat* (January 19, 1862) 4. Sanders, 33. *OR* 1, 7: 715 (Fertile Region). *OR* 1, 7: 105.
22. McKinney, 109, 125; *Confederate Veteran* Vol. 6, 128; *Richmond Times Dispatch,* August 1861; Among the 11 serving under General Thomas, the following staff officers were active at the Battle of Mill Springs: Captain George E. Flynt, Assistant Adjutant General, pre-war New York and Texas merchant, John Fitch, *Annals of the*

Army of the Cumberland (Philadelphia: J. B. Lippincott & Co, 1864) 66; Captain Reuben C. Kise, Assistant Adjutant General. Pre-war merchant in Indiana; John Eicher and David Eicher, *Civil War High Commands* (Stanford: Stanford University Press, 2001) 335; Captain Alvin C. Gillem, Quartermaster, West Point, 1851, Cullum's *Register* II, 44; Captain George S. Roper, Assistant Commissary of Subsistence, pre-war Illinois merchant with experience in a dry goods store, bookkeeping, and lumber business, boot and shoe dealer; *Portrait and Biographical Record of Winnebago and Boone Counties, Illinois* (Chicago: Biographical Publishing Co., 1892.) 1311–1312. These notes are not intended to include all staff officers serving on each side but, where possible, identify key positions and staff officers. As a result, aides-de-camp and other volunteers are not included.

23. Krick, 319; Among the 12 staff officers serving under Generals Crittenden and Zollicoffer, the following staff officers were active at the Battle of Mill Springs: A. S. Cunningham, Assistant Adjutant General; Captain J. G. Anglade, Acting Assistant Adjutant General; Krick, 314; Major John Lucien Brown, Quartermaster to Zollicoffer, prewar Law and Mexican War Commissary Officer with the 3rd Tennessee Volunteers. Born in 1800, he was 61 years old when he took this position. W. Woodford Clayton, *History of Davidson County, Tennessee* (Philadelphia: J. W. Lewis & Co., 1880) 414–416; Krick, 319; Major Giles M. Hillyer, Assistant Commissary of Subsistence, pre-war law; *OR* 7(1): 109; Krick, 333; In some cases, Krick does not include the officer rank.

24. Stuart W. Sanders, *The Battle of Mill Springs* (London: The History Press, 2013), 111.

25. Kelly, 391–92; Battles & Leaders I, 387–392.

Chapter 2

1. Benjamin Franklin Cooling, *Forts Henry and Donelson: The Key to the Confederate Heartland* (Knoxville: University of Tennessee Press, 1987) 45, 48; Charles P. Roland, *Albert Sidney Johnston: Soldier of Three Republics* (Austin: University of Texas Press, 1964) 285.

2. Cooling, 84.

3. Cooling, 83, 85–89. Richard M. McMurray, *Two Great Rebel Armies: An Essay in Confederate Military History* (Chapel Hill: University of North Carolina Press, 1989) 121–125.

4. Kendall D. Gott, *Where the South Lost the Civil War: An Analysis of the Fort Henry-Fort Donelson Campaign, February 1862* (Mechanicsburg: Stackpole Books, 2003) 54; St. John Liddell, "Liddell's Record of the Civil War," *Southern Bivouac* (December 1885) 1: 417–419.

5. Thomas Lawrence Connelly, *Army of the Heartland: The Army of Tennessee, 1861–1862* (Baton Rouge: Louisiana State University Press, 1967) 104–105.

6. Gott, 74; John Y. Simon, Ed. *The Papers of Ulysses S. Grant, 4, January 8-March 1, 1862*: 4 (Carbondale: Southern Illinois University Press, 1972) 90. Hereafter cited as Simon, *PUSG*.

7. Johnson and Buell, *Battles and Leaders of the Civil War 1*: (New York: Castle Books, 1956) 368–369.

8. Gott, 64.

9. *Johnson and Buell*, 430–436; Simon, *PUSG*, 4: 215; *ORN* (1) 22, 90, 791.

10. Timothy B. Smith, *Grant Invades Tennessee: The 1862 Battles for Fort Henry and Donelson* (Lawrence: University Press of Kansas, 2016) 269, 280, 322–326; *Johnson and Buell: 396–428*; *OR* 1, 7: 268; William Peters, *Recollections of William H Peters*, 1891; Robert C. Black III, *Railroads of the Confederacy* (Wilmington: Broadfoot, 1987), End Map.

11. Simon, *PUSG*, 4: 102, 104, 147, 171; Gott, 76–78, 86; McMurray, 52–53.

12. Steven E. Woodworth, *Nothing But Victory: The Army of the Tennessee 1861–1865* (New York: Vintage Books, 2005) 106.

13. Quoted in James McPherson, *Embattled Rebel* (New York: Penguin, 2014), 57.

14. Simon, *PUSG*, 4:215; McMurry, 81–83, 85, 90.

15. *OR*, 1, 7: 387; Smith, 281.

16. Johnson and Buell, 420.

17. *OR*, 1, 7, 121; Gott, 69; *PUSG* 4, 99, 103–04.

18. Gott, 205; *PUSG* 4, 215-16.

19. Simon, *PUSG* 4, 219.

20. Simon, *PUSG* 4, 215, 245, 266, 302; Selected Union staff officers at Fort Donelson included the following: Colonel Joseph D. Webster, Chief of Staff. Pre-war Engineer and Regular Army (1838–1854). John H. and David J. Eicher, *Civil War High Commands* (Stanford: Stanford University Press, 2002). Captain J. A. Rawlins, Assistant Adjutant General. Pre-war Law. Ezra J. Warner, *Generals in Blue: Lives of the Union Commanders* (Baton Rouge: Louisiana State University Press, 1986) 391–392. Lieutenant Colonel J. B. McPherson, Chief Engineer. West Point, Class of 1853, Cullum II, 515. Captain Reuben B. Hatch. Assistant Quartermaster. He was the son of Ozias M. Hatch, Illinois Secretary of State and former owner of Merchandise stores. This was one of Lincoln's political appointments. Captain John Parker Hawkins, Assistant Chief of Staff, Chief Commissary. West Point, Class of 1852, Cullum II, 513.

21. *PUSG* 4, 121.

22. *PUSG* 4, 215.

23. Ezra J. Warner, *Generals in Gray* (Baton Rouge: Louisiana State University Press) 89, 242–43.

24. Smith, 360.

25. *Johnson and Buell*, 422.

26. Gott, 205.

27. William Preston Johnston, *The Life of Albert Sidney Johnston* (Austin: State House Press, 1997) 455.

28. Simon, *PUSG*, 4:214.

29. Simon, *PUSG*, 4:245, 266, 302. Selected Union staff officers at Fort Donelson included the following: Colonel Joseph D. Webster, Chief of Staff. Pre-war Engineer and Regular Army (1838–1854). John H. and David J. Eicher, Civil War High Commands (Stanford: Stanford University Press, 2002). Captain J. A. Rawlins, Assistant Adjutant General. Pre-war Law. Ezra J. Warner, *Generals in Blue: Lives of the Union Commanders* (Baton Rouge: Louisiana State University Press, 1986) 391–392. Lieutenant Colonel J. B. McPherson, Chief Engineer. West Point, Class of 1853, Cullum's *Register*, II, 515. Captain Reuben B. Hatch. Assistant Quartermaster. He was the son of Ozias M. Hatch, Illinois Secretary of State and former owner of Merchandise stores. This was one of Lincoln's political appointments. Captain John Parker Hawkins, Assistant Chief of Staff, Chief Commissary. West Point, Class of 1852, Cullum's *Register*, II, 513.

30. *OR*, 7: 298.

31. *OR*, 7: 314.

32. *OR*, 7: 387.

33. *OR* 1, 7: 341.

34. Selected Confederate Staff at Fort Donelson. The author has chosen to emphasize General Pillow's staff as they were responsible for supplying his soldiers during the attempt to escape from the fort. General Buckner also participated in the action. Captain Gustavus A. Henry, Jr. Assistant Adjutant General to Pillow. He attended but did not graduate from West Point. He was the son of a Tennessee senator, and Fort Henry was named after his father, Gustavus A. Henry, Sr. *Journal of the Congress of the Confederate States of America* (Washington, Government Printing Office, 1904) 515; Captain Joseph Dixon, Chief Engineer Officer, originally with Johnston. West Point, Class of 1858, Cullum II, 700; Major John Wyatt Jones, Quartermaster, originally with Tilghman, from Kentucky, pre-war attorney; *The Lost Cause: A Confederate War Record*, Vol. 10, No. 2 (Louisville: United Daughters of the Confederacy, August, 1903) 39; Thomas Klugh Jackson, Commissary of Subsistence, originally with A. S. Johnston, West Point, Class of 1848, Cullum II, 359; Findagrave; Chief Commissary of Western Department under A. S. J. Captured at Fort Donelson while serving on the staff of General Buckner; Major William H. Haynes, Assistant Commissary Officer under Pillow; *OR* 7(1): 284; Also: Confederate Veteran, Vol. 8, No. 6 (Nashville: United Confederate Veterans, 1900) 287, "Cooperated in the erection of some of the largest mills in the south," Hot Springs: *Hot Springs New Era* (Oct. 27, 1921) obituary, FindaGrave.com; Major Jeremy F. Gilmer, Engineer Officer, originally served with General A. S. Johnston. West Point, Class of 1839, Cullum I, 740.

35. Johnson and Buell, 422.

Chapter 3

1. John D. Crabtree, "Recollections of the Pea Ridge Campaign and the Army of the Southwest," *Military Essays and Recollections: Papers Read before the Commandery of the State of Illinois, Military Order of the Loyal Legion of the United States*, III (Chicago, The Dial Press, 1899) 212, 213; William L. Shea and Earl J. Hess, *Pea Ridge: Civil War Campaign in the West* (Chapel Hill: University of North Carolina Press, 1992) 1–3; Edward A. Blodgett, "The Army of the Southwest and the Battle of Pea Ridge," *Military Essays and Recollections: Papers Read before the Commandery of the State of Illinois, Military Order of the Loyal Legion of the United States*, II, 291, 292; Unpublished typescript. Grenville M. Dodge, *Personal Biography of Major General Grenville Mellen Dodge from 1837 to 1871* I, 1914, 45.

2. Crabtree, 213. Ezra J. Warner, *Generals in Blue: Lives of the Union Commanders* (Baton Rouge: Louisiana State University Press, 1964) 107–8.

3. Shea and Hess, 5, 7, 9, 10.

4. Colonel Thomas E. Hanson, PhD. "Failure of Command at Pea Ridge, 1862." *16 Cases of Mission Command* (Fort Leavenworth, 2013) 1–2, 4–5; Franz Sigel, "The Pea Ridge Campaign," *Battles and Leaders of the Civil War* 1: (New York: Castle Books, 1956) 316; Mark M. Boatner III, *The Civil War Dictionary* (New York: David McKay Company, Inc., 1959) 215; Ezra J. Warner, *Generals in Blue*, 70–71, 352–353, 447–448.

5. Philip H. Sheridan, *Personal Memoirs of P. H. Sheridan* (New York: Charles L. Webster & Company, 1888) 1, 96; Dodge, 46.

6. Jay Monaghan, *Civil War on the Western Border: 1854–1865* (New York: Bonanza Books, 1955) 229; Sheridan, 96–97; Warner, 127–128, Dodge, 47.

7. Jarrod C. Bailey, "Civil War Logistics: Effects of Logistics on the Pea Ridge Campaign." (Master's Thesis. Jefferson City, Tennessee: Carson-Newman University, 2004) 63–64, 77–78; Sheridan, *Memoirs*, 49–50; Dodge, 48.

8. Ezra J. Warner, *Generals in Gray: Lives of the Confederate Commanders* (Baton Rouge: Louisiana State University Press, 1959) 200, 246–247, 314–315.

9. Shea and Hess, *Ibid*.: 20, 22.

10. *OR*, 1, 8: 286.

11. *OR*, 1, 8: 478, 541, 734, 736, 739–740, 746, 749, 750, 752; Shea and Hess, 23.

12. Blodgett, II, 298, 299; Crabtree, 216.

13. Shea and Hess, 33; *OR*, 1, 8: 752, 753, 763.

14. *OR*, 1, 8: 286; William H. Tunnard, *A Southern Record: The History of the Third Regiment Louisiana Infantry* (Baton Rouge, Longfellow. 1866) 129; Shea and Hess, 59; Hanson, 8.

15. Nathan S. Harwood, "The Pea Ridge Campaign," *Civil War Military Sketches and Incidents: Papers Read by Companions of the State of Nebraska, Military Order of the Loyal Legion of the United States* (Omaha: The Commandery, 1902)

117; Sigel, 319; Albert Castel, "A New View of the Battle of Pea Ridge," *Missouri Historical Society Review* (Columbia: State Historical Society of Missouri, 62, 2, January 1968) 141; Shea and Hess, 52; Dabney H. Maury, "Recollections of the Elkhorn Campaign," *Southern Historical Society Papers*, 186.

16. William H. Tunnard, *A Southern Record: The History of the Third Regiments Louisiana Infantry* (Baton Rouge, Longfellow. 1866) 132; OR 1, 8: 284, 304–306; Castel, 142. Shea and Hess, 84; Maury, 187.

17. Blodgett, 304; Shea and Hess, 90, 93, 94.

18. Tunnard, 134; Shea and Hess, 110, 115. OR 1, 8: 303.

19. Sigel, 324; Shea and Hess, 120, 144.

20. OR 1, 8: 92, 284; Maury, 188-89.

21. OR 1, 8: 316–318.

22. Bailey, 84–86; Shea and Hess, 231.

23. Bearss, 317; Crabtree, 225, 226; Shea and Hess, 303–305.

24. Stephen D. Engle, *Yankee Dutchman: The Life of Franz Sigel* (Fayetteville: University of Arkansas Press, 1993) 101–104; Hanson, 15.

25. Dodge, 52; Engle, 114–115; Shea and Hess, 220.

26. Blodgett, 300; Crabtree, 224; Castel, 138; Shea and Hess, 271.

27. Tunnard, 159; Shea and Hess, 111, 115, 138, 143.

28. Tunnard, 159-60; Crabtree, 218–223; Crabtee commanded Curtis's escort and rode with him on both days.

29. Shea and Hess, 224.

30. Nathan S. Harwood, "The Pea Ridge Campaign," *Civil War Military Sketches and Incidents* (Wilmington: Broadfoot Publishing Company, 1992), 115, 193.

31. John W. Noble, "Battle of Pea Ridge or Elkhorn Tavern," War Papers and Personal Reminiscences, 1861–1865, Read Before the Commandery of the State of Missouri, Military Order of the Loyal Legion of the United States, I (St. Louis, 1892) 224.

32. Shea and Hess, 92.

33. Selected Staff Officers in the Army of the Southwest under Samuel Curtis. Staff of 10 included the following men: Captain Thomas Irving McKenny, Acting Assistant Adjutant General and Inspector General. Pre-war businessman: Iowa real estate, railroads and building. Roger D. Hunt and Jack R. Brown, *Brevet Brigadier Generals in Blue* (Gaithersburg: Olde Soldier Books, 1990) 402. John H. and David J. Eicher, *Civil War High Commands* (Stanford: Stanford University Press, 2001) 380; Captain Arnold Hoepner, Engineer Officer. Fold 3.com. (H356) Justin S. Solonick, *Engineering Victory: The Union Siege of Vicksburg* (Carbondale: Southern Illinois University Press, 2015) 51, 227; Simon, *USG* 7, 78; Prime and Comstock's Official Report, Vicksburg Siege; Lieutenant David, Ordnance Officer; OR 1, 8: 203; Captain Philip Sheridan, Quartermaster and Assistant Commissary of Assistance, West Point Class of 1853, Cullum II, 550.

34. Tunnard, 125, 126.

35. Selected Staff Officers in the Army of the West under Earl Van Dorn. Staff of seven included the following men on March 22, 1862: Colonel Dabney H. Maury, Assistant Adjutant General, West Point, Class of 1846, Cullum II, 284, and Mexican War. Was actually on Earl Van Dorn's staff. OR 1, 8: 799; Thomas L. Snead, Assistant Adjutant General from staff of Sterling Price, pre-war Newspaper Editor, OR 1, 8: 799; *Confederate Military History*, 9, 74, *New York Times* (Obituary, October 19, 1890); Major James Harding, Quartermaster, pre-war auditor from staff of Sterling Price; OR 8(1): 799; *Confederate Military History*, 9, 74. Hess, p. 33; Major John William Reid, Assistant Chief Commissary, pre-war lawyer, OR 8(1): 799; *Confederate Military History*, 9, 74; Representative from Missouri, *Biographical Congressional Directory of the United States Congress*: 1774–1903 (Washington: Government Printing Office, 1903 (R000149)) 198.

36. Dodge, 51. Shea and Hess, 312.

Chapter 4

1. James Russell Soley, "The Union and Confederate Navies," 1, *Battles and Leaders* (New York; Castle Books, 1956) 624–29.

2. Henry Walke, "The Western Flotilla," *Battles and Leaders*, 1, 445; OR 1, 8: 110, 132, 797, 799, 804; OR 1, 10(2): 408.

3. ORN 1, 22: 279, 282, 359, 369; Boatner, 529; OR 1, 8: 125, 805.

4. Larry J. Daniel and Lynn N. Block, *Island No. 10: Struggle for the Mississippi Valley* (Tuscaloosa: University of Alabama Press, 1996) 3, 36, 40.

5. Henry Walke, "The Western Flotilla at Fort Donelson, Island Number Ten, Fort Pillow and Memphis," *Battles & Leaders* 1, 447–52.

6. Alvin P. Staufer, "Supply of the First American Overseas Expeditionary Force: The Quartermaster's Department and the Mexican War," *Quartermaster Review*: May-June 1950.

7. Chester G. Hearn, *The Capture of New Orleans 1862* (Baton Rouge: Louisiana State University Press, 1995) 31; Charles L. DuFour, *The Night the War Was Lost* (Lincoln: University of Nebraska Press, 1960) 43, 56; OR 1, 6: 59.

8. Hearn, 97–8, 125–29.

9. Chester Hearn, 181–82, 206, 234–35; ORN 1, 18: 7–8, 160–66.

10. Randolph H. McKim, *The Numerical Strength of the Confederate Army* (New York: The Neale Publishing Company, 1912) 25, 59; ORN, 1, 18: 166; Hearn, 192, 195.

11. Arthur and Ballard, *Second Bull Run Staff Ride* (Washington: U.S. Army Center of Military History, 2003) 29; OR, 1, 11(3): 479–484; OR I, 9: 37; Randolph H. McKim, 25, 59. McKim suggests that altogether, over 36 regiments from Louisiana,

Mississippi, Alabama, Tennessee, Texas and Arkansas traveled east.

12. Myron J. Smith, Jr. *The CSS Arkansas: A Confederate Ironclad* (Jefferson, North Carolina: McFarland & Company, Inc., 2011) 199; Isaac Brown, "The Confederate Gun-Boat Arkansas," *Battles and Leaders*, 572–573.

13. Woodworth, 261.

14. OR 1, 17(2): 462, 607; George W. Morgan, "The Assault on Chickasaw Bluffs," *Battles and Leaders*, 3, 463.

15. Woodworth, 266; Arthur W. Bergeron, Jr., "Martin Luther Smith and the Defense of the Lower Mississippi River Valley, 1861–1863," *Confederate Generals in the Western Theater,* 3 (Knoxville: University of Tennessee Press, 2003) 73–74; OR, 1, 17, 1(1): 683.

16. OR 1, 17(1): 607.

17. OR 1, 17(1): 625, 668.

Chapter 5

1. Charles P. Roland, *Albert Sidney Johnston: Soldier of Three Republics* (Austin: University of Texas Press, 1964) 289, 301, 310.

2. *PUSG* 4, 223; William Peston Johnston, "Albert Sidney Johnston at Shiloh," in *Battles & Leaders* Vol I, 549.

3. *PUSG* 4, 223. Timothy B. Smith, *Shiloh: Conquer or Perish* (Lawrence: University of Kansas Press, 2014) 30–31; OR 1, 8: 789–791; Larry Daniel, *Shiloh* (New York: Simon & Shuster, 1997) 47–48.

4. Roland, 313.

5. Thomas Lawrence Connelly, *Army of the Heartland: The Army of Tennessee, 1861–1862* (Baton Rouge: Louisiana State University Press, 1967) 136, 139, 175; Smith, 30, 428–32; Daniel, 65, 99.

6. Smith, 73; Daniel, 112–15, 140.

7. OR 1, 10 (2): 387. Johnston, "Albert Sidney Johnston at Shiloh," 1: 557.

8. Thomas Jordan, "Notes of a Confederate Staff-Officer at Shiloh," 1: 595. OR 1, 10 (2): 388.

9. Smith, 60–61, 84. Connelly, 155; Roland, 315, 324–325.

10. Smith, 97–98; OR 1, 10 (1) 581.

11. Smith, 115–117.

12. Smith, 133.

13. Smith, 213, 244, 245; Grant, "The Battle of Shiloh," 1: 473.

14. Cunningham, 206–303, 305–309; Smith, 209, 233, 245–246.

15. Daniel, 210; Beauregard, "The Campaign of Shiloh," 590; Smith, 246.

16. O. Edward Cunningham, *Shiloh and the Western Campaign of 1862* (New York: Savas Beatie, 2012) 342, 350, 351–365; Connelly, 158; Grant, 478; Smith, 253, 258, 263, 344, 362, 390, 412.

17. OR 1, 10 (1): 470; OR 1, 10 (2): 398; Cunningham, 368, 384–387; Smith, 412, 416.

18. Stacy D. Allen, "Shiloh," in *Blue & Gray Magazine* (Columbus, Ohio): Sesquicentennial Edition, 62–66; Cunningham, 421–424.

19. OR 1, 10 (1): 145, 279, 281; Allen, 18; Smith, 153–155; Grant, 471, 474, 475.

20. Beauregard, "The Campaign of Shiloh," I, 586; Smith, 103–104, 105, 130, 160, 218; Roland, 331; OR 1, 10 (1): 408, 465–466, 569.

21. Douglas Putnam, Jr., "Reminiscences of the Battle of Shiloh," in Sketches of War History [MOLLUS, Ohio, Vol. 3] (Cincinnati, Robert Clarke, 1890) 197–211; Cunningham, 159, 278, 309, 322; William T. Sherman, *Memoirs of General W. T. Sherman, Written by Himself,* I (New York: D. Appleton and Company, 1889) 266; Andrew Hickenlooper, "Battle of Shiloh," in (*Military Order of the Loyal Legion, Ohio Commandery,* 5 (Cincinnati: Robert Clarke and Company, 1903, 5) 435; "Sketches of War History, 1861–1865" in (*Military Order of the Loyal Legion, Ohio Commandery,* 5 (Cincinnati: Robert Clarke and Company, 1903); Grant, "The Battle of Shiloh," 468–469; Smith, 113, 145, 147, 173, 201.

22. Grenville M. Dodge, *Personal Recollections of President Abraham Lincoln, General Ulysses S. Grant, General William T. Sherman* (Glendale: The Arthur H. Clark Company, 1914) 115; Smith, 151.

23. OR 1, 10 (1): p. 403, 404, 547–549, 569, 621. Includes the report of William Preston, aide-de-camp to General Johnston. He was an eyewitness to Johnston's movements throughout the day. Roland, 331–332, 335–336.

24. Simon; *PUSG* 4, 364.

25. OR 1, 10 (1): 139–140, 304.

26. R. Steven Jones, *The Right Hand of Command: Use & Disuse of Personal Staffs in the Civil War* (Mechanicsburg: Stackpole Books, 2000) 85; OR 1, 10(2), 41; OR 1, 10 (1): 110; Dodge, 76; Grant's General and Personal Staff included the following officers: Colonel J. D. Webster, chief of staff and engineers possessed Mexican War, pre–Civil War Regular Army experience, and pre-war engineering. Jones, 69. Captain John A. Rawlins, Assistant Adjutant General, pre-war attorney. Captain Clark B. Lagow, aide-de-camp: "have a care to the amount of supplies on hand, both of *commissary stores* and articles of daily *consumption in the quartermaster's department*, such as coal, forage, &c." [Emphasis is mine.] A pre-war attorney, Lagow was in Grant's 21st Illinois regiment at the beginning of the war. Captain John P. Hawkins inspecting *commissary* for the Department of Missouri now assigned to District of West Tennessee. Pre-war West Point, Class of 1852. Cullum 2, 513 [Emphasis is mine]; Colonel John Riggin, Jr., aide-de-camp. Pre-war Business. Lieutenant Colonel James B. McPherson, Chief Engineer, West Point Class of 1853. Cullum II, 515.

27. OR 1, 10 (1): 110.

28. OR 1, 10 (1): 533, 534, 549, 582.

29. OR 1, 10 (1): 601, 567.

30. OR 1, 10 (1): 463, 469; OR 1, 10(1): Confederate Brigade Reports, 417–623.

31. Reviewing the General Staff from both General A. S. Johnston and General Beauregard, several men served in a variety of capacities. Their

assignments could and did change up to the moment of battle. On March 4, 1862, Braxton Bragg, Johnston's Chief of Staff, listed several staff appointments. These men served at times under Bragg or Johnston, or even Beauregard. Major George G. Garner, Assistant Adjutant General for Bragg at Shiloh, Krick, 329. Captain Theodore O'Hara, Assistant Adjutant and Acting Inspector General (AAIG) to Johnston, Krick, 346. Served as chief quartermaster under Gideon Pillow in the Mexican War and the failed filibustering expedition to Cuba in 1850. Served as a pre-war journalist. Spencer C. Tucker, ed., *Encyclopedia of the Mexican-American War: A Political, Social, and Military History*. Santa Barbara: ABC-CLIO, 2013. Colonel J. P. Villepigue, Chief of Engineers and Artillery for Bragg at Shiloh. Captain Hypolite Oladowski, Artillery, Chief of Ordnance for Johnston and Bragg at Shiloh. Krick, 346. Major J. J. Walker, Commissary of Subsistence, later under Bragg. Captain L. F. Johnston, Assistant Quartermaster, later under Bragg. Captain Henry P. Brewster, Assistant Adjutant General, Pre-war Lawyer with Mexican War experience. Served as secretary to Sam Houston and Texas Attorney General. Thomas W. Cutrer, Texas State Historical Association: *Handbook of Texas Online*. Krick, 318. Captain Nathaniel Wycliffe, Assistant Adjutant General, Pre-war Regular U.S. Army. Captain Jeremy Gilmer, Engineer Officer (EO), pre-war West Point under Johnston and Beauregard at Shiloh. *OR* 1, 7:921.

Johnston's Personal Staff also included the following political leaders: George W. Johnson, Governor of Kentucky; Thomas C. Reynolds Governor of Missouri; Isham G. Harris, Governor of Tennessee; Samuel Tate, President of the Memphis and Charleston Railroad, Roland, 269; William Preston Johnston, *The Life of Albert Sidney Johnston* (Austin: State House Press, 1997) 317.

Finally, General P. G. T. Beauregard's Staff, who served with A. S. Johnston's staff at Shiloh, included the following: Colonel Thomas Jordan, Assistant Adjutant General, pre-war West Point, Class of 1840. Cullum, II, 58. Major Albert J. Smith, Assistant Quartermaster. Robert E. L. Krick, *Staff Officers in Gray* (Chapel Hill: University of North Carolina Press, 2003.) 267. Colonel Richard B. Lee, Chief Commissary Officer, Pre-war West Point, Class of 1817. Cullum 1, 160. Major George W. Brent, Assistant Inspector General, Pre-war Lawyer. Krick, 82; Captain F. H Jordan, Assistant Adjutant General, in charge of General Headquarters. Major Eugene E. Mclean, Chief Quartermaster, West Point Class of 1842, Cullum 2, 146. *List of Staff Officers of the Confederate States Army: 1861-1865* (Washington: Government Printing Office, 1891) 111.

Chapter 6

1. D. Warren Lambert, *When the Ripe Pears Fell: The Battle of Richmond, Kentucky* (Richmond: Madison County Historical Society, 1995) 6; Ezra Warner, *Generals in Gray*, 279-280. *OR*, 1, 16(2): 567.

2. Ezra Warner, *Generals in Blue*, 343-44; Larry J. Daniel, *Days of Glory: The Army of the Cumberland, 1861-1865* (Baton Rouge: Louisiana State University Press, 2004) 117.

3. Daniel, 116; Lambert, 9-10; Hess, 96-7; Noe, 10, 19; Earl J. Hess, *The Civil War in the West* (Chapel Hill: University of North Carolina Press, 2012) 96-7; Kenneth W. Noe, *Perryville: This Grand Havoc of Battle* (Lexington: The University Press of Kentucky, 2001) 10, 39-40.

4. *OR*, 1, 16(2): 375; Kenneth A. Hafendorfer, *Battle of Richmond, Kentucky* (Louisville: KH Press, 2006) 36, 37; Ezra J. Warner, *Generals in Blue: Lives of the Union Commanders* (Baton Rouge: University of Louisiana Press, 1964) 40; Lambert, 11.

5. *OR*, 1, 16(2): 405; Warner, 83-84, 104-105, 310, 343-344; Hafendorfer, 37; Lambert, 12-14, 22, 35; James Lee McDonough, *War in Kentucky: From Shiloh to Perryville* (Knoxville: University of Tennessee Press, 1994) 117.

6. *OR*, 1, 16(2): 734; Hafendorfer, 115, 123; Lambert, 19, 26; McDonough, 118-19, 120, 122; Paul F. Hammond, "General Kirby Smith's Campaign in Kentucky in 1862," Rev. J. William Jones, ed., Southern Historical Society Papers, 9 (Richmond, VA: Wm. Ellis Jones Printer, 1816-1959) 250.

7. *OR*, 1, 16(1): 929; Hafendorfer, 158, 161, 165, 171; B. Kevin Bennett, "The Battle of Richmond, Kentucky" *The Blue & Gray Magazine*, 25, 6; Hammond, 250; Lambert, 22, 25; Frank Moore, ed., *The Rebellion Record* 5 (New York: G. P. Putnam 1861-63) 413; McDonough, 124; Hammond, 250.

8. Hafendorfer, 219, 221, 225; Bennett, 48; Hammond, 251; Noe, 213, 219, 225; McDonough, 137; *OR*, 1, 16(1): 913.

9. Hafendorfer, 241, 249, 251, 261, 269; Hammond, 253-54; Noe, 261, 269.

10. *OR*, 1, 16(2): 830; Hafendorfer, 15; Noe, 40-1; Kolakowski, 57-8.

11. *OR*, 1, 16(2): 745-46; *OR* 1, 17(2): 624; Lambert, 6; McDonough, 77; Steven E. Woodworth, *Jefferson Davis and His Generals: The Failure of Confederate Command in the West* (Lawrence: University of Kansas Press, 1990) 128-30.

12. Larry Daniel, *Days of Glory, The Army of the Cumberland, 1861-1865* (Baton Rouge: Louisiana State University Press, 2004), 117.

13. Lambert, 190-91; Daniel, 113. 156; Noe, 317, 318.

14. Lambert, 175; Noe, 315-16.

15. Lambert, 143-44, 191; McDonough, 139-41, 143.

16. McDonough, 139; Lambert, 68, 73, 79, 125, 136.

17. Lambert, 22, 131; General Mahlon Manson's Brigade Staff included the following officers: Captain Reuben C. Kise, Assistant Adjutant General. Pre-war Merchant. Hunt and Brown, *Brevet Brigadier Generals in Blue*, 338; *OR*, 1, 16(1): 915. Captain James Biddle, U.S. Regular Army. *OR*, 1, 16(1)

1: 915 and 3–4 civilians from the area. These men "composed my staff on the day of the battles." *Ibid*. While not a full listing of each staff member, these lists convey the general impression that both brigades and their staff officers were an ad hoc group of people. During the second and third stages of the battle, the following officers assisted Generals Nelson or Cruft: Captain Wickliffe Cooper, Acting Assistant Adjutant General Nelson's Staff: OR, 1, 16(1):915, 923. Captain Baldwin Nelson's Staff, *Ibid*.: 915. Captain J. Edward Stacy, Assistant Adjutant General. Nelson's Staff, *Ibid*.: 915. Captain J. Miles Kendrick Nelson's Staff, *Ibid*.: 915. Captain Charles C. Gilbert, Inspector General, West Point, Class of 1846, Cullum, II, 272. Nelson's Staff. Lieutenant J. T. Clark, Acting Brigade Quartermaster, OR, 1, 16(1):928. "got his trains safely away." Cruft's Staff. 5 civilian aides-de-camp. *Ibid*.: 928.

18. General Smith's General and Personal Staff included the following officers: Colonel John Pegram, Chief of Staff. West Point, Class of 1854. Cullum, II, 582. Colonel William R. Boggs, who lists himself as "Unassigned," West Point, Class of 1853, Cullum II, 522. William Boggs, *Military Reminiscences of General William R. Boggs, C.S.A* (Durham, N.C.: The Seeman Printery, 1913), 35. (He was also listed on July 2, 1862 and again on September 24 as Smith's Chief of Engineers; OR,1, 16(2): 717–18, 871; Lieutenant Colonel George W. Brent, Assistant Adjutant General, Pre-war Law. Boggs, 35. Major John Adams Brown, Chief of Artillery and Ordnance, West Point, Class of 1846, Cullum, II, 268. Boggs, 35. Major H. McD. McElrath, Quartermaster. Pre-war Merchant. Johnson, 257, Boggs 35. Major W. H. Thomas, Commissary of Subsistence, Boggs, 35. Captain John G. Meem, Jr. Chief Signal Officer and ADC. Pre-war Merchant. Boggs, 35. Lieutenant Henry P. Pratt, Acting Assistant Adjutant General, Later Assistant Adjutant General Krick, 349. Washington: U.S. War Department, *List of Staff Officers of the Confederate States Army 1861-1865*, 132. Note that this list includes three West Point graduates and two pre-war merchants with business experience; Lambert, 18, 27, 34; OR, 1, 16 (1): 935, 937; Bragg claimed that Confederates captured 200 wagons in the Richmond campaign. Noe, 343–44; Captain Joseph F. Belton, Assistant Adjutant General Krick, 82.

19. Lambert 29, 34; Quote from Colonel Henry C. Bunn, "Reminiscences of the Civil War," in Charles Edward Nash, *Biographical Sketches of Gen Pat Cleburne and T. C. Hindman* (Little Rock: Tunnah & Pittard, 1898) 214–15.

20. Lambert, 145, 190.

Chapter 7

1. Robert S. Cameron, *Staff Ride Handbook for the Battle of Perryville*, 8 October 1862 (Fort Leavenworth: Combat Studies Institute Press, 2005) 19; Christopher L. Kolakowski, *The Civil War at Perryville: Battling for the Bluegrass* (Charleston: The History Press, 2009) 22; D. Warren Lambert, *When the Ripe Pears Fell: The Battle of Richmond, Kentucky* (Richmond: Madison County Historical Society, Inc., 1995) 3–4; Larry Peterson, Decisions of the 1862 Kentucky Campaign (Knoxville: University of Tennessee Press, 2019) 10.

2. Basil Duke "Bragg's Campaign in Kentucky, 1862." *Southern Bivouac* 4 (April, 1886) 163, 217; Earl J. Hess, *The Civil War in the West* (Chapel Hill: University of North Carolina Press, 2012) 53, 92–93; James Lee McDonough, *War in Kentucky: From Shiloh to Perryville* (Knoxville: University of Tennessee Press, 1994) 36.

3. OR, 1, 17(2): 614, 623, 626; Kenneth W. Noe, *Perryville: This Grand Havoc of Battle* (Lexington: University Press of Kentucky, 2001) 28, 103, 369–380; Ezra Warner, *Generals in Gray*, 30–31.

4. OR, 1, 16(2): 701, 733–734; Duke, 161–162.

5. OR, 1, 16(2): 701–02; Noe, 32–33; Crist, ed., *Papers of Jefferson Davis*, 8, 322; Davis, *Jefferson Davis*, 465–66.

6. OR, 1, 16(2): 726–727; Hess, 94–5.

7. OR, 1, 16(2): 729.

8. OR, 1, 16(1): 732–38.

9. OR, 1, 16(2): 749; Kenneth A. Hafendorfer, Battle of Richmond, Kentucky (Louisville: KH Press, 2006) 389; Noe, 53–8.

10. Andrew Haughton, *Training, Tactics and Leadership in the Confederate Army of Tennessee: Seeds of Failure* (Portland, Frank Case, 2000) 29, 41, 49, 51; McMurray, 104–105, 109–110.

11. OR, 1, 16(2): 202, 741, 784; Kolakowski, 15; Noe, 31–2.

12. OR, 1, 16(2): 786–89.

13. OR, 1, 16(2): 830, 849, 850; Arthur Howard Noll, ed., *Doctor Quintard: Chaplain CSA and Second Bishop of Tennessee* (Sewanee, TN, 1905) Chapter 6.

14. Braxton Bragg Papers, in William Palmer Collection; OR, 1, 16(1): 987; OR 16(2): 876; Hess, 99; (Kolakowski, 53; Duke, 235; McDonough, 165, 183; Wheeler, 3, 10–11.

15. Vincent S. Esposito, *West Point Atlas of the American Wars*, 1 1689-1900 (New York: Praeger Publishing, 1978) Map 75; Larry Daniel, 109–112, 121; C. C. Gilbert, "Bragg's Invasion of Kentucky," *Southern Bivouac*, 1 (August 1885) 296–97.

16. Daniel, 123–125. OR, 1, 16(2): 266, 278.

17. Horace N. Fisher, "Historical and Memorial Paper," *Reunion of the Society of the Army of the Cumberland: Thirty-Second Reunion, Indianapolis, Indiana*, 1904 (Cincinnati: The Robert Clarke Company, 1905) 181.

18. James M. McPherson, *Tried by War: Abraham Lincoln as Commander in Chief* (New York: The Penguin Press, 2008) 116; Daniel, *Days of Glory*, 121–22.

19. OR, 1, 16(2): 567; Daniel, 126, 132–137; Hess, 101.

20. Daniel, 142; OR, 1, 16(2): 567.

21. Daniel, 144. Watkins, 69; C. C. Gilbert, 301; Kolakowski, 82–3; Wheeler, 15.

22. *OR*, 1, 16(2): 911–912; Noe, 130; Kolakowski, 83.
23. Noe, 152, 170; McDonough 220–21; *OR*, 1, 16(1): 1072, 1081 Sheridan; Kolakowski, 93.
24. Kolakowski, 123; Noe, 139–141; Daniel, 126–140, 145.
25. *OR*, 1, 16(1), 1024-25; Hess, 102; Noe, 151–152.
26. George Brent Diary Bragg Papers; Benjamin Cheatham, "The Battle of Perryville," Southern Bivouac 4 (April 1886) 704.
27. *OR*, 1, 16(2): 1133.
28. Cheatham, *Ibid.*; Judge L. B. M'Farland, "Maney's Brigade at the Battle of Perryville." *Confederate Veteran*, Vol. 30, p. 467; Surgeon Solon Marks, "Experiences with the Ninth Brigade." *War Papers, Being Papers Read Before the Commandery of the State of Wisconsin: Military Order of the Loyal Legion of the United States,* II, 107–108; Sanders, *Maney's Confederate Brigade*, 111.
29. Cheatham, 704; Judge L. B. M'Farland, "Maney's Brigade at the Battle of Perryville." *Confederate Veteran*, Vol. 30, 467; Kolakowski, 113–122; Stuart Salling, *Louisianians in the Western Confederacy: The Adams-Gibson Brigade in the Civil War* (Jefferson, NC: McFarland & Company, Inc., 2010) 69–70; Daniel C. Govan, "Patton Anderson: Major General, C. S. A." in Lawrence Lee Hewitt and Arthur W. Bergeron Jr., eds. *Confederate Generals in the Western Theater,* 1 (Knoxville: University of Tennessee Press, 2010) 219; Noe, 216, 283.
30. Arthur Howard Noll, ed., *Doctor Quintard: Chaplain CSA and Second Bishop of Tennessee* (Sewanee, TN, 1905) Chapter 6; Michael H. Fitch, *Echoes of the Civil War as I Hear Them* (New York: R. F. Fenno & Company, 1905) 65; Kolakowski, 123, 130–31. *OR*, 1, 7(1): 171.
31. John W. Headley, *Confederate Operations in Canada and New York* (New York: The Neale Publishing Company, 1906) 58; *OR*, 1, 16(1): 1127–28, 1129, 1132; Kolakowski, 116, 121.
32. Noe, 240; *OR*, 1, 16(2): 52. Thomas Claiborne, "Battle of Perryville," Confederate Veteran Vol. 16 (Nashville, 1908) 225, 227; Quintard, Chapter 6; Hess, 102–03; Kolakowski, 138–40.
33. Hess, 104–05; Wheeler, 19.
34. Horace N. Fisher, 181; Buell Commission *OR* 1, 16(1): 120.
35. *OR*, 1, 16(2): 549.
36. *OR*, 1, 17(2): 624, 628, 654–55, 658; *OR*, 1, 16(2): 645–46, 752–53. When Davis issued his General Orders No. 50 to redraw departmental borders, he left Bragg with a challenging task. Bragg was senior to Kirby Smith in date of promotion, but he was operating out of Kirby Smith's department; Noe, 36–9. On quartermaster issue, see August 24, 1862 letter from Bragg to Lucius Northrop at the War Department. Bragg Papers, Roll 2; Woodworth, *Jefferson Davis*, 135.
37. FM3-5. 2008, "Offensive operations are the means by which a military force seizes and holds the initiative." Author's Italics; Noe, 170–71, 333, 338; Hess, 103; Kent Masterson Brown, *The Civil War in Kentucky* (Mason City, IA: Savas Beatty Publishing Company, 2000) 202–03.
38. Curtius, "Field of Battle, Near Perryville, KY. Thursday, Oct 9, 1862. From Our Own Correspondent, Friday, Oct. 17, 1862," (*New York Times*) 8; Wheeler, 20–1; Testimony of McCook and Speed Fry. *OR* 1, 16(1): 106.
39. Michael H. Fitch, *Echoes of the Civil War as I Hear Them* (New York: R. F. Fenno & Company, 1905) 66.
40. Headley, 61; Noe, 22, 57, 338–39, 421; George Brent Diary in Bragg Papers, Roll 2; Woodworth, *Jefferson Davis*, 135, 156–59.
41. Marcus B. Toney, The Privations of a Private (Nashville, 1905). Printed for the Author. 1st Tennessee Regiment (Confederate), 41–42.
42. Sam R. Watkins, *Company Aytch* (New York: New American Library, 1999) 47, 48, 58; Kolakowski, 116, 121; Buell's General and Personal Staff included the following officers: Colonel James B. Fry, Chief of Staff. West Point, Class of 1847. Cullum, II, 314. Captain Henry C. Bankhead, Assistant Inspector General. West Point Class of 1850. Cullum, II, 430. Captain Nathan Michler: Engineer Officer. West Point Class of 1856. Cullum II, 348. Captain John Gorham Chandler, Assistant Quartermaster. West Point, Class of 1853. Cullum, II, 536. Captain Jeremiah H Gilman, Ordnance Officer. West Point Class of 1856. Cullum II, 656. Lieutenant Colonel Francis Darr: Chief Commissary. Pre-war Merchant. Hunt and Brown, *Brevet Brigadier Generals In Blue*, 148. Became Brevet Brigadier General Francis Darr, March 13, 1865. See also his witness statement in Buell's defense regarding the challenges of supplying Buell's army; *OR*, 1, 16(1): 602–619. While this list is not comprehensive in nature, it is designed to highlight staff officers who played important roles in the army's wellbeing. Aides-de-camp and other volunteers or assistants have not been included. *OR*, 1, 16(1): 1030.
43. *OR*, 1, 16(2): 752; Watkins, 69.
44. *OR* 16(1): 1093; Noe, 240; Kolakowski, 140; Peterson, 90.
45. Watkins, 48; Wheeler, 25.
46. Major General Braxton Bragg: Lieutenant Colonel George Brent, Assistant Adjutant General and Chief of Staff, pre-war Law, June Gow, "Chiefs of Staff in the Army of Tennessee Under Braxton Bragg," *Tennessee Historical Quarterly*, 27, 4. 341–360. (At times Brent served under both Generals Smith and Bragg during this campaign. He returned to Bragg on October 2. George Brent Diary in Bragg Papers, roll 2; Robert E. L. Krick, Staff Officers in Gray (Chapel Hill: University of North Carolina Press, 2003.) 267; *List of Staff Officers of the Confederate States Army: 1861–1865* (Washington: Government Printing Office, 1891) 111; Brent had been "loaned" to General E. Kirby Smith before Smith's advance on Richmond, Kentucky. Major John J. Walker: Assistant Chief of Staff. Krick, 360. Colonel David B. Harris:

Engineer Officer. West Point Class of 1833. Cullum, I, 542. Resigned in 1835 and became a pre-war tobacco merchant and planter. Lieutenant Colonel Hypolite Oladowski, Chief of Ordnance, pre-war Poland, New Orleans Armory, Krick, 346; Lieutenant Colonel Lawrence W. O'Bannon, Assistant Chief Quartermaster, Mexican War, U.S. Regular Army, Krick, 346. Colonel Meriwether L. Clark: Chief of Artillery. West Point Class of 1830. Cullum, I, 459. Resigned in 1833 to become an architect and civil engineer as well as a Representative in the Missouri House of Representatives. Larry Daniel, *Conquered: Why The Army of Tennessee Failed* (Chapel Hill: University of North Carolina Press, 2019) 62–70. While this list is not comprehensive in nature, it is designed to highlight staff officers who played important roles in the army's wellbeing. Aides-de-camp and other volunteers or assistants have not been included.

47. FM 3-1.
48. Curtius, 1; Noe, 338–39; Woodworth, Jefferson Davis, 159–61.
1. U.S. Grant, "Personal Memoirs of U.S. Grant," (New York: Da Capo Press, 1982), 193; Thomas L. Snead, "With Price East of the Mississippi," 718-19. *OR*, 1, 10(2): 144–45.

Chapter 8

2. Snead, 717.
3. Timothy B. Smith, *Corinth 1862: Siege, Battle Occupation* (Lawrence: University Press of Kansas, 2012) 21, 24; Snead, 719; *OR* 1, 10(1): 665.
4. Smith, 34–5, 84; *OR* 1, 10(2): 523, 545–46; *B&L* 2, 719; Snead, 720.
5. *OR* 1, 10(2): 543.
6. Smith, 108.
7. Martin Van Creveld, *Supplying War: Logistics from Wallenstein to Patton* (Cambridge: Cambridge University Press, 1977) 24.
8. Smith, *Corinth 1862*, 128–29, 130; 274.
9. Smith, 137, 274; Stacy Allen, "Crossroads of the Western Confederacy: A Visitor's Guide," *Blue & Gray Magazine* (Columbus: 2007) 49.
10. Ezra Warner, *Generals in Gray*: 130–131, 215–216; Peter Cozzens, *The Darkest Days of the War: The Battles of Iuka & Corinth* (Chapel Hill: University of North Carolina Press, 1997) 136.
11. Warner, 113–114, 198–199, 301, 470–471.
12. David A. Powell, "Arthur C. Ducat: One of the Men Behind the Man." Wordpress.com
13. *OR* 1, 17(1): 414. Court of Inquiry.
14. Smith, 147; D. A. Stanley, "The Battle of Corinth": (New York: MOLLUS, 1897) 272.
15. Smith, 151,156–167.
16. Cozzens, 214; Smith, 168, 169, 186, 193–94, 199, 207–08.
17. Smith, 202–03.
18. Smith, 210, 216.
19. Smith, 213, 217; Allen, 52, 53, 54; *OR* 1, 17(1): 715, 387.
20. Smith, 235, 252–53; Cozzens, 216; Allen, 56.

21. *OR*, 1, 17(2): 715; *OR* 1, 17(1): 163.
22. *OR* 1, 17(1): 160, 267, 169.
23. *Ibid.*: 214; Smith, 228, 237, 247.
24. Sword, *Shiloh*, 260; Edwin Bearss, The Vicksburg Campaign II (Dayton: Morningside Press, 1986) 642. In his trilogy on the 1863 campaign of Vicksburg, he noted: "Bowen's men had fought with their customary savage élan"; Philip Thomas Tucker, *The Forgotten Stonewall of the West: Major General John Stevens Bowen* (Macon: Mercer University Press, 1997) 1, 130, 132.
25. *OR*, 1, 17(1): 416, 417.
26. *Ibid.*: 422.
27. *Ibid.*
28. *Ibid.*: 422–424.
29. *Ibid.*: 431–433; Smith, 254–55.
30. *OR* 1, 17(1): Ducat, 160, 212; Prime, 114, 279; William S. Rosecrans's general staff included the following: Lieutenant Colonel Arthur Ducat, Chief of Staff. Pre-war engineering. Fitch, 48. Lieutenant Colonel Calvin Goddard, Acting Adjutant General, pre-war business, Fitch, 47. Captain Frederick E. Prime, Chief Engineer, West Point, Class of 1850. Cullum, II, 400, Captain Charles R. Thomson, Ordnance Officer, Pre-war Merchant, Fitch 53–54. Colonel John W. Taylor, Chief Quartermaster, Pre-war Business, Fitch, 47, 271. Lieutenant Colonel Samuel Simmons, Commissary of Subsistence. Pre-war Law, Fitch, 47, 280.
31. *OR*, 1, 17(1): 416–17.
32. *Ibid.*: 424, 425.
33. *Ibid.*: 439.
34. *Ibid.*: 437.
35. *Ibid.*: 440.
36. *Ibid.*: 435, 443, 450.
37. *OR*, 1, *Ibid.*: 431–432; Cozzens, 142; Smith, 231, 232, 253.
38. *OR* 1 (17)1, *Ibid.*: 169, 403, 443, 447; Earl Van Dorn's General Staff included the following officers: Major Edward Dillon, Chief Commissary. Lieutenant U.S. Army, 1857–1861. *OR* 1, 17(1): 443. Major Manning M. Kimmel (senior) Assistant Adjutant General Army of West Tennessee. West Point Class of 1857, Cullum, II, 691; *OR*, 1, 17(1): 395. Captain James M. Loughborough, Assistant Adjutant General. Pre-war Attorney. *OR* 17(1): 395; Captain Edward H. Cummins, Acting Inspector General. *OR*, 1, 17(1): 395, 415. Major J. H. Balfour, Assistant Adjutant General; *OR*, 1, 17(1): 395. Lieutenant Colonel James Patrick Major, Chief of Artillery, West Point, Class of 1852, Cullum, II, 655; *OR*, 1, 17(1): 448.
39. Smith, 252, 253, 255, 258.

Chapter 9

1. Scott E. Sallee, "The Battle of Prairie Grove," *Blue & Gray* 21, 5 (October 2004): 8.
2. Ezra J. Warner, *Generals in Gray* (Baton Rouge: Louisiana State University Press, 1959) 141; Douglas Southall Freeman, *Lee's Lieutenants: Manassas to Malvern Hill* (New York: Charles

Scribner's Sons, 1942) 97, 581, 614; Steven E. Woodworth, *Davis and Lee at War* (Lawrence: University Press of Kansas, 1995) 178. Sallees, *ibid*.

3. Ezra J. Warner, *Generals in Gray*, 137–138; Sallee, 9; Biscoe Hindman, "Thomas Carmichael Hindman," *Confederate Veteran* 38 (1938) 97–100.

4. Ezra J. Warner, *Generals in Blue*, 37–38; William Shea, *Fields of Blood: The Prairie Grove Campaign* (Chapel Hill: University of North Carolina Press, 2013) 72; Thomas L. Snead, "The Conquest of Arkansas," 3, 447.

5. Snead, *ibid*.

6. Michael E. Banasik, *Embattled Arkansas: The Prairie Grove Campaign of 1862* (Wilmington: Broadfoot Publishing Company, 1998) 517, 534.

7. Sallee, 15.

8. Sallee, 25.

9. *OR*, 1, 13: 899.

10. *OR*, 1, 13: 914; Snead, 16.

11. *OR*, 1, 22 (1): 805; Banasik, 534; Shea, 22, 85, 91, 92, 94, 114.

12. *OR*, 1, 17(2): 376; *OR*, 1, 22(1): 805.

13. *OR*, 1, 13: 50, 913, 914, 916, 917.

14. Shea, 120.

15. *OR* 1, 22(1): 140.

16. Banasik, 289, 291; Earlier Hindman issued 40 rounds per man and filled his limber chests in anticipation of the coming action but left the remainder back at Hogeye.

17. Captain S. T. Buffner, "Sketch of the First Missouri Battery, C. S. A." *Confederate Veteran,* 20 (1912), 417; Sallee, 20; *OR* 1, 22(1): 141.

18. Shea, 154; Banasik, 357.

19. *The Madison Journal*, January 3, 1863.

20. *The Madison Journal, ibid*.

21. *Confederate Veteran*, 5, 367–368. Letter from W. L. Morrison, Hamilton, Texas; Shea, 211.

22. F. M. Knox, "Captured and Released." *Confederate Veteran* 33. Knox was a member of Co. K, 16th Missouri Infantry, General M. M. Parson's Brigade; Shea, 225; Banasik, 432.

23. Sallee, 46.

24. S. T. Buffner, "Sketch of the First Missouri Battery, C. S. A." *Confederate Veteran*, 20, 418; *OR*, 1, 22(1): 101–02, 109.

25. James G. Blunt's staff officers in the Army of the Frontier included the following men: Major T. J. Weed, Assistant Adjutant General, No West Point or Regular Experience. Captain Lyman Scott, Jr., Acting Assistant Adjutant General, No West Point or regular army experience. Captain Oliver Barber, Assistant Chief of Staff, and Commissary Officer. Pre-war Manufacturer of woolen cloth and pork-packing. Kansas territorial and state politician. Alfred Theodore Andreas, *History of the State of Kansas* (Chicago: A. T. Andreas, 1883), 332. Major V. P. Van Antwerp, Inspector General and Chief Engineer. Attended West Point, three years as Isaac V. P. Van Antwerp. Pre-war Lawyer and Farmer. Wiki. Served as a Major and chief engineer under Blunt, 1861–62. Hunt and Brown, *Brevet Brigadier Generals* 630. Colonel Daniel Huston, commanding the 2nd Division in the field was a West Point graduate, Class of 1848. Cullum, 2, 364–65, *OR*, 1, 22(1): 77. Francis J. Herron's staff officers included the following men: Captain, Hyde Clark, Assistant Adjutant General. He was a pre-war banker. Hunt and Brown, 114. Captain Littleton, Commissary of Subsistence. Captain Brewster, Staff. Lieutenant Pettit, Staff. Lieutenan Shiras, Staff. Lieutenant Douglas, Staff. *OR*, 1, 22(1): 107.

26. *OR*, 1, 22(1): 142; Buffner, *Confederate Veteran*, 201, 203, 418.

27. Thomas C. Hindman's staff officers in the 1 Corps, Confederate Army of Trans-Mississippi included the following men: Colonel Robert C. Newton, Chief of Staff. Pre-war Education at Western Military Institute in White House, Tenn. Practiced law in Little Rock. Knew Hindman pre-war. Josiah H. Shinn, *A History of Arkansas* (Little Rock: Wilson and Webb, 1898) 297; Bruce Allerdice, *Confederate Colonels* (Columbia: University of Missouri Press, 2008) 290–91; Major John Phagan Wilson, Ark. Assistant Adjutant General. Fold3.com. Lieutenant S. B. Reardon, aide-de-camp, and Acting Chief of Ordnance. Colonel David Provence, Acting Chief of Artillery. Pre-war Planter. Allerdice, *Confederate Colonels*, 314. Colonel Archibald. S. Dobbins, Volunteer aide-de-camp. Pre-war planter in Arkansas. Allerdice, *Confederate Colonels,* 130. Major E. C. Boudinot, volunteer aide-de-camp. Surgeon J. M. Keller, medical director. *OR*, 1, 22(1): 143.

28. Sallee, 45.

29. *OR*, 1, 22(1): 143–144.

30. *Ibid*.

31. *OR*, 1, 22(2): 113; Shea, 233.

Chapter 10

1. James Lee McDonough, *Stones River: Bloody Winter in Tennessee* (Knoxville: University of Tennessee Press, 1980) 41; Larry J. Daniel, *Days of Glory: The Army of the Cumberland, 1861-1865* (Baton Rouge: Louisiana State University Press, 2004) 182.

2. Larry J. Daniel, 12, 185, 187, 188–190. Ezra J. Warner, *Generals in Blue,* 100–101, 294, 470; Jim Lewis.

3. Larry J. Daniel, 194–195.

4. Thomas Lawrence Connolly, *Autumn of Glory: The Army of Tennessee, 1862–1865.* Baton Rouge: Louisiana State University, 1971) 6–8, 17–18, 22, 25; Larry J. Daniel, 6. Dennis W. Belcher, *The Cavalries at Stones River: An Analytical History* (Jefferson, NC: McFarland & Company, Inc., 2017) 249; Jim Lewis, "The Battle of Stones River," *Blue & Gray Magazine* 21, 5 (2012) 7.

5. James Lee McDonough, 34–35. Joseph E. Johnston, "Jefferson Davis and the Mississippi Campaign," III: 473–474; McDonough, 37. Larry J. Daniel, *Stones River*, 26, 69. Connolly, *Ibid.*: 32, 38, 41. Belcher, *Ibid.*: 225. Matt Spruill and Lee Spruill, *Decisions at Stones River: The Sixteen Critical*

Decisions That Defined the Battle (Knoxville: University of Tennessee Press, 2018) 21, 29.

6. Daniel, 25–7.

7. Daniel, *Army of the Cumberland*: 199. Daniel, *Stones River*: 25, 33, 40.

8. Daniel, *Stones River*: 7, 46, 48, 62–64; Peter Cozzens, *No Better Place to Die: The Battle of Stones River* (Chicago: University of Chicago Press, 1990) 30; Connolly, 41, 42, 51. OR, 1, 20(1) 672–673; Lewis, "The Battle of Stones River," 19; Spruill, 49, 54–61.

9. Daniel, *Stones River*: 67, 68; Lewis, "The Battle of Stones River," 20.

10. McDonough, 97, 104–105; Cozzens, 91, 101; Daniel, *Stones River*: 95, 104; Daniel, *Army of the Cumberland*: 216–217.

11. Cozzens, 107; Connolly, 57.

12. Cozzens, 109, 159–161; But see Daniel, *Stones River*: 161 (He suggests that the delay might not have been as great as several historians have argued.); Spruill, 87–92; Christopher L. Kolakowski, *The Stones River and Tullahoma Campaigns* (Charleston: The History Press, 2011) 71.

13. Peter Cozzens, 162. Connolly, 58–60. G. C. Kniffin, "The Battle of Stones River," III: 623. Lewis, "The Battle of Stones River," 45; Spruill, 75–80, 93–97.

14. Daniel, *Army of the Cumberland*, 219; Cozzens, 172.

15. McDonough, 180–183; Cozzens, 181–182. Daniel, *Stones River*, 114, 175, 181, 185, 190; Spruill, 99–113.

16. Cozzens, 200; Daniel, *Army of the Cumberland*, 224; Daniel, *Stones River*, 198. Spruill, 113–15.

17. Larry Daniel, 211; Spruill, 126–127.

18. OR, 1, 20(2): 493; Daniel, 227–29; Archer Jones, *Confederate Strategy from Shiloh to Vicksburg* (Baton Rouge: Louisiana State University Press, 1991) 117.

19. Daniel, *Stones River*, 22; OR, 1, 20(2): 441.

20. Daniel, 64.

21. Earl J. Hess, *Braxton Bragg: The Most Hated Man of the Confederacy* (Chapel Hill: University of North Carolina Press, 2016) 105–108; Connolly, 69–89. Grady McWhiney, B*raxton Bragg and Confederate Defeat 1, Field Command* (New York: Columbia University Press, 1969) Index. The index to this book lists over a dozen individuals and groups opposed to Bragg by this time. I take the middle ground by suggesting that Bragg was neither supported strategically nor was he properly assisted by his own subordinates, and that upheld barely by his staff, he made enough mistakes on his own to nullify any of his positive contributions to the battle.

22. Fitch, *Annals,* 400; OR, 1, 20(1): 671.

23. Larry Daniel, *Conquered: Why the Army of Tennessee Failed* (Chapel Hill: University of North Carolina Press, 2019) 62–64; Christopher L. Kolakowski, 71.

24. Daniel, *Stones River*, 182.

25. Connolly, 61.

26. Daniel, *Conquered*, 68, 70.

27. *Atlas to Accompany the Official Records of the Union and Confederate Armies.* Washington D.C. U.S. Government Printing Office, 1891–95. Plate 30, 1.

28. OR, 1, 20(1): 671. Information on Lieutenant Colonel George Garner, *List of Staff Officers of the Confederate States Army*, 59; Krick, *Staff Officers in Gray*, 359; Lieutenant Colonel George Brent, Adjutant General, Pre-war Law; June Gow, "Chiefs of Staff in the Army of Tennessee Under Braxton Bragg," *Tennessee Historical Quarterly*, Vol. 27, No. 4. 341–360. Krick, 82; Captain S. W. Steele, Acting Chief Engineer, Robert E. L. Krick, 356. Lieutenant Colonel Hypolite Oladowski, Chief of Ordnance, pre-war Poland, New Orleans Armory, Krick, 346; Lieutenant Colonel James H. Hallonquist, Chief of Artillery, Krick, 321; Lieutenant Colonel Lawrence W. O'Bannon, Chief Quartermaster, Mexican War, U.S. Regular Army, Krick, 346; Major John J. Walker, Commissary of Subsistence, Krick, 360. Captain P. H. Thomson, Acting Inspector General, Krick, 358; Lieutenant Colonel William Kelly Beard, Adjutant and Inspector General, Krick, 316. While this list is not comprehensive in nature, it is designed to highlight staff officers who played important roles in the army's wellbeing. Aides-de-camp and other volunteers or assistants have not been included.

29. OR, 1, 20(2*)*: 115.

30. Fitch, *Annals,* 246–248, 647. OR, 1, 20(2): 102, 115, 117, 118, 135.

31. Fitch, *Annals*, 267–269; Daniel, *Stones River*, 28.

32. Lenette S. Taylor, *The Supply for the Tomorrow Must Not Fail* (Kent: The Kent State University Press, 2004) 95, 99, 102.

33. Fitch, *Annals*, 303, 352.

34. Lewis, "The Battle of Stones River," 50; Fitch, *Annals*, 271.

35. Fitch, *Annals*, 47–53; His volume contains several examples.

36. OR, 1, 20(1): 199; Fitch, *Annals*. Lieutenant Colonel Julius P. Garesché, Chief of Staff, West Point Class of 1841, Cullum, II, 84. Fitch 246–249. Major Charles Goddard, Acting Assistant Adjutant General, Pre-war Merchant. Fitch, 47. Captain Nathaniel Michler, Engineer Officer, West Point, Class of 1848, Cullum, II, 347; Fitch, 296. Colonel James Barnett, Chief of Artillery, pre-war hardware, Fitch 296. Lieutenant Colonel John W. Taylor, Chief Quartermaster, Pre-war Business, Fitch 272. Lieutenant Colonel Samuel Simmons, Chief Commissary, Pre-war Law. Fitch 280. Captain James Curtiss 15th U.S. Infantry, Assistant Inspector General, West Point, Class of 1851, Cullum, II, 461. Major William M. Wiles, Provost-Marshal General, Pre-war Business. Fitch, 286. Lieutenant Theodore Edson, United States Ordnance Officer. West Point, Class of 1860, Cullum II, 740.

37. Roy B. Basler, ed., The Collected Works of Abraham Lincoln (New Brunswick, N.J.: Rutgers University Press, 1953) 425.

Chapter 11

1. Charles Bracelen Flood, *Grant and Sherman: The Friendship That Won the Civil War* (New York: Farrar, Strauss and Giroux, 2005) 3–4; T. Harry Williams, "The Military Leadership of the North and the South: The Harmon Memorial Lectures in Military History Number Two" (Colorado: United Air Force Academy, 1960) 6–7; Earl J. Hess, *Braxton Bragg: The Most Hated Man in the Confederacy* (Chapel Hill: University of North Carolina Press, 2016) 276.

2. Lincoln to Joseph Hooker, quoted in David Herbert Donald, *Lincoln* (New York: Simon & Shuster, 1995) 434.

Appendix I

1. Bruce Levine, *The Spirit of 1848: German Immigrants, Labor Conflict and the Coming of the Civil War* (Chicago: University of Illinois Press, 1992) 57.

2. See individual chapter notes for details.

3. Bruce S. Allerdice, *Confederate Colonels*; Roger D. Hunt, *Colonels in Blue—Illinois, Iowa, Minnesota and Wisconsin*; Roger D. Hunt, *Colonels in Blue—Missouri and the Western States and Territories*; Roger D. Hunt, *Colonels in Blue—Indiana, Kentucky and Tennessee*; Roger D. Hunt, *Colonels in Blue—Michigan, Ohio and West Virginia*; Roger D. Hunt and Jack R. Brown, *Brevet Brigadier Generals in Blue*; Robert E. L. Krick, *Staff Officers in Gray*.

4. Bruce Levine, ed., *The German-American Soldier in the Wars of the U.S.* (Bowie: Heritage Books, Inc., 1996) 2, 7, 195.

5. Lenette S. Taylor, 1–3, 11, 12, 24, 33.

6. Robert O'Harrow Jr., *The Quartermaster: Montgomery Meigs* (New York: Simon & Shuster, 2016) 7–10, 13–15, 18–20; Earl J. Hess, *Military Logistics: A Study of Military Transportation* (Baton Rouge: Louisiana State University Press, 2017) 261.

7. George Edgar Turner, *Victory Rode the Rails: The Strategic Place of the Railroads in the Civil War* (Lincoln: University of Lincoln Press, 1953) 48, 54–60, 252, 289, 290; Hess, 42–43, 89–90.

Appendix II

1. Thomas S. Dickey and Peter C. George. *Field Artillery Projectiles of the American Civil War* (Arsenal Publications 2, Mechanicsville, Virginia, 1993) 14–15; Carl G. Carlson-Drexler, Douglas D. Scott, and Harold Roeker,"The Battle Raged...With Terrible Fury: Battlefield Archeology Of Pea Ridge National Military Park,"(Lincoln: Midwest Archeological Center Technical Report No. 112, United States Department Of The Interior National Park Service, 2008) 42–43; George F. Witham, *Shiloh, Shells and Artillery Units* (Memphis, Tennessee: Riverside Press, 1980) 88–89.

2. Shiloh National Military Park and Stones River National Military Park. Artillery Data graciously supplied by the National Park System.

3. Frank E. Vandiver, "Makeshifts of Confederate Ordnance" (Southern Historical Association: *The Journal of Southern History*, Vol. 17, No. 2. May 1951) 180–193; Larry J. Daniel, *Cannoneers in Gray: The Field Artillery of the Army of Tennessee, 1861–1865*,14–18, 44, 56, 68–69.

4. Larry J. Daniel and Riley W. Gunter, *Confederate Cannon Foundries* 61, 68, 70, 75.

Bibliography

Primary Sources

Agassiz, George R., ed. *Meade's Headquarters 1863-1865: Letters of Colonel Theodore Lyman.* Boston: Atlantic Monthly Press, 1922.

Andreas, Alfred Theodore. *History of the State of Kansas.* Chicago: A. T. Andreas, 1883.

Atlas to Accompany the Official Records of the Union and Confederate Armies. Washington, D.C.: Government Printing Office, 1891-95.

Badeau, Adam. *Military History of Ulysses S. Grant, from April 1861 to April 1865*, vol. 1. New York: D. Appleton and Company, 1885.

Balfour, J.H. List of *Staff Officers of the Confederate States Army, 1861-1865.* Washington, D.C.: Government Printing Office. 1891.

Basler, Roy B., ed. *The Collected Works of Abraham Lincoln.* 8 vols. New Brunswick, NJ.: Rutgers University Press, 1953.

Beauregard, Pierre G. T. "The Campaign of Shiloh." *Battles and Leaders of the Civil War*, vol. 1, 569- 593. New York: Castle Books, 1956.

Biographical Congressional Directory of the United States Congress: 1774-1903. Washington, D.C.: Government Printing Office, 1903.

Blodgett, Edward A. "The Army of the Southwest and the Battle of Pea Ridge," *Military Essays and Recollections: Papers Read before the Commandery of the State of Illinois, Military Order of the Loyal Legion of the United States*, vol. 2, 289–312.

Boggs, William. *Military Reminiscences of General William R. Boggs, C.S.A.* Durham, N.C.: The Seeman Printery, 1913.

Braxton Bragg Papers. William B. Palmer Collection. Series I, Folder 4, Roll 2. Cleveland: Western Reserve Historical Society.

Brown, Isaac. "The Confederate Gun-boat Arkansas." *Battles and Leaders of the Civil War*, vol. 3, 572-579. New York: Castle Books, 1956.

Buffner, S. T. "Sketch of the First Missouri Battery, C. S. A." *Confederate Veteran*, 20. 1912.

Bunn, Henry C. "Reminiscences of the Civil War," Charles Edward Nash, *Biographical Sketches of Gen Pat Cleburne and T. C. Hindman Together with Humorous Anecdotes and Reminiscences of the late Civil War.* Little Rock: Tunnah & Pittard, 1898.

Chamberlain, Samuel E. *My Confession: Recollections of a Rogue.* New York: Harper and Brothers, 1956.

Cist, Henry M. *Campaigns of the Civil War: The Army in Cumberland.* New York: The Blue & the Gray Press, ND.

Claiborne, Thomas B. "The Battle of Perryville." *Confederate Veteran*, vol. 16, no. 1. Nashville: S. A. Cunningham, Editor and Proprietor, 1908.

Clayton, W. Woodford. *History of Davidson County, Tennessee.* Philadelphia: J. W. Lewis & Co. 1880.

Crabtree, John D. "Recollections of the Pea Ridge Campaign and the Army of the Southwest," *Military Essays and Recollections: Papers Read before the Commandery of the State of Illinois, Military Order of the Loyal Legion of the United States*, vol. 3, 211–226. Chicago: The Dial Press, 1899.

Craighill, William P. *The Army Officer's Pocket Companion.* New York: D. Van Nostrand, 1862.

Crist, Lynda Laswell, Mary Seaton Dix, and Kenneth H. Williams, eds. *The Papers of Jefferson Davis*, vol. 8, 1995. Baton Rouge: Louisiana State University Press, 1971–1997.

Cullum, George W. *Biographical Register of the Officers and Graduates of the United States Military Academy.* Boston: Houghton, Mifflin, 1891.

Curtius, "Field of Battle Near Perryville, Kentucky." *New York Times*, October 17, 1862.

Dodge, Grenville M. *Personal Biography of Major General Grenville Mellen Dodge from 1837 to 1871: written and compiled by himself at different times and completed in 1914.* vol. 1. Unpublished typescript. https://archive.org/details/BiographyOfMajorGeneralGrenvilleM.Dodge.

Dodge, Grenville M. *Personal Recollections of President Abraham Lincoln, General Ulysses S. Grant, and General William T. Sherman.* Glendale: The Arthur H. Clark Company, 1914.

Duke, Basil. "Bragg's Campaign in Kentucky, 1862." *Southern Bivouac*, vol. 4, April 1886.

Dunbar, Roland, ed. *Jefferson Davis Constitutionalist: His Letters, Papers and Speeches.* Jackson, MS: Dept. of Archives and History, 1923, vol. 5.

Eicher, John, and David. *Civil War High Commands.* Stanford: Stanford University Press, 2001.

Field Manual 3-0: Operations. Washington, D.C.: U.S. Department of the Army. 2008.

Fisher, Horace N. "Historical and Memorial Paper," *Reunion of the Society of the Army of the Cumberland: Thirty-Second Reunion, Indianapolis, Indiana, 1904.* Cincinnati: The Robert Clarke Company, 1905.

Fitch, John. *Annals of the Army of the Cumberland*, Philadelphia: J. B. Lippincott & Co., 1864.

Gilbert, Charles C. "Bragg's Invasion of Kentucky," *Southern Bivouac*, vol. 1 (August 1885).

Grant, Ulysses S. "The Battle of Shiloh." *Battles and Leaders of the Civil War*, vol. 1, 465–486. New York: Castle Books, 1956.

Grant, Ulysses S. *Personal Memoirs of U. S. Grant*. New York: Charles L. Webster & Company, 1885–1886.

Hammond, Paul F. "General Kirby Smith's Campaign in Kentucky in 1862," the Rev. J. William Jones, ed., *Southern Historical Society Papers*, vol. 9. Richmond: Wm. Ellis Jones Printer, 1816–1959.

Harwood, Nathan S. "The Pea Ridge Campaign," *Civil War Military Sketches and Incidents: Papers Read by Companions of the State of Nebraska, Military Order of the Loyal Legion of the United States*, vol. 1, 110–121. Wilmington: Broadfoot Publishing Company, 1992.

Headley, John W. *Confederate Operations in Canada and New York*. New York: The Neale Publishing Company, 1906.

Hickenlooper, Andrew. "Battle of Shiloh," *Sketches of War History*, 1861–1865, 402–438. Cincinnati: Robert Clarke and Company, 1903.

Hindman, Biscoe. "Thomas Carmichael Hindman." *Confederate Veteran*, vol. 38. 1938.

Johnson, Timothy D., ed. *Memoirs of Lieut.-General Winfield Scott*. Knoxville: University of Tennessee Press, 2015.

Johnston, Joseph E. "Jefferson Davis and the Mississippi Campaign." *Battles & Leaders*, vol. 3. New York: Castle Books, 1956.

Johnston, William Preston. "Albert Sidney Johnston at Shiloh." *Battles and Leaders of the Civil War*, vol. 1, 540–568. New York: Castle Books, 1956.

Jordan, Thomas. "Notes of a Confederate Staff Officer at Shiloh." *Battles and Leaders of the Civil War*: vol. 1, 594–603. New York: Century, 1884–1887.

Journal of the Congress of the Confederate States of America. Washington, D.C.: Government Printing Office, 1904.

Kelly, R. M. "Holding Kentucky for the Union." *Battles and Leaders of the Civil War*, vol. 1, 373–392. New York: Castle Books, 1956.

Kniffin, G. C. "The Battle of Stones River." *Battles and Leaders*, vol. 3, 613–63. New York: Castle Books, 1956.

Knox, F. M. "Captured and Released." *Confederate Veteran*, vol. 33. United Daughters of the Confederacy. Nashville: S. A. Cunningham, 1925.

Liddell, St. John. "Liddell's Record of the Civil War." Louisville, KY: *Southern Bivouac*. December 1885.

List of Staff Officers of the Confederate States Army. Washington, D.C.: Government Printing Office, 1891.

Maury, Dabney H. "Recollections of the Elkhorn Campaign." *Southern Historical Society Papers*, vol. 2. New York: Kraus Reprint Company, 1977.

M'Farland, Judge L. B. "Maney's Brigade at the Battle of Perryville." Confederate Veteran, vol. 30.

Moore, Frank, ed. *The Rebellion Record*, vol. 5. New York: G. P. Putnam 1861–63.

NA. "Maj. John Lucien Brown," *Confederate Veteran*, vol. 6. Nashville: S. A. Cunningham.

NA. *Portrait and Biographical Record of Winnebago and Boone Counties, Illinois*. Chicago: Biographical Publishing Co., 1892.

Noble, John W. "Battle of Pea Ridge or Elkhorn Tavern," *War Papers and Personal Reminiscences, 1861–1865, Read Before the Commandery of the State of Missouri, Military Order of the Loyal Legion of the United States*, vol. 1, 211–242. St. Louis: 1892.

Noll, Arthur Howard., ed. *Doctor Quintard: Chaplain CSA and Second Bishop of Tennessee* (Sewanee, TN, 1905)

Peters, William. *Recollections of William H. Peters, Of Facts and Circumstances Connected with the Evacuation of the Navy Yard at Portsmouth, Virginia*. 1891.

Putnam, Douglas, Jr. "Reminiscences of the Battle of Shiloh," *Sketches of War History 1861–1865, Ohio Commandery, Military Order of the Loyal Legion of the United States 1861–1865*, vol. 3, 197–211. Cincinnati, Robert Clarke, 1890.

Reinhart, Joseph R., trans. and ed. *A German Hurrah! Civil War Letters of Friedrich Bertsch and Wilhelm Stängel, 9th Ohio Infantry*. Kent: Kent State University Press, 2010.

Sheridan, Philip H. *Personal Memoirs of P. H. Sheridan*. New York: Charles L. Webster & Company, 1888.

Sherman, William T. *Memoirs of General W. T. Sherman, Written by Himself*. New York: D. Appleton and Company, 1889.

Shinn, Josiah H. *A History of Arkansas*. Little Rock: Wilson and Webb, 1898.

Simon, John Y., ed. *The Papers of Ulysses S. Grant*. Carbondale: Southern Illinois University Press, 1972.

Simpson, John W. "A Boy's Story of the Battle of Mill Springs." *Confederate Veteran*, vol. 18, 335.

Soley, James Russell. "The Union and Confederate Navies," *Battles and Leaders*, vol. 1. New York: Castle Books, 1956.

Stanley, General D. S. "The Battle of Corinth: A Paper Read by General D. S. Stanley, U. S. A., December 4, 1895, Personal Recollections of the War of the Rebellion." *Commandery, Military Order of the Loyal Legion of the United States*, vol. 2, 267–279. New York: G. P. Putnam's Sons, 1897.

30th Congress, 1st Session. Senate Document 65.

Proceedings of the Two Courts of Inquiry in the Case of Major General Pillow.

Tunnard, William H. *A Southern Record: The History of the Third Regiment Louisiana Infantry.* Baton Rouge, Longfellow, 1866.

29th Congress, 1st Session. House Document 17. *Correspondence with General Taylor.*

29th Congress, 1st Session. House Document 197. *Dispatch from General Taylor.*

29th Congress, 1st Session. House Document 207. *Dispatch from General Taylor.*

29th Congress, 2nd Session. Senate Document 4. *Report of the Secretary of War.*

Walke, Henry. "The Western Flotilla," *Battles and Leaders of the Civil War*, vol. 1, 430–452. New York: Castle Books, 1956.

War of the Rebellion, A Compilation of the Official Records of the Union and Confederate Armies. Washington, D.C.: Government Printing Office, 1880–1901.

War of the Rebellion, A Compilation of the Official Records of the Union and Confederate Navies. Washington, D.C.: Government Printing Office, 1894.

Watkins, Sam R. *Company Aytch.* New York: New American Library, 1999.

Wheeler, Joseph. "Bragg's Invasion of Kentucky," *Battles and Leaders of the Civil War*, vol. 3, 1–25. New York: Castle Books, 1956.

Secondary Sources: Books

Alger, John I. *The Quest for Victory: The History of the Principles of War.* Westport: Greenwood, 1982.

Allerdice, Bruce. *Biographical Register of Confederate Colonels.* Columbia: University of Missouri, 2008.

Army, Thomas F., Jr. *Engineering Victory: How Technology Won the Civil War.* Baltimore: Johns Hopkins University Press, 2016.

Arthur, Billy, and Ted Ballard. *Second Bull Run Staff Ride.* Washington: U.S. Army Center of Military History, 2002.

Banasik, Michael E. *Embattled Arkansas: The Prairie Grove Campaign of 1862.* Wilmington, NC: Broadfoot Publishing, 1998.

Bauer, K. Jack. *The Mexican War, 1846–1848.* New York: Macmillan Publishing, 1974.

Bearss, Edwin. *The Vicksburg Campaign*, vol. 2. Dayton: Morningside, 1986.

Belcher, Dennis W. *The Cavalries at Stones River: An Analytical History.* Jefferson, NC: McFarland 2017.

Bennett, B. Kevin, "The Battle of Richmond, Kentucky" *The Blue & Gray Magazine*, 25, no. 6.

Black, Robert C. *The Railroads of the Confederacy.* Wilmington, NC: Broadfoot Publishing, 1987.

Boatner, Mark M., III. *The Civil War Dictionary.* New York: David McKay, 1959.

Boritt, Gabor S. ed. *Jefferson Davis's Generals.* New York: Oxford University, 1999.

Cameron, Robert S. *Staff Ride Handbook for the Battle of Perryville, 8 October 1862.* Fort Leavenworth: Combat Studies Institute, 2005.

Carlson-Drexler, Carl G., Douglas D. Scott, and Harold Roeker, "The Battle Raged...with Terrible Fury": *Battlefield Archeology of Pea Ridge National Military Park.* Lincoln: Midwest Archeological Center Technical Report No. 112. U.S. Department of The Interior, National Park Service, 2008.

The Century War Book: People's Pictorial Edition. New York: The Century Co., 1894.

Clary, David A. *Eagle and Empire: The United States, Mexico, and the Struggle for a Continent.* New York: Bantam Books, 2009.

Connelly, Thomas Lawrence. *Army of the Heartland: The Army of Tennessee, 1861–1862.* Baton Rouge: Louisiana State University, 1967.

_____. *Autumn of Glory: The Army of Tennessee, 1862–1865.* Baton Rouge: Louisiana State University, 1971.

Cooling, Benjamin Franklin. *Forts Henry and Donelson: The Key to the Confederate Heartland.* Knoxville: University of Tennessee, 1987.

Cozzens, Peter. *The Darkest Days of the War: The Battles of Iuka & Corinth.* Chapel Hill: University of North Carolina, 1997.

_____. *No Better Place to Die: The Battle of Stones River.* Chicago: University of Chicago, 1990.

Cullum, George W. *Biographical Register of the Officers and Graduates of the U.S. Military Academy at West Point, N.Y.: from Its Establishment, in 1802, to 1890, with the Early History of the United States Military Academy.* New York: Houghton Mifflin and Company, 1891.

Cunningham, O. Edward. *Shiloh and the Western Campaign of 1862.* New York: Savas Beatie, 2012.

Dalton, C. David. "He Died on the Field of Glory: Felix Kirk Zollicoffer and the Confederate Defeat at Mill Springs." *Confederate Generals in the Western Theatre*, vol. 4, 1–32. Knoxville: University of Tennessee, 2018.

Daniel, Larry. *Battle of Stones River: The Forgotten Conflict between the Confederate Army of Tennessee and the Union Army of the Cumberland.* Baton Rouge: Louisiana State University, 2012.

_____. *Cannoneers in Gray: The Field Artillery of the Army of Tennessee, 1861–1865.* Alabama: University of Alabama, 1984.

_____. *Conquered: Why the Army of Tennessee Failed.* Chapel Hill: University of North Carolina, 2019.

_____. *Days of Glory: The Army of the Cumberland, 1861–1865.* Baton Rouge: Louisiana State University, 2004.

_____. *Shiloh.* New York: Simon & Shuster, 1997.

Daniel, Larry, and Riley Gunter. *Confederate Cannon Foundries.* Union City, TN: Pioneer Press, 1977.

Daniel, Larry J., and Lynn N. Bock. *Island No. 10: Struggle for the Mississippi Valley.* Tuscaloosa: University of Alabama, 1996.

Davis, William C. *Jefferson Davis: The Man and His Hour.* New York: HarperCollins, 1991.

Dickey, Thomas S., and Peter C. George. *Field Artillery Projectiles of the American Civil War.* Arsenal Publications no. 2. Mechanicsville, Virginia, 1993.

Donald, David Herbert. *Lincoln.* New York: Simon & Shuster, 1995.

DuFour, Charles L. *The Night the War Was Lost.* Lincoln: University of Nebraska, 1960.

Dupuy, Trevor N. *The Evolution of Weapons and Warfare.* New York: The Bobbs-Merrill Company, 1980.

———. *Numbers, Predictions & War.* New York: The Bobbs-Merrill Company, 1979.

Eisenhower, John S. D. *So Far from God: The U.S. War with Mexico 1846–1848.* New York: Random House, 1989.

Engle, Stephen D. *Yankee Dutchman: The Life of Franz Sigel.* Fayetteville: University of Arkansas, 1993.

Esposito, Vincent S. *West Point Atlas of the American Wars, Vol. I. 1689–1900.* New York: Praeger, 1978.

Evans, David. *War: A Matter of Principles.* Fairbairn, Australia: Aerospace Centre, 2000.

Flood, Charles Bracelen. *Grant and Sherman: The Friendship That Won the Civil War.* New York: Farrar, Strauss and Giroux, 2005.

Freeman, Douglas Southall. *Lee's Lieutenants*, vol. 1. New York: Charles Scribner's Sons, 1942.

Gabel, Christopher R. *Rails to Oblivion: The Decline of Confederate Railroads in the Civil War.* Fort Leavenworth, KS: U.S. Army Command and General Staff College, 2002.

Goff, Richard D. *Confederate Supply in the Trans-Mississippi.* Durham: Duke University, 1969.

Gosnall, H. Allen. *Guns on the Western Waters: The Story of River Gunboats in the Civil War.* Baton Rouge: Louisiana State University, 1949.

Gott, Kendall D. *Where the South Lost the Civil War: An Analysis of the Fort Henry-Fort Donelson Campaign, February 1862.* Mechanicsburg, PA: Stackpole Books, 2003.

Hafendorfer, Kenneth A. *Battle of Richmond, Kentucky.* Louisville: KH, 2006.

Hagerman, Edward. *The American Civil War and the Origins of Modern Warfare: Ideas, Organization, and Field Command.* Bloomington: Indiana University, 1988.

Hart, B. H. Liddell. *Thoughts on War.* London: Spellmount Publishers. 1998.

Hattaway, Herman, and Archer Jones. *How the North Won: A Military History of the Civil War.* Chicago: University of Illinois, 1983.

Haughton, Andrew. *Training, Tactics and Leadership in the Confederate Army of Tennessee: Seeds of Failure.* Boca Raton: Psychology Press, 2000.

———. *Training, Tactics and Leadership in the Confederate Army of Tennessee: Seeds of Failure.* Portland, Frank Case, 2000.

Hearn, Chester G. *The Capture of New Orleans 1862.* Baton Rouge: Louisiana State University, 1995.

Henderon, G. F. R. "Strategy." *Encyclopedia Britannica,* vol. 25. New York: The Encyclopedia Britannica, 1902.

Hess, Earl J. *Braxton Bragg: The Most Hated Man of the Confederacy.* Chapel Hill: University of North Carolina, 2016.

———. *The Civil War in the West.* Chapel Hill: University of North Carolina, 2012.

Hughes, Nathaniel Cheairs, Jr., and Roy P. Stonesifer Jr. *The Life and Wars of Gideon Pillow.* Knoxville: University of Tennessee, 2011.

Hunt, Roger D. *Colonels in Blue—Indiana, Kentucky and Tennessee.* Jefferson, NC: McFarland, 2014.

———. *Colonels in Blue—Michigan, Ohio and West Virginia.* Jefferson, NC: McFarland, 2011.

———. *Colonels in Blue—Missouri and the Western States and Territories.* Jefferson, NC: McFarland, 2019.

Hunt, Roger D., and Jack R. Brown. *Brevet Brigadier Generals in Blue.* Gaithersburg: Olde Soldier, 1990.

Hunter, Louis C. *Steamboats on the Western Rivers: An Economic and Technological History.* New York: Dover, 1977.

Johnston, William Preston. *The Life of Albert Sidney Johnston.* Austin: State House Press, 1997.

Jones, Steven R. *The Right Hand of Command: Use & Disuse of Personal Staffs in the Civil War.* Mechanicsburg: Stackpole, 2000.

Keegan, John. *The American Civil War.* New York: Alfred A. Knopf, 2009.

King, Benjamin, Richard C. Biggs, and Eric R. Criner. *Spearhead of Logistics: A History of the United States Army Transportation Corps.* Washington, D.C.: Center of Military History, 2001.

Kolakowski, Christopher L. *The Civil War at Perryville: Battling for the Bluegrass.* Charleston: The History Press, 2009.

———. *The Stones River and Tullahoma Campaigns.* Charleston: The History Press, 2011.

Krick, Robert E. L. *Staff Officers in Gray.* Chapel Hill: University of North Carolina, 2003.

Kundahl, George G. *Confederate Engineer.* Knoxville: University of Tennessee, 2000.

Lambert, D. Warren. *When the Ripe Pears Fell: The Battle of Richmond, Kentucky.* Richmond: Madison County Historical Society, 1995.

Levine, Bruce. *The German-American Soldier in the Wars of the U. S.* Bowie: Heritage Books, 1996.

———. *The Spirit of 1848: German Immigrants, Labor Conflict and the Coming of the Civil War.* Chicago: University of Illinois, 1992.

Lewis, Jim. "The Battle of Stones River." *Blue & Gray Magazine,* 2012.

Mattis, Jim, and Bing West. *Call Sign Chaos.* New York: Random House, 2019.

McDonough, James Lee. *Stones River: Bloody Winter in Tennessee*. Knoxville: University of Tennessee, 1980.

———. *War in Kentucky: From Shiloh to Perryville*. Knoxville: University of Tennessee, 1994.

McKim, Randolph H. *The Numerical Strength of the Confederate Army*. New York: Neale Publishing, 1912.

McKinney, Francis F. *Education in Violence: The Life of George H. Thomas and the History of the Army of the Cumberland*. Chicago: Americana House, 1991.

McMurry, Richard M. *Two Great Rebel Armies: An Essay in Confederate Military History*. Chapel Hill: University of North Carolina, 1989.

McPherson, James M. *Embattled Rebel: Jefferson Davis as Commander in Chief*. New York: Penguin, 2014.

———. *Tried by War: Abraham Lincoln as Commander in Chief*. New York: Penguin, 2008.

McWhiney, Grady. *Braxton Bragg and Confederate Defeat*, vol. 1. New York: Columbia University, 1969.

Merry, Robert W. *A Country of Vast Designs: James K. Polk, The Mexican War and the Conquest of the American Continent*. New York: Simon & Schuster, 2009.

Mesh, Allen H. *Teacher of Civil War Generals: Major General Charles Ferguson Smith: Soldier and West Point Commandant*. Jefferson, NC: McFarland, 2015.

Miller, Francis Trevelyan, ed. *The Photographic History of the Civil War in Ten Volumes*. New York: The Review of Reviews Co., 1911.

Moat, Louis Shepherd, ed. *Frank Leslie's Illustrated History of the Civil War*. New York: Mrs. Frank Leslie, Publisher, 1895.

Monaghan, Jay. *Civil War on the Western Border: 1854–1865*. New York: Bonanza Books, 1955.

Moore, Jerrold Northrop. *Confederate Commissary General: Lucius Bellinger Northrop and the Subsistence Bureau of the Southern Army*. Shippensburg, PA: White Mane, 1996.

Murray, Richard M. *Two Great Rebel Armies: An Essay in Confederate Military History*. Chapel Hill: University of North Carolina, 1989.

Nevins, Alan. *The War for the Union: War Becomes Revolution*. New York: Konecky & Konecky, 1960.

Noe, Kenneth W. *Perryville: This Grand Havoc of Battle*. Lexington: University Press of Kentucky, 2001.

Northouse, Peter G. *Leadership: Theory and Practice*, 6th ed. Los Angeles: Sage Publications, 2013.

Nye, Roger H. *The Challenge of Command: Reading for Military Excellence*. Wayne, NJ: Avery Publishing, 1986.

O'Harrow, Robert, Jr. *The Quartermaster: Montgomery C. Meigs, Lincoln's General*. New York: Simon & Schuster, 2016.

Peskin, Allan. *Winfield Scott and the Profession of Arms*. Kent: The Kent State University, 2003.

Peterson, Larry. *Decisions of the 1862 Kentucky Campaign*. Knoxville: University of Tennessee, 2019.

Puryear, Edgar F. *American Generalship: The Art of Command*. New York: Ballantine, 2003.

Ramsdell, Charles W. "Some Problems Involved in Writing the History of the Confederacy," *The Journal of Southern History*, vol. 2, no. 2, May 1936.

Reinhart, Joseph R., ed. *A German Hurrah! Civil War Letters of Friedrich Bertsch and Wilhelm Stängel, 9th Ohio Infantry*. Kent: The Kent State University, 2010.

Rish, Erna. *Quartermaster Support of the Army: A History of the Corps, 1775–1939*. Washington: U S Army Center of Military History, 1988.

Roland, Charles P. *Albert Sidney Johnston: Soldier of Three Republics*. Austin: University of Texas, 1964.

Salling, Stuart. *Louisianians in the Western Confederacy: The Adams-Gibson Brigade in the Civil War*. Jefferson, NC: McFarland, 2010.

Sanders, Stuart. *The Battle of Mill Springs, Kentucky*. Charleston: History Press, 2013.

Shea, William L. *Fields of Blood: The Prairie Grove Campaign*. Chapel Hill: University of North Carolina, 2013.

Shea, William L., and Earl J. Hess. *Pea Ridge: Civil War Campaign in the West*. Chapel Hill: University of North Carolina, 1992.

Sigel, Franz. "The Pea Ridge Campaign." *Battles and Leaders of the Civil War*, vol. 1, 314–331. New York: Castle Books, 1956.

Smith, Justin Harvey. *The War with Mexico*. New York: Macmillan Publishing, 1919.

Smith, Myron J., Jr. *The CSS Arkansas: A Confederate Ironclad*. Jefferson, NC: McFarland, 2011.

Smith, Timothy B. *Corinth 1862: Siege, Battle Occupation*. Lawrence: University Press of Kansas, 2012.

———. *Grant Invades Tennessee: The 1862 Battles for Fort Henry and Donelson*. Lawrence: University Press of Kansas, 2016.

———. *Shiloh: Conquer or Perish*. Lawrence: University of Kansas Press, 2014.

———. "To Conquer or Perish: The Last Hours of Albert Sidney Johnston," Lawrence Lee Hewitt and Arthur W. Bergeron, Jr., eds. *Confederate Generals in the Western Theater*, vol. 3. Knoxville: University of Tennessee, 2011.

Snead, Thomas L. "The Conquest of Arkansas," *Battles & Leaders of the Civil War*, vol. 3, 441–460. New York: Castle Books, 1956.

Solonick, Justin S. *Engineering Victory: The Union Siege of Vicksburg*. Carbondale: Southern Illinois University, 2015.

Spruill, Matt, and Lee Spruill. *Decisions at Stones River: The Sixteen Critical Decisions That Defined the Battle*. Knoxville: University of Tennessee, 2018.

Sword, Wiley. *Shiloh: Bloody April*. Dayton: Morningside Bookshop, 2001.

Taylor, Lenette S. *The Supply for the Tomorrow Must Not Fail*. Kent: Kent State University, 2004.
Taylor, Robert L., William E. Rosenbach, and Eric B. Rosenbach, eds. *Military Leadership: In Pursuit of Excellence*. Philadelphia: Westview Press, 2009.
Tucker, Philip Thomas. *The Forgotten Stonewall of the West: Major General John Stevens Bowen*. Macon Georgia: Mercer University, 1997.
Turner, George Edgar. *Victory Rode the Rails: The Strategic Place of the Railroads in the Civil War*. Lincoln: University of Lincoln, 1953.
Tzu, Sun. *The Art of War*. Various editions.
Van Creveld, Martin. *Command in War*. Cambridge, MA: Harvard University, 1985.
_____. *Supplying War: Logistics from Wallenstein to Patton*. Cambridge: Cambridge University, 1977.
Vandiver, Frank E. *Ploughshares into Swords: Josiah Gorgas and Confederate Ordnance*. Austin: University of Texas, 1952.
Warner, Ezra J. *Generals in Blue: Lives of the Union Commanders*. Baton Rouge: Louisiana State University, 1964.
_____ *Generals in Gray: Lives of the Confederate Commanders*. Baton Rouge: Louisiana State University, 1959.
Way, Frederick. *Way's Packet Directory 1848-1994*. Athens: Ohio University, 1994.
Webb, Walter Prescott. *The Texas Rangers: A Century of Frontier Defense*. New York: Harper & Brothers, 1935.
Weigley, Russell F. *The American Way of War: A History of United States Military Strategy and Policy*. New York: Macmillan Publishing, 1973.
Wert, Jeffrey D. *Civil War Barons: The Tycoons, Entrepreneurs, Inventors, and Visionaries Who Forged Victory and Shaped a Nation*. New York: Da Capo, 2018.
Williams, T. Harry. *Lincoln Finds a General*, vol. 3. New York: The Macmillan Co., 1952.
_____. "The Military Leadership of the North and the South: The Harmon Memorial Lectures in Military History Number Two." Colorado: United States Air Force Academy, 1960.
Wise, Stephen R. *Lifeline of the Confederacy Blockade Running During the Civil War*. Columbia, SC: University of South Carolina, 1988.
Witham, George F. *Shiloh, Shells and Artillery Units*. Memphis: Riverside, 1980.
Woodworth, Steven L. *Davis and Lee at War*. Lawrence: University Press of Kansas, 1995.
_____. *Jefferson Davis and His Generals: The Failure of Confederate Command in the West*. Lawrence: University of Kansas, 1990.
_____. *Nothing But Victory: The Army of the Tennessee 1861–1865*. New York: Vintage Books, 2005.
_____. *Shiloh: Confederate High Tide in the Heartland*. Santa Barbara: Praeger Books, 2013.

Secondary Sources: Journals

Allen, Stacy D. "Crossroads of the Western Confederacy: A Visitor's Guide," *Blue & Gray Magazine*. Columbus: Blue & Gray Magazine, 2007.
_____. "Shiloh." *Blue & Gray Magazine*. Columbus, Ohio: Sesquicentennial Edition.
Bailey, Jarrod C. "Civil War Logistics: Effects of Logistics on the Pea Ridge Campaign." Master's Thesis. Carson-Newman University, Jefferson City: TN, 2004.
Bennett, B. Kevin. "The Battle of Richmond, Kentucky" *The Blue & Gray Magazine*, vol. 25, no. 6.
Carney, Stephen A. *The U. S. Army Campaigns of the Mexican War: The Occupation of Mexico, May 1846-July 1848*. U.S. Army Center of Military History, Publication 73-3.
Castel, Albert. "A New View of the Battle of Pea Ridge," *Missouri Historical Society Review*. Columbia: State Historical Society of Missouri, vol. 62, no. 2, January 1968, 136–151.
Govan, Daniel C. "Patton Anderson: Major General, C. S. A." in Lawrence Lee Hewitt and Arthur W. Bergeron Jr., eds. *Confederate Generals in the Western Theater*, vol. 1. Knoxville: University of Tennessee, 2010, 215–228.
Gow, June, "Chiefs of Staff in the Army of Tennessee Under Braxton Bragg." *Tennessee Historical Quarterly*, vol. 27, no. 4, 341–360.
_____. "Military Administration in the Confederate Army of Tennessee," *Journal of Southern History*, vol. 40, no. 2, 183–198.
Hanson, Colonel Thomas E. "Failure of Command at Pea Ridge, 1862." *16 Cases of Mission Command*. Fort Leavenworth, Kansas, 2013, 1–16.
Lewis, Jim. "The Battle of Stones River." *Blue & Gray*, vol. 21, no. 5. 2012.
Moore, John G. "Mobility and Strategy in the Civil War," *Military Affairs*, vol. 24, No. 2, Summer, 1960.
Powell, David A. "Arthur C. Ducat: One of the Men behind the Man." Chickamaugablog.wordpress.com. 2015.
Sallee, Scott E. "The Battle of Prairie Grove." *Blue & Gray*, vol. 21, no. 5., October 2004.
Sanders, Stuart W. "The Battle of Perryville." *Blue & Gray*, vol. 22, no. 5., December 2005.
Stauffer, Dr. Alvin P. "Supply of the First American Overseas Expeditionary Force: The Quartermaster's Department and the Mexican War." *Quartermaster Review*, May-June 1950.
Still, William N., Jr. "Facilities for the Construction of War Vessels in the Confederacy." *The Journal of Southern History*, vol. 31, no. 3, August 1965.
Vandiver, Frank E. "Makeshifts of Confederate Ordnance." *Journal of Southern History*, vol. 17, no. 2, 1951.
Walker, Peter Franklin. "Command Failure: The Fall of Forts Henry and Donelson." *Tennessee Historical Quarterly*, vol. 16, no. 4, 335–360.

Williams, T. Harry "The Military Leadership of the North and the South." *The Harmon Memorial Lectures in Military History,* Number Two. CO: United States Air Force Academy, 1960.

Yeakey, George W. "Situational Leadership," *Military Review.* January-February 2002.

Newspapers

Confederate Military History
Hot Springs New Era
Madison Journal
New York Times
Richmond Times Dispatch
The Weekly Pioneer & Democrat. Saint Paul, Minnesota

Electronic Sources

Civil War Digital.com
Fold3.com
NA. "Grant's Chief Engineer Left Mark on Corinth." nps.gov. https://www.nps.gov/shil/upload/Frederick-Prime.pdf.
Texas State Historical Association: *Handbook of Texas Online.* https://tshaonline.org/handbook/online

Index

ammunition 6, 18, 25, 26, 30, 31, 45–48, 54, 56–58, 62–64, 76, 77, 83, 86–88, 91, 97, 99–101, 107, 114, 119, 120, 134, 136, 144–147, 149, 150, 153, 158, 164, 167, 173, 174, 177–179
Anaconda Plan 36, 66
Anderson, Patton 112
Anderson, Robert 23
Anglade, J.G. 32
Arizona 9
Arkansas 1, 7, 49–51, 53, 54, 59, 63, 67, 71, 75, 76, 125, 139, 140, 142–144, 147, 150, 151, 156, 171, 173, 175
CSS *Arkansas* 66, 71
Arkansas troops: 9th Arkansas Battalion 88
Army of Northern Virginia 3, 7, 43
Army of Tennessee (Confederate) 119, 153, 156, 161, 168, 171
Army of the Cumberland 90, 115, 130, 155, 166, 167; *see also* Army of the Ohio
Army of the Mississippi (Confederate) 103, 104, 123
Army of the Mississippi (Union) 123, 127, 167
Army of the Ohio (Union) 90, 123
Army of the Southwest (Union) 50–52
Army of the Tennessee (Union) 123, 130
Army of the West (Confederate) 126, 132
Army of Trans-Mississippi 140, 142, 143, 147, 151
Army of West Tennessee (Confederate) 126
Army of West Tennessee (Union) 127
Asboth, Alexander S. 51, 60
Austin, Moses 11

Badeau, Adam 4
Baldwin, William 47
Bardstown, Kentucky 109, 118
Bauer, K. Jack 12, 13
Beauregard, Pierre G.T. 17, 36, 39, 40, 67, 69, 74–81, 83–85, 88–91, 105, 123–126, 171
Belmont, Missouri 35, 86
Benjamin, Judah P. 23
Benton, J.F. 150
Benton, Thomas Hart 14
Bentonville, Arkansas 51, 57
Black, Robert 38
Blunt, James G. 138, *139*, 141–152, 172, 173
Boggs, William R. 101
Bowen, John 85, 129, 133–136
Bowles, William A. 15
Bowling Green, Kentucky 22, 28, 32, 33, 45, 74, 108
Boyle, Jeremiah 93
Bragg, Braxton 10, 69, 75, 77, 79, 80, 84, 85, 88–90, 92, 93, 97, 98, 101, 102, 103, *104*, 105–122, 125, 126, 130, 151, 153, *154*, 155–165, 168, 169, 171–175, 182
Breckinridge, John C. 77, 84, 85, 133, 155, 157–*160*, 161, 162, 165, 168, 182
Brent, George W. 89, 101, 110, 120, 164
Brewster, Henry P. 89
Brown, Isaac 38, 71
Brown, John Lucien 25, 32
Buckner, Simon Bolivar 41, 43–45, 48, 112
Buell, Don Carlos 23, 24, 26, 28, 32–35, 39, 52, 74–76, 79–83, 86, 90, 92, 93, 97, 98, 103–*104*, 105–111, 113–119, 121–123, 125, 126, 130, 154, 161, 170–175, 179
Buena Vista, Battle of 12–15, 17, 19
Butler, Benjamin F. 69, 70

Cairo, Illinois 36, 37, 66
California 9, 12, 22

Camargo, Battle of 12
Camp Jackson, St. Louis 49
Carr, Eugene A. 51, 60
Carroll, William H. 25, 26, 29, 30
Casey, Silas 19
Cerro Gordo, Battle of 14
Chattanooga, Tennessee 90, 92, 104–108, 114, 115, 125, 154, 160, 161, 164, 170
Cheatham, Benjamin Franklin 109–111, 113, 114, 118, 157, 158
Chickasaw Bayou 65, 68, 71, 72, 171
Churchill, Thomas J. 99
Churubusco, Battle of 14
Civil War Logistics 6
Clay, Cassius 93, 94, 98
Cleburne, Patrick 78, 85, 88, 94, *95*, 96, 97, 99, 101, 113, 140, 157
Columbus, Kentucky 22, 33–35, 38, 39, 43, 45, 48, 65, 67, 74, 75, 133
Conestoga 37
Connor, David 13
Conquered 6
Contreras, Battle of 14
Cooling, Benjamin Franklin 34
Cooper, Samuel 23, 30, 105–107, 143,
Corinth, Battle of 53, 54, 127–137, 153, 154, 172, 174, 175, 178
Corinth, Mississippi 63, 65, 72, 74–76, 80, 81, 90, 103–105, 115, 123–137, 166, 171, 174, 175
Corps of Observation 11
Court of Inquiry 127, 133–136
Crittenden, George B. *22*, 24–33
Crittenden, Thomas L. 113, 114, 117, 154, 159, 163
Cross, Trueman 17
Cruft, Charles 94, *95*–101
Cumberland Gap 22, 23, 92, 93, 97–99, 106, 115
Cumberland River 21–28, 30,

Index

32, 34, 36, 39, 40, 42, 43, 48, 66, 74, 75, 106, 107, 171
Cunningham, A.S. 32
Curtis, Samuel 49, **50**, 51–64, 140–44, 147, 170–172

Daniel, Larry 6, 156, 158, 164, 165
Davies, Thomas A. 127, 128, 131, 132
Davis, Jefferson (Confederate) 3, 22, 24, 37–39, 41, 43, 52, 53, 59, 69, 74, 76, 77, 84, 98, 102, 103, 105, 126, 130, 140, 144, 155, 156, 161, 168, 171
Davis, Jefferson C. (Union officer) 51, 60, 109
Delaware 21
Department of East Tennessee 98
distribution 6, 7, 31, 45, 173, 177
Dixon, Joseph 47
Dodge, Grenville M. 4, 49, 52, 62, 63, 83, 87
Ducat, Arthur 127, 134
Duke, Basil 103–105
Duncan, James 17

Eads, James B. 36–38, 66, 68
Eastport 34, 39, 70
Elkhorn Tavern, Battle of 54–58, 60, 61, 63

Farmington, skirmish at 124
Farragut, David G. 66, 69, **70**, 71
Field Manual 100–104
Floyd, John B. **35**, 40, 41, 43, 44–46, 48, 171
Flynt, George E. 31, 32
food 1, 4, 6, 16, 18, 25, 30–32, 36, 45–47, 49, 51, 52, 56–58, 61, 62, 65, 77, 86, 90, 100, 101, 119, 120, 125, 128, 130, 134–136, 138, 145, 147–151, 153, 159, 164, 167, 171, 173, 174, 177–179
Foote, Andrew 37–40, 42–44, 66–68
Forrest, Nathan B. 47, 72, 105, 106, 156
Fort Donelson, Battle of 33, 34, 38–49, 65, 67, 74, 76, 80, 83, 86, 87, 90, 118, 126, 170–173, 178
Fort Jackson 69
Fort St. Philip 69
Fort Smith, Arkansas 55, 142, 143, 150, 151
Fort Sumter 21, 36, 38, 39, 74
Foster, John G. 17
Frankfort, Kentucky 94, 109
Fremont, John Charles 42, 49, 50, 166, 167, 171

Frost, Daniel M. 143fry
Fry, Speed 25, 28, 109

Gareschè, Julius 159, 163, 166
General Orders No. 21 86
Georgia 25, 26, 107, 125, 153–155
Gilbert, Charles 108–110, 113, 117, 121
Gillem, Alvin C. 26, 30–32
Gilmer, Jeremy 34, 47, 89
Gosport Navy Yard 38, 39, 69
Grant, Ulysses S. 4, 5, 10, 12, 13, **35**, 37–48, 51, 53, 72, 73–**75**, 76–83, 85–87, 90, 91 104, 106, 115, 123, 125–127, 130, 131, 134, 151, 155, 156, 167, 170–172, 174, 178
Green, Martin 57, 129, 132, 136
Gulf of Mexico 36, 37, 65, 66, 69

Halleck, Henry W. 33, 34, 39, 40, 42, 43, 49, 50, 51, 59, 74, 80, 81, 86, 90 103- 105, 108, 109, 115, 116, 123–125, 144, 151, 155, 161, 166, 170
Hamilton, Charles S. 127, 131
Hammond, Paul 97
Hardee, William 43, 77, 78, 84, 85, 88, 106, 109–**112**, 113, 118, 120, 125, 155–158, 161–165, 168, 173
Harding, Thomas 63
Harney, William S. 16
Harris, Isham 22, 43, 108
Harrodsburg, Kentucky 109, 110, 120
Hatch, Reuben B. 46
Hawkins, John P. 46
Haynes, William H. 46, 47
Hébert, Louis 56, 61, 126, 128–130, 132, 134, 136
Heiman, Fort 34, 39
Henry, Gustavus A. Jr. 47
Herron, Francis J. **141**–152, 173
Hess, Earl 6, 104
Hill, Benjamin J. 99
Hillyer, Giles M. 32, 45
Hindman, Thomas C. 138, **139**, 140, 142–152, 171, 173
Hitchcock, Ethan A. 17
Hoepner, A. 62
Holly Springs 53, 72, 73, 135, 155, 171
Holmes, Theophilus 140, 143, 144, 147, 151, 156
Hooker, Joseph 17, 174
Hurlbut, Stephen A. 78, 79, 82, 83

Illinois troops: 37th Illinois 146; 43rd Illinois 81
Imperial General Staff 4

Indiana troops: 10th Indiana 1, 25; 26th Indiana 146
initiative 2, 4, 5, 10, 14, 15, 20, 28, 30, 33, 43, 44, 48, 49, 59, 64, 81, 82, 91, 98, 99, 102, 106, 110, 116, 117, 122, 125, 129, 130, 131, 137, 143, 145, 147, 148, 151–153, 157, 162, 169, 172
Iowa troops: 4th Iowa 52; 9th Iowa 62; 19th Iowa 146
Island No. 10 51, 65–69, 71, 74, 80, 89, 90, 123, 126, 166, 170
Iuka, Mississippi 126, 127, 130, 153

Jackson, Andrew 53, 68, 69
Jackson, Claiborne 49
Jackson, James S. 98, 111, 112
Jackson, Thomas Jonathan 3, 43
Jackson, Thomas Klugh 47
Jesup, Thomas S. 17
Johnson, Bushrod 44, 45
Johnston, Albert Sidney 4, 5, 22–24, 26, 28, 31–34, 39, 40, 43, 45, 53, 59, 67, 74, **75**–81, 83–85, 89, 91, 104, 171, 173, 174
Johnston, Joseph E. 3, 17, 43, 80, 156, 161
Johnston, William Preston 29, 45, 77; kammerling 155
Jones, John Wyatt 47
Jones, R. Steven 87
Jordan, Thomas 77, 78, 88, 89

Kämmerling, 26
Kentucky 1, 7, 21–27, 32–34, 36, 37, 43, 45, 48, 51, 65, 67, 74, 75, 92–94, 97–99, 101, 103–109, 111, 113, 115–121, 125, 126, 130, 133, 153, 154, 160, 161, 165, 171, 173, 175
Kentucky River 93, 94, 97, 98
Kentucky troops: 4th Kentucky Cavalry 25, 28
Kise, Reuben C. 30, 32, 100
Kise, William C. 25
Knoxville, Tennessee 24, 26, 33, 104–106, 115, 116, 160

Lagow, Clark B. 87
Lane, Joseph 15
leadership 1, 3–5, 8, 10–13, 21, 22, 28–30, 41, 43, 44, 46, 48, 52, 63, 66, 79, 84, 91, 105, 106, 112, 122, 128, 130, 133, 136, 138, 147, 148, 153, 161, 163, 167, 170, 171, 173, 177, 178
Lee, Richard B. 89
Lee, Robert E. 3, 13, 17, 43, 71, 116, 140, 168, 171, 182
Lee, Stephen D. 73
Lexington 37, 79

Index

Lexington, Kentucky 94, 97, 98, 107, 109, 116
Lincoln, Abraham 23, 33, 36–38, 41, 42, 49, 50, 65, 66, 74, 81, 98, 104, 108, 109, 115, 116, 121, 153, 155, 156, 169–171, 174
Logan's Crossroads 21, 23; *see also* Mill Springs
logistics 4, 6, 7, 20, 30, 33, 36, 46, 48, 50, 64, 91, 102, 122, 134, 137, 151, 152, 169, 173, 174, 177, 179
Longstreet, James 3, 43, 121, 175
CSS *Louisiana* 66
Louisville, Kentucky 97, 98, 106, 108, 109, 115–119, 179
Louisville and Nashville Railroad 106, 166
Louisiana troops: 16th Louisiana 77
Lovell, Mansfield 69, 70, 75, 126–130, 132–136
Lyman, Theodore 4
Lyon, Nathaniel 21, 34, 49, 59, 167

Mackall, William W. 31, 67, 68, 89
Mallory, Stephen R. 66
CSS *Manassas* 66, 70
Manson, Mahlon 25, 94–98, 100, 101
Marmaduke, John S. 143, 145
Marshall, Humphrey 15, 103, 106, 115, 116
Maryland 21
Mason, Richard B. 17
Matamoros, Battle of 12
Maury, Dabney 54, 126, 127–129, 132, 136
McClellan, George B. 17, 23, 34, 40, 65, 66, 80, 115
McClernand, John 42, 44, 78, 79, 81–83, 86
McCook, Alexander McDowell 86, 109–**112**, 113, 117, 118, 121, 154, 157, 158, 163
McCook, Robert L. 28, 29
McCown, John P. 67, 89, 157
McCray, Thomas H. 99
McCulloch, Benjamin 21, 49–52, **53**–58, 60, 61, 63, 143, 173
McFadden's Hill 157–159, 161, 165, 168
McIntosh, James 56, 61, 63
McKean, Thomas J. 127, 128
McKenny, Thomas I. 62
McKenzie, Samuel 19
McKinney, Francis F. 26, 31
McLean, Eugene E. 89
McMurry, Richard M. 3
McNair, Evander 99
McPherson, James 42, 46

Meade, George Gordon 17
Meigs, Montgomery 36, 37, 156
Memphis, Tennessee 22, 34, 37, 65–68, 71, 72, 76, 80, 104, 106, 123
Mendenhall, John 163, 168, 182
Mexican War 9, 10, 11, 13–17, 19
Mexico 9–12, 14–16, 18–20, 24, 40, 68
Michigan troops: 12th Michigan 82
Military Department of Ohio 93
Mill Springs, Battle of 1, 21, 23–29, 31–33, 35, 74, 94, 115, 154, 170–173, 178
Mississippi 1, 7, 21, 36, 37, 65, 68, 72, 74, 75, 90, 105, 106, 123, 125, 130, 137, 139, 140, 156, 161, 171, 178
Mississippi River 21–23, 34, 35–38, 45, 48, 49, 51, 53, 59, 63, 65–68, 71, 72, 74, 80, 89, 104, 125, 139, 143, 144, 156, 178
Mississippi River Valley 36, 42, 65, 74
Mississippi troops: 6th Mississippi 135
Missouri 21, 34, 35, 37, 49–54, 59, 63, 67, 126, 139–144, 147, 151, 171, 175
Missouri State Guard 57, 61
Missouri troops: 1st Missouri 133, 135; 1st Missouri Light Artillery 147; 2nd Missouri Volunteers 52
Mobile and Ohio Railroad 72
Molino del Rey, Battle of 13, 16, 17, 19
Monterrey, Battle of 12, 14, 15
Morgan, George 93, 106
Morgan, John Hunt 105, 156, 165, 168
Morton, Oliver 93, 98
Munfordville, Kentucky 107, 108, 115, 117
Murfreesboro, Tennessee 75, 106, 118, 155–157, 162, 165, 167; *see also* Stones River, Battle of

Nashville, Tennessee 22, 23, 26, 32, 33, 39, 40, 43, 48, 65, 74–76, 80, 93, 97, 104–106, 108, 115, 116, 119, 123, 130, 153–156, 158–161, 164, 166, 167, 171, 172, 179
Nashville Pike 158–161, 165, 182
Native Americans 23, 50, 53, 55, 68, 139
Nelson, William 10, 81, 92–**94**, 95–100, 102, 109, 115, 117, 174
New Mexico 9, 12

Norfolk, Virginia 38, 66, 69
Nueces River 11

objective 2, 4, 5, 7, 8, 14, 20, 27, 33, 41–43, 48, 59, 64, 73, 80, 91, 97, 98, 102, 108, 115, 116, 122, 123, 130, 137, 138, 142, 143, 147, 152, 156, 161, 162, 169–171
O'Hara, Theodore 89
Ohio 23, 30, 36, 92, 93, 106, 109,
Ohio River 21, 36, 37, 67, 105, 107, 177
Ohio troops: 2nd Ohio Volunteers 50; 9th Ohio 25, 30; 95th Ohio 95
Oladowski, Hypolite 89, 119, 120
Old Whitey 12
Ord, Edward O.C. 126
Osterhaus, Peter J. 51, 56, 60
Overland Campaign 83

Paducah, Kentucky 37, 43
Palo Alto, Battle of 12
Patterson, Robert 16, 19
Pea Ridge, Battle of 49–64, 72, 76, 126, 127, 132, 133, 136, 139, 141, 146, 152, 170–174, 178
Pegram, John 101, 165
Pemberton, John C. 72, 73, 156
Pennsylvania troops: 79th Pennsylvania 112
Perkins, Simon, Jr. 167, 179
Perryville, Battle of 1, 7, 94, 102, 103, 106, 109–117, 119–122, 153–155, 160, 162–164, 171–175, 178
Peters, William 38
Pike, Albert 53, 56, 61
Pillow, Fort 68, 80
Pillow, Gideon 14, 16, 19, 21, 22, 39–**41**, 42–47, 171
Pittsburgh Landing 74, 77, 78, 80, 81, 86, 88, 179
Polk, James K. 10–15, 19, 41
Polk, Leonidas 21, 22, 34, 38, 39, 43, 67, 75, 77, 84, 85, 103, 106, 107, 109–**111**, 118, 120, 133, 155, 157, 158, 161–163, 165, 168, 171, 173
Pope, John 51, 66–**68**, 123, 166, 167
Prairie Grove, Battle of 63, 138, 139, 141, 142, 144–152, 156, 172, 173, 175, 178, 182
Prentiss, Benjamin 78, 79, 82, 83, 85
Price, Sterling 21, 49–**54**, 55–57, 60–63, 103, 106, 115, 116, 126–130, 132–137, 139, 174, 178
Prime, Frederick 134, 135
Principles of War 4, 73, 116, 170

Index

quartermaster 6, 17, 18, 25, 30, 32, 45, 47, 51, 59, 62, 86, 107, 116, 119, 164, 166, 167, 179
Quintard, Charles Todd 107, 113
Quitman, John A. 16, 19

Railroads of the Confederacy 38
Randolph, George W. 46, 105, 130
Rawlins, John A. 46, 86, 87
Rebel Brass 6
Reid, John W. 63
Resaca de la Palma, Battle of 12
resources 1–4, 7, 14, 19, 20, 23, 31–33, 38, 47, 48, 62–64, 66, 74, 90, 91, 102, 121, 122, 137, 150, 152, 158, 164, 166, 168, 169, 171, 173–175, 178, 181
Richmond, Kentucky 1, 7, 92–98, 101–103, 172, 174, 178
Richmond, Virginia 3, 21, 22, 24, 30, 38, 39, 41, 52, 69, 75, 80, 81, 98, 105, 107, 115, 116, 143, 147, 155, 161, 175
Richmond, Battle of 1, 7, 92–98, 101–103, 107, 170, 171–175, 178
Riggin, John, Jr. 87
Rio Grande River 11, 14
Roane, John S. 143
Roland, Charles 84
Roper, George S. 26, 32
Rosecrans, William H. 33, *124*, 126–132, 134, 135, 137, 153–**155**, 156–169, 171, 172, 175, 178
Round Forest 158

St. Louis 21, 34, 36, 49, 50, 51, 53, 59, 116, 141, 142, 151, 177
San Jacinto 11, 52
Sanders, Surgeon 30
Santa Anna, Antonio Lopez de 12, 19
Schofield, John 141, 142, 147, 151
Scott, Henry L. 17
Scott, John 97, 99
Scott, Winfield **9**, 10–20, 36, 44, 66, 69, 86, 92, 177
Scully, John 25
Seminole Wars 11, 23
Sheridan, Philip 51, 52, 59, 60, 62, 110, 157
Sherman, William T. 5, 13, 24, 28, 43, **72**, 73, 76, 78, 79, 81–83, 155, 171, 172
Shiloh, Battle of 4, 53, 59, 63, 72, 74–93, 103, 105, 106, 115, 118, 123, 133, 136, 140, 153, 157, 160, 170–174, 178, 181, 182
Shiloh Chapel 74, 76
Shoup, Francis A. 143, 145, 148
Sigel, Franz 51, 55–**58**, 59–61

Simpson, John 23
Smith, Albert J. 89
Smith, Charles S. 39, 40, 42, 44, 74, 81, 82
Smith, Edmund Kirby 92, **93**, 94–103, 105–109, 114–118, 121, 125, 147, 151, 157, 170, 173–175
Smith, Justin 12, 16, 18
Smith, Martin 73
Smith, Morgan L. 73
Smith, Preston 99
Smith, Tim 126, 128, 132, 134, 137
Snead, Thomas L. 63, 126
Spy Company 18
staff 2, 4, 6–8, 10, 12–14, 16–20, 28, 31–33, 42, 43, 45–48, 52–56, 61–64, 68, 71, 77, 79, 81–83, 86–93, 100–102, 108, 109, 113, 118–122, 126, 127, 129, 132–139, 142, 148–150, 152–154, 159, 163–169, 171–174, 176–179
Stängel, Wilhelm 30
Stanley, David S. 127, 128, 132, 154, 157, 163
Stevenson, Carter 156
Stones River, Battle of 18, 90, 112, 113, 118, 154, 157–169, 171–173, 175, 177, 178, 181, 182
strategic failure 3, 67, 103, 168, 171, 172
strategic success 2, 4, 7, 8, 10, 19, 20, 48, 63, 64, 90–92, 121, 122, 137, 153, 169, 172, 175
Stuart, J.E.B. 3, 162
Supplying War 125

Taylor, Jesse 40
Taylor, John W. 135, 166
Taylor, Zachary **10**, 11–15, 17, 19, 20, 52, 92, 154
teamwork 1, 3, 55, 112, 122
Telegraph Road 51, 150
Tennessee 1, 7, 11, 22–24, 26, 27, 30, 32–37, 39, 41, 43, 48, 51, 52, 65, 67, 68, 71, 72, 74, 76, 77, 80, 81, 90, 104–106, 108, 115, 116, 121, 125, 137, 139, 140, 153, 155, 156, 160, 161, 168, 169, 171, 172, 178
Tennessee River 21, 39, 43, 48, 66, 70, 74, 77, 78, 86, 106
Tennessee troops: First Tennessee Regiment 109; 3rd Tennessee 32; 9th Tennessee 112; 29th Tennessee 26
Texas 9, 11, 15, 21–23, 49, 67, 71
Texas troops: 2nd Texas 77; 6th Texas Cavalry 56
Texas War for Independence 11, 22, 52
Thomas, Charles 17
Thomas, George H. **22**, 23–34,
109, 113, 115–117, 123, 153, 154, 158, 159, 163, 170, 171, 174
Tilghman, Lloyd 39, 46
Totten, George M. 13, 17
Totten, James 141–143
Trans-Mississippi, Department of 52, 53, 63, 65, 71, 123, 139, 140, 142, 143, 147, 151
Tredegar Iron Works 3, 37, 66, 182
Tunnard, William 55, 61, 62
Tupelo, Mississippi 90, 105, 106, 125
Twiggs, David E. 15, 16, 19, 69
Two Great Rebel Armies 3
Tyler 37, 79

unity of command 5, 15, 16, 20, 28, 33, 44, 48, 59, 60, 64, 81–85, 91, 99, 102, 110, 117, 118, 122, 126, 131, 133, 134, 137, 152, 169, 172

Vandiver, Frank 6
Van Dorn, Earl **50**, 52–64, 71, 72, 75, 76, 103, 106, 113, 115, 116, 123, **124**, 125–137, 139, 140, 142, 150, 166, 171, 174, 175
Veracruz, Battle of 9, 10, 13–15, 18, 19, 86
Vicksburg, Mississippi 49, 65, 67, 68, 71–73, 80, 104, 125, 130, 143, 144, 151, 156, 168; *see also* Chickasaw Bayou
victory (conditions) 1, 121
Villepigue, John S. 89
CSS *Virginia* 66

Walker, J.J. 89
Wallace, Lew 44, 78, 80, 82, 83, 90, 93, 97, 172
Wallace, W.H.L. 78, 79, 81, 82, 83
Washington, D.C. 11–13, 21, 37, 41, 90, 98, 109, 116, 154, 161, 166
Watkins, Sam 109, 119, 120
Webster, Joseph D. 45, 46, 79, 86
Wellington, Duke of 13, 83
West Point 1, 7, 17, 22–24, 30–32, 39, 42–47, 50, 51, 53, 60, 62, 63, 81, 82, 84, 92, 111, 117, 119, 126, 127, 131–133, 135, 136, 138, 140–143, 145, 148, 154, 165–167, 177, 178
Wheeler, Joseph 106, 110, 114, 118, 155, 159, 162, 165, 167
Whiting, Henry 17
Wilder, John T. 107
Williams, C.C. 86
Wilson's Creek, Battle of 34, 49, 51, 52, 59, 141

Wisconsin troops: 18th Wisconsin 85; 20th Wisconsin 145, 146; 21st Wisconsin 112, 113
Wolford, Frank 29
Wool, John E. 13, 15

Worth, William 15–17, 19,
Wright, Horatio 93, 98
Wycliffe, Nathaniel 89

Yell, Archibald 15

Zahm, Lewis 109
Zollicoffer, Felix 1, 22–*24*, 25–31, 171, 173

www.ingramcontent.com/pod-product-compliance
Lightning Source LLC
Chambersburg PA
CBHW060343010526
44117CB00017B/2944